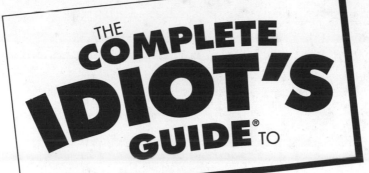

THE
COMPLETE IDIOT'S GUIDE® TO

Bringing Up Baby

Second Edition

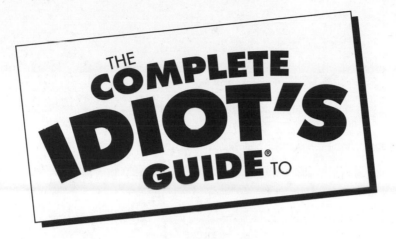

THE
COMPLETE
IDIOT'S
GUIDE® TO

Bringing Up Baby

Second Edition

by Signe Larson, M.D., and Kevin Osborn

ALPHA

A member of Penguin Group (USA) Inc.

ALPHA BOOKS

Published by the Penguin Group

Penguin Group (USA) Inc., 375 Hudson Street, New York, New York 10014, U.S.A.

Penguin Group (Canada), 10 Alcorn Avenue, Toronto, Ontario, Canada M4V 3B2 (a division of Pearson Penguin Canada Inc.)

Penguin Books Ltd, 80 Strand, London WC2R 0RL, England

Penguin Ireland, 25 St Stephen's Green, Dublin 2, Ireland (a division of Penguin Books Ltd)

Penguin Group (Australia), 250 Camberwell Road, Camberwell, Victoria 3124, Australia (a division of Pearson Australia Group Pty Ltd)

Penguin Books India Pvt Ltd, 11 Community Centre, Panchsheel Park, New Delhi—110 017, India

Penguin Group (NZ), cnr Airborne and Rosedale Roads, Albany, Auckland 1310, New Zealand (a division of Pearson New Zealand Ltd)

Penguin Books (South Africa) (Pty) Ltd, 24 Sturdee Avenue, Rosebank, Johannesburg 2196, South Africa

Penguin Books Ltd, Registered Offices: 80 Strand, London WC2R 0RL, England

Copyright © 2007 by Kevin Osborn

International Standard Book Number: 978-1-59257-596-1
Library of Congress Catalog Card Number: 2006932989

09 08 07   8 7 6 5 4 3 2 1

Interpretation of the printing code: The rightmost number of the first series of numbers is the year of the book's printing; the rightmost number of the second series of numbers is the number of the book's printing. For example, a printing code of 07-1 shows that the first printing occurred in 2007.

Printed in the United States of America

Note: This publication contains the opinions and ideas of its authors. It is intended to provide helpful and informative material on the subject matter covered. It is sold with the understanding that the authors and publisher are not engaged in rendering professional services in the book. If the reader requires personal assistance or advice, a competent professional should be consulted.

The authors and publisher specifically disclaim any responsibility for any liability, loss, or risk, personal or otherwise, which is incurred as a consequence, directly or indirectly, of the use and application of any of the contents of this book.

Most Alpha books are available at special quantity discounts for bulk purchases for sales promotions, premiums, fund-raising, or educational use. Special books, or book excerpts, can also be created to fit specific needs.

For details, write: Special Markets, Alpha Books, 375 Hudson Street, New York, NY 10014.

Publisher: *Marie Butler-Knight*
Editorial Director: *Mike Sanders*
Managing Editor: *Billy Fields*
Acquisitions Editor: *Paul Dinas*
Senior Development Editor: *Phil Kitchel*
Senior Production Editor: *Janette Lynn*

Copy Editor: *Krista Hansing Editorial Services, Inc.*
Cartoonist: *Richard King*
Cover Designer: *Bill Thomas*
Book Designer: *Trina Wurst*
Indexer: *Angie Bess*
Layout: *Chad Dressler*
Proofreader: *Aaron Black*

*To my children—Casey, Molly, Ian, and Megan—who were all very patient with
the on-the-job training of their parents*

Contents at a Glance

Contents

Introduction

"A baby is an inestimable blessing and bother."
—Mark Twain

Congratulations! Whether your new baby is the result of a happy accident, timely planning, or years of trial and error, she's finally arrived (or is at least on the way). You've been blessed—or soon will be—with a beautiful child.

Having a baby, however, is the easy part. Almost any idiot can manage that. Now that you have one, what are you supposed to do with her? How can you best care for her? How can you build a foundation of love and trust, and create a lasting bond between you?

You may feel somewhat confident in your parenting abilities. But no matter how sure you feel of yourself, you're still in for some surprises in the coming year. How will you handle the unexpected? Where will you turn for advice?

On the other hand, you may feel totally unprepared for parenting. And why shouldn't you? Before you can become an airline pilot, a doctor, a lawyer, or a forest ranger, you have to go through years of school and training. Heck, you have to endure a job-training program before you can work in a fast-food restaurant. But you can become a parent without any training or schooling at all.

Parenting: A Crash Course

Parenting, especially during the first weeks and months, involves intensive on-the-job training. Early on, you'll discover the pleasures—and occasional frustrations—of feeding your baby. Soon you'll become a master at the particular type of rocking, bouncing, cooing, and singing that your baby likes best. You'll become a quick-change artist, getting your baby into a clean diaper before he has a chance to make another mess (which may be no more than a minute or two).

Later on, you'll experiment with different methods of getting your baby to sleep—and getting him to stay asleep for more than 2 or 3 hours. You'll try to remain patient as your darling redecorates the kitchen walls with different shades of baby food. You'll hold your breath as your child learns first to crawl and then to stand. You'll discover just how much fun—and how much trouble—having a baby can be.

Indeed, over the next year, you'll learn so much about baby care that you will become an expert, at least where your own baby is concerned. You will learn through trial and error. You will learn through your baby's wise, forgiving, but not always patient teaching. And you will learn, hopefully, from *The Complete Idiot's Guide to Bringing Up Baby, Second Edition.*

This book provides you with essential information and advice you will need in the first year of your baby's life. Think of it as the owner's and operator's manual for your new baby. (Every child should come with one, but none does.)

In this new edition of *The Complete Idiot's Guide to Bringing Up Baby*, you will find information on developmental milestones during the first year, tips on how to master the basics and not-so-basics of baby care, cautions about pitfalls to avoid, and advance warnings about challenges that you're likely to face. You will also find discussions of the most vexing issues that confront new parents, from setting limits on your baby's behavior to finding time for yourselves—and for each other.

This book will do much more than help you become a confident and competent parent. Throughout you will find hundreds of practical tips and easy-to-use strategies that will help you become the best parent you can possibly be. You will discover not only how to help advance your baby's learning processes, but how to advance your own learning as well. As your child grows and develops, you'll grow and develop, too.

How This Book Is Organized

The Complete Idiot's Guide to Bringing Up Baby, Second Edition, aims to make baby care as entertaining, easy, and gratifying as possible for both you and your baby. The book is divided into five parts. Four address concerns that will come up in each of the four trimesters (3-month periods) of your baby's first year of life. In each of these parts, you will find information on your child's physical, mental, and emotional development; on health and safety concerns; and on making the most of playtime with your baby.

Each of these four parts also has special chapters that address challenges most often faced by parents during that trimester of their baby's life. However, because no baby sticks to a rigid schedule of development, each of these parts overlaps slightly with the next. The sixth month, for example, is considered not only the end of the second trimester (Part 2), but also the beginning of the third trimester (Part 3).

In addition to these four parts that anticipate your baby's chronology, the final part of this book addresses issues of special concern that may arise at any time during your baby's first year. This part features information and advice on how to work productively with your partner and how to take care of yourself and your own needs throughout the year.

Part 1, "The Newborn: 0–3 Months," covers the basics of baby care: breast-feeding and bottle-feeding, changing her diaper, sponge-bathing and dressing her, and keeping her healthy. Here you will also find information on …

- What your baby may look like at birth.
- What she can see and hear from the first days of her life.
- The instincts that determine newborn behavior.
- The development of more purposeful behavior.

It also offers advice on how to calm your crying baby and how to calm yourself if your baby is colicky. You will also find a chapter on how to communicate with your baby through words and through touch. Finally, it offers guidance on play and playfulness during your baby's first 3 months.

Part 2, "The Early Infant: 3–6 Months," points to the huge developmental leaps your baby will make in the second trimester. But it also provides advice on …

- Bathing your baby in a tub.
- Introducing solid foods.
- Traveling with your baby (whether to the store or to the shore).
- Toys, games, and exercises that will stimulate your infant.

Finally, it offers tips on how to make your home safe for your soon-to-be-mobile baby.

Part 3, "The Crawler: 6–9 Months," offers a guide to the rapid development from immobility to nerve-shattering mobility. You will also find pointers on …

- Setting limits on your newly mobile baby's increasingly dangerous behavior.
- Expanding your child's menu.
- Getting your baby to go to sleep by herself—and then sleep through the night.

Part 4, "The Pre-Toddler: 9–12 Months," points you toward the fun you'll have as your baby progresses toward her first steps—and her first words. Here you will also find advice on playing with your baby throughout the second half of the year. The final chapter looks ahead to your child's first birthday—and on how to keep your walking, talking toddler safe and sound.

Part 5, "Partners in Parenting: Issues for First-Year Parents," presents some of the great parenting dilemmas of our age. Here you will find advice on how to set aside a little time (even just half an hour) for yourself and your needs. This part also provides a discussion of the concerns of working parents, including guidance on how to find a good day-care provider. It also offers guidance on how to work together as parenting partners—and includes a special chapter directed at today's new fathers. It concludes with a chapter of advice on how to handle all the "friendly advice" you'll get during your first year as a parent—even from books like this one.

Extras

The Complete Idiot's Guide to Bringing Up Baby, Second Edition, offers clear, concise information and practical guidance on your baby's development and the more difficult issues that arise in the course of day-to-day parenting. Throughout the book, you will also notice an abundant supply of baby-care tips, words of wit or wisdom, superstitions, and health and safety warnings. You can easily spot these extras by looking for the following icons:

Q-Tip

These special tips offer advice on how to stimulate your baby's development, save time or money, make things simpler for yourself and your baby, and have more fun with your infant.

Babyproofing

These cautionary words will alert you to common dangers that might threaten your baby's health or safety. These boxes also offer advice on how to safeguard your child from these dangers.

Baby Talk

These wise and/or witty observations about babies and their parents will amaze or amuse you.

Baby Folklore

Here you will find entertaining bits of folk lore and superstitions regarding babies and baby care.

Baby Doctor

Here you will find medical information and advice on how to protect your baby's—or your own—health. These boxes will also alert you to situations in which you'll need to consult your pediatrician or another health-care professional.

Trademarks

All terms mentioned in this book that are known to be or are suspected of being trademarks or service marks have been appropriately capitalized. Alpha Books and Pearson Education cannot attest to the accuracy of this information. Use of a term in this book should not be regarded as affecting the validity of any trademark or service mark. Q-TIPS is a registered trademark of Chesebrough-Ponds, Inc.

Acknowledgments

We owe special thanks to a great number of people who contributed to the birth of this book. Nancy Mikhail and Richard Parks first brought us together. Jennifer Perillo, Carol Sheehan, and Mike Sanders offered critical editorial advice and guidance with patience and care.

Kevin Osborn would like to offer his greatest appreciation—and his undying love—to the five people who have taught him the most about parenting: his partner in parenting, Susan Kiley, and his babies: Megan, Ian, Molly, and Casey. This book—and my life—wouldn't be the same without you.

Part 1

The Newborn:
0–3 Months

You have a beautiful baby or are expecting one any day. Now what? No matter how much you've read or how much time you've spent with babies, chances are you feel both unprepared and overwhelmed. Just the basics of baby care—feeding, changing, soothing—seem to take all of your time. No sooner do you change a diaper than your baby dirties it. She probably wants to eat at least 10 or 12 times a day. When she needs anything, she cries.

Fortunately, newborns do one thing even more often than they eat, cry, and dirty diapers. They sleep. Take advantage of your baby's downtime. When you're not admiring her angelic sleeping face, remember to treat yourself to a little downtime yourself. It won't be long before you're needed again.

Chapter 1

Your Newborn's Appearance and Behavior

In This Chapter

- ◆ What your newborn may look like
- ◆ Normal blemishes and misshapen features that might worry you—but shouldn't
- ◆ Your baby's sensory perception
- ◆ Your newborn's behavior

Congratulations! Since you're reading this, you've probably just had a baby—or you're expecting one soon. In either case, your heart is no doubt filled with joy. Your baby is beautiful and hopefully healthy. Her coos and gurgles, peeps and squeaks sound like the song of an angel. When she sleeps, the serenity on her face radiates throughout your home. In these first weeks and months, even her poop smells sweet.

Despite your elation, however, you probably feel some anxiety. Questions bounce around in your head like an active baby in the womb during the final trimester. Why is my baby sleeping so much? Why doesn't she sleep more? Why doesn't she ever cry? Why is she crying so much? What's that mark on her back? How much can she see and hear? Why hasn't she smiled at me yet? Should her poop really be that color? Is what I'm seeing normal?

Relax. Try to enjoy this special time of your child's (and your) life. Your concerns are perfectly normal. Most parents have these worries when their children are newborns, and their children grow up healthy all the same. After all, babies are remarkably adaptable creatures.

Baby Talk

"Every baby born into the world is a finer one than the last."

—Charles Dickens

What does your baby most need from you? She needs you to feed her, change her diapers, and occasionally bathe her. But above all else, your baby needs your love. Whether you offer that love through a gentle touch, a soothing voice, a smile, or the glow in your eyes, your baby will thrive on it.

Beauty Is in the Eye of the Beholder: What Your Newborn May Look Like

As every parent knows, babies are beautiful—at least, to their parents. Yet in the first weeks of their child's life, even the most smitten parents may notice features that at first disturb or even alarm them. If you were expecting a smiling, perfectly rounded, smooth-skinned cherub, think again. Remember, your baby has just gone through an extremely difficult transition.

Considering what your baby has just accomplished, it would be remarkable if he emerged totally unscathed. So if your baby seems a shade too blue or his skin seems marred by a widespread rash, don't worry. These conditions are perfectly normal and should disappear as your child grows older. As these blemishes clear up, your child will grow more beautiful each day.

Too Big? Too Small? Or Just Right?

In the first weeks, you may be concerned about some of your baby's vital statistics:

◆ **Weight:** At birth, the average baby weighs around 7 or 8 pounds. Yet newborns who weigh as little as 5 pounds are considered normal. If your child weighs less than 5 pounds, your pediatrician may want to keep her in the hospital for a few days to monitor her feeding until she gains more weight. On the other end of the scale, newborns can weigh as much as 10 ½ pounds or more and still fall within the normal range. Even if your baby weighs more than this, you have little cause for concern.

◆ **Weight loss:** Newborns tend to lose weight during the first week or so. Don't worry. This weight loss is not an indication that you aren't feeding your baby properly. Your child will certainly let you know if she's not getting enough food.

◆ **Length:** Because newborns cannot stand on their own two feet, people seldom speak of a baby's height. Doctors and parents do, however, record a baby's length. The average child measures 18 to 22 inches long.

◆ **Head circumference:** The other important vital statistic for your baby is the circumference of her head. You may be startled at how big your baby's head appears. The head of a newborn takes up about one quarter of her entire body length— and even more if she is born early. (If this proportion held, an adult's head would be 15 to 18 inches long, which is roughly the size of a large watermelon!) At birth, the average child's head measures about 14 inches around. The normal range, however, spans from about 12½ to 15 inches. This size—and its steady growth—matters because it indicates the healthy development of the brain.

Babyproofing

Your baby's neck muscles will not develop until some time after birth. So until your baby can hold his head up by himself, you will have to do it for him. Whether carrying or lifting, always support the back of your baby's head and neck.

Why Is Your Baby's Head So Pointy?

You may be as concerned about the shape of your baby's head as its size:

◆ **Pointiness:** In most nonsurgical births, the baby's head travels through the birth canal first. Because the head is the biggest part of a baby's body, this makes for a tight squeeze. The pressure of the pushing that guides and forces the baby through the birth canal can temporarily alter the shape of his head. The skull bones, which are not completely joined or set in place, may need to move closer together in order to ease the trip. Normally, the head resumes its roundness within a week or so. But for the first few days, your baby may look a little like a conehead.

◆ **Lump:** Your baby may also have a fluid-filled lump on the top of his head. This lump is usually a result of the head banging against the mother's pelvic bones or unopened cervix and will disappear within the first week.

◆ **Soft spots:** To allow for rapid growth of the head and brain, the bones of your baby's head are not yet joined. For this reason, your child will have two soft spots, called *fontanels*, on his head. Over the first 2 years of his life, as your child grows and the bones of his skull join, these fontanels will close. The soft spot on the back of his head will disappear within several months, and the one on top will close before his second birthday. The fontanels open a small window to the brain, so take care to heed the cardinal rule of baby care: *never drop your baby on his head!*

The White Stuff

Many newborns, especially those born on or before their due date, are coated with a white waxy or greasy substance known as *vernix*. While your child was still inside the womb, this natural cream protected her skin from the fluids that surrounded her. Some hospitals wash off the vernix, but this is not necessary. Indeed, the vernix may continue to protect your child's skin from flaking after she is born.

During a baby's first week or two, the skin absorbs much of the vernix. In areas where excess vernix has gathered—in skin folds, around the genitals, and under the fingernails, for example—it turns into a powder that washes off fairly easily.

Baby Doctor

Flaky skin is most often found on the top of a newborn's head. This condition, known as *cradle cap,* is best treated by keeping your baby's scalp clean. Because different pediatricians approach cradle cap in different ways, ask yours what he or she recommends.

Blue Boy

Parents expect their newborns to have smooth, baby-soft skin. You may therefore be surprised to discover that your child's skin may be wrinkled and dry. Indeed, it may be so dry that it cracks and easily peels off.

You may also be surprised at your baby's color. Many babies are born blue! During the first days, the color of your baby's skin may react rapidly to changes in activity or temperature. Don't worry. As his circulatory system matures, your child's color will become more consistent.

African-American babies tend to have lighter skin at birth than they will have later in life. As your baby's body begins to produce *melanin*, a natural pigment, the skin will get darker. By about 6 months, your child's skin will have reached its permanent color.

Baby Folklore _____

If your child has a birthmark, think back upon your pregnancy. Did you ever drop anything—a bunch of grapes, some peanuts, a hairbrush—on your pregnant belly? Did a house pet—a cat, a dog, a ferret—jump on your abdomen? A 16th-century belief pointed to such incidents as the causes of birthmarks. It was believed that the shape of the birthmark reflected the impression of the object that landed on the belly.

Rash Assumptions

Although few babies emerge from the womb without one or more birthmarks or rashes, such marks still might surprise you when you first see them. Many birthmarks fade or disappear within the first year or two. Common birthmarks include the following:

Baby Doctor _____

Some rashes do demand professional attention. Consult your pediatrician if a rash persists or seems to be spreading, if it is accompanied by a cough or fever, or if a rash of blisters (raised bumps filled with fluid) appears.

- *Stork bites* are tiny pink birthmarks usually found at the back of the neck under the hairline. They generally disappear within the first 6 months.

- *Strawberry marks* are small red bumps, usually on or around the head, that sometimes grow larger during the first year but then disappear within the next.

- *Mongolian spots* are bluish-gray birthmarks that are often found on the backs or bottoms of dark-skinned infants (babies of African, Asian, or Southern European descent). They persist longer than other birthmarks, but they usually disappear within the first 4 years.

Many newborns also have one or more rashes in their first few days. Although rashes may bother you, they seldom bother infants. Rashes are generally harmless and nonirritating, and will go away without any attention:

- *Milia* are white dots that resemble pimples, commonly on the nose or elsewhere on the face. Resist the urge to squeeze them or try to scrub them off. They will clear up without any special care within a week or two.

- *Red blotches*, often with a raised white center, form another common rash. This will also go away on its own, though it may reappear during the first month or so before disappearing entirely.

◆ *Heat rash* consists of a collection of small red spots, especially on the face or bottom. If your baby has heat rash, make sure you haven't wrapped her up in too many blankets or too much clothing. Try to keep her skin cool and dry, but don't worry too much about heat rash. Heat rash results primarily from immature sweat glands. Your baby will grow out of it eventually.

Who's Got the (Belly) Button?

Immediately after birth, the umbilical cord will be clamped and cut. The remainder (the *umbilicus*) will be tied and probably washed with iodine. Within hours, it will shrivel and turn black.

Baby Doctor

If the umbilicus oozes, turns red, or emits a foul odor, it is probably infected. Consult your pediatrician as soon as possible.

The umbilicus needs to be kept clean and dry until it withers and falls off (usually within 3 weeks). Stick to sponge baths for the first week or two. Wash the umbilicus daily with alcohol and a sterile cotton ball. When diapering your baby, fold the top of the diaper down in the front to keep it from covering up the belly. Airing out the umbilicus—and keeping it free of urine—helps to prevent it from getting infected. (For more tips on bathing your newborn and later your older baby, see Chapters 3 and 12.)

Sense and Sensibility

If you're like most new parents, you wonder how much your baby can see and hear. How soon does he recognize your face and voice? Can he make out the features of your face? Do you have to be especially quiet to avoid hurting his delicate ears?

From the moment he came into the world, your baby began to look at, listen to, and learn about the world around him. In the few hours that he's awake, it may seem as though he's just lying there placidly (or fretfully, if he's colicky). Yet when alert, your baby is constantly using his senses and absorbing information.

Not only does your baby continually take in information, but he also begins to process it—even in the first days of life. Your baby uses the variety of sights, sounds, smells, and textures that he encounters to familiarize himself with his surroundings.

You and your partner stand out prominently among those surroundings. Studies have demonstrated that within days of birth, a baby can recognize his own mother's voice, smell, and face. So the action of the senses and the formation of sensory impressions and memories play an important part in establishing your newborn's place in the world.

Do You See What I See?

During the first week of life, your baby will have limited vision. She can focus best on objects that are 7 to 12 inches away from her eyes. (Conveniently, this distance approximates the distance of your face when you hold your baby in your arms to feed her.) Within weeks, the range of her sight will expand. Yet although she can now see objects that are farther away, she will probably show interest—through facial expressions or coos and gurgles—only for those objects that remain fairly close.

Most babies can also distinguish various patterns and shapes. Although they may not be able to make out all of the subtle features of the human face, most babies nonetheless like to look at faces more than any other pattern or shape. Take advantage of your baby's visual preference: make eye contact often and smile at your baby. She will return the eye contact almost immediately—and in time, she will return the smile, too.

Because newborns best perceive sharply contrasting patterns of light and darkness, the pastel pinks and blues traditionally used to decorate a baby's nursery have little benefit for your baby—at least in her first weeks.

Q-Tip

Because your baby might like pastels later, feel free to decorate her room in such colors even though she can't see them right away. But add touches that offer sharp contrasts: a black-and-white mobile hanging over the crib, a checkerboard or other black-and-white pattern on the wall next to the changing table, black-and-white toys or stuffed animals. You might also choose to wear clothes that present her with a sharply contrasting pattern to study.

Most babies also have a limited ability to track the movement of objects with their head and eyes or with their eyes alone. Babies can track movement only for a short distance and only if the objects move slowly.

Games such as peekaboo make little sense at this age. If you aren't in the direct line of your baby's sight, you are—for all intents and purposes—gone. Even if you just hide your face behind your hands, your baby no longer knows you're there.

Do You Hear What I Hear?

Most babies have a sensitive sense of hearing, and they pay careful attention to the noises in their world. Your baby can distinguish among a wide variety of different sounds. Like most newborns, he will probably show a particular fondness for human voices in preference to other sounds. Talking softly to your baby will stimulate his sense of hearing in a way he will enjoy.

Baby Doctor

Your baby will probably like repetitive, rhythmic sounds that mimic the vibrations or the heartbeat that he heard while he was still in the womb. Tapes of heart sounds, the beating of a tom-tom or other drum, and the loud hum of a vacuum cleaner will all be music to your baby's ears.

Babies can track sounds, just as they can track motion. Within several weeks of birth, your baby may even begin to look toward the source of your voice or another favorite sound—a remarkably early coordination of the senses of sight and hearing.

Your Baby Smells—and Tastes, Too!

Your baby's senses of taste and smell will also be active in the first days and weeks of life. Of course, babies are not gourmets. Your child won't experiment with a wide variety of tastes for quite some time. Indeed, breast milk and/or formula should make up your child's entire diet for several months.

Tests have shown, however, that newborns who are offered a wider variety of tastes demonstrate distinct preferences. Bitter or sour tastes provoke faces or crying from newborns. Not surprisingly, babies tend to have a sweet tooth—a good thing because both breast milk and formula taste very sweet.

Little is known about a newborn's sense of smell. Yet because the senses of smell and taste are so closely related, babies can probably distinguish among a variety of aromas. Just what babies prefer to smell is difficult to test.

Touch Me

Your newborn's skin is very sensitive to touch, especially his lips and hands. Long before he can voluntarily reach for objects, your baby nonetheless uses his sense of touch to establish contact with the outside world. By lying on different surfaces and coming into contact with different objects, he discovers the difference between hard and soft, hot and cold, smooth and rough.

By observing your child's responses, you can discover the textures and temperatures he prefers. Even without testing, however, you can safely assume that he likes being held close, cuddled, and kept warm.

What Your Newborn Can Do

Your baby has an extremely limited repertoire of activities, but don't judge her too harshly. She's expending an awful lot of energy simply absorbing and processing information through her senses, which leaves little energy left for, say, playing tennis, reading Shakespeare, or planting a flower bed.

Aside from discovering the world through a flood of sensations, most newborns engage in five primary activities:

♦ Sleeping

♦ Eating

♦ Dirtying diapers

♦ Crying

♦ Moving (mostly through the involuntary action of reflexes, at least initially)

Sleeping Like a Baby

Your newborn definitely spends more time sleeping than anything else she does. Most newborns sleep up to 16 hours or more a day. But not in a row!

Your baby's first sleep, recovering from the trauma of birth, may last from 12 to 24 hours. (You, too, may want to take advantage of this opportunity to sleep uninterrupted for more than 6 hours. It's probably the last chance you'll get for several months.)

Unless you have that rare baby who sleeps 8 hours a night from her first night home, your child will probably sleep in small doses that last anywhere from 2 to 6 hours before waking again. After a few hours (or even just a few minutes) of wakefulness, she'll drift off to sleep again.

Q-Tip

If you can, train yourself to take naps. Curl up with your baby for the afternoon. When your baby falls asleep at night, don't stay up too much longer yourself. In less than 6 hours—and sometimes much less—your baby will probably be awake again, demanding food and attention.

Most babies sleep very deeply, undisturbed by bright lights and loud noises (unless they are sudden). Moving your baby will also seldom wake her. In most cases, your baby will wake up solely due to the sensations or needs of her own body. She may be hungry or need to burp. She may have a dirty diaper or feel some pain. Or she may be too cold or too hot. Taking care of the source of her distress may allow her to fall back to sleep—or may leave her cheerful and awake.

You Are What Your Baby Eats

Your baby will begin eating—that is, nursing and/or drinking formula from a bottle—within the first few hours of birth. After he sleeps off the aftereffects of birth, your newborn will want to feed every 2 to 3 hours.

How will you know when to feed your baby? Don't worry; he'll let you know. When he's hungry, he will cry. For a detailed discussion of your baby's eating patterns, skip ahead to Chapter 4.

Baby Doctor

If your baby has not urinated in several hours, encourage her to drink more when you nurse or feed her. If you increase her fluid intake and her diaper still remains dry, contact your doctor. Your baby may have a urinary or other medical problem.

Highly concentrated urine, with a deeper yellow color, may also indicate a need for more fluids. If the urine remains strong—and especially if it begins to reek—contact your pediatrician. Your child may have a urinary infection.

Time for a (Diaper) Change

As often or even more often than she feeds, your baby needs a diaper change. Newborns typically go through anywhere from 10 to 15 cloth diapers (or 8 to 12 disposables) every day.

Many new parents seem preoccupied (and even fascinated) by the color of their child's bowel movements. In the first day or two, a black sticky substance called *meconium*, which filled your baby's intestines while in the womb, is excreted. After that, your child begins the transition to regular bowel movements. Your baby's poop will dazzle you with a rainbow of colors. Normal stools for newborns may appear greenish-gray, green, black, various shades of brown, or yellow. Excretions may also vary greatly in consistency, ranging from soupy to almost solid. None of these variations is a cause for alarm.

Your baby should urinate frequently. The average newborn wets six to eight diapers a day. As long as your baby is thriving and continues to gain weight, don't worry if she wets more than eight diapers. Too little urine may be a problem, though. An absence of urine in the diaper after a couple of hours have passed can indicate that your baby may not be getting enough fluids. Perhaps she has a fever or her blanket is too warm, so she needs more to drink. Try to increase the amount of fluid she drinks at feeding times.

For a detailed discussion of diapers, changing stations, diaper rash, and changing games, see Chapter 5.

Crybaby

Babies do not generally shed tears until several weeks or even months after birth. Yet they do cry because crying provides their primary means of communication. In time, you may even be able to interpret and understand your baby's specific cries. You may know, for instance, whether a specific cry signals hunger, pain, cold, or boredom.

In the first week of life, your baby may or may not make other vocal sounds as well. Taken together, his cries and vocal sounds allow your baby to convey basic emotions such as sadness, distress, anger, or happiness. For a full discussion of crying and communication, refer to Chapter 6.

Testing Reflexes: Involuntary Movements

As mothers know, most babies do move around a great deal long before they are born. Yet in the early weeks of her life, your baby has little conscious control of any of her movements. *Reflexes*—innate and involuntary responses to specific stimuli—control virtually all the jerky movements of your newborn's arms, legs, and hands. You might even notice that your baby sometimes moves involuntarily in time with the rhythms of your speech.

Babies have an amazing array of reflexes. Your child's instinctive reflexes help her eat and breathe, protect herself, and pave the way for future skills. Most babies exhibit all of the following baker's dozen of reflex actions:

- **Rooting:** The first of four feeding reflexes, rooting causes your baby to turn her head toward your finger or nipple if you gently stroke her cheek or the edge of her lips with it.

- **The Babkin reflex:** This reflex causes your baby to open her mouth if you gently press your thumb into her palm.

◆ **Sucking:** This reflex is the key to feeding, but babies apply it indiscriminately, sucking virtually anything that touches their lips. If your baby does *not* suck automatically, you can sometimes stimulate the sucking reflex by gently stroking the roof of her mouth.

◆ **Swallowing:** This reflex is the fourth and final feeding reflex.

◆ **Coughing and sneezing:** These reflexes clear your baby's throat or nose of fluids that commonly clog these passageways after birth.

◆ **Yawning:** Another respiratory reflex, yawning helps increase your baby's intake of oxygen.

◆ **Grasping:** The favorite reflex of family members, friends, and strangers (who tend to interpret this automatic response as a sign of affection), the grasping reflex causes your child to close her fist around any object placed in her palm.

◆ **The Babinski reflex:** When you stroke the sole of your child's foot, her toes spread out, the big toe rises higher than the rest, and her foot bends upward. (Curiously, an adult's foot reacts to the same stimulus by bending downward.)

◆ **The Moro reflex:** This reflex is the startle reaction, your baby's automatic response to any sudden movements, loud noises, or loss of support. Her body stiffens and may shake visibly as she quickly thrusts her arms and legs out and then immediately pulls them back in. She may look as if she is trying to hang on to the air to keep from falling.

◆ **The Shutdown response:** This reflex is a defense against overstimulation. When encountering a cacophony of sounds or an onslaught of competing visual stimuli, your baby may suddenly retreat from the world, instantly falling asleep no matter what she had been doing at the time.

◆ **The tonic neck reflex:** If you lay your baby on her back and turn her head to one side, she will extend the arm on that side straight out in front of her, putting her hand directly in line with the eyes. She will look like a fencer ready to parry an opponent's thrusts. This reflex may prepare her for future hand-eye coordination.

◆ **Automatic standing and walking:** If you hold your newborn upright and lower her toward a hard surface, she will automatically brace her feet and legs against the surface. Then she will alternately lift each leg, as if taking steps. Both of these reflexes tend to disappear within weeks of birth.

◆ **Automatic swimming:** If you hold your baby in water, she will begin to make swimming movements.

Although most movements result from reflexes, newborn infants do exhibit some voluntary movements—for instance, the tracking of sounds or movement. If you lay your baby down on her stomach, she may try to lift her head. (She may even succeed for a few moments.) She may also try to lift her head when you hold her on your shoulder. Finally, your baby might also makefaces at you, perhaps responding to or even imitating your own facial expressions.

Have fun playing with your baby's reflexes and observing her early activities. But keep in mind that no baby fits exactly a profile of "typical" newborn behavior. Try to avoid the temptation to judge your baby according to the skills she masters during the first week of her life.

From the moment they are born, babies are individuals. Each has a distinctive personality and a different path of development to follow. Some are active, some quiet; some are shy, and some are gregarious. So no matter how your baby behaves during the first days of his or her life, enjoy the precious time you have to get to know each other.

The Least You Need to Know

◆ Don't worry about your newborn's physical features or blemishes. Most blemishes will disappear.

◆ Babies can see, hear, touch, smell, and taste from the moment of birth.

◆ Newborns do little more than eat, sleep, pee, poop, and cry.

◆ Most newborn movements are reflex actions.

Health and Development

In This Chapter

- ◆ Developmental milestones in the first 3 months
- ◆ How to find the perfect pediatrician
- ◆ When you need to call the doctor
- ◆ Preparing for first aid

Babies don't grow quite as fast as the pod people in *Invasion of the Body Snatchers*—but almost. In just the first 3 or 4 months of your baby's life, he will grow from a gorgeous but largely immobile, inactive, and apparently inscrutable creature to a lively, rolling, smiling explorer.

Enjoy the first 3 months of your baby's life by getting to know him. Your baby will quickly develop preferences and express his likes or dislikes through facial expressions and sounds and, later, by directing attention to objects he likes and refusing to focus on things he doesn't like. As you get to know your child and the way he expresses himself, your confidence in your own parenting will grow.

The First Smile and Other Milestones

From the beginning, your child will show a great interest in people and a particular fascination with faces. Parents, friends, and strangers tend to smile when putting their faces in a baby's line of sight. At around 6 weeks, your baby returns the favor, usually upon hearing the sound of your voice. All babies' smiles are contagious. Her smiles prompt your smiles, and within a few more weeks, your smiles will spark hers.

Life of the Party

Your baby's smiles signal the dawn of a social being. At first, your party animal smiles at anyone. She clearly likes being with people and interacting with them. But by 3 months, your baby clearly recognizes and shows a preference for you above all other people. Oh, she still smiles at the faces of others, but your face brings the biggest smile.

During the first 3 months, parent-child bonding depends solely on your efforts: You offer caring, comfort, warmth, nourishment, and cuddling. By about 3 months, because you have earned her trust, she gratefully returns your affection.

Baby Folklore

Take care not to step over your baby while he is lying on the ground. It was once believed that this would permanently arrest the child's growth. If you do unthinkingly step over your baby, you can undo the damage by stepping over him again backward.

Rocking and Rolling

At birth and during the first weeks of life, your baby has almost no control over his movements. Between 6 and 12 weeks, however, he demonstrates gradually increasing muscular control, beginning with his neck muscles. At first, he balances his head when someone holds him upright. By the end of this period, he begins lifting his head up to look around when you put him down on his stomach. Soon after that, he begins to lift his shoulders off the ground, too.

By about 3 months, your baby no longer automatically curls up when you put him down. As his arms and legs gain strength, he begins kicking and waving—not merely through reflex now, but because he wants to move his arms and legs. The powerful thrust of his legs may make it seem as if he wants to jump out of your arms when you hold him upright with his feet in your lap.

Your baby's hands, which began as fists, begin to open up at about 6 weeks. Over the next several weeks, he discovers his hands and then practices using them. By 8 to 10 weeks, your baby delights in batting at the things he sees. Next, he begins exploring his hands by putting them (and anything else he manages to get his hands on) in his mouth.

By the end of 3 months, your baby may even begin rolling (although most babies do not begin to roll until the fourth month). At least initially, he probably will be capable of rolling only from his side to his back. But remember, he's only just beginning. Soon your baby will be on the move.

The Sweetest Sounds

During the first 8 weeks, your baby may make a wide variety of sounds. With the exception of crying, most of these are involuntary: burps, stomach grumbles, contented sighs, and discontented whimpers.

Baby Talk

"My God, the human baby! A few weeks after birth, any other animal can fend for itself. But you! A basket case 'till you're 21."

—Megan Terry

But by the third month, she makes all sorts of noises just because she likes to hear them: cooing, gurgling sounds, bubbling noises made with her saliva. Soon you will hear her burst out with full-body laughter when something amuses her.

Child Development Is Not a Race

One closing word about development, which applies not just to the first 3 months, but throughout your baby's early years: what matters is not when your child reaches each developmental stage, but only that he does so. Child development is not a race. Some infants progress in steady fashion according to the book; others progress in spurts. Avoid the temptation to compare the timing of your baby's development to any other child's (and politely ignore friends, relatives, and strangers who do these comparisons for you). It does your baby a disservice to be thought of as "better" or "worse" than any other child. After all, regardless of how fast or slow he acquires particular skills, your baby is always the best baby to you.

Finding the Right Pediatrician

Aside from choosing a trustworthy baby-sitter or day-care provider, picking the right pediatrician may be the most important personnel choice you make over the next 5 years. Finding a pediatrician is easy, but finding the right one may take a little time.

If you are still looking for a pediatrician, or if you become dissatisfied with the doctor who is currently examining your child, these steps will help you find a good one:

1. **Get recommendations.** Start by asking your obstetrician or midwife, friends, and other family members who have children for their recommendations. If you belong to an HMO, check the list of preferred health-care providers to see whether any of the recommended physicians are included.

2. **Meet the doctor.** After compiling a short list of viable candidates, meet with each of them. Some will charge you for the visit; some will not. Some will charge you for their time only if you decide not to choose them as your child's doctor.

3. **Ask questions.** Feel free to ask questions that will give you an idea of how the pediatrician operates. If it concerns you at all, it's not a silly question. Ask about the normal course of both routine and sick visits. Find out whether the doctor handles all aspects of examination or treatment. Many pediatricians, for example, try to maintain a good relationship with their patients by having nurses handle the more unpleasant tasks of giving shots and taking blood samples.

Baby Doctor

To find out whether your pediatrician is board certified, call your state or local medical society or physician-referral service. Or see whether your library has *The Directory of Medical Specialists,* which details the educational and career history of the nation's board-certified physicians.

What makes a good pediatrician? Different parents will give you different answers. All of the varying recommendations, however, probably boil down to the following important considerations.

Training and Competence

Your child's pediatrician should be well trained to handle not only regularly scheduled well-baby visits, but also those frantic calls and last-minute appointments that arise due to accidents and/or medical emergencies. If you have any questions or concerns, large or small, about your baby, you will understandably want to air them out with your pediatrician. So you should have confidence in the doctor's training and competence.

Find out whether the doctor is a board-certified pediatrician. Board certification means she has spent at least 3 years in an approved pediatrics residency training program and passed a standardized qualifying exam. This certification guarantees that the doctor is familiar not only with well-baby care, but also with a wide range of complicated childhood ailments.

Manner Toward Children

The way in which the pediatrician behaves with your child is of critical importance. Unfortunately, this quality is difficult to judge until you see him with your child. Still, you can observe these clues even before your baby meets the doctor:

- Do both the waiting area and the examination rooms seem child-friendly?

- Does the waiting area have a wide variety of toys, books, or things to look at?

- Do the toys seem clean and well cared for?

- When you bring your child for a visit, observe the way the doctor interacts with the baby. Does he attempt to distract your infant in any way before or during the examination? Does he talk to both you and your baby? Does he seem to like children?

If your pediatrician has not tried to create an atmosphere that welcomes children—or if he seems insensitive to the needs and feelings of your baby—you may want to consider finding a new doctor.

Rapport with Parents

If you can't talk openly to your child's doctor, her rapport with your child matters little. If you feel that the doctor has little time or patience for your questions, you won't ask them, and that means your baby may not get the care she needs. You need to feel welcome to share your priorities and your concerns with your child's doctor, or they won't get met.

Rapport between a pediatrician and parents depends, of course, as much on the individual parents as on the doctor. Some parents like their doctors to be friendly and approachable; others prefer their doctors to be businesslike. Some parents like to participate in making treatment decisions; others prefer to be told what to do. Some favor familiarity; others prefer authority.

Do you feel comfortable talking with the pediatrician? Does she make it easy for you to understand your baby's condition and the treatment plan she wants you to follow?

Does she ever offer you options regarding treatment and ask for your input? Does she hand down the law from on high: "Here's what we'll have to do …." Or does she explain her thinking in making a treatment decision? (Again, nothing is wrong with either of these approaches, but you want a doctor whose approach matches your preferences.)

Child-Rearing Philosophy

You need to have confidence that if you turn to your baby's doctor for guidance, he will offer advice that, in most cases at least, conforms to your own child-rearing beliefs and principles. To find out your doctor's philosophy, ask questions at your first meeting about such issues as the following:

- Breast-feeding versus bottle-feeding (see Chapter 4)
- Feeding on demand (see Chapter 4)
- Sleep disturbances (see Chapter 17)
- Pacifiers (see Chapter 6)
- The advantages or disadvantages of working parents (see Chapter 23)

The pediatrician's ideas regarding two or three of these issues should shed light on his overall child-rearing philosophy.

Treatment Philosophy

Different pediatricians may treat some of the same conditions in dramatically different but equally valid ways. The important thing is to find a pediatrician whose approach complements your own, even if you sometimes disagree. These are some of the issues you might want to explore:

- Is she aggressive in prescribing antibiotics?
- Does she prefer to take a wait-and-see approach?
- Does the doctor treat only medical conditions?
- Does she also offer psychological, behavioral, and/or nutritional advice?
- If you have interest in certain alternative medicines (homeopathy, acupuncture, herbal medicine), how does the pediatrician feel about them?

◆ Will she object if you consult not only her, but also an alternative practitioner? (You should ask the same questions of any practitioners of alternative medicine to find out how they feel about working with providers of traditional Western medical care.)

Availability

It does little good to find the perfect doctor if you can't ever see or speak to him. So before committing yourself to a pediatrician, find out about the following:

◆ **Office hours:** What are the doctor's office hours? Must routine visits be scheduled only between 9 and 5 on weekdays? Does he accommodate working parents by providing any evening or weekend hours?

◆ **Phone consultations:** Does your doctor personally return calls? If a medical emergency or illness arises after hours or on the weekend, can you reach him? How soon does he normally return a call?

◆ **Location:** Is the doctor's office in a convenient location for you?

◆ **Affiliations:** With what hospital(s) is he affiliated?

◆ **Practice:** Does he work alone or as part of a group? If it's a group practice, can you see the same doctor for all well-baby and most sick visits? In either case, who covers for the pediatrician during off-hours and vacations?

◆ **Insurance:** Is this pediatrician or the group practice covered by your health insurance plan?

In Sickness or in Health: Pediatric Visits

You will never see as much of your child's doctor as you do in your baby's first year of life. For well-baby visits alone, you will probably see your pediatrician half a dozen times. Typically, your doctor will want to see the baby at 1 month, 2 months, 4 months, 6 months, 9 months, and 1 year old. These visits provide your doctor the opportunity to measure and weigh your baby in order to monitor her growth, to answer any questions you may have about your baby's health or your parenting, and to immunize your child against common childhood diseases.

Q-Tip _____

Few parents have all the answers. So as questions arise in the course of parenting, jot them down on a piece of paper or in a small notebook that you can refer to on your child's next visit to the pediatrician.

You might also find it useful to keep a notebook that records your baby's behavior, development, and health history. A record of your baby's sleep patterns, rashes, teething, eating habits, frequency of bowel movements, crying patterns, and so on may help alert you to changes or disruptions that may signal illness. Software programs are now available that make it easy to record and organize all of the day-to-day data on your baby.

In addition to well-baby visits, of course, you will call on your pediatrician whenever your child gets ill. New parents are sometimes unsure when to call the pediatrician. They don't want to "bother" their doctor over nothing, but if it is "something," they don't want to delay calling. Try to allay these anxieties by observing the following rule:

If your child's appearance, behavior, or symptoms of illness concern you, it's not nothing.

A doctor's assurance that your child is well and normal can be just as important as her confirmation that your baby is sick. So feel free to call your doctor whenever your child looks or acts differently.

When to Call the Doctor

Certain conditions and symptoms demand professional attention. For specific ailments, illnesses, and emergencies, see Appendix D. In general, however, call your pediatrician if your child has any of the following:

- A **fever** greater than 100°F

- **Sweaty** or clammy skin

- Unusual and persistent **crying**

- An **injury** that causes more than 15 minutes of crying

- Disruptions in feeding patterns, especially a sudden **loss of appetite**

- Ingestion of anything you suspect may be **poisonous**

- **Vomiting** that differs in force or volume from normal spitting up

- **Diarrhea** that smells foul or shows blood or mucus, or is accompanied by a fever

- **Constipation** that is accompanied by vomiting

- Signs of **blood** in the urine or bowel movements

- Unusual **listlessness** or inactivity

- **Convulsions** or twitching fits

- Marked changes in **color** or behavior

- Any unfamiliar or widespread **rash**

- Any **burns** that result in blisters

- Difficulty in **breathing**

- A persistent **cough**

- **Redness** of the eyes or the discharge of pus from the eyes

Baby Folklore

Care to try some traditional cures for infant illnesses? If your baby gets whooping cough, put his godfather's or godmother's garter around his neck. Or hold the head of a live toad (wrapped inside a handkerchief) inside your baby's mouth. Doing the same with a live frog was once believed to cure thrush (a fungal infection). Of course, it didn't do much for the frog.

- **Discharge from the ears or ear pain,** which you may be able to recognize by the baby's constant turning of his head or pulling at his ear

- **Swelling or sinking of the fontanels** (the two soft spots in your baby's head)

Of course, just because a symptom is not on this list doesn't mean you shouldn't call. Feel free to call your child's doctor whenever you have concerns that cannot wait until the next scheduled visit.

Immunizations

The frequency of well-baby visits during your child's first year is largely determined by the immunization schedule. At almost every visit, your baby gets a shot and/or an oral vaccine to help prevent certain childhood illnesses. Immunizations help your baby develop the antibodies that protect her from such diseases as the following:

- Hepatitis

- Diphtheria (a bacterial infection that attacks the throat and airway)

- Tetanus (lockjaw)

- Pertussis (whooping cough)

- Hemophilus influenzae type B (HIB) (a bacterial infection that can cause meningitis)

◆ Polio (a viral infection that attacks the central nervous system, causing nerve damage and possible paralysis)

◆ Measles

◆ Mumps

◆ Rubella (German measles)

◆ Varicella (chicken pox)

◆ Pneumococcal

In addition, your pediatrician may recommend an influenza vaccine if your child has certain risk factors, such as asthma, cardiac disease, sickle cell disease, HIV, or diabetes.

Dead or weakened strains of the germs, when introduced into the body orally or through an injection, stimulate the protection of antibodies that fight disease. If your child later comes in contact with the germs that cause these diseases, she either will get a mild case of the illness or will not get it at all.

Your pediatrician will probably recommend that your child adhere to the immunization schedule outlined in Appendix B.

To Immunize or Not to Immunize?

Many parents today are reluctant to immunize their children against childhood diseases. Why? Let's enter into the debate:

POINT: Many of these diseases are now all but eradicated, and even on those rare occasions when they do occur, medical interventions now significantly reduce the risk of long-term damage. Some of these diseases are common only among certain segments of the population (usually the urban poor). Unless your child is at risk, why should you agree to have your child vaccinated?

COUNTERPOINT: Although some of these diseases may have all but disappeared, the germs that cause them have not been eliminated. The fact that children rarely get these diseases demonstrates the effectiveness of widespread immunization programs rather than a complete victory over the disease itself.

POINT: Some children have poor reactions to certain vaccines. For example, the side effects of the DPT shot (a combined vaccine against diphtheria, tetanus, and pertussis) may include 1 to 3 days of fever, loss of appetite, and general irritability.

COUNTERPOINT: Pediatricians can make adjustments to the vaccine to lessen the side effects. If, for example, your 2-month-old seems particularly out of sorts for an extended period of time following her DPT immunization, your pediatrician will probably agree to eliminate the pertussis vaccine, the most likely cause of this reaction, from all subsequent immunizations.

Ultimately, you will need to make your own decision about whether to immunize your baby. Discuss your concerns with your pediatrician, who may help you weigh the potential risks of vaccination against the risks involved in not immunizing.

Babyproofing

To minimize the transmission of germs to your baby, wash your hands frequently with a disinfectant soap. Have your guests wash their hands before holding or touching your baby, too. If friends or relatives are sick, wait until they get better before letting them come in close contact with your baby. Finally, if you are sick, let your partner handle as much baby care as possible.

Keeping Your Child Healthy

During the first 3 months of life, most babies have few, if any, health problems. Young infants are protected from most diseases in two ways. First, like most protective parents (especially first-time parents), you probably limit your child's contact with the outside world. Despite their sociability, most newborns have a very dull social life (and their exhausted parents probably don't socialize much, either). Friends or relatives who want to see your baby probably visit you in your home. So until your child begins day care, he seldom even comes into contact with most germs that cause illness.

Second, babies acquire their mothers' immunity to many diseases through the sharing of fluids in the womb. Much of this immunity continues in early infancy. If you breast-feed your baby, you will continue to pass on your immunity to many diseases through your breast milk.

Sun Screening

One health problem that many infants do have is overexposure to the sun. Because your baby's delicate skin has built up no protection from the sun's burning rays, you must protect your child as much as possible. You can keep her from getting a painful sunburn by sticking to these guidelines, especially during the first year:

◆ When you want to spend some time in the great outdoors, try to make it in the early morning or late afternoon. The intensity of the sun's rays peaks during midday (11 A.M. to 3 P.M.).

◆ Play in the shade whenever possible. When you do play with your child in the sun, limit the amount of uninterrupted time you spend in the sun. Alternate time in the sun with time in the shade.

◆ If your baby likes to go "swimming" with you, let her keep her shirt on (and maybe even her hat). Change to a dry shirt when you get out of the water.

◆ Have your child wear a hat with a brim wide enough to shadow her face when she goes outside.

◆ After your baby's half-birthday, use SPF 15 sunscreen on all exposed areas of the skin—except the hands (which too often end up transferring the sunscreen to the eyes) and face—even in nonpeak sun hours (before 11 A.M. or after 3 P.M.). Reapply sunscreen whenever necessary.

◆ Try to get your baby to wear UV sunglasses to guard against retinal burn. If she won't wear sunglasses, make sure she wears a wide-brimmed hat and keep her in the shade as much as possible.

◆ Use the sunshield on your child's stroller.

Fresh air and limited exposure to the sun are good for your baby. You certainly shouldn't keep her indoors all the time. But taking precautions to avoid *overexposure* will help keep your baby healthy.

In Case of Emergency: First Aid for Children

During the first 3 months of your child's life, you will hopefully have little need for first aid. Because your newborn has almost no mobility, he has few chances to injure himself. In all likelihood, you will need little more in the way of a first-aid kit than a thermometer, an accurate means of measuring out medications, and a bottle of acetaminophen drops.

Baby Doctor

An oral syringe generally provides the greatest accuracy in measuring medication. It also results in the least amount of spilled or lost medication. And when your child gets older, he'll probably enjoy squirting the medicine into his own mouth. (It also makes a great bathtub toy.)

Nonetheless, it's never too soon to learn about first aid and begin putting together a complete first-aid kit. (For information on when you should use your first-aid kit, see Appendix D.) Although you may not need many of these items in the first 3 months of your baby's life, you're sure to use most of the following as he grows older and more mobile:

- Adhesive bandages of various sizes (for cuts and scrapes)

- Large (1- to 2-inch) nonstick bandages (for larger wounds)

- Adhesive tape (for holding nonstick bandages in place)

- Sterile gauze or gauze pads

- Scissors (for cutting bandages, gauze, and tape)

- Thermometer (preferably a rectal one)

- Calibrated medicine dropper, spoon, or syringe

- Liquid acetaminophen

- Local pain reliever (herbal or medicinal) for teething

- Spray for relieving bee stings and insect bites

- Calamine lotion or other soothing lotion (for cooling the skin and reducing itching in case of sunburns or rashes)

- Hydrocortisone cream and/or benadyne (for allergic reactions)

- Antiseptic liquid (for washing your own hands before and after administering first aid)

- Ice pack (to reduce aching and swelling)

- Tweezers (for removing splinters)

- Complete family medical guide

Babyproofing

Unless your pediatrician specifically prescribes it, never give your baby aspirin or anything containing aspirin. When given in connection with influenza or chicken pox, aspirin has been associated with Reyes syndrome, a disease that can cause uncontrollable vomiting and liver damage.

Baby Doctor

Never give your baby syrup of ipecac, which was once recommended as a way to get babies to vomit up any poison they may have ingested. This can actually create further complications, and the American Academy of Pediatrics now recommends that parents never give their children anything that will make them vomit.

Also, please take special care to follow your pediatrician's instructions regarding the dosage and frequency of any medication, including acetaminophen.

If you use up any of these first-aid supplies, replace it as soon as you can so that it will be available if you need it again. Also check expiration dates on all medications regularly. You never know when you may need to use them.

Be Prepared: Infant CPR

If your child chokes or stops breathing, your knowledge of cardiopulmonary resuscitation (CPR) could save her life. The only way for you to be truly certain that you know how to perform CPR on your child is to take a CPR course. If you did not take a course in CPR for children prior to your baby's birth, take one in the first few months of her life.

Baby Doctor

To find a course on CPR for infants and children, consult your chapter of the American Red Cross, the American Heart Association, local hospitals and schools, parenting organizations, and the adult education programs offered in your community.

CPR instructors not only show you what to do, but they also provide you with the much-needed opportunity for hands-on experience. To pass the course and get your CPR certification, you have to demonstrate the techniques yourself.

In Appendix D, you will find a brief overview of the steps involved in CPR for infants. Do not fool yourself into thinking that you are prepared for an emergency just because you have read the brief description provided there. If you ever need to use it, you won't have the time to thumb frantically through this—or any other—book. So do yourself and your baby a huge favor: take an infant CPR class as soon as possible.

The Least You Need to Know

◆ Child development is not a race.

◆ Your baby will smile, make noise, and roll over at his own pace. Let him.

◆ Make sure your pediatrician is fully trained, has convenient hours, has a good rapport with you and your child, and shares your child-rearing philosophies.

◆ Call your pediatrician if anything about your baby's health or development concerns you.

◆ Learn infant CPR at the earliest opportunity.

Caring for Your Newborn

In This Chapter

- ◆ Keeping your newborn clean
- ◆ Dressing your baby
- ◆ Putting your newborn to sleep
- ◆ Sudden Infant Death Syndrome (SIDS)

Taking care of a newborn can be an intimidating responsibility for new parents. Your baby no doubt seems so small, so precious, and so vulnerable that you fear doing anything wrong. Faced with such a small creature, just the basics of baby care can seem overwhelming. In attending to the basics of baby care, you may feel as if your baby's fate—as always—rests solely in your hands.

Fear not. Although your baby's fate does indeed rest in your hands, the basics of newborn care—bathing your baby, dressing her, and getting her to go to sleep—are not that difficult. With a little experience, you will trust yourself to bathe your baby without drowning her. (Drowning is especially easy to avoid if you stick to sponge baths.) You will figure out how to dress your baby without either underdressing her or overdressing her. And easiest of all, you will find that your newborn will fall asleep when she's tired—with little or no help from you.

Early Sponge Baths

Bathing your baby will some day be fun for both your baby and you. Unfortunately, many newborns find bathing a disagreeable experience. In many cases, it's not so much the water, but the feeling of nakedness that newborns don't like. Fortunately, your baby won't really get very dirty until he becomes mobile, so in the first few months, you can concentrate on keeping clean those parts that do sometimes get dirty: his bottom and his genitals, and occasionally his hands or face.

For the first week or two of your baby's life, however, you won't have a chance to find out if he enjoys the bath. Until the umbilicus falls off (and a circumcision, if any, heals), avoid giving your baby a bath. Instead, you will have to clean him without immersing his belly (and perhaps his penis as well) in water. The best way to do this is with a sponge bath.

Are You Ready?

Because you want to get your baby clean, dry, and warm again as quickly as possible, have everything ready before you begin the sponge bath. Here's what you may need to have at hand:

- A towel on which your baby can lie or an empty portable tub in which she can lie
- A source of warm water (a sink or a large pitcher filled with warm water)
- Nondetergent soap
- Baby-safe shampoo
- A fine-tooth baby comb
- Cotton balls and alcohol (until the umbilicus has fallen off)
- A washcloth (the softer, the better)
- Cotton balls for washing the eyes (not necessary, but some babies like it)
- A towel or, even better, a hooded towel/robe
- Diaper cream
- A clean diaper
- A fresh set of clothes or pajamas

Before undressing your baby at all, make sure the room is warm (a toasty 75°F is ideal). Your baby will not like it (and will let you know it) if she becomes chilled.

Q-Tip _____

If you don't want to drive your heating bills up by turning the thermostat to 75°F, you can heat a small bathroom to that temperature quickly by shutting the door and running a hot shower for 2 or 3 minutes.

If your baby doesn't like total nakedness—and many newborns don't—then avoid ever completely undressing her, even for the bath. Keep your child's diaper on and her bottom half wrapped up in a towel while you wash her face, hands, arms, and chest. (You might want to keep the diaper on as long as possible to avoid accidents anyway.) Then dry off her head and torso, pull on a T-shirt, take off her diaper, and work on the bottom half.

How to Wash a Baby

To wash a baby, you need to work with one hand. Use your dominant hand to wash and the other hand to hold and support your baby. One hold that works well is to have your arm across your baby's back, gripping under his underarm with your hand and supporting his head and neck with your wrist. But as long as both you and your baby feel secure, any hold will do.

Using your free hand to wash your baby, start at the top and move down. As you work down your baby's body, pay special attention to all the creases: under the chin, on the neck, around the joints of the arms and legs, on the belly, around the bottom. You'll be surprised how much schmutz can gather in these creases. Unless your baby is very dirty, you won't need a lot of soap. In most places, water alone will suffice. Indeed, if your baby has very dry skin, soap can make this dryness even worse.

Here's how to do it:

1. Start by running a wet washcloth over his head. (Unless your baby has cradle cap, you won't need to use shampoo—which you can apply sparingly with a washcloth—more than once or twice a week.)

2. Next, wash his eyes with a warm, damp washcloth (not one that you've already used for shampoo) or clean cotton balls dipped in warm water.

3. Move on to the rest of the face, the neck, the shoulders, the arms and hands, and the chest.

4. After drying and wrapping your baby's head and torso, take off his diaper and wash his legs and feet.

5. Finally, turn him over on his hands and knees, supporting his head and neck with your forearm so that you can wash his back, genitals, and bottom. Always wash the genitals and bottom last—and in that order. For at least the first couple of months, this area may be the only one that requires soap.

Baby Folklore _____

You may want to skip washing your baby's hands. Superstition holds that hand-washing during the first year also washes away your baby's fortune or his luck. And how dirty could his hands get in a year anyway?

Baby Doctor _____

If you have not had your son's penis circumcised, wash it on the outside only. *Do not* pull back the foreskin to clean the penis. There's no need to clean under the foreskin, and you can do damage if you try.

If you have a daughter, you do not need to scrub the inside of her vulva vigorously. Just gently spread her labia, then wash and rinse them with soap and water from front to back. You may notice a white, cheesy substance inside the labia. Do not bother scrubbing it away. It is perfectly normal and, if left alone, will go away on its own.

If you have a son who has been circumcised, keep his penis dry until it has healed. (Even if the umbilicus has fallen off, avoid tub or sink baths until the penis heals, too.) Instead of washing, each time you change him, put a dab of Vaseline on the head of his penis and cover it with a small sterile piece of gauze. (In addition, double-diapering for the first day or two after the circumcision may provide some extra padding to protect the healing penis.)

Remember to keep the umbilicus clean—with alcohol and a sterile cotton ball—and dry until it falls off. (For more on umbilical care, see Chapter 1.)

You can continue with sponge baths for as long as your baby seems to enjoy them. However, anytime after the umbilicus has fallen off and the circumcision (if any) has healed, you can begin bathing your baby in a sink or tub (see Chapter 12 for tips on tub bathing).

Dressing Your Baby

Okay, now it's time to try out all those cute outfits that you received at baby showers and as gifts when your baby was first born. It's a good thing you got so many because between leaky diapers and occasional—or frequent—post-feeding spit-ups, your baby will go through a lot of outfits.

Your baby's body does not retain heat as well as an adult body does. For this reason, most newborns are generally not fond of complete nakedness. Even when the temperature seems comfortable to adults, a naked newborn will find it chilly.

This does not mean you have to dress your baby in winter woolens all the time—especially if you're staying indoors.

Dressing for Indoors

When your baby is inside with the temperature in the low 70s, this is all she needs to wear:

- A diaper (of course)
- A thin undershirt
- A lightweight outfit (onesie, or pants and shirt)
- Socks or booties

There now, that wasn't so hard was it? If you keep the indoor temperature in the mid- to high 60s, you may want to add another layer—perhaps a thicker undershirt. Also, if you put a skirt or dress on your newborn, you may want to dress her in tights or put on a pair of pants underneath her dress or skirt to keep her legs warm.

Dressing for All Seasons

What your baby should wear on your outings together—and taking your baby outside for a walk or an errand at least once a day will be healthy for both you and him—naturally depends on the weather. In the summer, your baby can go out in whatever clothes he's wearing inside for the day. Just make sure that you bring along a wide-brimmed sun hat in case you'll be spending more than a few minutes in the sun.

In the spring, a light jacket or sweater over his clothes and a hat to keep his head warm will usually suffice. In the fall, in addition to a hat, he will probably need a slightly heavier jacket and, on especially breezy days, a sweater underneath. Winter outings naturally involve the most dressing. Depending on the cold, your baby may need an undershirt, warm outfit, sweater, coat, and/or sweatsuit plus a warm hat and mittens.

Babyproofing

As long as you dress your child properly, you and he can brave almost any foul weather. In rain or snow or sleet or hail, you can safely take your baby out. But if it's uncomfortably hot and humid, you'd do better to keep your baby indoors.

The problems many babies have with winter outings are usually not related to getting dressed, but rather getting dressed too soon or undressed too late. Bundled-up babies get overheated easily, so avoid getting your baby all dressed up before you're ready to go. Get your own coat and hat on first. Then put your baby's coat or snowsuit on and whisk him outside before he gets too hot.

When you get wherever you're going, take your baby's outer clothes off if you'll be staying more than a few minutes. Even if you're staying for only a minute, consider at least loosening some of his outer clothes, if not taking them off entirely. (You might also want to loosen your baby's outer clothes before strapping him into his car seat, since the interior of your car is no doubt warmer than the wintry outdoor weather.) Your baby will get awfully cranky and overheated if you leave him bundled up indoors.

Sleepy Time

The average newborn sleeps about 16½ hours every day. So if you have an average baby, you and your partner should have plenty of downtime to rest yourself or get something else done besides baby care. Of course, your newborn is anything but average, so you may have more or less downtime than this. Some newborns sleep as much as 22 hours, while others sleep as little as 10 hours a day.

In any case, your newborn probably sleeps no more than 2 to 4 hours at a stretch, primarily because her tiny stomach won't hold enough food to sustain her for longer than that. By 3 months, however, your baby will probably be able to sleep 6 hours or more without waking.

Putting Your Baby Down

For most newborns, putting them down to sleep is not really much of a challenge. When your baby gets tired, chances are, he'll be cranky for a short time, you'll feed him and put him down in his crib, and he'll fall asleep. In fact, like many newborns, your baby may fall asleep before you get him to the crib—during nursing or bottle-feeding. Try not to view this as a cause for alarm. Yes, your baby will need to learn how to fall asleep without sucking and snuggling in your arms, but there's still plenty of time for that.

If your baby has difficulty falling asleep in the first few months of his life, here are some things you can try:

◆ **Nursing or bottle-feeding:** Many newborns fall asleep while feeding. If your baby falls asleep before finishing a feeding, you might want to wake him up a little to try to fill his stomach, which will allow him to sleep a little longer.

◆ **Swaddling:** Wrapping your newborn tightly in a blanket can help create a feeling of warmth and security, allowing him to drift off to sleep.

◆ **Rocking or swaying:** A slow, gentle rocking motion—whether by sitting in a rocking chair, walking slowly while swaying back and forth, or doing relaxed knee bends with your baby in your arms—may recall motion in the womb, lulling your newborn into a calm and drowsy state.

◆ **Traveling:** Taking a long walk after dinner (yours, your baby's, or both) while pushing your newborn in a stroller or carriage can help soothe him. As darkness approaches, he may drift off to sleep.

◆ **Sucking:** As your newborn gets a little older, you may find that giving him a pacifier or directing him to his thumb allows him to suck his way to slumber.

◆ **Binky:** Again, as your newborn gets a couple of months older, he may calm himself with a comfort item or "transitional object." This might be a soft blanket or a stuffed animal.

Whatever method you choose to soothe and lull your baby to sleep, try to do it close to your baby's crib. Not only will this make it easier for you to transfer your baby to the crib with little disruption, but it will also lay the groundwork for him to learn to fall asleep on his own. If your baby learns to associate his bedroom (or his corner of your bedroom) and his crib with calm and sleep, he may not mind as much later when you put him down while he's still awake. And that's the essential first step toward falling asleep on his own.

Crib Notes

If your baby does not sleep in your bed (see Chapter 17 for the pros and cons of this arrangement), she will need a crib. Make sure you buy one with adjustable mattress supports. These supports allow you to lower the mattress as your baby grows in both size and ability.

For the first month or two, the highest mattress level, as long as it's at least 4 inches below the guard rail, is fine. It will put less strain on your back and make it easier to put your sleeping baby in the crib without waking her. As soon as your baby can sit up, however, you must lower the mattress so that she can't accidentally spill over the edge.

Your crib posts will probably be one of the first things your baby uses to support herself as she pulls

Babyproofing

Never put your crib next to a window. The cords of blinds, shades, and drapes pose a strangling hazard for babies. For the same reason, remove any crib mobiles as soon as your baby can sit up.

herself up to standing. So be sure to lower the mattress to a level where the guard rail is as high as her shoulders will be when she is standing.

SIDS

Every year, about 1 in 600 healthy babies in this country die of SIDS (Sudden Infant Death Syndrome). Although the risk to the general population of babies is relatively small, SIDS, the sudden, unexplained death of an infant, is still the number-one cause of death among infants aged 2 weeks to 12 months.

Baby Doctor

If your baby is in a higher-risk group for SIDS, your doctor may recommend a SIDS monitor. This machine collects data on your baby's heart rate and breathing patterns while he is sleeping and signals alarm if either slows to a dangerous rate. Unfortunately, false alarms are common among monitored babies, and these alarms may create more anxiety rather than less.

Try not to obsess over the possible threat of SIDS. Your doctor will let you know if any concern is warranted. These factors increase the risk:

◆ One or more episodes of *apnea* (cessation of breathing that lasts more than 20 seconds), causing blueness and requiring resuscitation

◆ Serious heart or lung problems

◆ A strong family history (two or more siblings who died or nearly died) of SIDS

The American Academy of Pediatrics recommends that a healthy full-term baby sleep on his back or side rather than on his belly. This position may reduce SIDS rates significantly—up to 50 percent, according to one study.

If you haven't already done so, take a course in infant CPR (see Appendix D) and ask your partner and any probable sitters to do the same. Knowing that you may be able to save your baby's life may give you more peace of mind and let you sleep a little easier.

The Least You Need to Know

◆ Newborns should stick to sponge baths at least until any circumcision is healed and the umbilicus falls off.

◆ Try not to overdress or underdress your newborn. Loosening or removing warm clothing when coming indoors will help keep your baby comfortable.

◆ Your newborn may sleep anywhere from 10 to 22 hours a day—but probably little more than 4 hours at a time. Feeding, swaddling, rocking, and walking with your baby may help bring on much-needed sleep.

◆ The risk of SIDS is relatively small, but not small enough. One out of 600 healthy babies a year dies due to SIDS. Concern is warranted, but obsession is not.

Chapter 4

Breast-Feeding and Bottle-Feeding

In This Chapter

- The relative advantages of breast-feeding and bottle-feeding
- The basics of breast-feeding
- The basics of bottle-feeding
- Solutions to common feeding problems

What's the best way to feed your newborn? During the original post–World War II baby boom, most parents would have answered that bottle-feeding was the only way to go for modern parents. After all, baby formula is scientifically formulated to provide all the nutrition a newborn baby could need. Yet more and more of today's mothers are breast-feeding their infants. After all, mother's milk is the perfect food for a baby.

What's the right answer? Feed your baby lovingly, whether from breast or bottle. Hold your baby close, cuddle her, look at her, sing to her, talk to her, smile at her, hug her tight. Above all, have fun with your baby. Whether she drinks from the breast or the bottle, feeding time offers you a golden opportunity to delight in your newborn child, to marvel at her, and to begin forming a lasting and loving bond between you both.

Breast-Feeding Versus Bottle-Feeding: Pros and Cons

Both breast-feeding and bottle-feeding have their advantages. Because you need to make a decision now, let's consider each of them in turn. That way, you can make an informed choice.

Breast-feeding is better because …

- Your breast milk perfectly provides for your baby's nutritional needs.
- Your breast milk offers health benefits to your baby.
- You can get back in shape more quickly by breast-feeding.
- The physical act of nursing promotes bonding between you and your child.
- Breast milk is always available (as long as you are).
- Breast milk is cheaper.

On the other hand, bottle-feeding is better because …

- Both parents can participate equally in feeding and can take advantage of this opportunity to bond with their child.
- The mother has more freedom in terms of scheduling, dieting, and sexuality.
- Both you and your baby will have an easier time if you need to return to work in the months after his birth.
- It provides good nutrition for your baby if you have a very rare medical condition that dictates against breast-feeding.
- You can avoid any uncomfortable feelings you may have concerning the physical nature of breast-feeding, especially in public.

To help you make the decision that's right for you, let's take a brief look at these arguments.

Breast Milk Is the Best Milk

The American Academy of Pediatrics hails breast milk as the perfect food for the first 6 months of your baby's life. Just right in its mix of protein, fats, carbohydrates, and minerals, breast milk also provides most of the vitamins your baby needs (though it does come up somewhat short in vitamins A, C, and D).

Amazingly, your breast milk adapts its composition from day to day to suit the changing needs of your baby. In the first few days, your baby needs *colostrum*—a somewhat thicker, high-protein, low-fat liquid. Over the next 2 weeks or so, the consistency of breast milk changes. The colostrum is gradually replaced with mature breast milk, which is more liquid and higher in fat and cholesterol. (Unlike adults, babies make good use of a diet high in cholesterol and fat. Your baby's rapidly growing body needs these nutrients for the proper development of the brain, nerve tissues, and cell membranes.)

Commercial formulas may have come increasingly close to duplicating the essential composition of human breast milk, but formula will never be able to adapt its composition from day to day to suit the particular needs of your child.

Breast Milk Protects Your Baby's Health

Your breast milk contains antibodies that can destroy bacteria, viruses, and other germs that can make your baby sick. Breast milk can ward off everything from strep throat and tetanus to measles and chicken pox. It may also increase your newborn's resistance to many allergens. Because only the human body produces antibodies, formula cannot provide this natural immunity from diseases.

Buff Up with Breast-Feeding

Nursing your baby helps your body recover more quickly from pregnancy and childbirth. Breast-feeding helps burn off the fat that your body stored during pregnancy for milk production. It also activates a hormone that shrinks your uterus more quickly. Because you need to be relaxed to nurse your child properly, breast-feeding also forces you to sit down and rest. This rest promotes recuperation from pregnancy and childbirth, too.

Nursing may also, according to some studies, lower your risk of developing breast cancer later in life. Finally, breast-feeding can—but (alas!) does not always—delay the resumption of ovulation and menstruation for several months. Hooray, hooray!

Baby Doctor

The suppression of ovulation while breast-feeding is both temporary and unpredictable. You should never count on breast-feeding as a means of birth control.

Breast-Feeding Creates Intimacy

Breast-feeding undeniably creates a powerful bond between mother and child, not just physically, but emotionally as well. Feeling your baby's skin against your skin can be a source of tremendous pleasure and satisfaction for both of you. Knowing that you are nourishing your child with your own body can also be emotionally gratifying.

Of course, if you bottle-feed, you can (and should) also share love and intimacy with your baby during feeding times. But bottle-feeding doesn't offer quite as much warmth as breast-feeding. That's why most mothers who breast-feed insist that nursing is the ideal way to initiate bonding between a mother and her child.

You Never Have to Hunt for a Clean Breast

As long as you continue breast-feeding, you always have breast milk available. You'll never have to run out to the grocery store at 3:00 in the morning to pick up some breast milk. You won't have to go to all the trouble of sterilizing bottles and preparing formula.

Not only is breast milk a snap to prepare, it's always at the right temperature. So you won't ever have to worry whether breast milk is too hot or too cold.

Best of all, your breasts are extremely portable and you'll never forget to bring them with you when you take your baby on a walk to the park or anywhere else.

Save Money by Breast-Feeding

Breast milk is nearly free of charge (other than the cost of breast pads and nursing bras). You'll save on bottles, nipples, and—here's the biggie—formula. You'll never need to check expiration dates or throw away expensive formula because your baby wasn't very hungry at a particular feeding. Efficient and economical, breast-feeding generates absolutely no waste—except, of course, in your baby's diaper.

Now that we've looked at the arguments for breast-feeding, let's look at the other side of the issue: the advantages of bottle-feeding.

Dad Gets a Turn

If you choose to bottle-feed, your partner can take a much more active role in feeding your child. Bottle-feeding gives a father a chance to bond with his baby in a way that he can't when a mother breast-feeds exclusively.

Of course, even babies who breast-feed can occasionally feed from a bottle, giving the dad a turn. But only bottle-feeding gives both of you an equal opportunity to bond with your child as you feed her. (The father of a breast-fed child can, however, bond with his child in every other way besides feeding.)

Mom Gets a Break

When a new mother is breast-feeding, she has virtually no freedom at all. Because bottle-feeding allows the father and other caretakers to feed the baby, it can free up small pockets of time in a mother's schedule. So you will be able to sleep through the night once in a blue moon, go to the gym, or just give yourself a break from infant care.

Bottle-feeding also frees you to eat and drink whatever you want. You don't need to load up on calories the way a nursing mother does. You'll never need to worry whether you've had enough milk or whether that glass of wine you drank with dinner will make your baby tipsy or give him gas.

Baby Doctor

Contraceptive pills can interfere with the hormones that promote lactation. So if you decide to breast-feed, you may need to change your method(s) of contraception.

Bottle-feeding can also give you more sexual freedom (though your exhaustion may dampen your ardor somewhat). Certainly, breast-feeding does not have to interfere with new parents' sex lives; nonetheless, some parents insist it does. Lactation hormones, for example, can decrease vaginal lubrication, making it necessary to use artificial lubricants. In addition, both you and your partner may find your breasts less arousing when they function as the source of your baby's nourishment. Leakage of breast milk and tenderness of the breasts can also dampen sexual arousal. Bottle-feeding can eliminate all of these concerns. Nonetheless, studies have shown that, perhaps surprisingly, mothers who breast-feed tend to resume an active sex life earlier than mothers who bottle-feed.

Moms Who Need to Get Back to Work

Some working mothers have little choice but to bottle-feed their children (or combine bottle-feeding with morning and evening nursing). If you need or want to return to work within a couple of months of childbirth, you may decide to bottle-feed right from the start. On-the-job breast-feeding—or even expressing milk (drawing milk for later use) during work hours—is often impractical and sometimes impossible. Rather than suckling and then switching primarily to bottle-feeding, you may decide to forego breast-feeding altogether.

Baby Doctor _____

If you take any medications, consult your baby's pediatrician and your own doctor before beginning to breast-feed. Breast milk transfers any drug that you take to your baby. This warning also applies to illegal drugs, alcohol, and nicotine. If you abuse any of these drugs, quit. If you can't, don't force your child to take them, too: bottle-feed your baby.

My Health Won't Allow Breast-Feeding

You may have no choice but to bottle-feed. Less than 5 percent of all mothers produce too little milk to feed a baby, but you may be among that group.

Or you may have a chronic illness or medical condition (cardiac disease, kidney failure, or anemia, for example) that makes breast-feeding dangerous. Though some mothers with these conditions can and do nurse, consult your doctor before you try to nurse if you have any chronic diseases.

Highly infectious diseases such as AIDS, tuberculosis, or hepatitis can be transmitted through breast milk. So if you have an infectious disease, you should avoid breast-feeding.

I Can't Bare My Breasts in Public!

If you feel inhibited about your body, you may find it uncomfortable or even impossible to breast-feed, especially in public places. When your baby gets hungry, she's not likely to want to wait until you find a secluded place to feed her. She wants to eat right away. So if your inhibitions prohibit you from nursing in public, or if the idea of your baby feeding off of you seems creepy or makes you uncomfortable, you may decide to forego breast-feeding.

Modesty and discomfort are perfectly legitimate reasons to choose bottle-feeding. If you can't relax while nursing, your body will not respond well. Your baby will sense your discomfort and become frustrated with feeding. It makes no sense to try to force yourself to do something you can't.

Women who bottle-feed are no less loving and caring than those who breast-feed. What other people think shouldn't matter. You know best how to feed your baby. If you still can't make up your mind after considering the various arguments, try nursing first to see whether you like it. You can always switch to bottle-feeding if you change your mind. But you probably won't be able to switch in the opposite direction. Your body will stop producing milk if it's not being consumed.

> **Q-Tip**
>
> You can protect your modesty and still breast-feed. Try draping a baby's blanket over your shoulder and your baby's head while nursing. Or rather than unbuttoning your shirt from the top to nurse, unbutton it from the bottom or wear a shirt with no buttons. A lifted shirt can conceal most of your breast, your baby's head will cover the rest, and his body will cover any other revealed skin.
>
> If neither of these strategies makes you feel more comfortable, you can still breast-feed in private and bring along formula or expressed milk for public use.

Breast-Feeding Basics

If you've decided to try breast-feeding, start as soon after your baby's birth as possible.

First, find a comfortable position for yourself. You can nurse your baby while lying on your side or sitting up. If you are lying down, cradle your newborn's head in your arm. If you are sitting, make sure your arms are supported. You can use a firm pillow to cushion and support the arm that is holding the baby. Try to stay warm and comfortable when you nurse. Your milk flows more easily if you are warm and relaxed.

Your baby feeds and digests better if she's not lying flat, so hold her up at a slight angle with her head resting in the crook of your arm and her back nestled along your forearm.

> **Baby Doctor**
>
> The size of your breasts has nothing to do with the amount of milk you can produce. So don't fear that you might be inadequate just because your breasts are smaller than your sister's or your friend's.

Remember, your baby has never done this before; you have to teach her what to do. Start by taking advantage of the rooting reflex (see Chapter 1). To get your baby to turn toward your breast, gently stroke her cheek with a finger or your nipple. When she turns, lift your breast and gently guide your nipple into her mouth. She'll know instinctively what to do next. As she sucks, make sure she takes most of your areola into her mouth. If she sucks on just the nipple, she won't get the milk she needs, and your breasts will soon be sore, sore, sore.

During the first few weeks, while your baby gets used to feeding from your breast, feed her as little as possible from a bottle. Formula (or breast milk) flows much more easily from a bottle than from your breast. (You may find this hard to believe once your milk starts flowing—and leaking onto your shirts.) Bottles may confuse your baby and make it more difficult for her to learn how to draw milk from your breast.

No Need to Count Calories

At first, your baby nurses as often as every 2 hours or even more frequently. By the time he's 2 months old, though, he slows down to about once every 4 hours. He will, however, be eating more at each feeding than he did as a newborn.

Let your baby determine how much you feed him. Though you should switch breasts after 5 or 10 minutes, continue to feed him until he stops showing interest in sucking on the second breast.

Don't worry that you may run out of milk. Because your baby's sucking stimulates further milk production, your body makes as much as your baby needs. If he eats a lot, your breasts produce a lot. Only if your baby wets fewer than six diapers a day should you worry that you aren't producing enough milk or your child isn't eating enough.

When your baby has finished eating, release him from your breast by gently slipping a finger into the corner of his mouth. This action breaks the suction and makes it much easier—and a lot less painful—to slip your breast out of his mouth.

Q-Tip

Try to alternate the breast that your baby feeds from first because he is likely to suck longer on the first breast than the second. Use a safety pin on your bra strap as a reminder. Or start every morning with the same breast. Chances are, you'll know exactly how many times your baby has fed throughout the day, so it will be easy to remember with which breast to start (the first breast of the day at all odd feedings and the other breast at all even feedings).

Still Eating for Two: The Nursing Diet

To maintain your milk supply, avoid dehydration, and get the nutrients you and your baby need, you need to eat and drink more (and more carefully) while nursing than you usually do. Follow these guidelines:

- ◆ Eat 500 more calories a day than you normally would.

- ◆ Maintain a well-balanced diet that's high in protein.

- ◆ Avoid very spicy foods, which may give your baby an upset stomach.

- ◆ Drink plenty of fluids (between 2 and 3 quarts a day). Fluids with caffeine or alcohol, both of which dehydrate the body, don't count—and, in fact, require additional fluid supplementation.

- ◆ Drink extra milk or take calcium supplements to up your calcium intake.

- ◆ Drink little or no alcohol.

- ◆ Ask your doctor whether you should take iron or vitamin supplements.

As long as you are still eating for two, these dietary guidelines will keep you—and your baby—thriving.

Pumping Up: Expressing Breast Milk

Some breast-feeding mothers find it convenient to "express" milk from their breasts between feedings. Expressing your milk allows you to store your breast milk for later bottle feedings. You can maintain your baby's primary or exclusive diet of breast milk and still manage to take a break while other caregivers feed her.

You can express breast milk manually or with a manual breast pump. (Many women find the suction of electric breast pumps painfully strong.) Whichever you choose, you will want a quiet, private, relaxing place to do it. No matter how comfortable you feel breast-feeding with other people around, expressing milk will definitely not be something you want to do in public. So if you have returned to work and want to continue feeding your child primarily breast milk, ask your employer whether it's possible to arrange for the time (one or two 20-minute breaks) and space (ideally, a quiet room) you need to express your milk.

To express milk by hand:

1. Cup one breast in both hands with your thumbs on top.

2. Massage your breast with gentle but firm squeezes to stimulate the flow of milk. Start with the outer part of your breast, and then massage closer to your areola. After placing the thumb and fingers of one hand near the areola, press them gently and rhythmically against your ribs. This pumping action should stimulate a flow of milk.

3. Continue pumping for about 5 minutes, collecting the breast milk in a bowl or small pitcher. Then start all over again with the other breast.

4. Continue expressing milk until the flow slows down from a stream to drops.

To express milk using a manual pump:

1. Place the funnel-shape shield over your nipple.

2. Rhythmically squeeze and release the handle to create a vacuum that should draw out a flow of milk and transfer it directly into a bottle. If the pump is painful or doesn't seem to work, try another kind. Not all pumps work alike.

Whether using your hands or a pump, it may help stimulate the flow of milk if you first take a warm bath or shower or place a warm washcloth over your breast. Whichever method you use, stop and try again later if expressing your milk causes any pain. It should be a painless procedure.

> **Baby Doctor**
>
> *Do not* thaw or reheat breast milk in a microwave. Microwave heating may destroy the immunities that would otherwise be transmitted to your baby.

As soon as you have finished, put the milk into a sterile jar or bottle and seal it to keep it germ-free. Refrigerate or freeze it immediately so that it won't spoil. (Breast milk lasts up to 24 hours in a refrigerator; frozen milk lasts up to 6 months.) When you need a bottle, thaw or warm the milk by running it under warm water or letting it sit in a pan of warm water.

Bottle-Feeding Basics

Formula comes in ready-to-use cans or bottles, in concentrated liquid, or in powder form. Although ready-to-use formula is the most convenient, especially if you and your baby are away from home, it costs much more than powder or concentrate. If you choose to mix your own, make sure you make it exactly according to the manufacturer's instructions. Too much liquid may result in malnourishment, and too little water may cause dehydration.

Junior Chemistry

For bottle-feeding, you need between 6 and 10 bottles and nipples. Used bottles and nipples should be sterilized regularly for at least the first 2 to 4 months. (Your baby is more susceptible to germs during this time.) You can buy a fancy steam-sterilization unit, but the easiest way is to wash them thoroughly and then toss them into a covered pot of boiling water for 10 minutes. Most dishwashers also use water hot enough to sterilize bottles.

Q-Tip

If you use mixed formula, you'll find it convenient to make up more than one bottle at a time (formula lasts 24 hours if properly refrigerated). Again, mix formula carefully according to the directions on the can, but make a day's supply. Then be sure to store the mixed formula upright in a capped, sterile bottle.

If you use canned formula, whether in concentrate or ready to drink, always transfer all of the can's contents into sterile bottles as soon as you open it. *Never* store partially used formula in an open can, especially at room temperature, and *never* keep a thermos of warm, mixed formula. Both provide breeding grounds for bacteria.

When your baby gets hungry, warm a refrigerated bottle by placing it in a bowl of hot water or running it under hot water. Although nearly everyone warns parents not to warm a bottle in a microwave, almost every parent we know who bottle-feeds does so. If you do choose to use a microwave, however, please exercise extreme caution. Because microwaves heat unevenly, you must shake the bottle well, let it sit a minute, and then test the temperature.

Even if you don't use a microwave, always test the temperature of formula before feeding it to your baby. After washing your hands, pinch the nipple shut and shake it to restore uniform temperature. Then let a few drops fall on the inside of your wrist. The formula should be room temperature or warm, but never hot. As a general rule, better too cold than too hot. (Many babies don't mind cold bottles at all.) If you do overheat a bottle in the mad rush to get your baby fed, mix in a few ounces of cold formula until the temperature is just right.

Q-Tip

You might find it handy to keep a couple of ounces of extra formula in the refrigerator just in case you overheat a bottle. Your baby will have little patience to wait for an overheated bottle to cool or for you to make up another bottle. He wants to eat *now!* (Just remember not to use mixed formula that has been refrigerated for more than 24 hours—formula does not last any longer than 24 hours in the refrigerator.)

Once you have a bottle ready, find a comfortable position and hold your baby close, as described earlier in the chapter. Gently stroke your baby's cheek so that he turns toward the bottle. Then place the nipple in his mouth. Keep the bottle tilted upward and gradually increase the angle of inclination so that the inside of the nipple remains filled with formula. Otherwise, your baby will suck in lots of air and get gas bubbles in his stomach.

Make the most of your baby's feeding times. Don't just prop him up with pillows and stick a bottle in his mouth. Not only does this position deny him the bonding opportunity that feeding offers, but it could cause either choking (from ingesting too much formula) or serious gas pain and discomfort (from ingesting too much air). So cuddle your child and coo to him while giving him the bottle. Talk to him or sing to him. Look into his eyes and smile.

How Often and How Much Should You Feed Your Baby?

At first, your newborn drinks very little—perhaps an ounce or two at each feeding. But she wants to eat as often as every 2 or 3 hours. Within several weeks, however, her appetite increases. Though she eats more at each feeding, she gets full enough to allow you to space feedings further apart.

Babies change from day to day, and their appetites do, too. As your child grows, pay attention to feeding trends and alter the amount of formula you put in bottles accordingly. At the same time, be flexible and alert enough to respond to shifts in your baby's appetite.

Avoid the temptation to overfeed your baby. Don't insist that she finish everything you have prepared in her bottle. If you feed her too much, she will either vomit or get fat. (Some studies do suggest that formula-fed children are more likely to be overweight than breast-fed children.) When your infant stops drinking and no longer appears interested in the bottle, stop feeding her. Try to burp her and perhaps switch her to the other arm. Then see if she wants to finish the feeding. If she doesn't, don't force the issue.

By the same token, if your baby finishes an entire bottle and still seems hungry, don't stop there. Give her another 2 to 4 ounces until she seems full and satisfied. If this becomes a routine practice, start to make more formula in each bottle.

Just as you will need to adapt to your baby's appetite, you will have to adjust to her changing schedule as well. Few babies stick to the clock, eating every 4 hours on the dot. Feeding schedules may change from day to day. So don't automatically feed your baby just because she hasn't eaten in 4 hours. Don't worry: she'll let you know when she's hungry.

There is one exception to the go-with-the-flow rule: until your baby sleeps through the night, you might want to wake her up to feed her right before *you* go to bed. That way you might be able to get at least a few hours of uninterrupted sleep before the next feeding. But except for this bedtime feeding, try to avoid feeding your child until she asks for it.

For nighttime feedings, keep your supplies and an unopened can of ready-to-eat formula next to your bed. (Remember, room temperature is fine for your baby's bottle.) Or keep the powder and a sealed thermos of warm water next to your bed so that you can mix up a bottle without getting out of bed.

Common Feeding Problems

Feeding your baby—whether by breast or bottle—will not always go smoothly. But rest assured, both you and your baby will learn to cope as you go along.

Breast-Feeding Woes

Many new mothers have some trouble breast-feeding. If you do, too, you might find the solution here. If you have any other problems or questions, consult your pediatrician or a lactation specialist. Or contact the La Leche League at 1-800-LALECHE (1-800-525-3243).

Your Baby Refuses Your Nipple or Spits It Out

Try these solutions:

◆ Gently pull your breast back from your baby's face. Your breast may be covering his nostrils and making it difficult for him to breathe.

◆ Try to calm your baby by rocking or singing to him. After he has calmed down, try again. He may just be too fussy to feed at the moment.

◆ If he's a newborn, be patient and try again. He may still be trying to get the hang of feeding from the breast.

Your Baby Falls Asleep Soon After Beginning to Feed

Try these solutions:

◆ If he's a newborn, let him sleep. He'll wake again when he's hungry.

◆ If he's more than a few days old, let him sleep for half an hour or so, and then wake him and try again.

Your Nipples Are Sore

Try these solutions:

◆ Make sure your baby is taking the nipple and the areola fully into his mouth. He may be sucking solely on the nipple.

◆ Make sure you are holding your baby perpendicular to the breast. If you hold him too low, he will have difficulty taking in the areola.

◆ Keep your nipples dry between feedings.

◆ Try feeding your baby only from the pain-free breast (if any) for a day or so. Gently express milk from the sore breast for bottle feedings.

Your Baby's Sucking Causes a Sharp, Shooting Pain

If you're experiencing this problem, you probably have a cracked nipple. Stop feeding your baby from that breast until it has healed. You can still gently express milk from that breast.

Your Breasts Feel Too Full, Swollen, Hard, Tight, Hot, and/or Painful

Engorged breasts are not uncommon in the early weeks of breast-feeding, when your baby is still learning how to do it. Try these solutions:

◆ Consult your doctor, who may prescribe an ointment to prevent infection and speed healing.

◆ Try expressing some milk before feeding your baby. (Your baby will have difficulty latching on if your breasts are so full that they feel hard.)

◆ Take warm baths to stimulate the flow of milk.

You Have a Small, Hard, Painful Lump on Your Breast

If you have this symptom, you probably have a blocked milk duct. Try these techniques to solve the problem:

◆ Before feedings, apply warm washcloths to the breast and gently massage it.

◆ Encourage your baby to feed more often.

◆ Feed your baby from the blocked breast first.

◆ Make sure your baby empties your breast at feedings. If he doesn't, try expressing milk to empty the breast.

◆ Make sure your bra is not too tight.

You Have a Hard, Red, Painful, and Throbbing Area of the Breast. You May Also Have a Fever.

If you're experiencing these symptoms, you probably have a *breast abscess* (usually caused by an infection that enters the breast through an untreated crack). Immediately consult your doctor, who will prescribe antibiotics. If caught early enough, you can continue breast-feeding as usual. If you delay, however, the abscess will become extremely painful and you may need to feed your baby only from the uninfected breast.

 Baby Folklore

In eighteenth-century Scotland, nursing mothers used to wash their breasts clean with salt and water. It was believed that this treatment kept the breast milk from spoiling.

Caring for Your Breasts

Taking proper care of your breasts will go a long way toward eliminating many feeding problems. Keep your breasts clean by washing them daily with water or baby lotion. You can use moisturizer if you like, but avoid soap. (Soap can make a sore or cracked nipple even worse.)

Support matters, too. Choose a supportive nursing bra that opens in the front. Washable (or disposable) breast pads or a soft handkerchief that fits inside your bra can protect your clothes from leaks of milk, but change pads often to keep your breast and nipple dry.

Bottle-Feeding Problems

Bottle-feeding parents have their problems, too. If your baby has any trouble feeding from a bottle, try one of the solutions suggested here.

Your Baby Regularly Chokes on Too Much Formula

The hole in the nipple is probably too large. Buy nipples with smaller holes. To test the flow, turn a full bottle of formula or breast milk upside down. About one drop should fall every second.

Your Baby Never Drinks Much and Continues to Demand Frequent Feedings

The flow of formula is probably too slow, and your baby is getting too exhausted to finish eating. Slightly loosen the ring on the bottle to allow more air to flow into the bottle. If the hole of the nipple is too small, widen it by inserting a sterile, red-hot needle into the nipple. Or sterilize a small pair of scissors, insert one blade into the hole, and snip it open just a little. Test the flow and then, if necessary, snip a little more.

Your Baby Starts to Fuss a Minute or Two into Feeding

Baby Talk

"Babies on television never spit up on the Ultrasuede."

—Erma Bombeck

The bottle nipple may have become blocked. Check to see whether it still flows. Gently squeeze the bottle to try to unstop the clog. Or switch to a clean nipple.

If none of these feeding solutions works for you—or if you and your baby have feeding difficulties that aren't covered here—consult your pediatrician for further guidance.

Burping (and Worse)

All babies burp, but many babies don't mind gas. You may put your baby down after a feeding and she may rest quietly. Yet a minute later, an enormous belch may threaten to bring the whole house down. Despite the gas in her stomach, she was quite content. So you don't always have to help your baby burp before putting her down.

Regardless of whether you need to burp your baby, you may decide to make it part of your feeding routine. After she has finished eating—or in midfeeding if she suddenly seems upset—hold your baby so that her head rests on your shoulder. (You may want to drape a cloth diaper to protect your clothes from any spit-up.) Then stroke upward or gently pat her on the back. This action helps bring up any air bubbles. If she hasn't burped after 2 or 3 minutes, she probably doesn't have much gas.

Some babies spit up regularly due to a reflex action. Others spit up only when overfed. Whatever the cause, don't be overly concerned. If you worry that your baby spits up so much that she can't be getting enough food, wait a minute and offer her some more. If she refuses, she has probably eaten enough.

Baby Doctor

Spitting up is not vomiting. If your child vomits with great force, causing milk to fly several feet across the room, consult your doctor. True *projectile vomiting* of this kind can cause severe dehydration.

The Least You Need to Know

◆ Bottle-feeding mothers love their children as much as breast-feeding mothers do.

◆ Feed your baby by breast or by bottle on demand—that is, whenever he's hungry.

◆ Unless your baby's diapers run dry, don't worry that he's not eating enough.

◆ Don't force your baby to finish a bottle. Would you force him to finish a breast?

Chapter 5

Changing Your Baby

In This Chapter

◆ The arguments for and against cloth and disposable diapers

◆ Creating a special place for diaper changes

◆ Dealing with diaper rash

◆ Having fun while changing diapers (really)

Babies eat a lot, and they eat often. Unfortunately, what goes in one end comes out the other, so your baby needs a diaper change as often as he eats—or even more often.

Changing diapers is not nearly as awful as it sounds. Your darling's diapers will delight your senses, presenting you with a panorama of sights and smells. Not only will his stools come in a wide array of colors and consistencies, but the odors may change from day to day, too. As long as your baby eats nothing but breast milk, his poop will probably not smell strong and may even smell a little sweet. Yet as soon as you begin feeding him formula—and especially later when you start him on solids—your baby's dirty diapers will lose much of their early appeal.

Diaper Wars: Cloth Versus Disposable

Should you go with cloth or disposable diapers? Long ago in a far-away galaxy, everyone used cloth diapers. Then disposable diapers came on the market, and by the 1980s, nearly everyone had switched to them. As landfills became inundated with diapers, environmentalists urged a switch back to cloth diapers.

Environmental Arguments for—and Against—Cloth Diapers

Are cloth diapers better for the environment? Disposable diapers make up a huge part of the garbage we dump in our nation's landfills every year. On the other hand, washing cloth diapers raises environmental concerns, too. Laundering diapers uses a lot of energy and water, and detergents pollute the nation's waters. Some fans of disposables even argue that diaper-delivery trucks use up gas and oil and contribute to air pollution. Backers of cloth diapers counter that parents who make midnight runs to grocery stores and pharmacies to pick up another pack of disposables use much more gas than diaper-delivery trucks that map out the most cost-efficient route to serve their communities.

The debate over the relative impact of disposable and cloth diapers on the environment is not clear cut. The side you come down on depends on what aspects of the environment you value most. Disposables and cloth diapers each have their own advantages to you and your baby, as well as to the environment. So what you choose to do depends on which advantages you value most: convenience, cost, or comfort.

Convenience

No question, disposable diapers involve less hassle. When one gets wet or dirty, you just take it off, seal it up, and throw it away. The tape on disposable diapers makes them easier to take off and put on than cloth diapers. (Although Velcro on diaper wraps has made it much easier to change a cloth diaper, it's still not as easy as changing a disposable.) Cloth diapers are sometimes unwieldy. No matter how you fold one, you may find it difficult to fit it into a diaper wrap.

You can't just throw away cloth diapers. You need to store them in a diaper pail until your weekly diaper service pick-up or until you have enough to launder. The stench, especially after your baby has begun eating solid foods, can sometimes become overwhelming. Even if you use a diaper service, you'll have to wash the diaper wraps yourself. So cloth diapers require much more hands-on (excuse the expression) dealing with your baby's poop.

Q-Tip _____

Even if you do opt for cloth diapers, you will probably find it convenient to switch to disposable diapers when traveling. With disposable diapers, you have less to carry and you don't have to tote around wet, soiled, and smelly diapers until you get home.

Finally, disposable diapers do not leak as often as cloth diapers (as long as you change them often enough). So if your baby wears disposables, you will probably not have to change her entire outfit (not to mention the sheets in her crib or your bed) quite so often.

The advantages of disposable diapers all center on convenience. Yet cloth diapers offer convenience, too. Parents of babies who wear disposable diapers often run out at inconvenient times. But if you use a cloth diaper service, you'll never need to drop everything at quarter of 9 to fetch some diapers before your local store closes. You can order as many cloth diapers as you need every week and have them delivered to your door. Because cloth diapers are so absorbent, they also come in handy in wiping up your baby's spit-up and other spills.

Cost

As long as you're using a lot of diapers (80 or more each week), a diaper service is probably less expensive than purchasing disposable diapers. When the number of diapers you use falls to 60 or less, however, a diaper service is likely to be slightly more expensive due to the base delivery charge. Of course, if you're brave enough to buy and wash your own cloth diapers, that's by far the cheapest alternative of all.

Comfort

Babies who wear cloth diapers tend to get diaper rash less often than those who wear disposable diapers. Because it's not always easy to tell how wet a disposable diaper is, babies who wear disposables may sit in their own urine longer than those who wear cloth diapers, and continued contact with urine causes most cases of diaper rash. With cloth diapers, you can always tell how wet your baby is.

For this reason, cloth diapers also make it simpler to monitor your baby's urinary output. If you have any concern about how much food your baby is eating, you will find it much easier to keep tabs with cloth diapers.

Finally, cloth diapers probably offer your baby more comfort. If disposable diapers were more comfortable than cotton ones, we would all be wearing paper underwear. Try rubbing a cloth diaper and then the inside of a disposable diaper against your cheek. Which do you prefer?

Setting Up a Changing Station

You'll be changing an unbelievable number of diapers over the next 2 to 4 years. If your baby averages just eight diapers a day for the next 2 ½ years, you will change more than 7,000 diapers! So you may find it worthwhile to put a little effort into making your baby's changing station as pleasant and efficient a place as possible.

Babyproofing

If you want to eliminate any possibility that your baby might roll off the changing table, don't use one at all. Simply lay a waterproof pad down on the floor, get down on your hands and knees, and change her there.

If you like, you can outfit your changing area with a top-of-the-line changing table with drawers specially designed to hold all of the supplies you need. The top of a dresser or table, however, works just as well. Whatever you choose, make sure the primary changing surface is at least waist high. If the changing area is too low, you will put a tremendous strain on your back. After all, you'll be doing thousands of 10- to 40-pound lifts over the next few years.

On top of this surface, place a plastic changing mat. To make the mat cozier for your baby, you can buy fitted sheets just the right size for a changing mat. Or use a pillowcase or wrap the mat up in a soft bath towel. If you place a cloth diaper where your baby's bottom lies on top of the cover of your changing mat, you won't have to change the cover nearly so often.

Outfitting Your Changing Station

Here's what you should have on hand whenever you change your baby:

- A generous supply of washcloths, baby wipes, or cotton balls for wiping. Rather than using your everyday bathtub washcloths, get a separate supply for bottom-use only.

- Warm water (for washcloths) and/or baby oil (for cotton balls). (Filling a thermos of warm water and placing it near the changing table right before bed can save a lot of trouble in the wee hours of the night.)

- Plenty of clean diapers, cloth or disposable.

◆ Masking tape to repair a disposable diaper's adhesive tabs, which invariably come off in your hand when you're down to the last diaper in the house.

◆ At least a dozen diaper wraps, which are rubber-lined or otherwise waterproof covers (usually fastened with Velcro tabs) that hold a cloth diaper in place.

Babyproofing
Make sure that the baby wipes you buy do not contain alcohol. Alcohol will make your baby's bottom too dry.

◆ About a dozen diaper pins to hold the diaper wraps in place (after the Velcro has picked up so many other fibers in the laundry that it no longer works).

◆ Diaper cream for the treatment of diaper rash.

◆ A change of clothes for your baby, just in case what he's wearing has become wet or soiled.

◆ A diaper pail with a secure—and hopefully air-tight—lid.

Note that this list does not include soap. You can use soap, but it's usually not necessary. In fact, if your baby has a diaper rash, the detergents in most soaps can irritate his skin even more.

Make sure to place everything you need to diaper your baby within easy reach. Once you put your baby down on the changing table, you cannot leave him there while you run around the room searching for a diaper pin, dash to the bathroom for a warm washcloth, or get down on your hands and knees to find the diaper cream that's slipped under the table. Even if you have secured your baby to the changing table with a strap or belt, leaving him alone, even for "just a second," is unsafe.

Baby Doctor
Most pediatricians caution against using baby powder because inhaling particles of talcum or corn starch can be dangerous to your baby's health.

Keep your changing supplies constantly accessible, but at the same time, keep them out of your child's reach. Store supplies in changing table drawers or on a high shelf that your baby can't reach (even from the changing table, once he's standing). Or you can buy a decorative, pocketed wall hanging (not unlike a child-friendly shoe bag) made expressly for the purpose of holding diapering supplies.

Once you have set up your baby's primary changing station, establish satellite stations throughout your home. You will find it handy to keep a portable changing mat and a full set of diapering supplies on every floor of your house. That way, you don't have to trudge upstairs to the baby's room every time he needs a change.

A satellite station next to your own bed is especially handy if, like many parents, you bring your baby into your own bed for midnight feedings. Most newborns need at least one change in the middle of the night. (The best time is midway through a midnight feeding—halfway through the bottle or when you switch breasts.) If you have all the supplies you need next to your bed, neither you nor your baby will need to wake up fully for nighttime changes.

Special Tips for Cloth Diapers

The chief advantage of disposable diapers, as noted earlier, is convenience. They're simple to put on and easy to take off. But if you've chosen to use cloth diapers, you need a few pointers:

- If you're laundering diapers yourself, buy at least two dozen. That way, you have to wash them only every other day; your baby will probably go through about a dozen a day when she's a newborn.

- When buying diapers, go for quality. Though thicker, softer diapers cost more initially, they'll prove much more absorbent and will last much longer.

- If you use a diaper service, order many more diapers than you think you need. Because newborns go through 12 to 14 diapers a day, you need at least 100 diapers a week to start. As your baby grows older, she will need fewer changes but will still probably go through 70 or 80 per week.

Babyproofing

Always use diaper pins rather than safety pins. Safety pins can open more easily and hurt your baby.

- When you fold a diaper to fit it into a diaper wrap, make sure to put the thickest portion of the folded diaper where the baby needs it most. Boys wet their diapers in the front; girls near the center.

- After you fold a diaper, turn it over so that the folds face into the diaper wrap. That way, your baby has a smooth, soft diaper against her skin.

- If you use diaper pins, try running them through a bar of soap before you use them. Doing so makes it much easier to push them through a thick diaper.

Q-Tip

Parents who choose cloth diapers often find nighttime wetness a problem. No matter how thick the diaper, it is no match for a sleeping baby. When it soaks through, you have to change your newborn's pajamas and her sheets. To a new parent desperate for sleep, that's a real nuisance. Doubling up two cloth diapers may help stem the flood tide (though it will make your baby's bottom look as big as a basketball). But if you still find yourself changing sheets often in the middle of the night, you may have to resign yourself to using disposables at night.

Doing the Dirty Deed

Now for the fun part: wiping up your baby's mess. If the diaper is only wet, wipe with a wet washcloth, baby wipe, or baby oil applied with cotton balls. Wipe around the genitals first, and then anywhere else where the wet diaper touched your baby's skin. (Urine that stays too long on the skin causes most cases of diaper rash.)

If the diaper is soiled, begin by using any clean section of the diaper (usually the front) to wipe up as much of the poop as possible. Then use the wipe, washcloth, or cotton balls to clean the rest. Again, clean around the genitals first, and then clean the thighs and upper legs if they got dirty. Lift your baby by the ankles and clean the bottom last.

Naturally enough, differences in anatomy necessitate different rules for cleaning boys and girls. If your baby is a girl, follow these rules:

◆ Always wipe your baby from the front to the back.

◆ Never clean inside the lips of the vulva.

If your baby is a boy, follow these rules:

◆ If he is uncircumcised, never pull back the foreskin of his penis to clean it.

◆ Always point his penis down as you put on a clean diaper to prevent urine from leaking out of the top later.

Now that your baby's bottom is spanking clean, take off any of his clothes that have gotten wet or dirty. Put him in a new diaper, dress him, and wait 5 minutes. Chances are, he'll need another change.

Q-Tip

Many babies, especially boys, have a tendency to begin spraying as soon as a diaper is removed. You can (at least sometimes) avoid having to change everyone's clothes by employing these strategies:

- Always have a cloth diaper ready to catch—or block or mop up—any unexpected showers.
- Drape a cloth diaper over your son's penis whenever you change him.
- Roll up your baby's shirt and pull down the pants all the way to avoid wetness.
- Duck!

When you have finished diapering your baby, lift him off the changing table and put him down somewhere safe. Throw away baby wipes and cotton balls (as well as disposable diapers). Dump dirty washcloths (as well as soiled diaper wraps) in a covered pail filled halfway with water and about a cup of borax. The borax helps to minimize any foul odors that might emanate from your baby's diaper wraps.

If your baby wears cloth diapers supplied by a diaper service, dump most of the contents in the toilet. Then toss it into a well-sealed pail with a plastic liner.

If you own—and therefore clean—cloth diapers, first dump their contents into the toilet and rinse them. Then put them in a diaper pail. You can use the same pail as your washcloths and diaper wraps, or you can get a separate pail just for diapers. Adding baking soda to the diaper pail can help contain some of the stench.

Baby Folklore

Two centuries ago, English mothers would not clean their baby's first nappy (diaper). They would fling it out of doors and say a blessing for good luck. Needless to say, this is not as popular a custom as it once was.

If you wash diapers, *do not* use bleach. You can whiten your diapers by adding a cupful of vinegar to the washing machine during a rinse cycle. Vinegar also helps soften diapers and remove detergent, thereby helping prevent diaper rash.

Don't forget to wash your hands with an antibacterial soap when you're all done.

(Diaper) Rash Decisions

Nearly every baby gets diaper rash at one time or another. Most diaper rashes are caused by urine that rests too long against the skin. Bacterial action transforms urine into ammonia, which can irritate and burn your baby's skin. Diaper rash generally spreads from the genitals outward. It looks red and perhaps bumpy and can smell strongly of ammonia.

Here's what to do when your baby has diaper rash:

◆ Change your baby more often. Trapped moisture or feces can cause rashes.

◆ Give your child plenty of naked-bottom time; try to let her stay out of her diaper for at least 15 minutes every time you change her. Airing out her bottom can quickly cure many rashes.

◆ If your baby stays in roughly the same place when she naps, consider allowing her to sleep with a naked bottom. Keep the bedding dry by laying her on a rubber sheet and wedging a folded diaper under her.

◆ Switch, at least temporarily, from disposable to cloth diapers (or vice versa). The change may make a big difference.

◆ Don't use plastic or rubber pants that trap moisture next to your baby's skin.

◆ Check to make sure your baby wipes do not contain alcohol, which can dry your baby's skin too much. Consider switching to a clean, wet washcloth.

◆ Keep your baby's bottom clean, but use little or no soap. If you do use soap, try a special baby soap that is hypoallergenic and contains no detergents. Always rinse your baby's bottom with a different washcloth to remove the soap. Dry the area thoroughly after every washing.

◆ Grease your baby's bottom with vegetable shortening or petroleum jelly.

◆ Use an over-the-counter ointment to treat the rash. Cream that contains zinc oxide often does the trick. Try more than one brand if the first brand doesn't work.

◆ If you wash your own diapers, don't use bleach, and make sure you wash and rinse diapers thoroughly. (Use more than one rinse cycle.)

If, after trying all these ideas, diaper rash persists or worsens, consult your baby's pediatrician for further advice.

Diapering Can Be Fun—Well, Sometimes

You—and your baby—can have some fun during changing times. True, diapering is a chore. But it doesn't have to be drudgery. If you can distract your baby or keep him entertained while changing his diaper, he'll probably remain still and content, which will make it easier for you to clean up the mess.

Look at it this way: you're going to change thousands of diapers over the next year alone. If you see it as a chore, you'll build up resentment. If your baby doesn't enjoy it, he's going to kick and cry and make your life miserable every time he needs a change. So why not try to make changing fun?

Short and Sweet

Start by having everything you'll need within arm's reach so you can make the change as short and as sweet as possible. You can also speed the process along by unfastening the snaps on her clothes on your way to the changing area.

For Baby's Viewing Pleasure

Because you need to turn your attention to your baby's bottom, your baby may not be content simply looking at your face. Give him something fun to look at. Decorate the wall closest to the changing table with fun pictures and patterns. (Black-and-white images work best for newborns and infants.) Or hang a mobile over the changing table. Make sure that the objects, pictures, or images on the mobile face down toward your baby. After all, it should be designed for his viewing pleasure, not yours.

Something to Talk About

Even though you can't constantly look into your baby's eyes while changing her, you can hold her attention by talking to her. Recite a favorite nursery rhyme. Make up a short story. Provide a narrative of her life by telling her exactly what you're doing every step of the way. While talking, glance over at her and make sure your eyes meet every few seconds in order to hold her attention.

Now Batting ... Your Baby

Your baby will probably start batting at objects between the 10th and 16th weeks. When he does, hang a toy down within his reach. That way, he can take a whack at it while being changed.

Later, when your baby begins grasping and holding on to objects (at around 16 weeks), give him some toys to play with. You might even want to set aside certain toys for play only when he's on the changing table. This will make diaper changing the special time when he gets to play with those toys.

Make 'Em Laugh

Amuse your child with songs, games, or just plain silliness. Try making goofy faces at her. Wear a diaper on your head and ask her how she likes your new hat. (Yes, even preverbal children appreciate this silliness.)

Make up a special diaper-changing song that your baby will associate with the fun of changing time. If you like, you can use this one, but you'll have to come up with your own tune:

> Time to change your diaper, diaper, diaper
> Time to change your diaper because it's poopy.
> And it's kind of smelly, smelly, smelly,
> And it's kind of smelly—and a little goopy.

You can also keep your baby entertained by tickling her, but this technique works best only after she's clean. Otherwise, you may end up with the contents of her diaper kicked all over the room.

The Least You Need to Know

- ◆ You and your partner will change more than 7,000 diapers (per child).

- ◆ Keep changing supplies on every floor of your home.

- ◆ Change your baby often. Don't always wait until he has a bowel movement because urine that sits for too long against the skin can cause diaper rash, too.

- ◆ You'll be changing diapers a lot over the next 2 or 3 years, so you might as well try to have some fun with it.

Chapter 6

The Storm Before the Calm

In This Chapter

◆ Why your baby cries

◆ How to calm a crying baby

◆ The inconsolable crier

◆ Your baby's first attempts to "talk"

Like all babies, your baby will cry. That you can bank on. She will cry when she's hungry. She'll cry when she's wet. She'll cry when she's tired. She'll cry when she's hurt. She'll even cry for reasons you may never know. Some babies cry more than others, but all babies cry. So if your baby doesn't cry a lot, she's one of the lucky ones—and so are you.

What should you do when your baby cries? Respond quickly, not with alarm or panic, but with concern. She's trying to tell you something when she cries. What you need to do is try to figure out what she means.

Hey! I Need Something Here

Crying is your newborn baby's primary means of communication. Babies do not cry, as your grandmother might say, "just to exercise their lungs." Whenever your baby is not crying, you can generally assume that he doesn't need anything. Whether he is asleep or awake, silence usually signals contentment. But when he needs something, your baby lets you know in the only way he can: he cries.

Different cries, as you will soon recognize, mean different things. A steady, rhythmic cry that rises to a peak every second or so may signal hunger. By contrast, a louder and more intense cry that lasts up to 4 or 5 seconds per cry, punctuated with silences as he desperately refills his lungs, probably indicates pain or hurt of some kind.

It's up to you to find out what your baby needs when he cries. Fortunately, with young babies, the possibilities are not endless. When your baby cries, he's probably telling you that he feels one of these:

- Hungry

- Tired

- Uncomfortable or hurt because of gas, a full diaper, diaper rash, injury, cold, overheating, and so on

- Afraid

- Lonely or bored

- Frustrated or angry

Some babies appear to cry for no reason at all, but this apparent meaninglessness may be due to their limited ability to communicate and our limited ability to understand them. But just because we don't understand what they're saying doesn't mean that our babies aren't trying to tell us something.

Help!

Until your baby is about 3 months old, she cannot anticipate her needs. So when she cries, she's not saying, "I'm getting hungry," or "I'm getting tired." She's shouting, "I'm starving!" or "I'm exhausted!" Your baby is trying to alert you to immediate and pressing needs, so don't ignore her when she cries.

Some parents fear that they will spoil their babies if they respond "too quickly" to crying. You may think that if you give her what she wants, she'll just want more. But your baby doesn't merely want you, she desperately needs you—and the nourishment, love, care, and attention you can provide. How can you spoil her by giving her what she needs?

If you respond quickly and effectively to your baby's cries, then she'll know that her attempts to communicate were successful. This knowledge has immediate and long-term benefits. As she grows to trust that you will take care of what ails her, your baby will cry less often and for shorter periods. And later in life, your baby will likely be more outgoing and develop good communication skills.

By contrast, if you ignore your baby's cries and deny or delay gratification of her needs for attention and care, she may become withdrawn and shy throughout her life. In addition, studies suggest that she will probably cry more often and for longer periods during her first year.

So pick her up right away, look for the cause of her crying, and try to comfort her. The sooner you figure out what your baby needs and take care of the problem, the sooner she'll become quiet and happy.

Try to stay calm. If your baby won't stop crying, that's her way of saying, "No, that's not it." Panic, frustration, tension, or anger won't bring you any closer to understanding what your baby needs. What's more, your baby will sense your negative emotions and respond to them. How? By crying, of course. So remain calm, if possible, and try everything in your repertoire.

Baby Doctor

If your baby won't stop crying and you feel as if you may harm her if she doesn't shut up, seek help right away. Get your partner, a family member, or a friend to help you care for the baby. Then consult your pediatrician, a psychologist, a social worker, or another professional who can help you through this rough time.

Babyproofing

Before you offer your baby a finger to suck on, be sure to turn the finger up. That way, your fingernail won't scratch the roof of his mouth.

Feed Me, Feed Me!

If your baby is crying because he's hungry, then by all means you should feed him. Don't worry that feeding him "early" might throw him (or you) off-schedule. Your baby is likely to change his feeding schedule from day to day. When he's going through a growth spurt, for example, or when he's learning and quickly mastering a new skill, your baby will probably want to eat more often (and sleep more, too).

Try to feed your baby as soon as he starts to cry. If your baby tires himself out with crying, he may not have the strength to eat enough by the time you decide to feed him. A half an hour or an hour later, he'll start crying for more food and start the cycle all over again.

If your baby is truly hungry, merely sucking on something will not calm him. He needs breast milk or formula. But if your baby is full and apparently still wants to suck, let him. Babies find the simple act of sucking—apart from its value in feeding—remarkably soothing. When your baby is upset, sucking may calm him and eventually even lull him to sleep. So if you're sure your baby has eaten enough, offer him a bottle of water. Or wash your hands and offer him the top third of your pinkie finger to suck on. You'll be surprised how strong your baby sucks.

At 3 or 4 months, when your baby develops better hand-eye coordination, you can try to guide his thumb to his mouth for sucking comfort. (Though orthodontists might object to this strategy—especially if thumb-sucking continues beyond age 3—a self-soothing baby is a blessing to his parents.)

Pacifier Pros and Cons

If all else fails, try a pacifier. Pacifiers have a remarkably soothing effect on many babies. If your baby sleeps with a pacifier in her mouth, she may just start sucking when something disturbs her sleep. Indeed, she might not even wake up—and wake you up. Finally, if your baby uses a pacifier, she will probably not develop a thumb-sucking habit.

Yet pacifiers do have their drawbacks. If your baby uses hers regularly—not just for soothing, but as a routine habit—she will be unable to explore the world with her mouth when she gets a little older (one of the primary ways young babies learn).

In addition, your baby—and you—may come to rely on the pacifier too heavily as a soother. If, for example, your baby needs her pacifier to get to sleep, you will have to find it for her whenever she wakes up in the night and can't find it. You also might be tempted to use it as a cure-all instead of getting to know your baby's changing needs. Finally, like any habit, it may take years of effort to get your baby to stop using it once she has started.

If You Do Use Pacifiers ...

Here are some tips for parents who use pacifiers:

◆ Wash and sterilize them often by putting them in boiling water for 5 minutes.

◆ Avoid automatically using the pacifier whenever your baby starts to cry. Consider it the soother of last resort.

◆ Unless your baby is particularly fretful, try using one only at night.

◆ Scatter several pacifiers around your baby's crib at night to give her a better chance of finding one when she needs it.

◆ Consider trying to break the habit at about 6 months—before she is old enough to remember it (and therefore miss it) for very long.

I Need a Nap!

An often overlooked cause of crying is fatigue. If your baby is crying because he's tired, virtually anything you try will fail to soothe him. You may try bouncing your baby up and down, trying to get his attention with a toy, changing his diaper, or feeding him. Still he cries.

If you seem to be running into a brick wall in trying to get your baby to stop crying, consider the possibility of fatigue. Create a warm and peaceful sleep environment for your baby. Rock him gently for several minutes and then place him in his crib or in some other quiet, cozy place. As you cover your baby with a blanket to keep him warm, you may even hear a sigh of relief.

Ouch! That Hurts!

Obviously, if your baby gets hurt, she will cry, but discomfort may also cause your baby to cry. The source of your baby's discomfort may be any of the following:

◆ **Gas pains or overeating:** Your baby may have eaten too much or taken in too much air while eating, so her belly aches. Try burping her (see Chapter 4). If she has gas pains, a big burp might help her feel better. If she ate too much, burping her may cause her to spit up, so have a cloth diaper ready. Despite the mess, she'll feel much better after spitting up.

◆ **A full diaper:** A wet diaper tends to get cold if it sits for very long. Understandably, your baby may object. A wet or dirty diaper can also cause an uncomfortable rash. Change the diaper and treat the rash, if any (see Chapter 5).

◆ **Injury:** If your baby cries loudly in long bursts (about 5 seconds each) that seem to rob her of her breath, she's probably hurt. Perhaps a diaper pin came loose and is sticking her. Maybe her bottle is too hot. Or she may have bumped her head. Whatever the source of the pain, your baby first needs comforting. What was she doing when she started crying? This may give you a good clue about how your baby got hurt. Comfort and cuddle your baby first, and then take care of what ails her.

◆ **The temperature:** Babies do not conserve heat well. When your baby feels cold, her crying not only communicates discomfort, it also generates some heat to warm her. Feel your baby's hands and feet. If they're cold and she's breathing quickly, warm your baby by holding her close to you, feeding her, adding another layer of clothing, or wrapping her up tightly in a blanket. If, on the other hand, your baby is too hot, take off a blanket or layer of clothing.

Q-Tip

The ideal surrounding temperature for a newborn is a steamy 85°F. When the temperature falls below 85°F, a new baby's body burns up a lot of energy creating warmth. Fortunately, you don't need to turn the thermostat up that high. With a room temperature of about 70°F, two layers of light clothing and a blanket will bring the surrounding temperature up to 85°F.

When you need to change your baby's diaper, keep her warm by draping a blanket over her until she's fully dressed again.

The Fear Factor

Any loud noise, bright light, or sudden movement can startle your baby. If you pick him up or put him down too fast, your baby thinks he's going to fall. In fact, many times when a baby gets hurt, the shock of a sudden bump may cause as much crying as the pain itself.

If your baby seems frightened, pick him up—slowly and gently. Slide your arms under his head and bottom. Talk to him before you lift him and continue talking to him while you pick him up. Remember to support his head until he can support it himself. Then hold your baby close to help him feel warm and safe. Gently rock him and sing or talk softly to him. Or try lying down and laying your baby on top of your chest. The feeling of closeness and the sound of your heartbeat may calm him down. Swaddling also can often help calm a frightened newborn. Wrap your baby tightly inside a blanket to keep him feeling warm and safe.

Nobody Wants to Play with Me!

Your baby may want nothing more than you and your attention. Your baby is a social creature. She likes to command the attention of others—you more than anyone else. If your baby is lonely or bored, she may stop crying if you hold her.

Of course, you can't hold your baby all the time. After all, you have other things to do besides taking care of your baby. So if you need to do some chores while your baby is awake, let her come with you. Prop her up in a baby seat or lay her down on her belly near where you are washing the dishes or making the beds or vacuuming. As you go about your chores, talk to her, describing what you are doing. If your baby still insists that you hold her, try putting her in a carrier. That way, at least you have one or two free hands for your chores.

Don't Make Me Mad!

Your baby may cry because he can't satisfy his needs. Perhaps the hole in the nipple of his bottle is too small, so he can't get food fast enough to satisfy his hunger. Or maybe you took your baby off the breast or bottle to burp him too soon. Perhaps your timing is off: you want to bathe or change your baby when what he needs most is to eat or sleep, or you put him down when he needs to be held.

In later months, his frustration gives way to anger. Crying will still be his main way of communicating, of course, but with this angry cry, he'll be saying, "Stop that!" or, "Don't you dare leave me here!" or, "No, I want it now!" The best solution to your baby's cries is to try your best to discover and satisfy his needs.

Rock, Rhythm, and Soothing Sounds

Unless your baby is crying because she is hungry or tired, you can try a number of different methods to soothe her.

Rocking motions are very calming. Hold your baby close while rocking—about one rock per second seems an ideal speed—in a rocking chair. Walking with your baby in your arms also provides her with the sensation of rocking. Or try rocking your baby in a cradle or a baby swing. Gently bounce her up and down in your arms. Do vigorous knee bends while holding your baby. Or ask her to slow-dance with you.

A baby carrier or sling can help if your arms get too tired to carry your baby any longer. But be fore-warned: your baby may not like it as much if the carrier places a barrier between you and her.

You might also want to try taking her for a ride in her stroller or the car. The rhythmic swaying may soothe her to sleep.

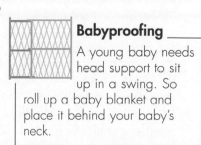

Babyproofing
A young baby needs head support to sit up in a swing. So roll up a baby blanket and place it behind your baby's neck.

Baby Talk

"There are 152 distinctly different ways of holding a baby—and all are right."

—Heywood Broun

Certain sounds can calm your baby, too. Anything that provides a loud, steady whir or hum, such as a dishwasher, a washing machine, a hair dryer, a fan, or a vacuum cleaner, may remind your baby of the wash of sounds within the womb. The constant purr of a car engine—especially because it couples soothing sounds with calming motion—is especially effective in pacifying a crying baby. Soft music with a steady rhythm or a tape of heart sounds from within the womb may also soothe your baby.

Your voice is naturally soothing to your baby, too. Talk gently and calmly to your baby. You may find that she likes it even more when you adopt a sing-song voice. Try singing a lullaby or other song to her. Don't worry about whether you can carry a tune; your baby won't care.

You've Really Got a Hold on Me

Whatever method you find works best to calm your baby, it will almost always begin with holding. Hold your baby close, with his head against your chest. That way, your baby hears the soothing sound of your heartbeat as he snuggles into the warmth of your body.

Often just holding your baby reduces his cries to snuffles. If not, it's still a good starting place to find out what is causing the crying. Whether you feed your baby, walk with him, rock him, talk to him, or play with him, it all begins with picking him up and holding him.

Every New Parent's Nightmare: Colic

If your baby has colic, nothing is likely to soothe her. *Colic* is a pattern of unexplained, inconsolable, and intense crying that can continue for up to 3 months. Neither an illness nor a disease, colic apparently does no harm to the baby, but it can drive the baby's parents crazy. Unable to console their child, parents can feel like failures. Despair, frustration, and anger commonly result.

If your baby does develop colic (though let's hope not), it will probably make its first appearance when she is 3 or 4 weeks old. Once a day, usually in the late afternoon or early evening, your colicky baby will begin crying. Her cry will sound much more intense and higher pitched than it does when she is hungry, hurt, cold, or lonely. Your baby will not just cry; she will scream. Often a baby with colic draws her legs up to her chest or belly (as if it ached terribly). She may also clench her fists, appear restless, and become red with crying.

If your baby has colic, your attempts to discover and deal with the cause of her crying will meet with only fleeting success, if any. When you try to feed your baby, give her a pacifier, burp her, rock her, caress her, or sing to her, she may stop screaming—for, at most, a minute. Even then, she will continue to sob and tremble before starting to scream again. The crying will last anywhere from 1 to 4 hours. Then, as suddenly as it began, the screaming will stop.

The good news: this crying jag generally happens just once a day. The bad news: it happens every day, almost always at about the same time. At all other times, your baby will seem perfectly normal. She may eat and sleep well. When she gets hungry, tired, lonely, or hurt, she will cry—but it won't be anything like that daily dose of colic. Her needy crying will have a cause—and a remedy.

Q-Tip

Your baby does not have colic if one of the following is true:

◆ She cries for quite some time but then falls asleep.

◆ Her crying sounds no different from her usual cry.

◆ Her crying ends within a half an hour.

◆ Your efforts to soothe her work for more than a minute or so. (If the crying has an identifiable cause, it's not colic.)

◆ Her crying starts again only when you stop doing whatever worked to halt the crying.

◆ Your baby stays happy for at least 15 minutes and then starts crying again.

The Mystery of Colic

If the cause of colic could be pinpointed, it could also be treated and perhaps even cured. Unfortunately, no one yet knows the cause. Current theories suggest that it may be caused by cramps or spasms of the intestinal tract. However, you may want to take this theory with a grain of salt. In the past, colic has been attributed to the following:

◆ Milk flowing too fast, causing overfeeding

◆ Milk flowing too slowly, causing underfeeding

Babyproofing

If at all possible, get some help during these colicky hours. You need all the support you can get from your partner, family, and friends. Help that allows you to take a break from the screaming will ease some of your frustration and stem negative feelings that you might be developing toward your child.

◆ Milk that was too hot

◆ Milk that was too cold

◆ Milk that was too strong (not enough fluid)

◆ Milk that was too weak (not enough nutrients)

◆ Gas

◆ Appendicitis

◆ Gall-bladder ailments

◆ Allergies

None of these theories ever proved true.

What to Do (Besides Tearing Out Your Hair)

Whatever the cause, if your baby has colic, you're in for a very stressful couple of months. You can't just let your baby cry until he's done. So try everything suggested here and keep trying—but don't expect anything to achieve lasting results.

Because you can probably set your watch by your baby's colic attacks, schedule your day around them. Whenever you can, free your afternoons and evenings of all other activities. That way, when the screaming starts, you'll be able to deal with it as best you can.

Be as patient as you can and wait it out. Yes, it's going to be rough, but colic almost never lasts longer than 12 weeks—and sometimes much less. (Granted, that's still a lot of time to listen to your baby's screaming.) Remind yourself that it won't last forever. And hang in there.

The Least You Need to Know

◆ Your baby's crying means he's trying to tell you that he truly needs something (unless he has colic).

◆ Responding quickly to your baby's cries will not spoil him. In fact, quick responses may reduce the amount and intensity of cries in coming months by building your baby's trust in you.

◆ Colic, no matter how horrible and difficult on a parent, will not last forever and will not harm your child.

◆ Listen to your baby and talk to your baby. Neither of you will understand each other's words, but the feelings underlying them will be clear.

7

Bonding with Your Baby

In This Chapter

- ◆ How to talk to an infant
- ◆ Conversation and other language-building tools
- ◆ The miracle of touch and other nonverbal communication
- ◆ The benefits of infant massage

Communication and bonding with your baby began even before birth. Both you and your partner no doubt developed loving, tender, and protective feelings toward your baby while he was still in the womb. Perhaps you talked or sang or cooed to him or gently stroked his head (or at least what you thought was his head) through the belly.

Then when he was born, you bonded with your baby—and perhaps even more important, your baby bonded with you—in a thousand different ways:

- ◆ You nursed him or fed him a bottle.
- ◆ You held him.
- ◆ You rocked him.
- ◆ You danced with him.

- ◆ You comforted him.

- ◆ You changed him.

- ◆ You bathed him.

- ◆ You played with him.

- ◆ You talked to him.

- ◆ You sang to him.

- ◆ You whispered to him.

- ◆ You read to him.

- ◆ You smiled at him.

- ◆ Even better, he smiled at you.

Each of these everyday events offered an opportunity to bond with your baby, to grow closer to each other, and to enhance the warm feelings between you. The months ahead will provide many more chances for you to cement that bond through word and deed.

The bonding between parent and child is no small matter. Psychologists and other researchers have linked early parent-child bonding to everything from future mental development (such as language learning) to future social skills (such as the ability to form intimate and lasting relationships). In this first year of your child's life, bonding depends on building trust and security. If you respond to your child's crying and other expressions of need by providing for your baby as best you can, he will develop trust in your ability to understand him and in your willingness and ability to take care of him. If you communicate your love to him as often as you can, he will feel secure, nurtured by the warmth of your affections. And that's what bonding is all about.

My Word Is My Bond

The key to bonding with your baby is communication. You no doubt communicate with your baby with and without words. Through gestures, caresses, and actions, you show her that you love her and that you understand what she needs. You no doubt talk, coo, sing, and murmur sweet nothings in your baby's ear, too.

Just as important as your communication with your baby is her communication with you. Intimate bonding requires not only actively transmitting the messages you want to send, but actively listening to the messages being transmitted to you. So by all means, keep talking to your baby. But stop and listen to what she has to say, too.

Sounding Off

During the first 3 months, your baby communicated primarily through an assortment of cries. He may have started gurgling, humming, or blowing bubbles with his saliva sometime during his second month. Then during the third month, he may have started cooing a little, producing such vowel sounds as *aaaah, eh, ooooh, oh,* and *uh.* But for the most part, his attempts to communicate (rather than just make noise) centered on crying.

During the fourth month, however, your baby will probably try to put his ability to make sound to work. You may notice a certain intensity in his eyes as he makes some of his favorite vocal sounds. It seems as though now that he has become aware that the sounds are coming from him, he wants to direct them toward some audience.

Baby Talk

"When the first baby laughed for the first time, the laugh broke into a thousand pieces and they all went skipping about, and that was the beginning of fairies."

—J. M. Barrie, *Peter Pan*

By the end of the fourth month, your baby will already have amassed quite an array of sounds: cries, gurgles, squeaks, squeals, puffs, sighs, bubbles, raspberries, vowel sounds, and, best of all, giggles and belly laughs. If you listen carefully, you may notice that some of these sounds seem reserved solely for "conversation," and others are used indiscriminately.

The Tower of Babble

Your baby's repertoire of sounds and syllables starts to expand between now and her first birthday. Over the next few months, she'll slowly begin adding consonants, beginning with the explosives *P* and *B* and the humming *M.* The combinations of vowels and consonants will, for the first time, make it sound as though your baby is talking to you. She may sound, for example, as though she's saying, "Maaaamaaaa, Maaamaaa" and "Paapaa, Paapaa." But don't kid yourself. Your baby's probably not calling you by name just yet. These words mean just as much (or as little) to her as "Baaabaaa, Baaabaaa." At this stage, she's just having fun making noise.

By 5 or 6 months, your baby will string sounds together in a meaningless yet always sweet-sounding babble. This babble serves as good practice for later conversations. Don't expend a lot of time and energy trying to understand what your baby is saying. She's probably not saying anything yet. (Real words don't usually come until around the first birthday.) For now, she's just trying to make sounds with her mouth and be sociable—just the way she has seen you do it.

By 6 months, your baby will probably want to practice her new "language" skills with anyone who's willing to listen. Six months is a very social age. Your child will most likely welcome the company of others and will start talking (saying *gaga* or *baba*) to almost anyone.

Q-Tip

The social months from about 5 months old until stranger anxiety grows toward the end of the year are a great time to introduce your baby to different people: not just grownups, but other children as well. Take your baby out for visits and playdates, or invite people into your home. Before long, you may even be able to teach her to wave bye-bye.

Can We Talk?

As soon as your baby starts making vowel sounds, he starts to consider himself a real conversationalist. It hardly matters that you can't understand him and he can't understand you. (After all, the same is true of many conversations between adults.) Your baby wants to talk to you the same way he has heard you talk to others.

You may be surprised the first time your baby seems to wait for you to respond to his babbling. It seems incredible that in just 6 months, he has picked up the nuances of conversational style. When he starts pausing (perhaps to make sure you're listening), you can have an entire babbling conversation. First your baby talks and you listen; then he knows it's his turn to listen and your turn to talk. Indeed, because he stops to listen when you talk, you may find your infant much more civil than many adult conversationalists.

When your baby tries to have a "conversation" with you, be polite. Respond to your baby as you would to any adult who starts to talk to you.

- Stop what you're doing (at least some of the time) and engage in face-to-face conversation.

- Listen to his babbling.

- When your baby pauses, he's probably waiting for your reply. (You may even hear his voice rise just before he pauses, as if he were asking you a question.)

- You can respond using real words, or you can echo your baby's sounds.

- As soon as you stop talking, your baby may start up again, trying to keep the conversation going.

Q-Tip _____

Imitate and echo your baby a lot during the next few months. Before long, your baby will begin to mimic and echo you, too. Okay, so he'll probably do that even if you don't imitate him, but in the meantime you'll both have fun babbling, and your baby will enjoy these conversations with you.

Talking to your baby is not only polite; it speeds up your child's learning process. In general, the more you talk, the more your baby will try to talk. When your baby starts babbling conversations with you, at least initially, he's getting some social practice. But in the coming months, your conversations will become a tool for your baby to learn more complex sounds. Talk a lot to your baby if you can, but don't monopolize the conversation. Remember to give your infant a chance to talk while you listen.

Watch Your Language

What's the best way to talk to your baby? Let's start with a basic guideline: try not to feel too silly talking to her. Even though your baby can't understand your vocabulary, she's beginning to understand the conversational process. The more you talk with her, the more she learns.

Feel free to talk to your baby in the same high-pitched, sing-song voice that parents have used with infants for centuries. Infants respond better to higher-pitched sounds, so using a high voice will more readily capture your baby's attention.

Talk naturally. You don't need to simplify your words or grammar for your baby's sake. Remember, no matter how much you simplify your language, your baby doesn't understand what you're saying (at least, not until around the sixth month). Your baby is not listening to you because she's fascinated by your ideas or your stories. She listens because she's fascinated by anything you do. Your baby just loves to interact with you. She could care less whether you're talking about the weather, your chores, or the thermodynamics of nuclear fusion.

By the end of the sixth month, long before she utters her first word, your baby begins to understand a few simple things that you say. So now's the perfect time to start providing a blow-by-blow of your life with baby. In addition to describing what you are doing (or she is doing), point out objects as you name them. Concentrate on immediate sights and sounds. The more you talk to your baby about the here and now, focusing on the moment and describing what's there or what's going on, the easier it will be for her to make connections between the sights and sounds and tastes she perceives and the words you attach to them.

Q-Tip _____

Get in the habit of providing your baby with a narrative of your life together even before she can understand any of what you're saying. Whenever she's alert, tell her what you are doing. "Okay, I'm going to change your diaper now. First we have to take off your pants …."

Also describe to her what she is doing. "Look at you! Holding that rattle all by yourself. Can you shake it and make a sound? Good!" Your talking will hold your baby's interest, help her polish her social skills, and lay the groundwork for learning words.

From 6 months (or even earlier) to a year, speak slowly and clearly to give your child a better chance to understand and distinguish individual words. Emphasize important words, especially nouns (person, place, or thing), through vocal stresses and frequent repetition. If you stress the same nouns often enough, your child will soon understand that these sounds she keeps hearing are the names of the things in her world: bottle, diaper, Mama, Dada. (Even if she doesn't understand their naming function, your baby will at least begin to associate the names with the objects.)

Same Old Song and Dance

Although conversation with you should provide the bulk of your child's preverbal language learning, other avenues can teach your baby about language, too. Like all learning tools for infants (and toddlers and preschoolers, too), the ones that teach language best are those that encourage your child to have fun learning:

◆ **Songs:** Whether it's a bathtub song that you sing while washing up, a diaper-changing song that you've invented, silly sing-along songs by the likes of Raffi or Tom Paxton, "circle time" songs that encourage activity, or soft-sung lullabies at bedtime, your child will love it if you sing to him. The rhythms and melody of music may also facilitate language learning. A year from now, your baby's first extended strings of words may be those he's learned from listening to songs.

If you buy commercial children's music, don't let the CDs or tapes do all the work. Your child will respond much more readily to you singing along with taped music than he will to a disembodied voice through a speaker. So listen to the music with your child and work on memorizing the lyrics so that you can sing along, or sing your baby's favorite songs on your own when the CD player or tape deck is not available.

Q-Tip

If you or your baby likes children's music, you can choose from a huge selection of children's CDs and tapes. Most are well worth the investment. As long as the CD or tape features songs with simple, catchy melodies and easy or silly lyrics, your child will enjoy listening to it over and over again. Some favorite recording artists for young children (including infants) are the Wiggles; Raffi; the music of *Sesame Street;* Tom Paxton; Joanie Bartels; Peter, Paul, and Mary; and everyone from Tony Bennett and Johnny Cash to Celine Dion and Linda Ronstadt.

◆ **Nursery rhymes:** Read or recite nursery rhymes often. Repeat the same rhymes over and over again. Your baby will not mind the repetition (although you may tire of it). In fact, your baby will appreciate the familiarity of favorite pieces. At this age, he learns more from the repetition of a half-dozen or dozen well-chosen rhymes than he would from hearing 300 different rhymes with no reruns. With repeated hearings, your baby will start to pick out different words, if not to speak, at least to anticipate and recognize.

Beginning around your baby's half-birthday, he will especially love nursery rhymes and songs that involve activity: bouncing on your knee ("This Is the Way the Gentlemen Ride" and others), clapping ("If You're Happy and You Know It"), and finger play ("Pat-a-Cake"). Later in the year, when he begins standing up, he will also enjoy rhymes and songs that involve standing up and sitting down ("Ring Around the Rosy," "London Bridge," and the like).

◆ **Books:** Even at this early age, many children appreciate the worlds that books open up to them. In buying or borrowing books before your baby's first birthday, pick ones that feature just one colorful illustration of a single object per page. Busy pages that depict full scenes with painstaking detail may be more interesting to you, but they will confuse your baby, who won't know what to look at.

Q-Tip

Start your child on the road to reading early. Get your baby books of his very own that he can read with you or play with by himself. At this age, however, avoid books with paper pages. Your child will not just "read" his books, but will pull on them, tear at them, chew on them, spit up on them, throw them, and drop them. Sturdy board books, with pages made of thick cardboard, hold up well. So do bath books with pages made of padded vinyl or plastic. Cloth books will probably survive your child's infancy, and texture books like *Pat the Bunny* will get a lot of use before your child manages to rip out all the pages.

Reading, singing songs, and reciting nursery rhymes can all encourage the development of your infant's language and communication skills. But the main appeal of these activities to your baby is the sound of your voice and the loving attention you give him.

Words Fail Me: Nonverbal Communication

Your infant still cannot communicate through words, but she has other means of letting you know what she thinks, feels, or wants. Crying (see Chapter 6), of course, still serves your baby well as a means of communicating her needs. By around 5 months, however, your baby begins to communicate in other nonverbal ways. She increasingly uses facial expressions and gestures to get her message across.

> **Baby Talk**
>
> "Life in all its phases possessed for him unsounded depths of entertainment, and in the intervals of uncontrolled laughter at the acts and words of his astonished elders, he gave way to frequent subtle smiles resulting from subjectively humorous experiences unguessed by the world at large."
>
> —Josephine Dodge Bacon

Your baby has expanded her repertoire of gestures. She now points and reaches toward something she wants. She opens her arms wide and reaches toward you when she wants you to pick her up. She also may push away a toy or food that she doesn't like.

You can also see a broad range of facial expressions by 6 months. Your baby may scrunch up her face when presented with a new food. She may frown when something puzzles her (as so many things do). She will open her mouth wide with surprise. She may stick out her tongue and make a "blah" face if something displeases her. And of course, whenever you walk into the room, she smiles and smiles.

Do You Have the Magic Touch?

You, too, communicate with your baby in nonverbal ways. You reward him for grasping a toy or sitting up with your smiles and claps (as well as your words of praise). You wave bye-bye when you're going somewhere. You comfort him with a hug or a kiss. But most of all, you hold him.

Communication with a preverbal child of any age begins and ends with a parent's touch. Remember that when your baby cries in an attempt to communicate with you, your first response should always be to pick him up and hold him. This magic of touch helps form a secure basis for any further communication between you. Through recognition of his cry, common sense, or guesswork, you may then find out what your baby wants, but you may also discover that all he really wants is for you to hold him.

Close physical contact in these early years is the cement that bonds parents and infants together. Any loving action you take with your baby in your arms helps build the bond of trust between you. Whether you hold him, rock him, hug him, read to him, play with him, sing to him, or coo to him, you send a nonverbal message of love that your baby understands and appreciates.

When you hold your baby in your arms, he feels safer, more secure, and calmer. When you respond to his cries by quickly picking him up and hugging him tight, your baby learns to trust that you will try to make everything all right. By about 3 or 4 months, your baby may even stop crying as soon as you bring him up to your chest. He knows you now and trusts you to take care of his needs.

Because physical closeness means so much to your baby, give him as much as he wants. Like all babies, your baby will love to be held, hugged, rocked, caressed, and massaged. Indeed, research has shown that most babies prefer caresses even to food. So use gentle touch to communicate and bond with your baby. Hold him, cuddle him, and snuggle with him as often as you can. Lie down with your baby and let him cuddle up close. Let him take in the warmth of your skin and the aroma of your body (and your partner's, too). Let him lie on your chest so that he can hear your heartbeat. In all likelihood, you'll love this close physical contact almost as much as your baby does.

There's the Rub: Infant Massage

Massage has special benefits for infants:

- ◆ It helps to establish a special degree of physical intimacy that shows your baby that you love her.

- ◆ If you doubt your own gentleness, massage can help you get accustomed to handling your baby tenderly and lovingly.

- ◆ It stimulates your baby's circulatory, digestive, and respiratory systems.

- ◆ It can ease your baby's gas pains, calm her, and quiet her when she seems fussy.

- ◆ Studies have shown that massage even improves the growth and development of babies born prematurely. (Whether it does the same for full-term babies is not yet known.)

Babyproofing

You don't need to use any special oils to massage your baby. A little moisturizer rubbed into your own hands allows you to rub her smoothly. If you decide you want to use oils anyway, rub a little on your baby's arm about 30 minutes before starting the massage. That way, if she has an allergic reaction, you can avoid applying it to her whole body.

In short, massage can give great pleasure to both your baby and you. If you want to try infant massage yourself, here's how to do it:

1. Choose a time when you will least likely be interrupted or distracted. Unplug the phone or let the answering machine take your calls.

2. Find a warm, quiet, comfortable place. Lay your baby on her back on a warm towel. If she objects to being totally naked (as some babies do), then just take off her shirt to start and then cover up her torso and take off her pants when you start massaging her lower half.

3. Work from the head down and from the center out. Start by gently massaging the top of your baby's head, her forehead, and the sides of her face. Then move down to her neck and shoulders. Use tender squeezes as you move down her arms. Then gently rub her chest and belly. Apply gentle squeezes down her legs, ankles, feet, and toes. Finish with long, light strokes all the way down her body from head to toe.

4. Use light, gentle, and even strokes throughout the massage. Some babies like a circular motion. Look into your baby's eyes often and smile as you massage her. Quiet talk (perhaps a narration of the massage) may help keep her calm, but your touch itself should also have a soothing effect.

5. If your baby seemed to enjoy the massage, turn her on to her belly and massage her back, again working from the top down. But if she's getting restless, don't force the issue. Remember, one of the benefits of infant massage is building feelings of physical closeness—not physical struggle!

Remember to use very tender strokes. After all, she's just a baby. Chances are, she doesn't have sore or pulled muscles that require extensive physical therapy. So focus on gentle, loving touches that both you and your baby will enjoy.

The Least You Need to Know

- Listen to your baby and talk to your baby. Neither of you will understand each other's words, but the feelings underlying them will be clear.

- In talking to your baby, focus on the here and now, just as he does. He may begin to associate the words he hears with the sights, sounds, smells, tastes, and feelings he's experiencing when you say them.

◆ Introduce your baby to the wide scope of language through conversation, songs, nursery rhymes, and books.

◆ Your baby wants (and needs) warm hugs and gentle caresses from you more than anything else in the world—even food.

Chapter **8**

The Play's the Thing

In This Chapter

◆ Creating a stimulating play space

◆ Encouraging your child to develop and explore through play

◆ How to play with (or like) a baby

◆ Ideal first toys for your infant

Play is fun for both you and your baby. But for your baby, play is much more than fun. Play can help your baby explore his world, discover new things, see how different objects feel or move, learn new abilities, and practice and master new skills.

You and your partner are your baby's first and best teachers, and toys and play are your best teaching tools. Through games, toys, and play, you can stimulate all of your baby's senses as well as his physical and mental development. By choosing age-appropriate games, toys, and play throughout this first year, you can make learning enjoyable for both you and your baby. The love for learning that you create in your baby now can establish a pattern that will last throughout his life.

Welcome to the Fun House

Whether your baby sleeps in her own room or in a corner of yours, try to make this playspace a safe, loving, stimulating environment. Decorate it, including the walls next to the changing table and the area around the crib, with toys and pictures that excite your baby's interest.

Everything's in Black and White

During the early months, your baby sees objects and images that present sharp color contrasts best: especially black on white or white on black. Make the most of your baby's ability by showing him pictures of black-and-white patterns. Simple geometric patterns, such as a black-and-white checkerboard or alternating black and white circles that make a bull's-eye, as well as images of faces and animals are particular favorites.

Nowadays you can buy many black-and-white toys, specifically designed for young infants, in any toy store: stuffed cows and other animals, books with black-and-white faces and patterns, or plastic pattern cards. You can also easily make your own checkerboard patterns, circles, black-and-white pictures of faces, and so on.

Hang some of these black-and-white pictures next to your baby's crib. Place others on the wall next to the changing table. For your baby to see these stimulating images, they need to be less than 1 foot away from her head. Your baby will also love it if you hang a mobile of black-and-white images about 10 inches over her crib or changing table. (Make sure all of the images on the mobile face down where your baby can see them, rather than to the side where you can see them.)

Q-Tip _____

Don't go overboard on decorating your newborn's room (or corner of your room). One or two pictures on the wall next to the changing table, one or two black-and-white toys for the crib, and perhaps a crib mobile provide all the visual stimulation your baby can handle during the first few months. Overstimulation only creates a confusing blur for your baby.

As your baby's vision improves, she will enjoy bold primary colors: red, yellow, and blue. (Pink or pale blue pastels, long a favorite color scheme for baby nurseries, are virtually invisible to newborns and hold little visual interest for infants.) She will still enjoy black-and-white decorations, but you might want to change them or add to them to give her something new to see. Try hanging some pictures cut out of magazines, photographs of yourselves, wrapping paper, or your own drawings.

Playspace

For an infant, every place is a playspace. It doesn't matter whether your baby is in his crib, in his playpen, lying on his stomach on the living-room rug, or resting on a soft blanket stretched out over the grass. Any space can easily become an arena for play.

In addition to offering black-and-white (and later boldly colored) visual stimuli, you can enhance your infant's playspace during the first 3 months by providing the following:

◆ **Rattles:** Even before your baby can grasp one himself, a rattle entertains him with both sight and sound. And rattles can serve an important function around the third month: they can help your infant discover his own hands. At first, he will simply notice the random movements of the rattle in his hands and the sounds these movements produce. But soon your baby will associate movement, sight, and sound and get his first gleanings of the principles of cause and effect.

◆ **An activity center:** Long before your baby figures out how to use an activity board, he will enjoy watching and listening to it as you spin the dials, roll the rollers, push the buttons, and ring the bells. Around the third month, when your infant begins swatting at things, he may even bang into it or slap it accidentally on his own. Watch the surprise and delight on his face as he turns his head toward the activity center and waits for it to make more noise. (Now he'll probably need your help again.)

◆ **A crib mirror:** A mirror placed in the crib or playpen delights most young infants. By around the eighth week, your baby will enjoy looking at "that other baby" in the mirror. But even when he's not looking at himself, your baby can enjoy the mirror because what he sees in it changes depending upon where he is. When your baby lies in one corner of the crib, he may see the changing table and the pictures on the wall beside it. From another corner, he may see the frame of a window. And if he manages to move his head just an inch or two, he'll see something completely different.

Babyproofing

Before putting any mirror where your child can reach it, make sure it's a child-safe baby mirror (metal enclosed in a plastic frame) rather than a glass one.

Child's Play

Don't worry too much about stimulating your child to give her a "head start" on learning. Just because you and your partner are your baby's first teachers doesn't mean that you have to put pressure on yourselves to teach her anything. Your child learns from everything in her world: the things she sees, touches, hears, smells, and tastes. She doesn't need a set of fancy flashcards or other learning aids, at least not yet. As you play with your infant, keep in mind that play is supposed to be fun. Both you and your child will have more fun if you keep the pressure to learn to a minimum.

During these first few months especially, what your baby needs from you is your love, your attention, and your time. More than anything else (even food), she wants and needs you to …

Baby Doctor

Never swing an infant (or even pick him up) by holding just his hands or arms. Until your baby's bones become more set, at around 1 year, even a small amount of tension can easily dislocate his shoulder or elbow.

- Hold her.
- Sing to her.
- Play with her.
- Talk to her.
- Coo to her.
- "Read" to her.
- Praise even the smallest of successes.
- Cuddle with her.

Q-Tip

Don't feel as if you always have to be "on." Both you and your baby will have "downtimes," and you need to respect these moods by providing calmer, quieter activities.

Timing is everything. Your baby will be most responsive to your playfulness when she is both alert and unfussy. If you try to play when your child is hungry or tired or sick or upset, both you and she will gain nothing but frustration.

Your Child's Favorite Plaything

During the first 3 months of your baby's life (and for several years more), you will be his favorite toy. He will enjoy lying on top of you, exercising his developing muscles with your help, rocking with you, grabbing at your nose and hair, listening to you talk and sing, and making you smile and laugh.

Your games with your baby need not be very complex. Simply making faces at each other can provide many minutes of delight. Or just hold your baby on your lap facing you, lean into him, and say something nonsensical like, "Ah-boo!" Repeat it for as long as it entertains your baby. You could play peekaboo, but don't ever hide for too long. If you hide your face behind a blanket or towel, your baby won't know where you are. And because a baby's attention span is so short, if you hide for more than a second or so, he won't even know he's playing a game.

Don't be afraid to play rough-and-tumble physical games with your baby in the third month, once he has gained control of his neck muscles. Okay, maybe not *too* rough-and-tumble, but you can be physical:

Baby Talk

"To every job that must be done, there's an element of fun. Find the fun and, snap, the job's a game."

—*Mary Poppins* (Bill Walsh and Don DaGradi, screenwriters)

- ◆ Lie on your back, bend your knees, and place your baby face-down on your legs to let him fly like an airplane.

- ◆ Pull your baby up to a sitting position.

- ◆ Bounce him up and down on your knees in rhythm to a favorite nursery rhyme.

- ◆ Hold him by the waist and swing him around securely in your arms, lifting him up and down as you spin like a tilt-a-whirl.

Everything you do with your baby can have an element of play in it. Changing a diaper can include playing with a toy or watching a mobile spin above him. Dressing, especially pulling a shirt over his head, lends itself to a quick game of peekaboo or "Where's the Baby?" Feeding can involve singing lullabies.

Choosing Age-Appropriate Toys

During your baby's first 2 months, she doesn't need or want any toys. Your baby won't even discover her own hands until she's about 2 months old. Your baby may instinctively clutch a toy that you put in her hand, but she can't really play with it. She may enjoy looking at a plaything or listening to it, but she'd much rather look at and listen to you.

From 2 to 3 months, however, when your baby's hands open up and she first discovers them—and all the things she can do with them—toys become much more valuable as learning tools. Noisy toys are great at this age. (Just make sure they're soft because your baby will probably hit herself in the head with them.)

Soft rubber squeak toys, lightweight rattles, rattling bracelets, and easy-to-hold plastic keys do more than entertain your baby. They focus her attention on what her hands are doing. You can almost see the connections forming in your baby's brain:

noise = hands → hands = moving → moving = me

my hands = moving = noise → look what I can do!

From about 10 to 14 weeks, your baby will enjoy taking a kittenlike swipe at toys. Hang toys of various shapes, textures, and sounds (a rattle, a fuzzy ball, a plastic or rubber ring, a small doll or stuffed animal, and so on) above your baby's crib. Or tie a string to them and hold them above her while she lies on the floor. When she connects with the toy, your baby will be delighted at the way it swings and the sounds it makes, if any. This activity also helps your baby make connections between what she does with her hands and what happens.

Introducing Toys

When you pick out toys for an infant, keep in mind what he will be doing with them. From the third month on, your baby will take any toy—or anything he can reach—and explore it. How does your baby explore an object? He grasps it, feels it, looks at it, perhaps bangs it against the floor (or himself), and invariably brings it to his mouth and sucks on it. Yum.

Fun Toys

Until he can move on his own, you are the filter through which your baby explores the world. He cannot explore anything unless you bring it to him. To encourage your baby's exploration, give him toys and other objects that have varying textures, shapes, weights, colors, sounds, and even smells. Your child will love to explore these items:

◆ Textured activity blankets

◆ Activity boxes with sounds and movement

◆ Soft blocks

◆ Balls

◆ Plastic cars, trucks, and trains

◆ Pop-up books

Because everything is new to him, your baby will have fun with almost anything you give him. Just make sure that what you give your baby is safe. This means no sharp edges, no glass objects, and nothing toxic. Don't give your baby anything so heavy that it will hurt when he drops it (as he soon will). Finally, make sure that what you offer your baby is too big (at least 2 inches in diameter) for your baby to swallow or choke on.

> **Q-Tip** _____
>
> Not all your baby's playthings need to be store-bought toys. You can find dozens of suitable playthings throughout your house. Look in the kitchen. Your infant will love playing with wooden and plastic spoons, measuring spoons, spatulas, pots, pans, lids, plastic colanders, funnels, plastic bottles, plastic jars, plastic cups, and plastic plates. Your baby will also love the sound he makes if you lay him on his back and hold a cookie sheet where he can kick it. Fruits and vegetables can be fun to play with, too.
>
> Look in a desk drawer. You'll find delightful plastic rulers, pieces of paper (crumpled or flat), and transparent tape that you can wad up into a big, sticky ball.
>
> If your baby is playing with something you need—a spatula or other cooking utensil, for example—give him another plaything. By offering your baby a trade, you can retrieve the object you need with little or no fuss.

Introduce new objects for your baby to play with one at a time. Your baby can focus attention on only one thing at a time anyway. If you spread out a wide selection of toys, your baby won't know which to choose.

Be Flexible

Different babies have different personalities, so a rattle that appeals to one baby might not interest another at all. Indeed, your own baby's mood may change from day to day—or even hour to hour. So just because your baby enjoyed playing with a fuzzy rattle yesterday doesn't mean it will capture his attention today. Even if your baby usually likes bouncing up and down on your knees, the game will lose its appeal whenever he's tired or hungry. You may therefore need to adjust your play to your baby's changing moods.

Q-Tip

From about 3 months on, keep those toys coming. Your baby will appreciate a variety of objects as long as he knows basically what to do with them. If you give your baby the same toy again and again, you deny him the opportunity to explore the world in all its diversity. But if you give him a series of soft rattles, hard rattles, wrist rattles, key rings, rattles with beads, rattles with bells, and so on, your baby can explore and discover new shapes, textures, and sounds. So try rotating toys every few days or so. You can help expand your baby's horizons by occasionally changing the objects hanging from his crib or changing-table mobile, too.

Whenever you introduce a new toy or game, carefully watch the way your baby responds to it. Let him help you get to know him better and recognize and appreciate his likes and dislikes. By tuning in to his reactions, you will know whether your baby enjoys a particular toy, game, or kind of play.

If your baby likes it, he will focus his attention on it and, if he's old enough, reach for it. When your baby starts to get bored with a toy or game or just tired of playing, he will turn his head away or start to fuss or cry. (This might be from the very instant you offer the toy.) These signals are fairly obvious, but many parents overlook them in their enthusiasm to entertain and enlighten their babies.

Your baby has the attention span of a baby. Even the most fascinating of toys and games will not likely hold his interest for more than a couple of minutes. So try to provide variety in activities, toys, textures, sounds, and every new thing you introduce to your baby.

Remain flexible; let your baby make up the rules of play. If he seems bored with a particular toy or game, try something else. Let your child know from his first months on that his interests are important to you and that he can play, or not play, with whatever he chooses (as long as it's safe, of course).

The Least You Need to Know

◆ For your baby, play is not idleness. It allows her to develop new abilities and explore the world.

◆ You are your baby's favorite plaything throughout her first year and beyond. So relax and have fun with your child.

◆ Your baby doesn't need a lot of store-bought toys. Safe household objects are just as much fun and give her just as much opportunity to grow and explore.

◆ Use playtime to get to know your baby better. If you pay attention, your infant may clearly indicate her likes and dislikes.

◆ If your baby shows signs of being bored, give her a rest. She doesn't need you to entertain her all day.

Part 2

The Early Infant: 3–6 Months

Has it been 3 months already? It probably seems like just yesterday that your baby was born or that he first looked up at you and smiled. Now the real fun begins. Your baby is becoming more and more conscious of his own movements. Over the next few months, he will become increasingly active: grasping and crudely manipulating objects, rolling over, and perhaps even sitting up.

One or two teeth may make their first appearances, too. Even if they don't, you'll start to feed your baby real food—or at least a soupy mush that once resembled real food. Although spoon-feeding can get messy, you will delight in each discovery your child makes: whether it's something new to eat or something new that he can do.

Early Infant Health and Development

In This Chapter

◆ Rolling over, sitting up, and other clever tricks

◆ Reaching, grasping, banging, tasting: your baby's active exploration of the world

◆ Determining whether your baby is too fat, too thin, or just right

◆ Caring for first teeth (and teethers)

Your child transforms herself during the second 3 months of her life. Socially, she becomes more friendly and eager to make contact. Mentally, she begins coordinating the activities of her various senses: making connections between what she hears and sees, what she sees and touches, what she touches and tastes. Physically, she starts rocking and rolling and reaching and grasping and sitting and perhaps even moving. By 6 months, your lively, active infant hardly resembles the peaceful newborn she was before.

My Body, Myself: Physical Development

As you begin the second trimester of parenthood, your baby is still probably immobile for the most part. Oh, she kicks her legs and waves her arms when you lay her down on her back, and she picks up her head and maybe her shoulders when she's lying on her stomach. She may even surprise and delight herself (and you) by rolling over once in a while. But for the most part, if you put her down on a blanket on the floor and leave the room for a minute, you know exactly where she'll be when you come back.

Going Mobile

Between the fourth and sixth months, your baby becomes increasingly mobile. This means you need to watch him even more closely than you have during his first 3 months.

If, like most babies, yours didn't develop the ability to roll over during his third month, you can be sure that he'll figure it out during the fourth. First, he'll probably flip himself from his back to his side, and then he'll learn that he can flop down onto his belly from there. (Though most babies start rolling this way, some do flip from belly to back first.)

> **Babyproofing**
>
> If your baby has begun to roll over at all, or even if she gives you an inkling that she might be ready, avoid putting her down by herself on your bed—or anywhere other than the floor. Any mobility at all on her part could lead to a nasty fall.

A few days, weeks, or months later (remember that these milestones don't come along according to a strict schedule), your baby will begin reversing this process. flipping over from front to back. By 6 months, he will probably be able to roll all the way over from his belly to his back and then onto his belly again. In this way, your baby (and you) may soon discover that he can move about a room quite quickly just by rolling.

Even if your baby doesn't discover the joys of *logrolling*, he may discover other ways to get around a room long before he starts to crawl. In the third or fourth month, your baby begins lifting his head up off the floor when he's lying on his stomach in order to look around and survey the territory. In the month that follows, he starts to use his arms to push his chest up off the ground, giving him even more territory to scope out. In the sixth month, you may even see him trying to swim across the floor by rocking back and forth on his stomach with his arms and legs lifted and outspread.

Few babies crawl by 6 months, but although your baby may not crawl yet, he's certainly working toward that goal. Through kicking, thrusting, pushing, and stretching, your baby is giving his arm, leg, and back muscles quite a workout. Indeed, by 6 months, he may have built up the strength of his muscles so much that he can get across a room on his belly by propelling himself with his legs and/or pulling himself with his arms.

By 6 months, your baby may even be able to get his bottom off the floor and get up on his knees. If he manages this feat, he may discover yet another way to move himself across a room. By rocking back and forth on his knees, he can build enough momentum to throw himself forward several inches at a time.

Granted, your baby moves (if he can get around at all) in fits and starts rather than in one smooth motion, but moving will become smoother in the seventh and eight months. Your baby's ability to move himself at all is a cause for celebration—and increased caution.

Sitting Pretty

At 4 months (or even earlier), your baby loves it when you pull her to a sitting position. She now has enough control over her back and neck muscles to keep her head from flopping over and leaving her nose in her navel. At first, however, her head might fall backward somewhat while you pull her up. Once upright, though, she can probably hold her head fairly steady—at least, for a short time. As your baby gains more and more control over her muscles during the fifth (or perhaps sixth) month, she will be able to keep her head in line with her chest and shoulders even while being pulled up.

Sitting up gives your baby so much more to see and learn that she won't be able to get enough of it. Once she's learned that you can pull her up to sitting, she probably won't even wait for you to offer anymore. Instead, she'll reach out imploringly—and you'll be unable to resist.

Babyproofing

Although your baby may be able to hold a steady sitting position for some time by 6 months, she is still working very hard to maintain her balance. So don't leave her sitting up on a bed, couch, or chair.

When she's sitting on a hard surface, scatter plenty of pillows around her for the inevitable time when she flops over. Even then, don't leave her. If she falls face first and her body lands on top of her arms, she may not be able to lift her face from the pillows.

By her half-birthday (or perhaps a little later), your baby will probably do much of the work involved in pulling herself up to sitting. All you need to do is give her the fingers she needs to support herself while she pulls.

Once she's sitting, your baby may also be able to hold herself in that position without any support for a little while if you set her up just right. Plant her on her bottom and spread her legs in a V position for balance. Then pull her arms together and place her hands on the floor between her legs. (She will have to lean forward a bit to reach the floor.) By supporting herself on her outstretched arms and balancing herself with her legs, she can sit almost upright. With a little practice, she may even learn to support herself with just one hand.

Babyproofing

If you pull your baby to a standing position, remember to pull gently. Jerking him could result in a dislocated elbow or shoulder. Remember also never to pick your child all the way up by the hands or forearms.

Sooner or later, your baby will lose her strength, concentration, or balance and topple over. But in the meantime, she gains a whole new perspective on the world.

Onward and Upward

Sitting, although fun and fascinating, won't satisfy your baby for long. Once he's discovered the joys of sitting up, he will want to go even higher. During the fifth or sixth month, your baby will probably start bearing some weight on his legs, so he will love it if you help him to pull himself up from sitting to a standing position. To start, you can pull your baby up while he is sitting in your lap, facing you, and holding your hands. But soon you can gently pull him to standing anywhere—as long as he has some place to plant his feet without slipping.

Like all your baby's physical skills, sitting and standing improve with practice. Practice allows him to strengthen and coordinate the muscles needed to maintain balance and stability. With practice, your baby may even be able to remain standing for a short time by his half-birthday—just as long as he has something to hold on to for support.

Living from Hand to Mouth

Your baby's hand-eye coordination undergoes dramatic development during these 3 months. At 2 months, your baby didn't even know that he had hands. By 3 months, he had discovered that hands are great for swatting at things, grasping things, and perhaps even bringing things to his mouth. But during this trimester, your child really starts using his hands.

In the fourth month, your child becomes even more adept at grasping and handling objects. By 16 weeks, he can track objects all the way across his field of vision, from left to right or right to left. Now he's ready to take things into his own hands.

By 16 to 18 weeks, your baby begins deliberately reaching out for things and handling them. This action seems so simple to us that we forget what a complex process is involved. It requires focusing on the object of desire, gauging its distance and direction, and coordinating the movement of the arm and hand to first reach out and then grasp the object. Don't worry if your baby's judgment of distance seems a little off at first. He'll get better with practice.

By the sixth month, your infant may have even mastered the hand-off: passing a toy, a bit of food, or another object of interest from one hand to the other. As he comes to recognize the concept of *object constancy* (the realization that an object doesn't cease to exist just because it has disappeared from sight), your child may even begin looking for something that he's dropped (though he may not look for long).

Babyproofing

Your baby's improving manual dexterity, his growing curiosity, and his tendency to explore everything with his mouth make it essential that you keep anything dangerous—that is, small, sharp, or poisonous—well out of his reach.

Your child also uses his hands to touch and explore the world around him. He reaches out and strokes things such as books, toys, flowers, blankets, foods, and your face or hair, exploring their textures.

Upon discovering his hands, your baby becomes more and more active physically and mentally. No longer content merely to soak up information that comes to him passively through sights, sounds, and other sensations, your infant actively seeks out knowledge. For example, he may see a squirrel dart up a tree and crane his neck to get a better look. He may hear your voice or the doorbell and look around for the source of the sound. Or he may see a rattle and reach out to grasp it. Then he may shake it or bang it or squeeze it to discover the sound it makes. And invariably, he will bring it to his mouth to find out how it tastes. Yummy!

Physical Training

By about 6 months, your baby gains at least some control over most of the muscles in her body. She doesn't really need your help to discover how to use them. She'll develop, practice, and master the physical skills described in this chapter with or without your help. Nonetheless, you may move along the process (and have a lot of fun doing it) by helping your baby exercise and build her muscles.

Here's what you can do:

◆ **Give her the floor.** Your baby will take advantage of almost any opportunity to explore her new skills and the world around her. So don't keep her cooped up all day in her crib, playpen, stroller, baby carrier, baby swing, or baby bouncer. Give her some free time as well.

◆ **Keep her mouth open.** Limit her use of a pacifier to those times when she needs it to calm or soothe herself. Otherwise, give her free rein to explore safe objects through her favorite sense: taste.

◆ **Give her a hand.** Help your baby to practice her new skills by pulling her to sitting or standing, giving her bottom a little push to help her roll over, and putting safe toys or other objects within her grasp for her to explore. But provide only as much help as she needs. Let her do as much of the work in sitting up, for example, as she can. Or start putting objects down next to her rather than in her hand.

Baby Talk

"A child is fed with milk and praise."

—Mary Lamb

◆ **Give her some exercise.** Put your baby through a calisthenics routine: not to give her an intense workout, but just for fun. Help her to reach her hands over her head or touch her toes or clap her hands or kiss her knees. Help her do sit-ups. Or play bouncing games on your knees.

◆ **Give her a round of applause.** Praise her warmly and enthusiastically for each new skill she demonstrates.

You don't need to put pressure on your baby to develop her physical skills. But if you offer playful encouragement, you'll both enjoy discovering just how much she can do.

All Shapes and Sizes

As the months pass, you may become concerned about your child's size or shape. Is your baby growing properly? Is your child getting too fat? Or is he not growing fast enough?

Too Fat?

Like all healthy babies, your baby was born with a certain amount of padding. Until he begins to develop and exercise muscles, this baby fat is perfectly natural.

How round is too round? If your baby is not gaining weight during this first year, then he's not growing properly. As long as your baby is gaining both height and weight, weight gain shouldn't be a problem. That's why your pediatrician (or a nurse) measures your baby's height and weight at each visit—and one of the reasons well-baby visits are scheduled so frequently. But if your baby's weight gain is consistently outstripping his gain in height (see the height and weight charts in Appendix B), your pediatrician may advise you to take one or more steps to try to slow your baby's weight gain.

If your pediatrician does suggest that you need to monitor your baby's weight, observe the following do's and don'ts when trying to regulate your baby's weight gain:

- ◆ Do try to soothe or calm your baby using something other than the breast or bottle (or, later, something other than solid foods or juices).

- ◆ Don't automatically push food on your baby when he's upset. He may want something else but accept food as a substitute. This situation can set up an unhealthy pattern of comfort eating that, unfortunately, can last a lifetime.

- ◆ Do offer your baby water instead of formula or breast milk "between" feedings. If your baby seems to want to drink or suckle within an hour or two of a previous feeding, he may be thirsty rather than hungry, or he may just want something to suck on.

- ◆ Don't dilute formula (by adding more water) unless your pediatrician specifically instructs you to do so.

- ◆ Do dilute juice with water.

- ◆ Don't nurse your baby (or feed him with a bottle) as much when you start him on solid foods, but don't wean him altogether either. The increase in solid foods should be balanced with an equivalent decrease in the amount of formula or breast milk he drinks.

- ◆ Do encourage your baby to be more active. Give him more free time on the floor. Do baby calisthenics, bending your baby's joints and exercising his muscles by hand. Help him practice pulling up to sitting (or even standing). Encourage him to bounce while standing and holding your hands.

Babyproofing

Do not alter the mix of your baby's formula without your doctor's explicit instructions. Diluting it can reduce the amount of nutrition that your baby gets. On the other hand, going light on the water used to mix formula can result in dehydration. So unless your pediatrician advises you otherwise, stick to the proportions recommended on the label.

Whatever you do, don't take *any* measures to control weight gain without first discussing your concerns with your pediatrician. Just because you think your baby looks fat doesn't mean that he needs to go on a diet. Get a professional opinion first.

Too Thin?

Another common concern among parents in the first year is that their baby isn't growing fast enough. How thin is too thin? In all likelihood, you have no need to be concerned about a thin baby. Most lean babies are healthy and very active. If your baby is very active, she may burn away almost as many calories as she consumes. In addition, if both you and your partner are lean, your genes may have influenced your baby's body type.

Unless your child's weight gain continues to drop over 2 or 3 months, you probably have no cause for concern. (If you are concerned nonetheless, talk to your pediatrician.) If your child's weight gain does slow significantly or come to a halt, consult your pediatrician. Your pediatrician may encourage you to do one of the following:

- Make sure your baby is still nursing or bottle-feeding at least five times a day

- Begin feeding her solids

- Alter the mix of your baby's formula

Whatever you do, don't underfeed your baby in the hopes that it will set her off on the path to lifelong slimness. Your baby needs more food (per pound of body weight) and more fat than an adult or even an older child needs. Undernourishing your child will retard her development, regardless of whether it controls her weight gain.

Nothing but the Tooth

Sometime around your child's half-birthday, his first tooth begins to poke out through the gums. (If you breast-feed your baby, you may notice the tooth long before it makes its appearance.) The first tooth is most often one of the lower incisors, followed by a second lower incisor. Two upper incisors follow, usually at about 7 months. By 12 months, your baby should have a full set of incisors: four on top and four on the bottom.

Most babies don't begin cutting a tooth until they are at least 5 to 7 months old. Some babies get their first tooth a little earlier; some get it a little later. Even if your child doesn't have any teeth by 9 or 10 months though, don't worry. Like all aspects of your baby's physical (or mental) development, cutting teeth is not a race.

Baby Folklore _____

Although rare, some babies do have teeth at birth. What does the future hold for these children? Different superstitions have offered quite contradictory predictions. Some suggested that a child born with teeth would grow up to be extremely clever. Others gravely insisted that a baby born with teeth would eventually be hanged as a murderer.

The Tooth Is Sometimes Painful

Contrary to popular belief, first teeth usually come in relatively painlessly. Because the first eight teeth are all incisors (the relatively flat, sharp front teeth), they cut through gums fairly easily. True, the gums often become inflamed in response to the cutting of teeth, and this can sometimes cause pain. But many babies suffer virtually no pain from teeting until cutting the first molars, which are broader and larger than incisors (some time after their first birthday).

So don't assume that your baby is teething just because she is cranky, and don't assume that she'll be cranky just because she is teething. Your baby's fussiness may be the result of another cause. If, for example, your baby's irritability is accompanied by fever, diarrhea, or vomiting, then illness rather than teething lies behind it. Teething cannot cause any of these symptoms.

Baby Folklore _____

According to English lore, if your baby teethes early, you will soon have another baby—and many more to follow.

Baby Doctor _____

If your baby cuts short several feedings in a row or drastically reduces his intake of breast milk or formula and solid foods for several days running, consult your pediatrician.

Cutting first teeth *can* cause ...

◆ Red and swollen gums.

◆ A trace of white on the gum or a lump underneath the swollen area that you can feel with your finger.

◆ Extra salivation.

◆ Dribbling or drooling (although drooling alone, which begins at about 3 months, is not necessarily a sign of teething).

◆ An intense desire to chew on almost anything hard.

The excess saliva may have an effect on your baby's bowel movements, loosening them somewhat (but not causing diarrhea). The saliva also might prompt a little coughing. But none of these symptoms should cause concern unless they are accompanied by other symptoms, such as fever.

If your baby is a heavy drooler, you may want to have her wear a terry-cloth bib for most of the day. The absorbent bib will not only keep clothing dry, but you can use it to keep your baby's mouth and chin dry if they begin to look red and/or chapped.

 Babyproofing

If you use a teether that contains gel, be sure to examine it regularly for cracking or other signs of wear and tear.

Do not offer food as a teether until your baby has begun eating solid foods. Even after he's started on solids, stay with him and stay alert if you offer him a hard food to use as a teether. Take special care that your baby doesn't choke on any piece that breaks off in his mouth. Be ready to fish out any small piece of food with your finger.

Chew on This

Certainly, teething may also cause some irritability, if not from the pain, then from the pressure of the teeth against the underside of the gums. Unfortunately, your child's primary means of solace, sucking, offers him little comfort when he is teething. In fact, sucking may increase the pressure on his gums and any pain he feels.

Your baby is in an impossible position: he wants to suck because of its soothing effects, but he doesn't want to suck because it causes him pain. As a result, your teething child may lose some of his appetite for nursing (or bottle-feeding)—and maybe for solid foods, too. If he does drink from the breast or bottle, your baby may stop short and then start again many times. Try not to worry. Once the tooth has cut through the surface, his appetite will return.

Because sucking doesn't do the trick, you need to try something else to relieve the pressure on your baby's gums. Teethers, especially cold ones, are likely to offer your baby some much-needed comfort. By biting down on a teether, your baby can balance the pressure from under the gums. Cold teethers have the added benefit of numbing the gums to extend the relief.

Any of the following items make great teethers:

◆ A teething ring, especially one designed with a gel inside that cools when stored in a refrigerator

◆ A hard, smooth toy with no pieces that might break off

◆ A toothbrush

◆ A bagel

◆ A frozen banana

◆ Something cold to eat

◆ An ice cube

◆ A cold, wet washcloth

◆ A small piece of ice wrapped inside a washcloth

Your baby will also find his own "teethers":

◆ The handle of a rattle

◆ The railing of his crib or playpen

◆ An unsuspecting relative's finger

◆ His mother's breast

Q-Tip

If your baby bites down on your breast or fingers when teething, remember that he's not trying to hurt you. To relieve the pressure from under the gums, he will bite down on virtually anything you put in his mouth.

So try not to get angry with your baby. If you must, say (but don't shout), "Ow!" Then gently but firmly draw him away from your breast. Look into his eyes as you tell him, "No biting!" Then return him to the breast if he's still interested. (Be patient. It may take more than one lesson for your message to sink in.)

If none of these teethers works for your baby, try rubbing the tooth and/or gum firmly with your own finger. (You may want to dip your finger in ice water first to chill it.) Consult your pediatrician before using liquid acetaminophen (or any other medication) to ease pain associated with teething.

Babyproofing

Never use a touch of alcohol to numb your child's gums. Even a small amount of alcohol can poison a small baby.

The first teeth, which are always the front ones, are not for chewing, but rather for biting. Although your baby won't use these teeth to chew, he still starts to chew food around the time his first teeth come in. Even before the molars start coming in, your baby learns to chew using just his gums. Actually, your baby probably started to practice chewing on toys at around 3 or 4 months. But by 5 or 6 months, he needs food to practice on, too (see Chapter 11). Again, watch your baby carefully whenever he's chewing on anything. If he swallows something without chewing it thoroughly, he may start to choke.

Tooth Care

Unless your baby develops some problem with her teeth, you won't need to take her on her first visit to a dentist until she is 2 or 3 years old. But just because she isn't yet seeing a dentist doesn't mean that you should neglect dental care.

Caring properly for baby teeth is important. Your child's baby teeth determine where her adult teeth will grow in. If your child develops tooth decay and it spreads under the gums to the bone, the damage might make them unable to support adult teeth properly. Tooth decay in baby teeth can also create spacing problems for the adult teeth to come.

You don't need to begin brushing your baby's teeth until about 18 months—when she has about 16 teeth, all in a row, that can easily trap food between them. But that doesn't mean you shouldn't do anything to care for your baby's teeth.

Start brushing your baby's teeth, if you like, but don't be surprised if she resists the proper use of a toothbrush, preferring instead to bite down on it. Because your baby has few teeth and they're all up front, rubbing a washcloth or a small square of damp gauze gently over her first teeth is easier than using a toothbrush. Clean the gums, too, in order to remove food particles and bacteria that can cause plaque. Look out for any food that might get stuck between her teeth and remove it, if possible.

Q-Tip

Encourage your baby to drink water for the health of her teeth. Water contains no sugar and is therefore better for your baby's teeth than juice. In addition, drinking water helps to wash out other foods that get trapped between her teeth.

As for fluoride, your pediatrician may prescribe it in liquid vitamins (if the amount in your local water supply is inadequate), but you don't need to use a fluoride toothpaste just yet (although it won't hurt to use a tiny dab to flavor the gauze or brush).

Although brushing is unnecessary, you may want to give your baby her own tooth-brush just to familiarize her with something she'll have to get used to a year from now. Choose one that has very soft bristles and let your child hold on to it herself. Then let her watch you when you brush your teeth. With an older infant, you can even turn this ritual into a game: you brush and your baby imitates you. Don't worry about your baby's brushing technique at this point. Just have fun and let your baby familiarize herself with the toothbrush.

The Least You Need to Know

◆ Give your baby a chance to exercise his muscles, but be gentle and let him do as much of the work as he can.

◆ Give your baby the opportunity to explore by offering him plenty of free space. Keep his mouth free by limiting pacifier use to when he really needs it.

◆ Eating habits can be established as early as infancy. So avoid setting up a pattern of using food as an automatic comforter or of underfeeding to promote slimness.

◆ Just because your baby is cranky does not necessarily mean he's teething. Don't ignore possible signs of illness, such as fever and digestive disturbances, that teething cannot cause.

Chapter 10

Home, Safe Home

In This Chapter

◆ Why you need to babyproof now!

◆ Overall strategies to guard against fire, electric shock, choking, and serious falls

◆ Room-by-room babyproofing to prepare for the crawler

◆ Safety in the yard

Unless you keep your baby locked up in a fully padded room with no furniture, you can't prevent your child from ever having an accident. But you can take safety measures to minimize accidents—and to make sure that those that do happen don't have serious consequences.

There's No Time Like the Present

In a few months, when your baby begins to crawl, he will begin actively exploring and investigating his world. One of the best ways to encourage your baby's curiosity is to allow him to examine, explore, and develop an understanding of everything in his world. Of course, you cannot let your baby roam through your house wild and free. But you can give him a relatively free rein—as long as you first make sure that everything he can get his hands on will be safe for him to explore.

Infants are true sensualists. If your baby sees, hears, or smells something fascinating, he cannot resist the urge to find out what it is. As long as he can get his hands on it— and he'll do everything he can to do so—your baby will grasp it, handle it, scrutinize it, shake it, listen to it, smell it, and taste it. That's how he learns about the world and its objects.

Babyproofing creates a safe environment in which your baby can explore to his heart's delight. You won't need to worry about what he's getting into because you'll know that whatever it is, it will be safe. Oh, sure, he'll still find a way to have an accident or somehow hurt himself, but because you've babyproofed your home, you'll know that he probably won't suffer any serious or long-lasting harm from these minor accidents and injuries.

Although you can begin babyproofing anytime before or after your baby is born, you certainly should babyproof your entire home before your baby starts to crawl. If you haven't yet begun, start now.

The best overall strategy in babyproofing your home to prepare for a crawler is to go where your baby will go. Adopt a crawler's-eye view as you go from room to room in your home. Get down on your hands and knees so that you're about the same height (or even a little taller) than your baby. Getting on your own hands and knees will help you discover dozens of potential dangers. Almost anything you can get your hands on while you're on the floor, your soon-to-be crawler can get his hands on, too.

Look around. What catches your eye? Is it that corner of the tablecloth hanging down from the kitchen table? Ooh, a colorful extension cord! A wastebasket! What's in there anyway? Wow, a wall socket! I wonder what might fit in those slots? What's this cord hanging down from the window blinds? Hmmm, what's inside this floor-level cabinet?

You need to bar your child's access to such obvious dangers as electrical outlets, house-hold cleaners, and decorative glass or ceramic knickknacks. But don't stop there. If you can reach anything, even something that's not obviously dangerous to your baby, give it a firm tug to see whether it moves or topples over. If it does, you may want to put it elsewhere or keep it in storage.

Establishing a Safe House

Danger is your baby's middle name. As she starts to crawl throughout your home in search of new adventures and discoveries, she will invent new ways of getting herself into trouble. You and your partner need to serve as your young adventurer's scouting party: explore the terrain first and eliminate anything that poses a serious threat to your baby's health and safety.

Fire Fighters

Do you have a working **smoke detector** on every floor of your home? You should. Fire safety depends on early warning and planning for an emergency. If you haven't yet mapped out fire escape routes from every room of your home, do it now. You should also keep a **fire extinguisher** in your kitchen and perhaps one on every other floor of your home, too.

You have to have heat in your home, but **heat sources** can sometimes get very hot themselves, posing a serious risk of burning. The most dangerous source of heat is a **portable space heater.** Don't use one at all, if possible. If you really need a space heater, avoid the type that features electric bars or coils that will attract your baby with their glowing reddish-orange color.

Babyproofing

Never, ever leave your child alone in a room with a space heater or an electric fan on. For that matter, don't even leave him alone if the space heater or fan is off, unless you have unplugged it and put an outlet cover over the electric outlet.

Any open **radiators** also pose a danger. In the winter, they get scorching hot, so get guards or covers that will keep your baby's hands away from them. If you have a **fireplace,** make sure the fire screen fits securely into place. Store fireplace matches on the mantle and other matches high out of your baby's reach.

Shock Treatment

Electric outlets pose a significant danger because most are located right at the level of a crawling baby's eyes. Make it impossible for her to shock herself (or worse) by sticking anything into an outlet. Any outlet not being used should be shielded with a plastic outlet cover. Outlets that are used can also be protected from your baby's curiosity. Special outlet safety boxes that fit over both the plug and the outlet will prevent your baby from pulling the plug.

Loose **electric cords** can also be hazardous. If your crawler's hands or feet get tangled up in the cord, she can unwittingly pull a lamp or other appliance down on top of her. If she can grab a loose cord, she can also deliberately pull a clock or iron down from a table or counter. Even more dangerous, your baby may suck or chew on an exposed electric cord—which can cause shocks or serious burns, or even start a fire.

Q-Tip

Carry some outlet covers in your baby's diaper bag so that you can use them for any extended visits with grandparents or friends who don't have babies of their own.

Babyproofing

Make sure that you've put protective outlet covers on all outlets, inside and out.

Keep all electric cords out of reach, if possible. Thread them behind furniture and under rugs as much as you can. Those that need to remain exposed should be secured with tape or special electric cord staples. You can also tie up any excess length of cord with rubber bands.

If an electric cord looks cracked or frayed, replace it immediately. Make sure the rest of the electrical system is safe and up-to-date, too. All electric outlets and appliance cords should be grounded (use three-holed sockets for three-pronged plugs).

Baby Food? No!

If your baby can pick something up, he will almost surely put it in his mouth. That's why it's so important to get down on your hands and knees when babyproofing. What can your baby reach? Poisons? Small objects that might block his windpipe? Any sharp objects? As you crawl about your home, clear your floor and any low tables of all **choking hazards, toxins,** and anything else that might do your baby harm.

Most **poisons** are not kept out in the open where your baby can reach them. But many, including household cleaners and medicines that don't fit in the medicine cabinet, are traditionally stored in under-sink cabinets that your baby can easily reach. You can install babyproof locks on any low cabinets to keep their contents off-limits. But if you or any of your guests ever forget to relock the cabinet, you will be making poisons immediately accessible to your baby.

Because the ingestion of toxins can have grave consequences, you should move all toxins out of low cabinets. Lock them up high where your baby will have no chance to reach them even after he becomes a toddler and a climber. These "high-cabinet" items include the following:

- Household cleaning products

- Polishes (including shoe polish)

- Air fresheners, deodorizers, and moth balls

- Laundry supplies, especially bleach and spray starch

- Pesticides

- Kerosene or other lamp oil

- Cosmetics

- Alcohol, cigarettes, and other drugs (including vitamins)

In searching your home for poisons, don't overlook plants. A variety of **plants and flowers** commonly found in homes and gardens are poisonous if eaten. These plants include willow, rhododendron, laurel, lily of the valley, tomato leaves, irises, daffodils, hyacinths, and buttercups. Be sure to place those tasty-looking plants on high shelves or hang them from ceiling planters.

All **medicines** should be stored in high, locked medicine cabinets. If you need to take a certain medication daily, don't keep the bottle out to remind yourself to take it.

Because many drug poisonings result not from accidental discovery, but rather from improper dosage given by parents or other caregivers, always check the label and consult your physician before giving your child any medicine. Check to make sure you've picked the right bottle and double-check the expiration date. Never cut adult pills into what you consider to be child-size doses.

In removing all possible dangers from your baby's reach, don't forget to check—or chuck—your **wastebaskets.** If your baby finds a wastebasket, he will almost definitely dump it. Whatever you've thrown away will suddenly become accessible to him. Your bathroom wastebasket may contain razors, old medicines, and poisonous cosmetics. A desk wastebasket may have sharp staples, old pens or pencils, or toxic printer cartridges. The kitchen wastebasket probably has plastic bags that could smother your baby, discarded food that could make her sick, and "nearly empty" bottles of household cleaning products. In addition, all of these wastebaskets probably contain objects small enough to choke your baby. Either monitor everything that goes into your wastebaskets to make sure they're safe or remove wastebaskets from any room in which your baby plays. Covered garbage pails will limit your baby's access and therefore provide much more security.

Baby Doctor

If your baby eats anything that you even suspect might be toxic, call your pediatrician or poison control center immediately. Do not give your child syrup of ipecac (to induce vomiting) until you have first talked to a doctor or poison authority.

Babyproofing

When your parents or in-laws (or any other guests who might take a number of different medications) visit, let them know your safety rules regarding medicines and ask them to adhere by them, too.

Finally, keep all poisons, whether cleaners, other household supplies, or medications, in their original, **childproof containers.** When using any of these products, take what you need and immediately recap the container and put it away.

> **Q-Tip**
>
> When it comes to toxins and choking hazards, one babyproofing session, no matter how thorough, never does the trick. You must exercise extreme vigilance to protect your baby from new poisons or choking dangers that may enter your home on any given day. Don't ever allow yourself or your guests to put hazardous objects—anything sharp, small, or toxic—anywhere near where your child might reach it.

Bye-Bye Boo-Boos

As you crawl around the floors babyproofing, check all furniture for **sharp corners.** You can fit any furniture that has low sharp corners with rubber or soft plastic "bumpers" that will round and cushion their impact. Don't forget to check and bumper the corners on the underside of furniture as well. Until after her first birthday, your baby is much more likely to smash her head on the underside of furniture (getting up) than crash into the top (falling down).

You might also choose to put certain pieces of **furniture,** especially low, glass-topped tables, into **storage** for a few years. Other objects you may want to consider putting into storage or moving are table lamps, fragile decorative items, and anything else that might get broken by and/or injure your child. Pay special attention to the items you normally keep on end tables, coffee or cocktail tables, and bedside tables or nightstands.

Although your crawler doesn't have far to fall yet—and the many times she's planted her face in the carpet show that she can fall without injury—she will not be just a crawler for long. When she starts using legs of chairs, tables, and people to pull herself to standing, her falls can become more damaging. **Rugs and carpets** can help soften your baby's falls as she begins to practice standing (although slippery throw rugs can actually cause more damage than they prevent). Pillows can cushion the blow but may also cause your baby to fall as she gains a little mobility while standing.

Blocking and Locking

Stairs can cause the most serious falls. So whenever you're not there to spot your baby as he crawls up the stairs, you need to make them totally inaccessible. Install two safety gates on every set of stairs in your house (unless the staircase is behind a locked door): one at the top and one at the bottom. Of course, your baby is not about to fall up the stairs, but once they learn to crawl, most babies love to climb. If you don't put a safety gate at the bottom of the stairs, your baby may climb all the way up and risk falling all the way down.

At the bottom of the stairs, you can install either a latched gate or a **pressure gate.** But never use a pressure gate, which expands to fit snugly between a newel post and a wall, at the top of a flight of stairs. A baby who falls against a pressure gate or uses it to pull himself to standing may cause it to pop loose. If this happens at the bottom of the stairs, it's no big deal. You'll hear the crash, turn to see your baby lying under the gate (crying, no doubt, but not seriously hurt), and put it back in place. But if a pressure gate pops loose at the top of the stairs, it will come crashing down the stairs with your baby right behind it. So take the trouble to install a **latched gate** at the top of every staircase.

Open stairways are particularly dangerous for crawlers (and for toddlers as well), so install **banisters** on any open stairways to prevent your baby from falling over the edge. With any banister, make sure that all railings are no more than 4 inches apart so that your baby doesn't get his head wedged between them.

Q-Tip

A pressure gate will fit in almost any standard doorway. This adaptability makes a pressure gate ideal for temporarily blocking your crawler out of certain rooms that you want to keep off-limits.

When your baby does crawl or climb upstairs, make sure you stay right behind him, with your hands and arms ready to catch him, every step of the way. Then when he wants to come down the stairs, try to teach your baby how to come down safely by crawling backward. Again, stay right below your toddler at all times on the stairs. Since your baby will have enough trouble getting up and down stairs without having to negotiate an obstacle course, try not to use the stairway as a way station for "things to go upstairs."

If you can get yourself into the habit of using them, **locks** can also keep certain dangers off-limits. Basement doors (including outside storm doors), garage doors, workshop doors, and tool-shed doors should be kept locked at all times. Your baby cannot open even an unlocked door yet, but getting into the habit of locking doors prepares you for the day (probably some time during his second or third year) when he can open a door. It also provides you with the cer-

Q-Tip

You can encourage your child to improve his skill at climbing up and down stairs by investing in either a playroom set of sturdy wooden steps or a baby slide that has three or four steps.

tainty of knowing that you have indeed remembered to pull the door shut. Use **safety locks** (or rubber bands or bungee cords) on the doors of any cabinets or drawers that contain things your baby should not regard as playthings.

Try not to lock up every cabinet or drawer. Leave a few, perhaps those with pots and pans or plastic measuring cups and plastic cookie cutters, open for your infant to explore. First make sure, however, that everything you put in these cabinets or drawers will be safe in the hands (and mouth) of your baby.

Window Treatments

Windows, like doors, should remain locked to prevent your baby from opening them, whether by accident or on purpose, and falling out. In the summertime, however, you may need to keep many windows open most of the time. But you can still take one of the following steps to protect your baby from the danger of falling:

- ◆ Open only the top halves of windows rather than the bottom halves, if possible.
- ◆ On upper-story windows, consider installing window grates that make falls next to impossible.

Q-Tip

In many cities, owners of apartment buildings are required by law to install window safety grates in the apartments of tenants with small children. If you live in an upper-story apartment, ask the owner of the building to do so.

- ◆ Install special window guards that prevent windows from being opened more than 4 inches.

Finally, make sure that you make it a practice to shorten or tie up all **cords of window shades,** blinds, and drapes so that they never dangle down to where your baby can reach them. Your baby could easily get tangled or strangled in these kinds of loose cords.

The Grand Tour

All the previous suggestions should be implemented in every room of your home, but every room also has its own particular hazards. Let's take a grand tour of your home to see what specific steps you can take to increase the safety of every room.

Someone's in the Kitchen

What do you do in the kitchen? You cook. So what's the greatest risk to your child in the kitchen? Burning, of course. To reduce the risk of burns, start with this basic rule: never hold your baby while you're cooking or serving hot food. Your child has too many ways of squirming and wriggling into trouble to hold her anywhere near a hot surface, hot pots, or very hot food.

Whenever you cook, try to use the back burners before using the front burners, to minimize the risk of spilling a scalding hot pot. You should also point all pot handles toward the back of the stove rather than out toward you.

Once your baby can pull herself up to a standing position, you may need to install plastic guards that will prevent her from turning the **stove and oven controls.** If you don't have guards for the controls, then pull off the knobs when you're not cooking.

Small appliances, such as blenders, coffee makers, and food processors, are another major danger found in the kitchen. To prevent your baby from pulling one down on top of herself, store all small appliances away from the edge of the kitchen counter and tuck the electric cords behind them. Also, when you're not using a kitchen appliance, unplug it so that your baby can't turn it on by accident.

Babyproofing

Stoves, ovens, toaster ovens, coffee makers, irons, and pots and pans all retain heat long after you've stopped using them. So keep them well out of your baby's reach until you're sure they've cooled down enough to touch safely.

Babyproofing

If you drink coffee or tea, keep your cup well out of your baby's reach at all times. One cup of piping hot coffee or tea, if spilled on your baby, can cover more than 80 percent of her body with third-degree burns.

In looking around your kitchen for potential hazards, use your common sense:

- ◆ Store knives, scissors, and anything else that's sharp in locked drawers.

- ◆ Keep glass and other breakable dishes in high cabinets that your baby can't reach.

- ◆ Move plastic bags to higher drawers or cabinets.

- ◆ Remove anything toxic from the cabinet under the sink.

- ◆ Move popcorn, nuts, hard candy, spices, and other potentially dangerous foods to high cabinets or shelves.

Consider putting away all **tablecloths** for the next few years. If you leave them on the table, your budding magician might try the old tablecloth trick and pull everything on the table down on top of herself.

Folding chairs are also not a great idea for crawlers (or even toddlers and preschoolers). Most easily collapse when weight is concentrated on the back of the seat and can send your baby crashing to the floor or perhaps crush fingers that get caught in the joint. If you have folding chairs, consider replacing them with something a little more substantial.

A Tale of Two Bedrooms

With the exception of the changing station, everything in your baby's bedroom should be totally safe for your baby. That way whenever your baby is in the nursery, whether playing, sleeping, or getting changed, you will be virtually worry-free.

In the play area, store the toys your baby likes best somewhere he can easily reach them. Leave everything in plain sight on low, **open shelves.** If your baby sees something he wants to play with, he can get it himself without having to climb. Until he can stand and do something with his hands (lifting the lid) at the same time, a toy chest will not allow your baby this degree of independence, yet you may prefer the tidiness of a toy chest to open shelves (or you may have so many toys that you need both). If your baby's room does have a **toy chest,** make sure it cannot slam shut, crushing your baby's fingers.

Q-Tip

If you have inherited a classic wooden toy chest (or if you find one at a garage sale), chances are, it has no safety features. You can create your own safety zone for fingers, however, by gluing small blocks of cork onto the two front corners of the opened chest. Virtually all modern toy chests incorporate a built-in space between the lid and the chest to guard against crushing fingers.

Arrange the furniture so that your **baby's crib,** as well as any other furniture that he might climb on, is not next to a window. Then make it a rule that the side rail of the crib must be raised to the locked position whenever your baby is in the crib. If it gets cold, provide your baby with an appropriate number of thermal blankets, but never place an electric blanket in your baby's crib. An electric blanket and a wet diaper are a hazardous combination.

Speaking of diapers, make sure to keep your **diaper pail(s)** covered except when you're using them—not just for safety's sake, but to contain the smell as well. If you can, make the diaper pail inaccessible, too—perhaps behind a closed closet door (if your changing station is right next to the closet). Store diaper creams, diaper pins, and other hazardous supplies on a shelf above the changing table or in a pocketed wall hanging. Everything you need to diaper your baby should be out of his reach but well within yours. That way, you'll never need to leave your baby alone on the changing table, even for just a second.

You will also need to take certain safety measures in your own bedroom. Again, remove or make inaccessible anything that might endanger your baby if he gets his hands on it:

- Hang your purse on a high hook in the closet or keep it on top of your dresser.

- Hang all ties, scarves, and belts well out of your child's reach.

- Store coins and jewelry, as well as hair pins, safety pins, buttons and other sewing supplies, staples, thumb tacks, paper clips, and the like, on high shelves or on the tops of very high dressers, where they will be not only out of your baby's reach, but out of his sight, too.

- Throw away dry-cleaning bags. They aren't safe anywhere in your home.

Dear John

Until your baby starts to use the toilet (unfortunately, still a year or more away), your baby will probably spend little time in the bathroom when she's not taking a bath. (For bathtub safety tips, see Chapter 12.) Yet a couple of hazards outside the tub deserve your attention, too.

Horrifying but true, infants and toddlers have been known to drown in a **toilet.** So either keep the bathroom door shut when it's not being used or install a toilet-seat latch. These precautions will keep your baby—not to mention bath toys, soap, washcloths, your toothbrush, and nearly anything else your baby can reach—out of the toilet.

As mentioned in the section on poisons, always keep **medicines and cosmetics** stored in a locked medicine cabinet. Also keep less toxic products that you use every day, such as soaps, shampoos, conditioners, and razors, out of your baby's reach. A shower caddy that slips over the shower nozzle serves the purpose nicely.

The Great Outdoors

Once you've made sure everything inside is safe and sound, turn your attention to the great outdoors: your yard, if you have one. If you have a porch, deck, or balcony, any **railings** should be spaced less than 4 inches apart, to prevent your child from falling through or getting his head stuck. In addition, you should remove any horizontal bars that your baby might someday use to climb up and over the fence.

Babyproofing

If your railings are spaced too wide, you can fix the problem by adding more railings or by adding screening.

Keeping up with **lawn maintenance** will help keep your yard safe for your baby. Eliminate ditches or holes that become drowning hazards when filled with water by leveling the ground as much as possible. Regularly mow your lawn to avoid the high grass that ticks and other insects love. Check daily to make sure that no passersby has used your lawn as a trash basket or doggie dumping ground. Finally, put up a fence or a row of thick hedges to keep your baby in the yard and to keep animals out.

If you decide to put up a swing set, slide, or other **playground equipment,** check the equipment regularly for rust and exposed screws or bolts. Make sure to put a couple of inches of wood chips, sand, or other loose material under all playground equipment to soften your baby's landing if he falls.

Be sure to store all toxins or potential hazards, hedge clippers and other gardening tools, fertilizers and plant food, gasoline and charcoal fluid, and barbecue supplies on a high shelf in the garage or **tool shed.** (Don't forget to lock it up tight.)

Finally, make sure your yard offers adequate **shade.** Your baby's skin has had little or no exposure to the sun, making it particularly susceptible to sunburn. Avoid the mid-day sun, which can burn your baby's skin in less than 30 minutes. When you do let him out, use at least SPF 15 sunscreen on all exposed areas of his skin. However, do not use sunscreen until your baby is 6 months old. When you do put sunscreen on your baby, avoid his hands. Sunscreen on your baby's hands will sting his eyes if he rubs them. Avoid his face, too. Instead, insist that he wear a wide-brimmed hat to keep his face shadowed.

There! Perfectly Safe?

All done babyproofing your home, inside and out? Good! Now start all over again. Babyproofing is not a one-shot deal. Whether you've done it once or 20 times, babyproofing is an unending process. Keep an eye on your child when she begins to crawl. She'll happily show you what you missed by getting into trouble with it.

In addition to following your baby's lead, repeat the hands-and-knees survey of your home every time your baby demonstrates a new physical ability: crawling, standing, cruising, and walking. Each new skill brings with it an ability to find new dangers. No matter how many hours you spend crawling about your home in search of potential hazards, your baby will quickly find or invent new dangers once she's mobile. To keep your baby safe, keep an eye on her as much as possible once she starts crawling. Stay close, stay alert, and stay aware of what she is doing.

In the months and years to come, you and your partner will need to serve not only as your baby's guardian angels, but also as her teachers. Remember that even though your baby doesn't yet speak, she still understands a lot of what she hears. In any case, she almost certainly knows the word "No!" So put an end to any unsafe behavior not just with your actions, but with your words as well.

Accidents Happen

No matter how thoroughly you have babyproofed your home and how strictly you police your baby, accidents will happen. So be prepared. Make sure you have a well-supplied first-aid kit in your home (see Chapter 2). Take a class in CPR for infants and children (see Appendix D), and keep an emergency information card next to every phone in your home.

Your emergency information cards should have all of the following information:

- ◆ Your names and your child's name, age, and weight, as well as any special medical conditions or allergies that she has

- ◆ Your own home address and phone number (most people forget this one, but baby sitters, even relatives, may not know this information offhand)

- ◆ Your work addresses and phone numbers

- ◆ Your pediatrician's name and number

- ◆ The address and phone number of the nearest hospital

- ◆ Names, addresses, and phone numbers of two or three neighbors, friends, or nearby relatives

- ◆ Phone numbers for the police, the fire department, and the local poison control center

Hopefully, you'll never need to use this card. But if you do need it, you'll be ready.

The Least You Need to Know

- The more you babyproof, the freer your child will be to explore the world safely.

- The best way to babyproof before your baby crawls is to get on your hands and knees and crawl across the floors yourself. Anything you can reach, he can reach, too.

- If you can't make a room safe, make it off-limits to your baby.

- Babyproofing never ends. Your baby will point out the things you missed. Try to catch them before he gets hurt.

- Accidents happen even in the most thoroughly babyproofed homes. So take CPR, post emergency information next to every phone, and hope that you'll never have to use it.

Food for Thought: Introducing Solids

In This Chapter

- How to know when your baby is ready for solid food

- When, where, and how to feed your baby solid food for the first time

- First foods that find favor

- Foods to avoid feeding your baby

As your baby grows bigger and becomes more active, he needs to consume more calories. And unless you want to go back to feeding your baby every 2 to 3 hours, including in the middle of the night, breast milk or formula may no longer provide your baby with all the calories he needs.

To meet your baby's growing needs, you eventually need to introduce him to solid foods. Solids not only fulfill your baby's dietary needs, but also stimulate your baby's sense of taste by familiarizing him with different flavors and textures of foods.

Getting Ready for Dinner

Your baby will give you clues that indicate his readiness for solid foods. These clues include the following:

- His age
- His weight
- His appetite
- The number of times you feed him
- His physical readiness
- His interest (or lack of interest) in the foods you eat

Let's examine each of these clues in a little more detail to see whether your baby is ready to start on solids.

Old Enough to Eat

When should you start introducing solids into your baby's diet? Unless you have a very large baby, you should not start to feed her solids before she is at least 4 months old. Before that, your baby's immature digestive tract cannot yet break down and absorb complex foods. In addition, introducing solid foods too early may lessen your baby's desire to suck, which may result in your baby not getting the nutrition she needs. Finally, feeding your baby too soon may set the stage for years of mealtime melees. She may develop the habit of rejecting foods, and you may develop the habit of pushing food on her.

On the other hand, if you wait too long—until your baby is 7 or 8 months old, for example—your baby's total dependence on the breast or bottle for nourishment may cause her to reject new tastes and new ways to nourish herself. (If you wait still longer, she may even resist developing the skill of chewing and swallowing solids.)

The range between too soon and too late is clear: start your baby on foods when she is between 4 and 6 months old.

What a Big Baby!

Your baby needs to consume about 3 fluid ounces for every pound he weighs. So by the time your baby weighs 14 pounds, he needs 42 ounces—that's six 7-ounce feedings a day! At this point, you should seriously consider supplementing your bottle- or breast-feeding with solid food.

I'm Hungry!

Your baby can probably drink little more than 7 ounces of formula at a single feeding. Her stomach cannot hold much more than that. If your baby is finishing her bottle at almost every feeding—and especially if she seems dissatisfied or still wants more after a feeding—then it's time to break out the baby cereal.

Please, Sir, May I Have More?

For many parents, the first big clue that their baby is ready for solid food comes when their infant begins regularly demanding an "extra" feeding. If your baby suddenly needs one more feeding than you're used to giving him, then he probably needs more than just breast milk or formula. If this extra feeding comes in the middle of the night—especially when your baby has gone 1 or 2 months without midnight feedings—you have plenty of motivation to begin feeding him solids.

Ready or Not

You cannot begin feeding solids to your baby until she is physically ready to eat food other than breast milk or formula. Your baby must, for instance, be able to hold her head steady for quite some time while sitting upright. If her head flops over after a minute or so of sitting, hold off on feeding solids.

Your baby may instinctively know that she's not ready. A reflex that protects a young baby from choking causes her to push out her tongue whenever something is placed in her mouth. By the time your baby is ready to begin eating solid foods, this reflex should have abated to some degree.

Q-Tip

You can test the "rejection" reflex by offering your baby a few spoonfuls of rice cereal mixed with breast milk or formula. If the cereal all comes out again, your baby's probably not ready for solid food. Of course, even after your baby is physically ready, a lot of food will come back out when you first introduce solid foods to your baby because the experience will be so new to her. But if none of the food seems to be getting past her tongue, put off trying to feed her solid food for another week or two.

I'll Have What She's Having

Some babies show an interest in eating solid foods sooner than others. If your baby sees you eating and indicates that he wants to eat something like it, you won't do him any harm by giving him a taste, unless it's one of the foods to watch out for (see the following information). But whatever you give your baby as his first food, you first need to turn it into an almost liquid mush by grinding it down and adding some water, breast milk, or formula.

First Foods

When giving your baby solid foods for the first time, take it slow and easy. Your child is not likely to sit down to three square meals of carbohydrates, fruits and vegetables, and protein. First foods are intended only to supplement, not instantly replace, bottle- or breast-feeding. Breast milk and/or formula should still make up the bulk of your baby's diet for the first month or two of solid feedings.

Baby Doctor

Don't mix your baby's cereal with cow's milk unless and until your pediatrician gives you the okay. In some rare cases, cow's milk can cause allergic reactions or other health complications when consumed by young infants.

In choosing what to feed your child, keep in mind that breast milk or formula still supplies almost everything your baby needs in terms of balanced nutrition: protein, calcium and other minerals, and most vitamins. As long as your baby's nutritional needs are met by breast milk or formula, you won't need to fret over introducing a balanced diet of solids. You can serve him anything he likes (as long as it's safe).

Start Me Up

The American Academy of Pediatrics recommends baby cereal as the best start-up food for a baby. It's simple to make and easy to alter the consistency by adding more or less liquid to suit your baby's needs. Baby cereal (rice, barley, or oats) is also easily digested and unlikely to cause an allergic reaction. In addition, because most baby cereal is fortified with iron (which breast milk lacks almost entirely), it's an especially good first food for a breast-fed baby.

Don't succumb to the temptation to sweeten your baby's cereal before he has had a chance to taste it plain (that is, mixed with water only). To you, it may seem bland this way, but you have had considerably more experience with food. Most babies seem to like plain baby cereal. If your baby does turn up his nose at plain cereal mixed with water, try sweetening it with a bit of formula, expressed breast milk, or a clear juice such as apple, pear, or—later—grape. There's no need to add sugar.

Varying the Menu

As soon as your baby has begun to accept the basic concept of eating solids, you can begin to introduce greater variety into her diet. With your guidance, your baby will be excited to discover that foods have different flavors and different textures.

Be sure to introduce just one new food at a time in very small amounts. Then wait 2 or 3 days before offering her anything else new (although you can, of course, give her anything she's enjoyed before). By introducing new foods one at a time, you'll instantly know which food is responsible if your baby has a food reaction (indigestion or an allergy marked by diarrhea, a rash, or otherwise unexplained crankiness). If your baby does have an adverse reaction to a particular food, don't offer it to her again for a couple of months. By then, she may tolerate it better.

As you gradually add variety to your baby's diet, aim to provide balanced nutrition. Breast milk and formula, for example, are both rich in protein. So if you still nurse or bottle-feed your baby several times a day, she will need little more in the way of protein (fish, meat, soy products). Instead, load up on grains (cereal, bread, pasta), fruits, and vegetables during the first months of feeding solids.

- ◆ **Grains:** After starting with rice cereal (the easiest to digest), move on to the greater variety and complexity of barley, oat, and mixed baby cereals. You can gradually add bread and pasta (macaroni or spaghetti cut into small strands) during the fifth or sixth month.

- ◆ **Fruits and vegetables:** Most babies love fruits, and many love vegetables, too. However, it might be wise to introduce vegetables before you introduce fruits. Otherwise, your baby may develop such a taste for sweet foods like fruits that she rejects vegetables. Start with vegetables that seem to find the most favor (carrots and sweet potatoes), and then move on to green vegetables: peas and beans. Your baby will also enjoy a wide variety of fruits, including apples, pears, bananas, apricots, peaches, plums, and prunes.

- ◆ **Meats:** Hold off on these high-protein foods until your baby is at least 7 or 8 months old (see Chapter 16).

- ◆ **Eggs and dairy products:** The American Academy of Pediatrics does not recommend introducing eggs, milk, or milk products (including yogurts, cheeses, and, of course, ice cream) before a baby's first birthday. If you want to introduce dairy products earlier, wait until your baby is at least 8 to 10 months old. Even then, consult with your pediatrician first—especially if your baby hasn't tolerated cow's-milk-based formula.

Q-Tip _____

As you introduce new foods into your baby's diet, keep in mind that the tastes she develops during her infancy and childhood will probably be the ones she prefers throughout her life. So pave the way for a lifetime of healthful eating habits by choosing foods for her wisely.

When your baby starts eating solids, she should also start drinking liquids other than breast milk or formula. A half-ounce to an ounce of water or diluted fruit juice should do at first. After all, she gets plenty of liquid through the breast or bottle. As your baby's breast-feeding or bottle-feeding begins to wane, however, be sure to increase not only the amount of solids she's eating (to replace lost calories), but also her liquid intake (to replace lost fluids). Otherwise, your baby may become dehydrated. (By the sixth month, encourage your baby to drink all fluids other than breast milk or formula from a sipper cup rather than a bottle.)

Home Cookin'

As much as you can, try to strike a balance between jars of commercial baby food and home-prepared foods. True, cooking your own baby food is not as easy as opening a jar. But it's not that hard, either—especially if you're just grinding up, straining, and adding some liquid to whatever you are eating (before you add spices).

Jars of baby food do have a lot to offer:

◆ They're convenient.

◆ They're extremely portable.

◆ They're economical.

◆ They're easy to clean up after.

They're also generally pretty nutritious, with most low in sugars, salt, and fats (though you should always check the label to make sure). In fact, jarred baby food contains more nutrients than most leftovers, which lose a lot of vitamins and minerals through reheating.

If you use jarred baby food, avoid feeding your baby directly from the jar unless you're relatively sure that he will eat the whole thing. Your baby's saliva may contaminate any leftover food. Similarly, don't use the same spoon that's been in his mouth to scoop out seconds if your baby wants more.

Once you've opened it, jarred baby food won't last more than 24 to 48 hours, even if refrigerated. A good rule of thumb: if you aren't sure how fresh a jar of baby food is, it's too old. Toss it!

If you want to make your own baby food …

Babyproofing

Avoid cooking your baby's food in copper pots. Copper may destroy the vitamin C in the food.

1. Steam or boil the food until it gets mushy. (Steaming retains more vitamins.)

2. Use a blender, food processor, hand mixer, or food mill to purée it to a soupy consistency.

3. Push the puréed food through a strainer with small holes to remove any seeds and skins and break up any remaining chunks. (If the cooked food is mushy enough, you probably don't need to purée it. Just straining it will yield the right consistency.)

4. If the food isn't soupy enough, add a little water until you get the right consistency.

5. After cooking, puréeing, and straining your home-cooked baby food, put it in a sealed dish and cool it in the refrigerator. Or cool it quickly by stirring in an ice cube. But don't let it sit on a counter to cool at room temperature—doing so will make it a breeding ground for bacteria.

Q-Tip

You can freeze freshly puréed foods. If you freeze them in ice cube trays or in dollops on cookie sheets (covered with plastic), you can thaw them for quick meals or meals on the road. But thaw baby foods in the fridge, under cold water, in a double boiler, or in a microwave (on defrost setting). Do not thaw them at room temperature because this may make them susceptible to bacterial growth.

If you do use a microwave, remember to mix food thoroughly before serving it to your baby, since microwaves heat food unevenly.

Continue puréeing and straining all food that you cook for your baby until he is at least 6 months old. Because he cannot chew yet, he might choke on a chunk of food. Even if the food doesn't cause him to choke, your baby will certainly not like swallowing anything so big.

Remember, whether buying or making your own baby food, be sure to start with single ingredients so that you can gauge precisely your child's physical reactions to different foods.

Warning: Do Not Feed the Baby

Your baby will probably eat almost anything you offer her, so do your best to make sure that the foods you offer her are safe. Avoid the following foods:

- Citrus fruits and juices (due to their high acidity)
- Strawberries and other berries (common allergens)
- Tomatoes (high acidity)
- Peanuts and other nuts (choking hazards and allergens)
- Eggs, even just the whites (allergens)
- Cow's milk and milk products (allergens)
- Wheat and corn (allergens)
- Fish and shellfish (allergens)
- Chocolate (allergen)
- Salt (too much can strain or damage an infant's kidneys)
- Other spices (can cause indigestion and may be allergens)
- Sugar or sugar substitutes (difficult to digest)
- Soda (high sugar content)
- Butter or other added fat (difficult to digest)
- Honey (may cause botulism in infants and 1-year-olds)
- Alcohol and caffeine, of course (both are drugs)

Your baby doesn't need any of these foods before her first birthday. But if you have a particular desire to see how your child likes any of them, you can start introducing most of them around 8 months. (The exceptions are alcohol and caffeine, which you should avoid giving your child altogether; honey, which you should avoid until your child is 2; and dairy products, which you may be wise to avoid until your baby's first birthday.)

Timing Is Everything

If you want to introduce solid food to your baby, you need to time it right—not just in terms of her age and readiness, but also in terms of her day-to-day scheduling. Don't choose a meal when your child is beside herself with hunger, such as the first feeding of the day. Also avoid feedings when your baby is sleepy, especially the feeding before bedtime. These are times when a bottle or breast works best for feeding. Instead, choose one of your baby's meals between late morning and early evening (but not right before a nap): a time when your baby is awake and hungry, but not ravenous.

Q-Tip _____

If you're breast-feeding your baby, you may notice that at certain daily feedings your milk supply consistently seems lower than at others, certainly lower than first thing in the morning or right before your baby's bedtime. Try feeding your baby solids at one of these times, when supply and demand are lower.

When you first introduce solid foods, try offering your baby some spoonfuls of food in the middle of breast- or bottle-feeding. Again, timing is everything. If you try to feed your baby solids for the first time before offering her a bottle or breast, you may just upset her. (Remember, she won't know how to eat this way.) But if you wait until after your baby has finished with the breast or bottle, she may be too dopey, and her stomach may have no more room for solid foods.

Between breasts or halfway through a bottle, pause and give your baby a few small spoonfuls of food. If she likes it, continue feeding her 10 or 20 spoonfuls. Then wipe her face (and probably her hands), return her to the breast or bottle, and let your baby finish.

In addition to choosing the right time, make sure you have enough time. If you have only 20 minutes to breast-feed or bottle-feed your baby, that's a lousy time to try to introduce solid foods. Your baby needs time to get used to this new experience and to master the art of spoon-feeding, and you need time (lots of time) to clean up the mess that the two of you make.

Someone's Been Sitting in My Chair

Where should you give your baby his first meals? For first feedings, you probably don't need a high chair or other baby seat yet. First of all, your baby may not be able to sit up straight on his own for very long. Second, if you're feeding him from the breast or bottle, your baby is already securely planted on your lap, and he may balk at the disruption of being moved into a high chair or baby seat in the middle of his meal.

Sitting your child up in your lap will probably be the easiest and least disruptive way to feed your baby initially. Yes, it may be a little messy, and you might prefer having two hands to feed him. But you need only one hand to hold the spoon, and, as you'll soon find out, feeding him is going to be messy wherever you choose to do it. So you might as well do it in the least disruptive and most convenient place possible: your lap.

> **Q-Tip**
>
> Plan in advance for your baby's first meals. Before you begin nursing or bottle-feeding, have everything you'll need within reach: the bowl of food, the spoon(s), and plenty of cloth diapers for easy clean-ups. If you want your baby to wear a bib, put it on before you offer the breast or bottle. That way, when you stop midway through the feeding, you won't have to do anything but slightly adjust your child's position and pick up a spoonful of food. The smoothness of your transition may make it easier for your baby to accept this new way of eating.

If you do decide that you want to use a high chair or other baby seat right from the start, let your baby get used to sitting in it for a week or two before you try to feed him in it. Just as you would avoid introducing two new toys at the same time, don't introduce the new experiences of sitting in a chair and feeding at the same time. (If your child slumps or sags in his high chair, try propping him up with some padding. Towels work best because they're easy to clean afterward.)

Spooning

You know how to use a spoon, of course, but your baby doesn't—at least, not yet. Try to make it as easy as possible for her. Choose a plastic-coated spoon that has a small bowl. The plastic coating makes the spoon softer against your baby's tender gums. The small bowl makes it more likely that you will get the spoon in or near your baby's mouth and less likely that she will gag on too much food.

Q-Tip

Give your baby her own spoon to hold, too. The extra spoon will keep her hands busy: handling it, spinning it, banging it, dropping it, and trying to pick it up again. With so much to occupy her, your baby will be less likely to grab or swat the feeding spoon each time it heads for her mouth or each time you try to pull it away to refill it.

To feed your baby, hold the spoon up to your baby's lips, brush it gently against them, and then let her suck the food off the spoon. Introducing spoon-feeding in this way is the most natural method because your baby begins by eating the only way she knows how: by sucking.

Don't try to shovel the food into your baby's mouth. If you put the spoon too far into her mouth, your child may gag on either the food or the spoon. On the other hand, if you put the food on the front of your baby's tongue, she won't be able to get the food far enough back in her mouth to taste or swallow it. The food will just dribble out, frustrating both of you.

Q-Tip

You don't need to worry about heating your baby's first foods. Room temperature is just fine. If it makes you feel better about it, feel free to warm the food slightly. But your baby probably won't care one way or another.

At first, give your baby just 2 or 3 teaspoons of solid food at a sitting. (This amount is more than a dozen spoonfuls from a baby spoon.) Then, as her interest in and appetite for solid foods increase, gradually increase the amount you feed her.

Eat Everything on Your Plate?

Don't ignore your baby's signals about eating. At the same time, don't be deceived by facial expressions. If your child makes a face when tasting something new, he may be reacting to the novelty of the experience as much as the new taste itself. So despite the face he makes, offer your baby a second spoonful. If he opens his mouth for more, you know you have a hit.

When your baby doesn't like the taste of a particular food, or when he has lost interest in eating from a spoon, he will send a clear signal. He might do one or more of the following:

◆ Turn his head away

◆ Close his mouth

◆ Spit the food out

◆ Push the food back out with his tongue

◆ Get cranky

Don't give up too soon. Keep in mind that a lot of food will come back out or get pushed out during the first months of feeding. But when nearly all of the food you give your baby starts to come right back out, then you know that he's done.

When introducing solids, your aim should be to make eating as fun and pleasurable as possible for both of you. If you try to force your baby to eat things he hates or to eat when he's bored, exhausted, cranky, or already full, you will make eating from a spoon an unpleasant experience: something he will not soon want to try again.

Be as responsive to your baby when introducing solid foods as you would be when introducing a new toy. If he's not interested (or loses interest) in a new toy, you probably won't continue shoving it into his face. Why respond any differently when introducing a new food?

Baby Talk

"A man finds out what is meant by a spitting image when he tries to feed cereal to his infant."

—Madeline Cox

Respect your infant's likes and dislikes. If he indicates he wants more of something, by all means give him more. But if he doesn't seem to like a particular food, give him something else instead. Then try the rejected food again in a few weeks. Who knows? His tastes may have changed by then.

The patterns you establish in the first months of feeding may influence your child's attitudes toward eating for many years to come. If you put pressure on him, you will create an air of tension around the act of eating that may last a lifetime. But if you can relax and have fun, your baby will probably do the same.

How Much Food Should My Baby Eat?

At first, your baby will eat very little solid food. But as your baby becomes adjusted to eating from a spoon, she will eat more and more. By her half-birthday, she may become so eager about spoon-feeding that she puts off the breast or bottle until afterward. Even then, she may want only a small amount of milk or formula.

If your baby is still drinking four full bottles or has four ample breast-feedings a day, then she needs only about 200 calories from solids. That's approximately one serving of cereal and two jars of baby food. But if she has begun drinking less breast milk or formula, then she depends more on solid food to provide energy and continued fuel for growth.

By 5 or 6 months, many babies eat three "meals" a day, plus several snacks from the breast or bottle and a major nighttime or morning feeding to make up for the long break from dinner to breakfast. Because your baby can't eat as much as you can at a single sitting, she needs more frequent meals and snacks than you do.

Your baby's appetite will not remain consistent. It will fluctuate greatly depending on growth spurts, her level of activity (or inactivity), and her degree of interest (or disinterest). Let your baby tell you (through her nonverbal signals) how much she wants to eat. If she consistently leaves food in her bowl, don't pressure her to finish. Simply start serving smaller meals.

Try not to worry that your baby isn't eating enough. Concern yourself with the quality of baby food rather than the quantity. In general, babies do not let themselves go hungry. As long as you continue to offer her foods that she can eat, your baby will not starve herself. Keep in mind that, especially at the beginning, your baby is also feeding (indeed, is primarily feeding) from the breast or bottle. Don't expect her to have a huge appetite for solid foods. As long as your baby continues to grow steadily and remains active and alert, she's getting plenty to eat.

The Least You Need to Know

- Your baby has no nutritional need for solid foods until at least 6 months because breast milk or formula supplies virtually all the nutrients he needs. Don't feel you need to rush into feeding him solids.

- Good timing helps to make first feedings successful. Avoid introducing solids during the first or last feedings of the day. Instead, choose a midday meal when you have plenty of time (and patience).

- Introduce new foods one at a time and then wait 2 to 3 days before introducing another. If your child has an adverse reaction to a particular food, you will immediately know which food caused it.

- Pay attention to your baby's signals that he's had enough. Never force your infant to eat something he doesn't like or to eat more than he wants.

Chapter 12

Splish, Splash, I Was Taking a Bath

In This Chapter

◆ Washing your baby from head to toe

◆ Tub time

◆ Hair and nail care

◆ Keeping your baby safe in the tub

◆ Water play and bathtime fun

The smell, feel, and sight of a freshly washed baby are something special indeed. Even beyond the pleasant odor of baby shampoo and mild baby soap, a sweetness wafts up from your baby. The softness of her bare skin and the glow that seems to envelop her makes the experience even richer. Unfortunately, your baby may not agree. Even after the first few months, many babies find bathing an uncomfortable experience—although most babies warm to the joys of bathtime by around 6 months. So no matter how pleasing you may find it, keep in mind that your baby doesn't need to take a bath every day. Until she's crawling around and starting to get into everything, your baby won't get very dirty. So if your baby doesn't seem to like bathing, concentrate on keeping clean only those parts of her body that tend to get dirty: her bottom and genitals, her hands, and after the introduction of solid foods, her face. One or two sponge baths or dips in a sink or portable tub per week should be plenty to keep her clean. On the other hand, once your baby starts to enjoy the bath, even though she doesn't necessarily need one every day, it can be a wonderful daily ritual for both of you.

Taking the Plunge

As long as he doesn't object, your baby can begin taking sink or tub baths several weeks after birth, as long as the umbilicus has fallen off and a circumcision (if any) has healed. Until your baby can sit up on his own (and even long after), you need to hold the slippery devil tightly—or at least keep one hand on him to provide support and safety. In addition, you need to lean over and wash your baby with your other hand, without once relaxing your grip. If you're kneeling by the side of a conventional tub and leaning over the edge, you can strain your back. That's why most parents bathe young babies in a sink or portable tub.

Most kitchen sinks have the advantage of being at approximately the right height for the average adult to wash a baby (like washing dishes) without significant back strain. They have a ready supply of water (though be sure to swing the spigot away from the sink or cover it with a washcloth to prevent unpleasant bumps). Kitchen sinks often also have the advantage of a sprayer attachment that makes rinsing easy (and, for some babies, fun). If you use a sink, be sure to line the bottom of it with a towel, a rubber mat, or the foam-rubber insert from a portable tub to keep your baby's bottom from slipping and sliding.

Q-Tip

If you put one foot up on a stool (or open the under-sink cabinets and put one foot on the ledge) while bathing your baby, you will probably feel considerably less back strain.

Portable tubs have the advantage that you can use them anywhere (including outside, if weather permits). The need to have access to a source of warm water and the likelihood of considerable splashes and spills, however, make it most practical to set up the portable tub in the kitchen or bathroom. Choose a surface (a kitchen counter, a table, a vanity) where …

- ◆ The tub sits securely.
- ◆ You have plenty of room around the tub for all the essentials (soap, shampoo, towel, diaper, clean clothes, and so on).
- ◆ You do not need to strain your back by bending over so much.

Come On In! The Water's Fine!

Successful baths often come down to timing. If you bathe your baby 3 to 4 hours after she eats, she may be getting so hungry (and cranky) that she has no patience for the bath. On the other hand, if you bathe her right after she eats, the jostling may make her spit up. Aim for a bathtime between an hour and 2 hours after a meal. Many parents find that sandwiching bathtime between the evening meal and the final feeding of the day sets up a warm and relaxed atmosphere that makes it easier for the baby to nod off.

Remember to set all of your bath supplies (see list in Chapter 3) next to the sink or tub before getting your baby undressed. You will want everything within reach so that you won't have to leave your baby unsafe for even a second.

Be sensitive to your baby's reactions. If she violently objects to being put in the water, remember that she doesn't have to take a bath. After all, you're not likely to overcome her fears by immersing her in them. Instead, continue giving her sponge baths (see Chapter 3) and try again once a month or so until she feels more comfortable with all that water.

Before putting your baby in the water—indeed, before you even undress her completely—test the water temperature with your elbow to make sure it is comfortably warm. (Don't use your hands as a gauge; they may be less sensitive to heat.) After you test the temperature, undress your baby and, with one hand gripping her thigh and supporting her bottom and the other hand gripping her shoulder and supporting her neck and head, lower her bottom gently into the water. Maintain a secure hold and talk to her in calm tones in order to minimize her startle reaction. If your baby tenses up in the water, continue to hold her securely with both hands until she feels more relaxed. Give her time to get used to it. If your baby doesn't get upset by the water (or if she calms down after her initial shock), maintain your firm grip on her shoulder (and your support of her head and neck), but release the hand on her thigh.

Babyproofing

If you can, set your water temperature at a maximum of 130°F. Also, when you run a bath (in a sink or tub), always turn the hot water tap off first. That way, if water drips into the tub, it will be cold—which your baby may find unpleasant but not dangerous.

If the water cools too much while your baby is in the sink or tub, take her out. Because water temperature from a tap can change suddenly, refilling or rewarming the sink or tub while your baby is in the water can be dangerous.

Now that you have a free hand, you can begin washing your baby. As you did with sponge baths, start at the top and move down. Again, wash and (if you use soap) rinse one part at a time before moving on to the next part. If you soap up your entire baby before rinsing, you're almost sure to lose your grip. A wriggling, soapy baby is like a greased pig: impossible to hold and then impossible to catch.

When you're done, always use two hands to lift your baby out of the tub (Caution: Slippery When Wet). Immediately wrap her in a towel. If you're not using a hooded towel, be sure to cover your baby's head to keep her warm and cozy. Finally, when drying your baby, make sure to dry the many creases and folds in her skin just as carefully as you washed them. Trapped moisture in these creases can lead to a nasty rash.

Would You Like a Shampoo and Manicure with That?

You don't need to shampoo your child's hair with every bath (though it wouldn't hurt to run a washcloth over his head). Unless your child has cradle cap and your pediatrician has advised you to shampoo more often, once or at most twice a week should be enough shampooing for most babies.

Baby Folklore

To clip or to nibble? Well, keep this in mind when making your decision: thieves and pick-pockets steal, it once was said, because their mothers cut their nails instead of biting them during their first year.

And save those nail clippings. Tying up nail and hair clippings in a linen cloth and placing them under your baby's cradle, according to Irish tradition, will cure convulsions.

This news may come as a relief to you because most young babies don't like having their hair washed. Probably the least upsetting way to shampoo your baby's hair is to lay him down on his back on a towel placed on the kitchen counter. Cradle his head and neck over the sink with one hand and wet, shampoo, and rinse his hair with the other. (You can use the sprayer for wetting and rinsing.)

Many babies, however, feel insecure putting their head back in this way, despite a parent's supporting hand. If your baby balks at lying back over the kitchen sink, try washing his hair while sitting him up, using the tub hold described earlier. A kitchen sprayer or a shower attachment in the tub can provide controlled wetting and rinsing, but the devices frighten some infants.

Another alternative, the shampoo visor, allows you to wash your baby's hair while protecting his face and eyes from running soap and water. Unfortunately, some babies hate the visor, too. Chances are, your baby won't love having his hair washed. So try different ways of doing it and settle on the one that he finds least objectionable.

Bathtime can also be a good time to trim your baby's nails. Because nail clippers require two hands, one to steady the fingers and the other to snip, you may need to call in reinforcements. (You need a third hand to support your baby.) Or you can cut them yourself right after the bath, when your baby is warm and snug in a towel. Or you can forgo the clippers entirely and nibble the nails off with your teeth. Or you can notch the side of your baby's nail with your own nail and then easily peel off the top of the nail, which is perhaps the safest way to trim a baby's nails.

No matter how you choose to trim your baby's nails, you need to do it regularly to keep them very short. Your baby's nails grow very fast. If you don't keep them closely cropped, his manual explorations will result in many scratches. If nail trimming at bathtime seems to upset your baby, then try cutting or nibbling the nails after he's fallen asleep.

Water Safety

When can your baby start to use the real tub for baths? Your child is ready when she can sit relatively steadily on her own. (You still need to support her while she's in the tub, however. That sitting position never lasts very long.)

Even with only a couple of inches of water, the big tub can be intimidating when confronted for the first time. If you've been bathing your baby in a portable tub, make the transition easier for her by first placing her familiar tub inside the big tub and bathing her there for a week or so. Or get in the bath with her for the first week if you've been bathing her in the sink. Just keep in mind that she will not like the water temperature nearly as warm as you do. Don't forget to leave a towel by the side of the tub, too, so that you can quickly wrap up your baby when it's time to get out.

Q-Tip

If you're bathing with your baby and your partner or someone else can scoop the baby out of the tub, dry, and dress her, take advantage of the opportunity. Add some warmer water and relax for 10 or 15 minutes once you're alone.

In the big tub, a bath seat—a molded plastic seat secured to the bottom of the tub with suction cups—will relieve you of the need to provide constant support, but don't let down your guard just because your baby is in a bath seat. She still needs constant supervision because she may slump in the seat or, despite safeguards, slip out and under the water. Until your baby can sustain a sitting position for more than a minute, continue to keep your arm under her armpit for support even when she's in a bath seat. Kneeling beside the tub works better than bending over the tub.

Babyproofing

Because the faucet is hard and your baby's head is soft, be sure to cover the tub spout with a specially designed foam cover. Placing a washcloth on the bath seat under your baby's bottom can eliminate or minimize slipping. Also, if you keep razors, shampoo, or bubble bath on the side of the tub, remove them. It's not just your tub anymore.

No matter how well your baby sits up on her own, never, never, never leave her alone in any bath (whether kitchen sink, portable tub, or adult tub) even for a second! If the phone rings, ignore it and let the answering machine pick up. If the doorbell rings, scoop your baby out of the tub, wrap her in a towel, and bring her with you. Have everything you might need during or after the bath ready before putting her in the tub. If you forget something, forget it. Don't go to the linen closet to pick out a fresh towel or to your baby's bedroom to get some pajamas. Better she get a little chilly than risk drowning.

Water Sports

Bathtime can be a fun time for your baby. Although he may not have liked the water—or the nakedness—in his first month or two, by the third or fourth month, your baby will probably love both. Water is an amazing substance for your baby to discover. He can see it, hear it, feel it, and taste it. But try as he may, he can't hold it. In just a few inches of bath water, your baby also gets the chance to experience some sense of weightlessness or floating. Most of all, water is just plain fun to splash, kick, pour, catch, and (later) blow bubbles in.

Let your child have fun in the tub. Unless your bathroom is in serious danger of flooding, try not to discourage splashing or kicking. And now's the time to break out the toys! Old favorites such as rubber duckies or other floating animals will delight your baby. Almost anything else that floats (so long as it's safe) will also be a big hit:

◆ Plastic stacking cups or other unbreakable containers (plastic measuring cups or bottles) are great for filling and emptying with water.

◆ Cups with one or more holes in the bottom are terrific for creating his own stream. If you hold the cup above his hands, he'll have fun trying to catch the water, too.

◆ Floating balls, boats, bath books, and foam toys give him a chance to practice reaching out and grasping.

◆ Washcloths, whether plain, imprinted with cartoon characters, or designed as puppets, are always fun to suck on.

◆ Unbreakable mirrors give your baby a chance to see how much fun he's having.

Q-Tip _____

Drying bath toys immediately after use and storing them in a dry place minimizes the build-up of mildew. Unfortunately, anything that takes water inside it (rubber ducks or dolls, squeak toys, and the like) will probably acquire some mildew anyway.

Later in the year, you can add …

◆ Bath crayons or fingerpaint soap, which he can enjoy using to scribble or spread on the side of the tub.

◆ Bathtub stickers, which he can slap on the side of the tub and then peel off.

◆ Bathtub activity centers, which let him explore and play with water in many different ways.

Babyproofing _____

Young infants do not need bubble baths. Your baby will have a lot of fun with bubble baths when he gets a little older, but for now the bubble bath can dry his skin. Even when he gets older, try to limit bubble baths to once a week or so to prevent dry skin.

Try not to rush your baby in and out of the bath. Allow plenty of time for him to enjoy himself and get clean. If, despite your efforts to turn the bath into a water park, your baby still doesn't like it, then bathe him just once or twice a week. Just make sure to wash his hands before and after meals, his face after meals, and his bottom during diaper changes, and your baby will remain clean enough. If your baby does take to the bath like a fish takes to water, make it a joyous daily ritual.

When your baby is 2 or 3 months old, you might want to try letting him have some time to play naked before or after the bath—as long as it's warm enough and he no longer objects to nakedness. Naked play allows your baby to practice more sophisticated movements without getting tangled in his clothes or hampered by bulky diapers. Naked play also gives your baby the chance to discover new sensations: the feel of the blanket or rug against his naked skin, the warmth of the sun on his back, the touch of a breeze on his belly.

The Least You Need to Know

◆ Your baby doesn't need to take a bath every day. If she likes it, great. But if she doesn't, then bathe her only once or twice a week.

◆ Until your baby can sit up for quite some time without toppling, always support her with at least one hand, even when she's in a bath seat.

◆ Never leave your baby alone in the tub.

◆ Don't rush the bath. If you give your baby time to enjoy herself, she will—and you will, too.

Chapter 3

Out and About with Your Baby

In This Chapter

◆ Everything you could possibly need in a diaper bag

◆ Making it easier to shop, dine out, and even go to the movies with your baby

◆ Planning a travel itinerary with baby in mind

◆ How to survive traveling with a baby by car, plane, or train

You will never find it easier to travel with your child than you will during this first year of her life. That doesn't mean, of course, that you can go anywhere you want with your baby on the spur of the moment. Even a 20-minute outing may require nearly as much time to plan and get ready. With so many baby supplies needed even for short errands, you may feel somewhat like a pack mule.

But your infant is much more likely to be flexible about running errands or going on long trips with you now than she will be in a year or two. She probably enjoys riding in the car or stroller and may even take advantage

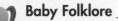

Baby Folklore

Want to keep your baby safe from the witches and evil fairies? Of course you do. When you take him out of the house for the first time, especially at night, do what they once did in Wales: put a pinch of salt in his pockets. Or wrap up a piece of bread in the baby's clothes, as they once did in England. Either charm protects your child from evil.

of the opportunity to take a nap while she's strapped in. When you get to your destination, she won't be running all over the place, which makes it much easier to limit what she gets her hands on no matter where you go.

So if you need to run a few errands, don't hesitate to bring your baby along with you. Your outings together will give your baby new perspectives on the world and exposure to many new people. Likewise, if you're planning a vacation or an overnight stay somewhere, do it now. No matter how you travel—by car, plane, or train—your trips will only become more difficult as your baby becomes older and more mobile. So what are you waiting for? Get up and go somewhere.

On the Town

You or your partner can start going out and about with your baby on the first day home from the hospital (although you may not feel up to it yourself). Some "helpful" friends and relatives might advise you otherwise. "He'll get sick," they'll warn. "He'll get too hot (or too cold)." Despite such warnings, you don't need to isolate your baby from the world any longer than the hospital or birthing center does. If he's been discharged, then you're free to go.

Yes, your baby is fragile, but that doesn't mean that you have to keep him indoors. Yes, your baby is susceptible to infection, but as long as you guard against the transfer of germs, you can keep him pretty safe from illness. Your baby is extremely sensitive to changes in temperature, too, but if you dress him appropriately, he'll be okay.

You can go almost anywhere with your baby:

◆ Get into the habit of taking your baby out for a stroll or a ride.

◆ Go to the park or just on a walk through the neighborhood.

◆ Visit your friends, whether they have children or not.

◆ Take him with you on errands to the grocery store, the mall, the bank, the post office, or the library.

◆ You can even take your baby to museums, restaurants (even fancy ones), or out to the movies. If you time it right and bring along a carrier seat, your baby may even fall asleep at any of these quiet places.

Everyday Errands

Your baby can come with you on nearly any errand you have to run. You'll have an easier time, though, if you do some advance planning. Gather everything you need near the front door before you start getting your coats on. Before you go out the door, establish your priorities. If you're planning on making four stops, do the most important first. It may be more efficient in terms of gas and miles driven to make the loop of post office, library, bank, and grocery store. But if the grocery store is the one thing you absolutely have to do, don't save it until last. Your baby may go ballistic long before you reach your final stop—and what does that do to your efficiency?

Don't feel as if you always have to arrange your schedule around your baby's. If your outings interfere slightly with your baby's nap schedule, for example, he'll adjust. The motion of the car and steady hum of the motor may put your child to sleep if he's ready for a nap. If he does fall asleep, you may be able to transfer him to a baby carrier—or if your car seat converts to a baby carrier, snap it out—and complete your errands without waking him.

Babyproofing

Never let your baby loose on a restaurant floor, even if she hasn't yet learned how to crawl. Waiters are often too busy serving customers to notice an infant on the floor. With trays of steaming food being toted around, this situation can result in a serious accident.

Dining Out: Table for Three?

Restaurants, unless they are fast-food joints, often require a special etiquette on the part of parents with babies. If you take your child to a restaurant (especially a fancy one) to celebrate a special occasion, you will have a more relaxed and enjoyable time if you …

- Go early, when most restaurants are less crowded. Your baby will not want to wait for a table and won't appreciate having to sit and wait long for your food.

- Choose an out-of-the-way table, if possible. You'll be less likely to disturb other diners or interfere with waiters.

- Order as soon as you can after sitting down, and then eat quickly. Who knows how long you'll be able to stay?

- Bring some quiet entertainment (a few favorite toys or books) for your baby, but save it until you really need it. She may be content just to look around or to play with a spoon for a while.

◆ If your baby has already started on solids, be sure to bring some food for her. Some dry cereal can keep her happily occupied.

◆ Be considerate of other diners. Be prepared to take your baby on a brief walk outside if she starts getting unbearably loud or can't possibly sit still any longer.

◆ Bring along a baby carrier, just in case she falls asleep.

◆ Be flexible. If your baby remains fussy or restless, consider taking turns with your partner (unless, of course, you're dining alone—well, not quite alone). First one of you eats while the other takes the baby, and then switch halfway through the meal. Or if necessary, get a doggy bag and transform your romantic evening out into a night of terrific take-out.

An occasional night off from cooking is essential for new parents. So treat yourself to a restaurant once in a while. Even if it means getting a baby-sitter, you will find the experience well worth it.

Our Feature Presentation: Movie Time

You can even go to the movies with your baby, as long as you are considerate of the others in the audience. Try to avoid taking your baby to the movies during the peak hours from around 6:30 to 9:00 in the evening. Instead, choose matinees and late, late shows. For one thing, your baby is more likely to fall asleep if the theater isn't packed with people. For another, if he doesn't go to sleep, you'll disturb fewer people if the theater isn't crowded. If your baby does start to make a lot of noise, take him into the lobby and walk or play with him there. If that settles him down, then try again—but stay in one of the back rows where, if necessary, you can get out again quickly. If it doesn't, then try again another night.

Your Bag of Tricks: The Complete Diaper Bag

Your days of traveling light are over. Wherever you go with your baby, and however briefly you plan to stay, you need to go fully equipped. For local trips and everyday errands, here's what you'll need in your bag of tricks:

◆ Plenty of cloth or disposable diapers. Always bring more than you think you need and restock the supply regularly.

◆ Diaper wipes, not only for your baby's bottom, but for her hands (and yours as well).

Q-Tip

Rather than carrying the whole bulky box of diaper wipes, try streamlining. Buy a travel pack of wipes that you can refill whenever the supply runs low. Or just fold up a bunch of wipes and put them in a sealed plastic sandwich bag.

If your baby needs a new diaper while you're out and about, try changing her in the hatch of a hatchback, on the tailgate of a station wagon, in the trunk of a sedan, or in the back of a minivan. You'll find this setup much easier and more comfortable than crawling into the back seat with her. Just put down a blanket and the changing pad, and you're ready to go to work.

- Diaper cream—just in case your baby develops a sudden case of diaper rash.

- Several cloth diapers for spills, spit-up, and other messes. Nothing absorbs better than a thick cloth diaper.

- A compact, waterproof changing pad to protect beds, couches, and other furniture when you need to change your baby on the go.

- A few large plastic bags for dirty diapers, dirty clothes, dirty bibs, and leaky bottles or jars.

- At least one extra set of clothes (depending on how long you plan to be out) in case of spit-ups, spills, and/or overflowing diapers.

- One or two pairs of socks or booties, in case her feet get cold.

- A light jacket or sweater, in case it gets cold.

- A hat, in case of cold (make sure it fits snugly) or sun (make sure it's wide-brimmed).

- A small bottle of baby sunblock for when you and your baby find yourselves outdoors.

- A set of safety covers for electric outlets. Once your baby has learned to sit up on her own, you may need to do an impromptu babyproofing job when visiting the homes of friends or relatives who don't have children.

- One or two pacifiers in a sealed container (if your baby uses them).

- A baby blanket, stuffed animal, or other comfort object (if your baby has one).

- Two or three small and simple playthings, in case your baby needs some entertainment on the run.

◆ Two or three teethers. The extras will come in handy when the first teether gets dirty (as it inevitably will).

◆ One or two sealed bottles of ready-to-use formula (if your baby bottle-feeds) or sealed bottles of water and a tightly closed container of powdered formula (with a measuring spoon).

◆ A bib (once your child has started on solids), to minimize the need for complete changes of clothes.

◆ Several snacks (if she eats solid foods). This item will become easier to pack once your child is ready for finger foods. But in the meantime, you can probably make do with one or two unopened jars of baby food. (You should also bring baby food in addition to snacks if you plan to be out for very long.) Don't forget the spoon.

◆ A plastic bottle of water or one or two juice boxes.

Q-Tip

Dry cereal and/or crackers will remain fresh for more than a month if you store them in small, airtight containers until you need them.

When you get home, clean out dirty diapers, soiled clothes or bibs, and any food that you've opened (except dry foods). Take a minute or two to restock any items that are running low, and then put the diaper bag away. That way, the diaper bag will be ready whenever you need it. If you have to go somewhere in a hurry, you can just grab it and go.

For longer trips, you may want to pack more of each of the items in the preceding list and add the following:

◆ A new toy that you think she'll like

◆ Something interesting to look at: board books, pictures cut out of magazines

◆ Extra finger foods (chunks of cheese, bananas, and so on), to minimize pit stops if you're traveling by car and to make sure that you have safe, appropriate, and nutritious food if you're on a plane or train

◆ A first-aid travel kit with thermometer, adhesive bandages, gauze pads, antibacterial cream, tweezers, infant's acetaminophen, and syrup of ipecac

A complete diaper bag makes you ready for anything that might happen. You may not use every item in the diaper bag on every trip you take, but if you need something, you'll know it's there.

Packing for a Long Haul

For longer trips involving car, plane, or train travel, your baby probably doesn't need a separate suitcase. Nearly everything he needs is in the diaper bag. The only other things you'll need to pack for him are the following:

◆ As many disposable diapers, plus 8 to 10 more, as you'll likely need en route. (The extras are for unforeseen events such as diarrhea and to give you a little time to settle in once you arrive.) Unless you're heading for the wilderness, plan on buying diapers when you arrive at your destination.

Q-Tip

If you normally use cloth diapers, consider going disposable for your trip. Disposables are much more convenient than cloth diapers while traveling. If you refuse to use disposables under any circumstances, then you'll need to bring along extra sealable plastic bags or other airtight containers for carrying used diapers. Otherwise, you risk seriously offending your fellow travelers. (Of course, changing a diaper on a plane or train can in itself offend some people—but that can't be helped.)

◆ Ten or fifteen of the most convenient-to-change, easy-to-wash-and-dry, light-weight outfits your baby owns. This supply should last you a week before you'll need to do any laundry, barring a series of major accidents.

◆ Any medications he takes and a prescription for each one, in case you lose it, spill it, or run out.

◆ Medical insurance information cards and your baby's medical records.

◆ A baby monitor to give yourself a little more freedom of movement when he's sleeping.

◆ A night light if he's used to sleeping with one in his room.

In addition to what you pack, you will find it helpful to have a baby carrier or light-weight umbrella stroller if you need to get around an airport or train station. If you bring along a stroller, you can hang one or two of your bags on the handle. But test it carefully first to make sure that when you let go of the stroller, the weight of the bags doesn't cause it to tip over backward. If you are traveling by plane, you may need to check your stroller at the end of the gate, right before you get on the plane. Airline personnel (in a perfect world) will bring it to the door of the plane for you upon landing.

Finally, if you're not traveling by car, consider bringing your own car seat along with you. Otherwise, you'll need to rent a car seat at your destination. (If you're renting a car, the agency should be able to provide you with a car seat, or make sure your rental has a built-in car seat.) If you take your car seat, you can check it directly from your car to the luggage handlers before you park. Or you can bring it on the plane or train with you. If the seat next to you is empty, you can use it as a safety seat for your baby. (However, unless you buy a seat for your baby, usually available at half the adult price, there's no guarantee that you'll get the opportunity to use the car seat.)

If you'll be staying with relatives at your final destination, ask them to look into borrowing or renting a crib. (Have them look up *Baby Rentals* or *Rentals* in the Yellow Pages.) If they can, you will have one less piece of bulky baby equipment to lug around with you. Other items you might want to consider renting or borrowing at the other end include a high chair or other feeding seat and a playpen (although many portable cribs now double as playpens).

 Babyproofing _____

Use your baby's car seat (and your own seat belts) religiously. Never leave your baby in a parked car if the weather is hot (or even warm). Your baby may quickly suffer heat stroke or worse if confined in that hot metal box.

Wherever you're staying—hotel, motel, cottage, guest house, or the home of a relative or friend—take a few minutes shortly after you arrive to check the room (or the entire house) for safety (see Chapter 10).

The Long Haul: Vacations with Your Baby

Traveling will never again be quite so carefree or spontaneous as it might have been before your baby arrived. You can't just drop everything on the spur of the moment and take off for a beach weekend or a week on the slopes. Heck, you probably can't even go to the grocery store without spending 20 minutes packing diapers, food, baby toys, and the rest. But even though spontaneity has become impractical, don't let that discourage you from planning a vacation trip with your family. It may involve a little more hassle to get anywhere else than it once did, but you may find it well worth the effort.

 Q-Tip _____

Consider planning a vacation with friends, especially those who have infants of their own. When two or three families who get along well travel together, all of the adults have a chance to take turns relaxing or seeing the sights. By rotating child-care responsibilities, at least two parents at a time get a chance to kick back or go off somewhere on their own.

Plane Planning

When traveling by plane, reserve seats in advance. Airline travel is subject to enough delays as it is without adding the uncertainty of whether you'll be able to get seats on the next plane to your destination. Your baby will tire of the airport ambiance quickly if she is forced to wait around.

When purchasing tickets, here's what to request, if available:

◆ **Bulkhead, first-class, or front-row seats in coach.** These seats give you extra room in front of the seat (often enough to accommodate a baby carrier or bassinet). Some bulkhead seats even come equipped with built-in, fold-away bassinets. (Ask your reservation clerk about bassinets.) The extra room will make it easier for your baby to sleep at your feet. (During takeoffs and landings, you'll have to hold your baby whenever the seat belt light is on.)

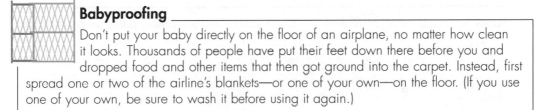

Babyproofing

Don't put your baby directly on the floor of an airplane, no matter how clean it looks. Thousands of people have put their feet down there before you and dropped food and other items that then got ground into the carpet. Instead, first spread one or two of the airline's blankets—or one of your own—on the floor. (If you use one of your own, be sure to wash it before using it again.)

◆ **Uncrowded seats.** Ask the reservation clerk if it's possible to seat you next to an as-yet-unoccupied seat. Although the airline may sell that empty seat after you have made your reservation, you'll have a free seat for your baby if it remains unsold.

You may be able to increase the odds in your favor if you ask about three seats in a row and then reserve the two seats on the ends. The lone seat between you will probably be one of the last to be sold. (If it does get booked, then you can always ask the stranger to change seats with you or your partner so that you can sit together.)

◆ **Aisle seats.** Aisle seats allow you to take your baby for as many walks as she likes without repeatedly imposing on those next to you.

◆ **Nonemergency seats.** Be sure to tell the reservation clerk that you will be traveling with your baby (even if you're not buying a seat for her). By law, parents with small children are not allowed to sit next to emergency exits because people seated there are expected to assist other passengers in case of emergency.

By getting the seats that you need as new parents, you will make the trip easier for everyone: for your baby, for yourselves, and for your fellow passengers.

Q-Tip

To increase your odds of getting the seating reservations you want, consider traveling during off-peak hours. (Ask the reservation clerk what those hours are.) You will be more likely to get bulkhead seats, aisle seats, and/or seats next to empty seats if the plane is not full.

Leaving on a Jet Plane

Flying in a plane offers limited options for relief to a cooped-up baby. You can't exactly ask the pilot to pull over for a while so that your baby can take a walk. Nursing or a bottle will offer relief, but try to hold off feeding your baby until you are at the end of the runway and about to take off. Sucking and swallowing will help equalize the ear pressure and minimize or eliminate the ear pain associated with air pressure changes in the cabin during takeoff and landing. Try to feed your baby during takeoff and again during landing. If your baby won't drink, don't get overly concerned about stifling her cries. Like sucking, swallowing, and yawning, crying will help clear your baby's ears.

Change your baby's diaper just before boarding the plane. The tight space in airplane bathrooms makes it nearly impossible to lay your baby down to change her. If you have an empty seat next to you, don't feel shy about changing your baby's diaper right there; it's the safest place on a plane to change a diaper. Be considerate, however: use a changing pad to protect the seat. Also, have everything ready before you open up Pandora's box so that you can be as quick and efficient as possible.

If your baby must have a warm bottle, ask a flight attendant to warm one up for you. Exercise extreme caution, however, because the flight attendant will undoubtedly use a microwave, which heats unevenly. To protect your baby from scalding, shake the bottle thoroughly and then test the temperature on the inside of your wrist before you feed her. Better yet, bring powdered formula or liquid concentrate on the plane and mix one or two ounces of boiling water (which is available for tea-drinkers) into several ounces of cold water. Then add the proper amount of formula, shake the bottle, and test the temperature before feeding your baby.

If your child starts bawling, try to take it with good grace. Do anything you can to soothe her, but don't put extra pressure on yourself just because you have 200 to 300 witnesses, some of whom may resent your baby's (and your) existence.

Q-Tip _____

Try not to introduce any major changes in your baby's sleeping or feeding patterns in the week or two before traveling by plane. If possible, plan departure times right before your baby's regular bedtime or naptime. The white noise of jet engines is likely to put your baby to sleep for much of the flight. If you fly at a time when she would otherwise be awake, any napping she does on the plane will disrupt her normal sleep schedule even more than you might expect with air travel. If so, don't expect your baby to stick to her usual sleep schedule after you arrive at your destination—or let you stick to yours.

After the plane lands, try not to be in a rush to get off. You'll probably have so much to carry (baby, diaper bag, other carry-ons) that you'll find it easier to get up the aisles when just a few passengers are left. Also, if you're trying to gather everything together among the crush of deplaning passengers, you might easily leave something behind. (Let's hope it's not the baby.)

Foreign Affairs

If you are planning on traveling abroad, you need passports not only for yourself and your partner, but for your baby, too—no matter how young he is. So get your baby's passport information in order before you plan on leaving the country.

Schedule a well-baby visit with your pediatrician the month before you go abroad. At that time, share any health concerns you may have regarding traveling with your baby. Make sure your baby has received all the immunizations he needs, too. (For trips to certain countries, he may need to get additional immunizations.)

Baby Doctor _____

If your child gets sick or injured while you're away from home, head straight for the emergency room of the nearest hospital or contact the local medical society for a recommendation on a pediatrician. Better still, ask your own doctor before you leave home if she or he can recommend anyone in the area where you'll be staying.

Rules of the Road

The most important rule to help maintain your sanity on a long car ride with your baby is: allow extra time to arrive at your destination and stop often along the way.

Baby Doctor

Make sure you schedule your visit to your pediatrician at least a week before your departure date. That way, if your baby does need immunizations, any reaction will have passed by the time you leave.

If your baby falls asleep, drive as far as you can before she wakes up. But if she's awake, don't expect to go more than 100 miles without stopping.

Whenever and wherever you stop, take your baby out of her car seat and take a stroll with her to stretch your legs a bit. Then, when you're ready to go, offer your baby the breast or bottle first. Some soothing sucking and a full belly might make her more willing to get strapped in again.

Know in advance where you will be sleeping every night of your trip. If you're going to a single destination and it's within a day's drive, this won't be a problem. But if you're planning an on-the-road tour or driving somewhere more than a day away, make reservations at a hotel, motel, or inn before you set out.

When you make hotel reservations, always ask if the hotel can supply a crib, even if you won't need one because you're bringing a portable crib of your own. If the hotel does not offer cribs, then the management and staff probably do not welcome or accommodate the needs of families very well. You might want to consider making reservations elsewhere.

With a baby, you should plan your overnight stops no more than 300 to 400 miles apart. Even the youngest of infants is not likely to want to remain strapped in a car seat for more than 6 or 7 hours in a day.

If your baby starts to get bored along the way, switch places with your partner. Unless the switch freaks her out, take turns driving and entertaining, calming, and feeding your baby.

Are We There Yet?

After you arrive, kick back and relax as much as you can. Try not to schedule your whole vacation. Instead, be as loose and flexible about making plans as you possibly can. Remember that your baby will have a loud say in what you can do and when you can do it.

Even though you're on vacation, try to adhere as closely as possible to your baby's normal schedule of naps and meals. This consistency will benefit not only him, but you as well. You will be able to go more places, do more things, and enjoy more of your trip if you do what you can to help your baby avoid getting tired, hungry, and/or cranky.

Finally, wherever you stay, take advantage of this rare and wonderful opportunity to spend a little time alone with your partner. If you're staying with friends or relatives, ask them if they would baby-sit for an evening or two. If you're at a hotel, ask the concierge or bell captain if the hotel will arrange for a sitter. After all, you deserve a vacation, too.

The Least You Need to Know

◆ You can take your infant everywhere, so do so now while you still have the chance. (When she's a toddler, you may not be able to take her anywhere.)

◆ You have room in a diaper bag for only the bare minimum you need to feed, clothe, protect, and entertain your baby.

◆ Aim for off-peak hours. Whether you're going to a restaurant, catching a movie, traveling by car, or making reservations for planes, trains, or hotels, avoid the crowds by choosing the least popular times.

◆ If you're traveling with your baby, always allow extra time, in case you need to stop along the way.

Chapter 14

Fun and Games

In This Chapter

◆ Play and learning during early infancy

◆ Exercises for your early infant

◆ Toys to bat, grasp, hold, handle, and "eat"

◆ Toys that delight your baby's senses

◆ How to choose appropriate toys for your baby

During the first 3 months of your baby's life, toys meant little or nothing to him. Oh, sure, he probably enjoyed visual toys like mobiles, which moved and entertained him without requiring any action on his part. In the third month, he may have begun enjoying a few toys that he could grasp, especially if they jingled, rattled, or squeaked—but he didn't need much more than that.

You (and perhaps a select group of other people) were his favorite toy—and you still will be for the second three months of his life. As your baby's hand-eye coordination improves, he will delight in grabbing your nose and hair and ears, taking off your eyeglasses, poking you in the eye, putting his fingers in your mouth, and so on. Yet your child's interests will now expand beyond you and other people who provide him loving entertainment.

From about 3 months on, the toy story begins. With his manual dexterity improving daily, your baby needs the opportunity to practice manipulating playthings. Toys to grasp, look at, make noise with, suck on, and pass from hand to hand give him invaluable practice.

Opportunity Knocks: Playing Is Learning

Your child learns through everything she does, but if you can challenge the skills she's developing naturally at each age, you can greatly enhance (and perhaps even accelerate) her learning. By playing with her, you provide her with the opportunity to learn.

A Daily Workout

A playful daily workout gives your baby the chance to exercise his muscles. Put your baby on your lap or a clean carpeted floor and let him practice his new *gross motor skills* (those used to perform big movements): rolling, sitting, kneeling, crawling, pulling to standing, and so on. Long before your child can do any of these actions on his own, you can give him a hand (or two). With your guidance and support, your baby will begin to realize all the wonderful things his body can do.

Lap Dance

Your baby will love it if you take time to play games with her in your lap. You don't need to do much. She will find these simple exercises endlessly entertaining:

◆ Pull her up to sitting.

◆ Pull her up to standing.

◆ Hold her hands to help maintain her balance while standing (or sitting).

◆ Help her do deep knee bends and "jumping."

In the coming months, your baby will enjoy nursery-rhymes that involve bouncing her on your knee. (You can find delightful bouncing rhymes in any good book of nursery rhymes or play rhymes. Ask your local children's librarian to point you in the right direction.) Start with a basic rhythmical bounce: "Ride a Cock Horse to Banbury Cross." Then vary speeds with "This Is the Way the Gentlemen Ride." Finally, you can move on to "Trot Along to Boston," with its surprise ending (opening up your legs and letting your baby "fall" through—but don't let go of her hands).

Give Your Baby the Floor

Floor time gives your baby a chance to develop and practice new skills such as rolling over, getting on his hands and knees, and sitting up. Make sure that the floor or ground is soft enough that he won't hurt himself when he plops down face first. Putting your baby down on a quilt or a thick blanket can soften a hard floor or tightly packed earth.

> **Q-Tip**
>
> You can help your baby learn how to roll (if he hasn't already started on his own). When he's lying on his back on the floor, take a knee in your hand and cross it over the other knee. After you've helped him flip the bottom half of his body, all he needs to do is flip his hips and his shoulders will follow. Support his hips in your hands and then gently rock them back and forth until you've built enough "momentum" to flip him over onto his belly. Pretty soon, he won't even need you to get him started anymore.

If it's warm enough (indoors or out), you can also start giving your baby a regular dose of naked time. By 3 or 4 months, your child will probably begin to enjoy the sensual experience of letting it all hang out. In addition to stimulating all of his senses, naked time gives your baby total freedom of movement, unencumbered by one-piece outfits and bulky diapers.

When your baby can sit up by himself for more than a minute or so, try rolling a big, colorful ball to him. At first (assuming you have reasonably good aim), your baby's body will just stop the ball without any active intervention on his part. But before long, your child will start anticipating and reaching out to stop the ball. Encourage him to roll the ball back to you. When he does, you'll have a real game going.

> **Babyproofing**
>
> Make sure that the strings or straps on your crib gym are no longer than 6 inches, to prevent the risk of your baby's strangling. Once your child can sit up by herself, be sure to remove the crib gym. Otherwise, she might use it to boost herself up and out of her crib.

Babyproofing _____

Make sure the legs that support a baby swing are far enough from the swing that your baby won't get her hands caught. With a baby bouncer, make sure the hook or clamps that hold it up are secure. Finally, no matter how secure and happy your baby seems in her swing or bouncer, never, never leave her alone while she's up in the air.

Exercise Equipment

At around 4 months, your baby will begin making good use of a cradle or crib gym. She will enjoy lying on her back and batting at or kicking, and later reaching out and grasping, the rings and bars that hang above her. By around 6 months, she may even grab rings or a bar and use it to pull her back off the ground.

Once she can sit up, your baby will also love swinging, now and for years to come. Outdoor swings and slides, whether found in a park, a playground, or your own yard, provide hours of entertainment. An automatic baby swing can also keep your baby entertained and is handy to have around. As an added bonus, many parents find that a baby swing can sometimes lull a baby to sleep when all else seems doomed to failure.

A baby bouncer or jumper may also delight your child. The baby bouncer consists of a canvas seat attached to a door frame or ceiling hook by elastic cords. Your baby can dance and jump and spin in the baby bouncer; it also gives her a new, upright perspective from which to view her world.

Fun is the whole point of both of these pieces of equipment. If your child doesn't like them, by all means take her out. If she loves them, then let her have as much fun as she wants, but be sure not to use the equipment so much that your baby has little or no opportunity to practice her motor skills while on the floor or in your lap. Although swings and bouncers provide plenty of movement, neither does much to exercise or develop your baby's skills.

Babyproofing _____

Walkers are especially dangerous near stairs. Never put your baby in a walker if she has even the remotest access to a down staircase. Keep the basement door shut and locked. Use chairs, tables, or other furniture to block off your baby's access to all other down staircases. (A gate may give way to the combined weight of baby and walker.) Or better yet, whenever your baby's in a walker, keep her in a room (or rooms) with a closed door.

Walker/Don't Walker

Like automatic baby swings and baby bouncers, a baby walker, which is a canvas or plastic baby seat set inside a table framework with a wheel at the base of each leg, does little to advance your baby's development of physical skills. Indeed, too much time in a walker may retard certain precrawling and prewalking skills that cannot be practiced in a walker:

◆ Getting on all fours

◆ Pulling up to a standing position

◆ Balancing

◆ Falling safely

If you make sure your baby gets adequate floor time in order to practice these skills, a walker—used safely and sparingly—may delight your child and expand his horizons. Like a swing or bouncer, a walker gives your baby a new, upright view of the world. Unlike a swing or bouncer, however, a walker enables your baby to get somewhere. He can move himself around by pushing his legs against the ground. (Of course, he will probably go backward for quite some time before he figures out how to move forward.)

The ability a walker gives a baby to move about is both the chief appeal of a walker and the chief danger. Every year, more than 5,000 infants in this country receive medical treatment for injuries sustained in walkers. So if you do let your baby use a walker, supervise him constantly. With the help of a walker, your baby can go a long way very quickly and reach many places where he probably shouldn't be. If you plan to use a walker, you'll need to babyproof everywhere in your home (see Chapter 10).

Hand Jive

During your baby's third month, she will discover her own hands. Though your baby will find these wondrous objects fascinating, she will not recognize her connection to them—at least not at first. (Your baby's toes will fascinate her, too—although when they're not in her hands, in front of her face, or in her mouth, she may forget they are there altogether.)

Q-Tip

As soon as your baby has discovered her fingers and toes, the time is ripe for starting to play finger, toe, and clapping games. Favorites include "This Little Piggy," "Pat-a-Cake," and "Itsy Bitsy Spider."

Babyproofing

Take care not to leave any toy with a ribbon or string longer than 6 inches anywhere where your baby can reach it on her own. Your baby could strangle herself with a longer string or ribbon.

Once your baby recognizes that she has some control over these strange and beautiful things called hands, she will want to find out what she can do with them. Indeed, your baby's hands will become one of her favorite "play-things." At first, your baby will just swat at objects. Crib gyms and activity centers will give her a chance to exercise this skill. You can also help her practice by tying a ribbon or string around almost any soft toy and holding it above your baby as she lies on her back. This play offers your baby immediate gratification: as soon as she connects with a toy, it moves (and perhaps even makes a pleasing sound).

Your baby won't be content with merely swinging at objects for very long. From about 14 weeks on, your baby will want to hold on to toys. You can help advance this skill by holding out toys so that your baby can reach out for them.

Mastering the art of grasping will take time and effort. Your baby needs to gauge the distance, look back and forth from her hand to the toy, and finally coordinate her hand and eyes to reach for it. So try to avoid impatiently giving your baby the toy she is struggling to reach. When she finally reaches out and touches the toy, put it securely in her hand. Don't forget to lavish your baby with praise for her accomplishment. After all, she's learning a complex process.

Reach Out and Touch Something

When your baby has gained some proficiency in the art of grasping, provide him with toys that offer a wide variety of shapes and textures to stimulate his sense of touch. Texture books such as the classic *Pat the Bunny* let your baby experience the feeling of soft, rough, scratchy, and furry. You can also make your own texture books with small pieces of felt, sandpaper, textured wallpaper, yarn, and anything else that has a unique or interesting feel to it (as long as it's safe). Stuffed animals of various sizes and textures will also stimulate your baby's sense of touch.

Beanbags make a great grasping toy for babies this age because the shape gives way to the grasping hand, making it easier for your baby to hold on to it. Your baby will also love handling, mouthing, and dropping them.

Q-Tip

You can easily make your own beanbags by filling rectangular scraps of cloth with rice, dried peas, crunchy dry cereal, or coffee beans and then sewing them shut. Using different types of cloth and different fillers offers much more variety of texture than store-bought beanbags can provide. For a change of pace, you can also use crinkly cellophane, tissue paper, or cotton balls as filling, too.

Almost any toy that is safe for your baby will give him the opportunity to practice reaching, grasping, handling, banging, mouthing, and other ways of exploring objects. Here are a few toys to try:

◆ Activity centers can stimulate both hand-eye coordination and the development of *fine motor skills* (those used to perform small, delicate movements: grasping, pressing a button, turning a knob, and so on). The rewards of a ringing bell, a squeaky noise, a spinning pattern, or a dancing figure will make the activity center one of your baby's favorite playthings during these months. As your baby plays with it, you also get a reward: seeing how quickly his skills improve.

Babyproofing

Until age 2 or 3, stuffed animals that have embroidered mouths, eyes, and noses will be much safer for your baby to enjoy (especially on his own) than those with buttons or glass eyes.

◆ Soft blocks are terrific toys for the second (and third) trimester. If you build a tower of soft blocks right in front of your baby, he will gleefully swipe at it to knock it down. Build it up again, and he'll knock it right down again. Now you've got a game going!

◆ Balls—fuzzy balls, rubber balls, plastic balls, jingly balls, squishy balls—give your baby a fun way to practice new hand-eye coordination skills. Your baby will love rolling, holding, squeezing, and "eating" almost any ball you offer him.

◆ Mixing spoons, measuring cups, colanders, pieces of paper or magazines, and other baby-safe household objects will also stimulate your baby's interest.

Stimulating the Senses

In addition to exploring the sense of touch, your 3- to 6-month-old baby will want to make full use of her other senses. By offering your baby toys that stimulate one or more of her senses, you will encourage her sensual exploration of the world around her.

The Eyes Have It

You don't need to do a whole lot to stimulate your baby's sense of sight. After all, he probably spends most of his waking moments delighting in (and trying to make sense of) what he sees. You can, however, expand your baby's horizons and provide him with fun visual activities, games, and playthings.

Your baby will probably enjoy taking a visual tour of the house and neighborhood. You can serve as the tour guide, carrying your baby and pointing out all the sights that might interest him. When you feel you've exhausted the possibilities of the home tour, take your baby out to a park, on errands, or on a special trip to a museum or botanical garden to introduce him to a score of new sights (and sounds).

> **Q-Tip**
>
> If you have a fish tank, your baby will probably love watching the fish gliding through the water, the air bubbles floating to the top of the tank, and even the colorful gravel. Simultaneously stimulating and soothing, an aquarium consistently delights most young infants.

The second 3 months of your baby's life are also a terrific time to introduce visual games such as peekaboo, covering a toy with a handkerchief, or hiding your face behind your hands. Peekaboo helps teach your child the concept of *object constancy* (the realization that something doesn't cease to exist just because it disappears from sight). Around the end of the sixth month, your baby may begin to play peekaboo himself: hiding his face with his hands, a diaper, or a blanket; making a noise to attract your attention; and then laughing and squirming as he waits for you to "find" him.

Mirrors (nonbreakable, of course), which can stand free or be attached to the side of a crib or playpen, will also delight your child at this age. Your baby will find it fascinating to see another baby who does everything he does.

Mobiles entertain your baby while they stimulate his sense of sight. You will find it well worth the price to buy one with an electric or wind-up arm that rotates the mobile. This mechanism keeps the mobile's motion (and often music, too) going for as long as it's on—or for a minute or two, if it's a wind-up mobile. As an added bonus, when it's time to sleep, your baby may find the mobile soothing.

Q-Tip

Crib mobiles are intended to delight your baby, not you. So try lying on your back and holding the mobile above you to get an idea of what it will look like from your baby's perspective. Also, remember to keep any crib mobile well out of your baby's reach; remove the mobile when your baby learns to pull himself up to a standing position.

All Ears

A common gift at baby showers and births, rattles hold little interest for babies during the first couple months. But once your baby begins to grasp objects, rattles give your infant practice at grasping and shaking, and reward her efforts with a delightful sound. For many babies, rattles provide the first consistent and repeated lessons in the principles of cause and effect, and allow your baby to be the cause. Whenever your baby shakes the rattle, it makes a sound. Once she recognizes this fact (and she soon will), she gains a new sense of her own power, control, and mastery. She now knows that she can make the rattle noisy at will.

To supplement traditional rattles, you can make terrific noise-makers by filling sealable containers such as plastic food-storage boxes, coffee cans or other cans with plastic lids, and metal flour shakers with rice, sugar, metal lids from baby-food jars, beads, paper clips, or marbles. Even colored water (prettiest when placed in a clear, sealed plastic container) makes a swishing sound.

Babyproofing

Make sure that any homemade noise-makers that have small objects inside are securely sealed. You don't want your baby to be able to get the objects out of the container and inside herself.

Your baby will enjoy almost anything that makes a noise when she swats, bangs, shakes, pushes, squeezes, or drops it as if it were a rattle. She will shake stuffed animals or other safe playthings that have small bells inside. She will squeeze (and probably shake) rubber squeak toys, too.

Toyland

Today's toy stores offer thousands of products from which to choose, and that's just in the newborn and infant aisles. Unless you want to turn your home into a toy store, you need some criteria to help narrow the field.

Here's what to look for:

◆ **Age-appropriateness.** Your baby will enjoy a toy only if he can use it. An age-appropriate toy encourages or challenges your baby to practice and improve one or more developing skills. A toy that doesn't offer any challenge may bore him. On the other hand, if it's too hard to use, a toy may frustrate your infant. By the time he develops the skills needed to enjoy a toy he received prematurely, he may have lost interest in it entirely.

◆ **Safety.** Although toy manufacturers' age recommendations do take safety into account, you should carefully examine any plaything you plan to give your baby. During the first year, your baby will bang, drop, kick, pull, throw, bite, and suck on any toy you give him. To hold up under this kind of treatment, a toy needs to be **durable, nontoxic, washable**, and have **no small parts**. If it is breakable, your child will no doubt break it into pieces. If it has small parts, your baby will break them off. To prevent choking, avoid toys that have any parts smaller than 2 inches in diameter. Because your child will undoubtedly chew on his toys, they should be painted or finished with nontoxic materials. Finally, they should be easily washable so that you can keep them (relatively) clean and (relatively) free of germs.

In addition to these major safety concerns, you should consider the weight of any toy. Avoid toys that will hurt him when he inevitably drops them on his toes or bangs them into his face. Also avoid any plaything with sharp edges or with strings or ribbons long enough to wrap around your baby's neck.

Babyproofing

You can find a great variety of used toys for your baby—often in good condition and at a cheap price—if you frequent garage, yard, or tag sales. But examine every used toy especially carefully to make sure that it is safe and appropriate for your baby.

◆ **Stimulation.** If used correctly, a good toy will do something to stimulate one of your baby's senses (especially touch, sight, or hearing) or his developing abilities (hand-eye coordination, gross motor control, fine motor control, and so on).

◆ **Variety.** Try to select toys that offer your baby colors, textures, shapes, and sounds different from those you already have. By opting for variety, you expose your baby to the myriad possibilities the world has to offer.

◆ **Simplicity.** In general, the simpler the toy, the longer it will last. Simple toys have fewer parts and therefore prove more durable than more complicated toys. Simple toys also tend to offer more versatility. Today your child can hold it, next month he can throw it, and next year he can use it as a prop for make-believe play.

Whatever toys you choose, let your baby play with them in any way he chooses. After all, just because you know the "right" way to play with a certain toy doesn't mean that your baby can't come up with new and ingenious uses on his own.

The Least You Need to Know

- ◆ Playing with your baby gives her the opportunity to practice developing skills and discover new ones.
- ◆ No matter how much your baby enjoys a baby swing, baby bouncer, or walker, make sure she also gets plenty of free time on the floor.
- ◆ Never let your baby use a walker without supervision.
- ◆ When buying toys for your baby, choose a variety that are safe, age-appropriate, stimulating, and simple.

Part 3

The Crawler: 6–9 Months

Horses run almost immediately after birth. Ducks swim in their first days, too. So why does it take human babies more than 6 months before they begin to crawl, much less walk? Because it takes human parents half a year to get used to all the other aspects of baby care before we can even fathom the responsibilities (and anxieties) involved in keeping up with a baby on the move.

Time's up. Now that your baby's on his hands and knees, you'll really need to be on your toes. No matter how safe you make your home, and you should make it as safe as possible, you will now need to be your baby's constant companion and guardian angel. There's a whole world out there (or even just in your house) that your baby is eager to explore. Get ready, world. Here he comes!

Sound and Movement: Development from 6 to 9 Months

In This Chapter

◆ Your baby's developing control over his body

◆ Your baby's move toward mobility: crawling

◆ Your baby's rapidly increasing verbal understanding

◆ The progression from babble to speech sounds

By the time your baby reaches her half-birthday, her muscles will have grown much stronger and her balance will have improved. She also will have developed greater control over her upper body. She can now turn her head to keep track of movement. She can lift her head and shoulders up off the floor with her arms. She can reach out and grasp objects, though she's probably still working on perfecting this art.

Over the next few months, your baby will gain even more strength, balance, and control in her lower body (her hips, her legs and knees, and her feet). Just about the same time she learns to sit by herself, your baby will probably begin to crawl. So watch out! Your baby's on the move.

Creeping and Crawling

Over the next 3 months, your baby will progress rapidly toward full mobility and her first steps. Although every infant develops at his or her own pace, most babies follow this approximate progression:

- Sitting with support (5 to 7 months)
- Getting on hands and knees (5 to 8 months)
- Standing with support (5 to 8 months)
- Sitting on her own (8 to 9 months)
- Crawling (8 to 10 months)

If your baby is an early stander, she may even be standing, or even inching along the edges of furniture, by the ninth month!

Again, keep in mind that all the ages listed here and elsewhere in the book are approximate. Just because your child doesn't crawl until 11 months (or skips crawling altogether), while your best friend's baby crawls at 7 months, does not mean that your baby is in any way backward. The age at which a child begins sitting, crawling, or standing does not have any known correlation with intelligence, talent, or future abilities.

Have a Seat

Though your baby has by now gained steady control over the muscles in the upper half of his body, he still has not perfected the ability to maintain his equilibrium. If you sit your baby up on the floor when he is 6 months old, he may remain seated for 1 or 2 seconds, but he will inevitably topple over. Once he can sit up on his own for a few seconds, though, you should give your baby more and more practice at balancing while sitting on his own. But make sure he remains under your watchful eye.

Sitting on his own is a big step for your baby. It gives him a whole new view of the world around him. For the first time, your baby can see things all the way across a room. Although your baby will still love it if you pull him up into a sitting position, soon he will pull himself up on you.

If you want to help your baby practice sitting, set him down on the floor. Be sure to have plenty of pillows scattered closely around your baby so that he won't get hurt when he falls, as he most certainly will. At first, your baby will probably need a little extra support. A small beanbag chair will mold around your baby's bottom and give him the support he needs. Or you could sit cross-legged on the floor and place your baby's bottom in the middle of your legs. That way when your baby falls back, he'll land in his favorite place: your arms.

Do not leave a room where your baby is sitting up in a beanbag chair or surrounded by pillows. If your baby falls face first into the beanbag or pillows, he may try to lift his head up using his arms and upper body. But if the fall traps your baby's arms under his body, he could smother in the pillows.

As your baby gets more secure, you can have him sit on his own between your straddled legs, or you might try jamming pillows around your baby's hips and under his bottom. These pillows will support your baby's sitting for a little longer than he can manage on his own. Still, in less than a minute, your baby will probably tumble over.

Try to cut down on the amount of time your baby sits in a baby seat, stroller, or car seat at this stage. The more time your baby spends in a baby seat, the less opportunity he has to build up the muscles and coordination needed to sit on his own for longer periods. Certainly, any of these seats allows your baby to sit, but none of them gives him the valuable practice time he needs in order to improve his balance. While sitting in a baby seat, stroller, or car seat, your baby still rests most of his weight on his back, where the seat provides ample support. But to sit on his own for more than a few seconds, your baby needs to lean forward a bit and put more weight on his bottom.

Babyproofing

Don't sit your baby up in a chair or on a bed yet. A fall from this height probably won't do any serious damage (although it could), but your baby will get hurt and frightened. The experience might scare him away from any further attempts at sitting for a while.

Once your baby can sit up, you must always use safety straps when he is in his stroller, carriage, or high chair. (Of course, you should have been using them all along, but now you really need to make a point of it.) When your baby couldn't lift himself up, he had less risk of falling out (though he did have a risk of sliding down and out). But now the danger of falling is always present.

Portable baby seats at this stage not only slow your baby's development of balance and muscular control, but they may be dangerous, especially if you're in the habit of putting the baby seat on a table or counter so that you can talk to your baby while you cook or do other chores. Your baby will want to sit up to get a better look at what you're doing. Yet his efforts to sit up will always end with your baby falling back with the full weight of his body. This sudden force can easily tip over a baby seat, which could lead to a serious injury if the seat falls off a table.

By 7 or 8 months, your baby may sit up for longer periods by leaning forward. Unfortunately, he's likely to lean too far forward and need to use his outstretched arms and hands to prop himself up. Your baby can't do anything while he's sitting this way because his hands are in use keeping him from falling and his leaning over limits his range of vision. Eventually, your baby may learn to hold himself up with just one arm, freeing the other hand for reaching out and grasping treasures.

As your baby's balance improves over the next month or so, he learns to lean forward, but not too far forward, for more control. Though your baby does not need those pillows for support anymore, he still needs them for safe landings. By 8 or 9 months, your baby may be able to maintain balance without arm support for a minute or longer. But he probably can't shift his balance yet. If he tries to move, your baby will fall. But that's not a problem because around this same time (9 months), your baby performs a new miracle: getting himself into a sitting position all by himself.

On All Fours

Most babies crawl before they walk, but not all do. A few babies skip crawling altogether. So don't worry if your baby hasn't begun crawling yet, even as she approaches 9 or 10 months old. Your baby may have figured out another way to get around, or she may just skip crawling and go straight from sitting to standing to walking. The description here offers an average or typical portrait of the crawler, but no baby is typical in every respect.

Your baby may begin to prepare herself for crawling at around 6 months. That's when you may notice your baby pulling her knees up and supporting herself on her arms. Your baby may look ready to crawl, but she isn't. Your baby can balance on all fours; that's a very steady base. But she does not yet know how to lift an arm or a leg without toppling over.

Just because your baby doesn't know how to crawl at 6 months doesn't mean she can't get around a room, though. Babies are remarkably ingenious. If your child loves to roll around, she may discover that with some sustained effort, she can roll from place to place. Soon your baby may be rolling with a definite destination in mind. Your baby may also pull herself across an uncarpeted floor, combat-style, using nothing more than her elbows. Your baby may even discover that she can sit up and use one hand to "bump" her bottom across a floor.

During your baby's seventh or eighth month, you may think, "Okay, now she's really ready to crawl." After getting up on her hands and knees, your baby rocks back and forth. She looks as though she might start to move forward at any moment. Indeed, she may move forward by "throwing" her body forward. Your baby will not find this a very efficient way of getting where she wants to go, however. It can also produce some hard landings.

Most babies begin to crawl around 9 months. Like many babies, your child may crawl backward first, even when she wants to crawl forward. (How frustrating!) That's because she still has greater strength and control of her upper body than her lower body. Don't worry, she'll get the hang of it and be crawling forward within a few weeks.

Just as every baby has his or her own individual pace for starting to crawl, every baby has an individual style of crawling. Your baby may crawl on her hands and knees. She may crawl on her hands and feet. She may even crawl on her hands, one knee, and one foot. But how your baby crawls doesn't matter; the important thing is that she's doing it at all. Your baby deserves heaps of praise (and hugs and kisses) for figuring out any way to get where she wants to go.

You can help your baby teach herself how to crawl. To encourage and accelerate the process, your baby needs three things from you:

- **Opportunity.** Give your baby plenty of floor time. (Carpeted floors provide a softer landing than hard wood or linoleum floors.) Don't keep your baby cooped up in a playpen whenever she's not in your arms or asleep.

- **Motivation.** Lay your baby down on her belly and put a toy or something else she likes just out of her reach. Don't forget that what your baby likes best is still you, so try sitting just beyond where she can reach. Hold out your arms and call your baby's name. If she starts bawling, give up the game and comfort her. But if your baby manages to get to you—or even if she just tries hard but doesn't quite make it—reward her with encouragement and praise.

- **Supervision.** Don't leave your baby alone on the floor even for a minute. If you have to leave the room—even just to answer the phone or get yourself a glass of water or put the pasta in boiling water—put your baby in a playpen or bring her with you.

Clearing the Way: Safety for the Crawler

Once your baby starts crawling, you have to work 10 times harder to keep him safe. By now, you should have already babyproofed your entire home and yard (see Chapter 10). If you haven't yet done so, take the time to make sure you have made your baby's everyday surroundings safe.

When your baby starts crawling, be sure to double-check the following precautions:

◆ Keep all electric cords out of reach or secured to the floor. If your baby can grab a cord, he's sure to pull a lamp or clock or iron down on his head.

◆ Shield all electric outlets with safety caps. If your baby manages to stick a finger or a plaything into an outlet, he may get a nasty shock.

◆ Avoid leaving anything on the floor unless it's safe for your baby. Your baby will soon be able to cover lots of ground very quickly, so rid your floor of any choking hazards, toxins, and anything else that might do your baby harm.

◆ Install safety gates that block off stairs at both the bottom and the top. Crawling on stairs, especially going upstairs by himself, will be lots of fun for your baby. You may even want to encourage your baby's skill at climbing by getting a playroom set of sturdy wooden steps or a toddler slide that has three or four steps. However, you need to make sure that your baby doesn't go upstairs on her own whenever she pleases. When your baby crawls upstairs, stay right behind her. When he wants to come down again, try to teach her how to crawl down safely by going backward. Again, stay right behind your baby at all times. And use those safety gates!

Babyproofing

Although pressure gates work fine at the bottom of a flight of stairs, they provide inadequate protection at the top of the stairs. If your baby falls into a pressure gate, uses it to pull himself up, or even just pushes hard, he may pop it right out of place and crash down the stairs with it. So be sure to install a safety gate that bolts into the wall or newel post at the top of the stairs.

Now that he's on the move, your baby needs constant supervision. Otherwise, you'll find him getting into everything that's less than 2 or 3 feet off the floor.

Shortly after he begins crawling, he may start to pull himself to standing, or at least to kneeling. So he'll empty out your rack of CDs, cassette tapes, or videos, and somehow remove each one from its case. He'll dump wastepaper baskets. He'll pull things off of tables and other surfaces. To prevent mishaps, keep an eye on your baby at all times and never let down your guard.

Standing on Her Own Two Feet (Well, Almost)

Although you don't necessarily have to crawl before you walk, you do have to stand. At 6 months, your baby can stand if you hold both of her hands for support. If you pull her up to standing in your lap, your baby may practice flexing her knees to make herself "jump." A month or so later, your baby may even start lifting first one foot and then the other, but neither her feet nor her body is moving forward at this point.

At around 9 months, your baby may begin "walking"—as long as you continue to hold both of her hands. By this point, she's definitely making forward progress: she puts one foot in front of the other (rather than on top of the other). Many parents get very excited at this point, thinking either that their baby is really walking now or that she will soon. But if a baby needs help to walk, she isn't really walking yet.

Your baby still has a long way to go. At this stage, she still needs to learn how to support her weight with her legs and how to balance herself while standing. Give your baby time. After all, she's probably just now learned how to balance while sitting.

> **Baby Talk**
>
> "When I was born, I was so surprised I couldn't talk for a year and a half."
>
> —Gracie Allen

Babble On

Just as your baby may not walk until he is 13 or 14 or 16 months old, he will probably not utter a "real" word until after his first birthday. Nonetheless, the development of listening skills, an appreciation for language, verbal understanding, and speech sounds during the second 6 months prepare him for talking in just the same way that the development of control over his hips, legs, feet, and balance paves the way for walking.

Don't bother trying to rush your little one into uttering his first words. After all, your baby doesn't need to talk at all yet. He generally gets pretty much what he needs or wants by crying and sometimes by pointing. Nonetheless, your baby probably loves to babble and loves to hear other people talking. Why? Because your baby's a social being from the very start.

Know What I Mean?

Your baby learns language by listening to you and others use it. Though your baby certainly doesn't understand everything you say, she no doubt picks up glimmers of meaning here and there. Especially if you speak to your baby a lot, she will understand dozens of words before she utters anything recognizable.

One of the first words your baby will probably understand is the word *no*. By around 6 months, your baby will begin to associate a sharp "No!" with the idea that she has to stop doing whatever she's doing. By 9 months, she may understand a few simple phrases that are often directed toward her, such as "Wave bye-bye" or "Drink your bottle."

If you want to check your child's understanding of words, even before she speaks, try these two games:

◆ Ask your baby to find a favorite object. "Where's your blanket?" "Where's your teddy bear?" If she turns toward it, your baby probably knows what *blanket* or *teddy bear* means. This game works even better with your baby's favorite people. If you have several visitors for your baby to choose from, have your partner hold the baby and ask, "Where's Mama?" or "Where's Daddy?" If she turns toward you, you're golden.

◆ See whether your baby can do what you ask if you make simple requests. Some examples include, "Wave bye-bye," "Sit down," "Give me a hug," "Throw the ball," "Drink your juice," or "Fetch my slippers." See how many your baby understands.

If your baby does what you've asked her to do, let her know how pleased you are. If she doesn't, then ask her to do something else or drop the game for a while. (Of course, just because your child refuses to do what you've asked doesn't necessarily mean that she has failed to understand you. She may just be loathe to perform on command.)

Sound Bites

During the past couple months of your baby's life, he was limited to one-syllable bites of sound: *la*, *ma*, *ba*, and so on. But around the seventh or eighth month, you will hear a wide range of new sounds. Suddenly, your baby will shout out two-syllable sound bites: *ama*, *booboo*, *umum*, *poopoo*, *immi*, and the ever-popular *gaga*. These two-syllable sounds become more and more distinct as your baby tries new consonant sounds.

Hearing so many sounds coming out of your baby's mouth will be exciting for you, but your baby will be even more thrilled. He will love the sound of his own voice (not unlike many adults), and he'll talk in a steady stream whenever he's happy, regardless of whether anyone else is there to listen or reply.

Q-Tip

Pay attention to all the sounds your baby makes. Like many infants at this age, your baby may develop a special sound (a cough, a squeak, a gleeful shout) that he consistently uses to gain your attention. What he's trying to say is, "Psst. Over here!" Reward him for this bit of cleverness with an enthusiastic response.

By 8 or 9 months, your baby listens carefully to any speech sounds he hears. If you watch your baby when you're having a conversation with someone else, you'll notice that he resembles a spectator at a tennis match. He turns his head back and forth from person to person as each speaks. His expression may convey the impression that he's trying to follow the conversation of two people who don't speak the same language he does, and that's exactly what he is doing. After watching for a while, he'll suddenly burst into the conversation with a shout, as if to say, "Hey, I'm here, too. Talk to me!"

After all this careful listening, your baby tries to imitate sounds. Although your baby appears to be saying his first words, he isn't. This imitation is not really language; it's mere echoing of sounds. Few (if any) of these imitative sounds will have meaning for your baby.

Q-Tip

If you want to make good use of your baby's talent at mimicry, start teaching him your favorite tunes. Because songs add the force of rhythm and the enchantment of melody to words, they are often more fun—and more memorable—than words alone. So sing a lot of songs to your baby during the second 6 months. Just as your baby echoes your speech, he may imitate not just the words but also the melodies you sing. And when he first joins in for a few notes, you may be surprised how well your baby can carry a tune.

Around the ninth month, language building progresses quickly. First, your baby begins to appreciate and imitate the tones of conversations he's heard. He begins to stress certain vocal sounds and add inflections to some "words." Now his babbling sounds like an adult conversation, sprinkled with statements, questions, jokes, and soft-spoken confidences.

Your baby may also begin to construct chains of vocal sounds that become longer than two syllables: *moomoomoomoo* or *lalalalalala*, for instance. On the heels of these verbal chains and the addition of intonation come fully inflected "words" that may combine several different speech sounds: something like *pagoolamida*, *zippadeedooda*, or *moo-googaipan*.

He seems so close to speaking that you or your partner may expect him to launch into Hamlet's soliloquy any day now. In truth, however, your baby will probably practice and hone the sounds and inflections of these verbal chains for another month or two. His first words are unlikely to come until at least the tenth or eleventh month and probably even later.

Baby Talk?

You can help your baby master the nuances of a difficult language and learn to speak without resorting to complicated phonics programs or rote repetitions of the names of objects. You need to do only two things: talk to your baby and listen to her.

Your baby will learn language more quickly from you, her primary caretaker(s), than from anyone else. Because your baby knows you best, she's learned to recognize the way you speak: your tones, your inflections, your facial expressions. So talk around your baby and talk to your baby. Speak naturally and clearly (though you may want to slow down your speech slightly to make the words more distinctive).

Devote at least some time to talking to your baby one on one. Your baby will learn much more from direct conversation than she will by trying to follow a conversation that doesn't include her. Oh, she'll still listen to a two-way exchange and might pick up some valuable sounds and intonations, but any discussion that involves three or more people will probably confuse your baby. It's just too hard for a new listener to try to sort out sounds coming from all corners of a room.

When you talk to your baby, talk about the present as much as possible. Your baby's memory is not yet her strong suit. So talk about what's happening right here and now ("Wow! An airplane. Look up in the sky, Megan. It's an airplane.") Your baby can then form meaningful connections between what she's seeing or hearing or touching or tasting or smelling or feeling and what you're saying. Talking about what happened earlier will not necessarily evoke associations for your baby, unless, of course, you helped her make those associations by also talking about them when they were happening.

Pro Nouns, Anti Pronouns

The indefinite and continually changing meaning of pronouns confuses infants. For example, *it* is probably one of the most used words in the English language, but think of what must be going through your baby's brain as he struggles to understand what that pronoun means. *It* means a ball now, but a minute ago *it* meant the spoon, and 2 minutes ago *it* meant a rattle. Or *they* means the books now, but I thought *they* meant Grandma and Grandpa.

Personal pronouns may be even more confusing. To a listener, hearing *you* means me, and hearing *I* means you. But *I* also means your partner, who said it just a few minutes ago. *You* also means your partner because your baby overheard you talking to your partner by that name earlier. (This confusion will become more apparent next year, when your baby starts using these pronouns. Many toddlers reverse the two terms, speaking of their things as *yours* and your things as *my* or *mine*.)

Instead of pronouns, use nouns and names when you speak to your baby. "Mama's looking for Ian's spoon" will mean much more to your baby than "Where is it?" or even "Where is your spoon?"

Context Counts

Don't just give your baby words to parrot. Certainly, you will do no harm in holding up a ball and saying, "Ball. See the ball? This is a ball. Now say ball, sweetie." Indeed, your baby, who loves both imitating and pleasing you, may even say "Ba." But just because she makes the sound doesn't mean that your baby knows that *ba* refers to that colorful, round, bouncing thing in your hand.

Your baby will learn much more about language by associating sounds she hears many times, in a variety of contexts, with what she observes during those moments. That's why talking to your baby about the present, what you or she is doing or what she sees or hears, is so important. For example, if your baby hears the word *diaper* as you check it, pull the top of it away from her to take a peek at what's inside, put her on the changing table, take it off, get her a new one, put it on, and fasten it, her neurons will be firing with the connections made. Before long, she will realize that *diaper* refers to that thing she wears on her bottom.

Talk in full sentences to your baby and trust that she will pick out the sounds she hears again and again. If she hears it often enough, your baby will associate these sounds with whatever the occasions had in common. Remember, your baby is listening carefully to you, trying to make connections. Even before she tries to master the inflections and vocal sounds that seem to make up this appealing new language of yours, your baby will try to understand what you are saying.

Because your baby is listening so carefully to you, you owe it to her to do the same. During the babbling stage, give your baby your full attention as she chatters away. Then "answer" your baby's babble with adult language. This exchange enables your baby to initiate a "real" conversation with you to practice social interaction.

The Least You Need to Know

♦ Your baby will sit up, crawl (or not), and stand when he is ready. Help him, but don't rush him.

♦ Once your baby is at all mobile, he needs constant supervision.

♦ Your baby listens to everything you say and understands much more than he can say.

♦ Talking to your baby and around him will do more to advance his developing language skills than anything else you can do.

Chapter 16

Food, Glorious Food

In This Chapter

◆ Encouraging your baby to feed herself

◆ Expanding your baby's menu

◆ From spoon-feeding to finger foods

◆ When and how to wean your baby from the breast or bottle

By your baby's half-birthday, she has become an experienced eater. She has tasted a variety of cereals, fruits, and vegetables. She has smeared food all over her face, her hair, her hands, and you. She has probably finger-painted her high chair and perhaps the nearest wall with food, played "Drop the Spoon," and thrown food onto the floor. Your baby has had her fun with food. Now it's time to get down to the serious business of eating. (Actually, you should continue to allow and encourage your baby to have fun while eating. The more your baby enjoys eating solid foods, the easier time you will have feeding her.)

Up until now, your baby's consumption of solid foods has been merely supplemental. Soon that will no longer be the case. By the seventh or eighth month, solid foods should begin providing more and more of your baby's nutritional needs. Instead of serving as a midmeal break, solid foods will begin to replace one or two breast or bottle feedings. What you feed your baby will change, too. In the coming months, you will add more and more variety, in terms of both taste and texture, to your child's diet.

Helping Those Who Help Themselves

From the beginning, try to offer your baby a degree of independence when feeding him. Letting your baby feed himself (or at least take part in feedings) is a great way to improve his hand-eye coordination and overall manual dexterity. The food that makes it all the way into your baby's mouth and then down to his stomach serves as a positive reward for your baby's efforts to coordinate hand, eye, and mouth.

Of course, you can't just plop your baby's food down on the tray or table in front of him and expect him to feed himself. But while continuing to do the bulk of feeding, you can still offer your new eater his own spoon (in addition to the one with which you feed him), his own cup, and at least samples of his own food on the tray or table. That way, your baby can squeeze and squirt the food between his fingers and (who knows?) once in a while even bring some of it up to his mouth.

Of course, you should never force your baby to participate in feeding himself, but you probably won't need to convince him. If you give him foods he likes and the tools and the opportunities he needs, he'll be more than happy to help feed himself. Be sure to allow extra time at mealtimes because it will take a while for him to learn how to feed himself. Try not to get impatient with him. If your baby is having trouble manipulating his spoon, for example, he's probably frustrated enough without adding your frustration into the mix, too.

Given enough opportunities and encouragement, your baby will probably be able to feed himself a lot by the eighth or ninth month, but you'll need to give him a little leeway. Your baby will use whatever means are necessary (a cup, a spoon, his hands, or a few licks directly off the tray) to get food into his mouth. Don't worry about your baby's atrocious table manners; etiquette lessons can come later. For now, just concentrate on making eating solid foods and drinking from a cup as enjoyable as possible.

Table for One

When your baby can sit up with support for a reasonable amount of time (say, 5 to 10 minutes), you will probably want to start feeding her in a high chair or a baby seat that hooks onto the top of the kitchen or dining-room table. For safety reasons, your baby's high chair should have a wide, stable base and come equipped with a safety belt (including a crotch strap to prevent her from sliding down under the tray). A wide-rimmed, removable tray will catch most major spills and be relatively easy to clean.

For safety's sake …

◆ Be sure to lock the high chair in the open position before you sit your baby in it.

◆ Place the high chair in the middle of the kitchen or dining room, or with its back against a wall.

◆ Keep the high chair a safe distance away from anything (a table, a counter, or a wall, for instance) that your baby might kick her feet against. With the power in her thrusting legs, she could easily propel herself backward with enough force to knock the high chair over.

◆ Be sure to strap your baby in securely and yet supervise her at all times. (It will help if you set up in advance so that you'll have everything you might need at hand before you strap your baby into the high chair.)

Your baby will enjoy having her very own spoon. At first, she may bang it, wave it, put it in her mouth (whether her mouth is full or empty), and bite it. But she'll never discover how to use a spoon properly if you don't give her one.

By around 8 months, your baby will begin using her spoon to feed herself. At first, she'll just dip her spoon into some food and lick it off. But within a few weeks of this initial experiment, your baby will be dipping or scooping her spoon and then opening her mouth and putting the food in it, at least some of the time. Your baby may find it helpful if you fill one spoon with food and then trade it for the empty spoon in her hand. This sleight of hand will greatly increase the efficiency with which she feeds herself.

> **Babyproofing**
>
> If you use a baby seat that hooks onto the top of a table, be sure to lock it securely in place before seating your baby in it. Though she may look somewhat precarious hanging in midair in this kind of seat, resist the temptation to put a chair under the seat to shorten any potential fall. By thrusting her powerful legs on the chair, your baby may pop the baby seat loose.

When your baby does want to try to feed herself with a spoon, try to make it as easy as possible for her to succeed. The soupiness of jarred fruits and vegetables, for instance, make it more likely that they will run off the spoon and on to your baby's chin, chest, lap, or high chair than reach her mouth. (To make jarred food easier to keep on the spoon until your baby can get it to her mouth, mix a little baby cereal in with it.) Your baby will have much better luck if you offer her "sticky" foods such as oatmeal, mashed banana, mashed potatoes, and thicker homemade fruit or vegetable purées.

In addition to providing a special chair and her very own spoon, you might want to consider giving your infant her very own cup. Choose a plastic "sipper" cup, ideally with two handles, that has a weighted bottom and a secure lid on top. These last two features will make the cup "spillproof" (although your baby will probably find a way to spill almost any allegedly spillproof cup). Sipper cups do provide a valuable transition between the breast or bottle and a regular cup. Most allow your baby to get the water, juice, or other liquid out of the cup and into her mouth through either sucking or drinking. (Your baby's talent at sucking may also make it easy to cultivate the skill of drinking with a straw at this early age.)

In introducing your baby to the art of drinking from a cup, start with very small amounts of water or diluted juice. Then, once you're sure she can handle drinking from a cup, you can fill the cup up more and more in the weeks to come. Let your baby control her drinking as much as she wants. If she shows no interest in or protests against drinking from a cup, then put it away and try again in 2 or 3 weeks. But if she does want to hold her cup, go ahead and let her.

Q-Tip

You might want to try introducing a sipper cup at bathtime. That way you won't have to worry about spills while she's getting used to drinking from it. At the table, try to indulge your baby's spills and messes without blaming her or groaning. It takes a while to master the skill of drinking from a cup, so she'll need all the patience and support you can muster.

You should sterilize the sipper top of your baby's training cup every day. A dishwasher generally uses hot enough water to sterilize the top. But if you don't have a dishwasher, be sure to allow the top to drip dry in a rack rather than rubbing it dry with a dishtowel. (Kitchen towels are like beach blankets for bacteria.)

Mess Hall

Remember, for your baby, feeding (especially during the first few months) is not merely a matter of absorbing nutrition—it's fun time. Expect your baby to make a mess by playing with his food, and you won't be disappointed. Food is for eating, yes. But food is also for smearing, painting, slapping, spilling, and generally wallowing in.

Try not to get too upset, no matter how messy things get. Just keep telling yourself that everything, your baby included, will wash off.

The more you allow your baby to take part in feeding himself, the messier things will get. But the clean-up will be well worth it because your baby will learn more quickly how to feed himself.

To cut down on some of the clean-up, you'll need a bib for your baby. Plastic bibs are easy to clean, but if your baby is still eating drippy, puréed baby foods, they do little more than protect his shirt by shifting the spills to his pants. Cloth bibs absorb more food, but they need constant laundering. Plastic bibs with a pocket at the bottom are sometimes too bulky, but they will protect your baby's shirt while catching most spills before they reach his pants. If your baby rebels against wearing a bib (as many infants do) and you want to avoid a prolonged battle, forget the bib and take his shirt off before feeding him. Just make sure the kitchen (or dining room) is warm enough for him.

Expanding the Menu

By 6 or 7 months, your child should have sampled two or three dozen different foods: a few cereals, bread and pasta, and at least a dozen different fruits and vegetables. In the months to come, you should continue to make an effort to expand your baby's culinary repertoire. Continue to add variety in fruits and vegetables. During the seventh or eighth month, you can begin adding more sources of protein: cooked tofu, legumes, and meats.

When introducing meats into your baby's diet, start with beef or poultry. If they cause no adverse reactions, then you can try adding some fish. You can buy jars of puréed meat, stews, or casseroles, or you can make your own almost as easily. Just add a little water before you purée the meat, and you should come up with the right consistency.

If you want your baby to be a vegetarian, she can get the protein and calcium she needs from formula as well as a variety of beans, peas, and green, leafy vegetables. If, however, you are raising your baby as a vegan (eschewing all animal products), you may need to take extra care to ensure your

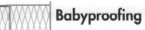
Babyproofing

If you make your own baby food, always cook it thoroughly, especially meat, poultry, and fish. Never feed raw or even soft-cooked eggs to your baby. (Indeed, most pediatricians would advise you to hold off on eggs altogether until after your baby's first birthday.)

child's normal growth and development. To provide nutritional balance, continue to breast-feed your baby throughout the first year, if at all possible. When introducing solid foods, serve whole-grain cereals, breads, and pasta. Make sure she also eats plenty of high-protein foods (tofu, brown rice, beans, and peas) and calcium-rich foods (broccoli and green, leafy vegetables). Finally, ask your pediatrician whether your baby might need a calcium supplement and/or a vitamin-and-mineral supplement that supplies iron, vitamins D and B_{12}, and folic acid.

Whether feeding vegans, vegetarians, or meat eaters, try to provide nutritional balance as your child eats more and more solids and less and less breast milk or formula (though your baby will still need about 24 ounces of breast milk or formula every day). You can't go wrong if you offer your baby essentially the same balanced meals that (ideally) the rest of the family eats. But you'll need to mash, purée, or strain the food to a thick, liquid consistency and serve it in much smaller quantities.

Keep in mind that a balanced diet does not mean that your baby always needs to eat something from each of the major food groups every day. Try to take a more long-term approach to balancing your baby's diet, by watching what she eats over the course of a week or two. If your baby eats nothing but chicken for 2 days, for example, she will—with your guidance—balance it out with lots of carbohydrates and fruits and vegetables for the next few days.

As for consistency, your baby's food should remain smooth and almost liquid until the sixth or seventh month. But once your baby has started to chew her food, regardless of whether she has any teeth yet, you will no longer need to purée everything she eats. Your baby may still enjoy certain puréed foods, but you won't need to grind up her food as rigorously. You can start to add small chunks of vegetables, meat, or fruit to her diet.

Fun Finger Foods

As you well know by now, everything is a finger food for your baby. No matter how earnestly he tries to use a spoon, sooner or later he abandons it for the much more successful use of his fingers. From the soupiest of puréed vegetables to the stickiest oatmeal, every food seems perfect for picking up (or dipping) with his hands.

You can begin offering "real" finger foods almost as soon as you begin to feed your baby solid foods. Until he can chew, however, he can only suck on most finger foods: a slice of apple or a bagel. Although he cannot eat these foods yet, your baby may still enjoy discovering their different flavors. You can also offer your baby a few finger foods that he can eat: bite-size dry cereals, zwieback, and toast will all "melt" in your child's mouth through the action of his saliva.

By 6 or 7 months, your baby will be ready for more finger foods that he can chew (or gum, as the case may be). Finger foods offer a terrific opportunity to introduce greater variety into your baby's diet. You can introduce these foods:

◆ Cooked, grated vegetables

◆ Cooked, sliced vegetables (carrots, beans)

◆ Chunky mashed potatoes

◆ Sliced banana or very small pieces of fruit (even a grape is too big)

◆ Cubes or triangles of bread, plain or smeared with cream cheese or margarine

◆ Dry, relatively unsweetened cereals

◆ Macaroni or other pasta

◆ Rice

◆ Rice cakes

◆ Low-salt or no-salt pretzels

◆ Small cubes of well-cooked meat or poultry

Eating with his fingers is fun, fast, and efficient for your baby. It allows him not only to experience the tastes of a wide variety of foods, but also to feel their texture with his hands as well as with his mouth and tongue. Eating finger foods also helps to exercise your baby's rapidly improving hand-eye coordination. Best of all, finger foods not only encourage your baby to learn to feed himself, but also keep his hands busy enough to allow you to shovel in the food he needs.

Baby Folklore

When are the best and worst times to wean your baby? According to Christian folklore, Good Friday is the best day of the year (though Ash Wednesday, the beginning of Lent, seems more appropriate). May is considered a very unlucky month for weaning. Folklore also advises against weaning your baby under a waning moon, for your child's health will then decline until the moon begins to wax again.

Babyproofing

Certain finger foods present a serious choking hazard: store popcorn, nuts, hard candies, and other dangerous finger foods out of your baby's reach. Until your baby can chew, stay nearby when he has a hard finger food (a bagel, for instance). If he breaks off a piece, quickly sweep it out with your finger so that your baby won't choke on it.

Weaning Isn't Everything

Now that your baby is practiced at eating solid foods, you may be thinking of weaning her from the breast or bottle. When's the best time to wean your baby? If you're breast-feeding, then it may depend more on your needs than on your baby's. If you have to return to work, for example, you may wean your baby from the breast to a bottle or perhaps cut down to a single nighttime nursing at 3 months or even earlier. Or you may decide to wean your baby when she begins showing more and more interest in eating solid foods.

If you've never really enjoyed breast-feeding (or if the thrill is gone), you may want to begin weaning her sooner rather than later. But on the other hand, if you enjoy breast-feeding and have no pressing reason to give it up, there's no need to wean your baby completely during the first or even the second year. At this point, your child will suck only for comfort rather than for nourishment. But what's wrong with that?

Similarly, if you bottle-feed your baby, you may decide to continue letting your baby suck from a bottle for comfort until she is a toddler or even older. Your dentist may argue that the sugar in formula will lead to tooth decay (especially when given before bed, but after brushing). Your orthodontist would also discourage prolonged use of a bottle. Nonetheless, your baby may find the bottle an irreplaceable source of comfort for many months to come.

If you leave it up to your child, she'll probably be content to drink from the breast or bottle forever. You'll have to draw the line somewhere. But take your time. There's no need to rush into anything—or out of anything either.

Ready or Not?

Just because your baby has started to eat some solid food doesn't necessarily mean that he's ready for weaning. (Of course, whether you're ready or not is an entirely different question.) Your baby sucks on a bottle or breast to satisfy both nutritional and emotional needs. Although solid food can, in time, replace most of the nutritional needs that until recently were met entirely through the breast or bottle, it cannot make those emotional needs go away.

Don't withhold the breast or bottle in an attempt to force your child to eat more "real" foods. Let him dictate the pace by the interest he shows in eating solids.

Just because your baby has begun teething doesn't mean it's time to wean him either. If you breast-feed your baby, it may take a little while before you get used to his having teeth, but you'll both get the hang of it. Just remember that when your baby bites you (as he inevitably will), he doesn't mean to hurt you. He may have bitten you by accident, or he may have meant it playfully. Either way, though, it will hurt. When your baby does bite you, just say "No!" firmly and take the nipple from your baby's mouth. Then give it back only if he stops biting. He'll quickly get the message.

> **Q-Tip**
>
> Don't be surprised if, after having gotten into the habit of eating solids, your baby suddenly wants only breast milk or formula and shuns solid food for several days at a time. Your baby may revert to exclusive breast-feeding or bottle-feeding for either physical or emotional reasons. He may return to old habits when feeling sick or especially tired. He may also resume old ways of feeding (and comforting) during times of rapid change. When starting day care, for example, or moving into a new house (or just a new room), or beginning to crawl or stand, he may need the extra security that sucking offers.

A Weaning Attitude

Whenever you decide to wean your baby from the breast or bottle, whether at 3 months, 6 months, 9 months, or 18 months, do it gently and gradually. If you suddenly and arbitrarily refuse to let your baby suck from your breast, she will feel rejected. "Cold turkey" weaning will cause discomfort and even pain for you, too. Because your breasts will continue to produce milk at the same rate for several days, they will become painfully overfull if you try to go from three to six feedings a day straight down to zero.

Take it slow and easy. Most babies wean themselves at least partially as they eat more and more food. When your baby begins to eat three meals a day (around 6 or 7 months), the fun and fascination of eating foods will probably cause her to abandon at least one of her mealtime breast or bottle feedings—or perhaps simply suck (without really feeding) for a few minutes after a solid meal. She will want to eat more and suck less. Within a few months of beginning solids, your baby may be down to just two or three bottles or breast-feedings a day:

> **Baby Doctor**
>
> If you breast-feed your baby, the gradual, one-meal-at-a-time reduction of her sucking will reduce the supply of milk produced in your body without causing as much discomfort. But be sure to wait until your breasts have adjusted to the elimination of one feeding before you try to cut out a second one.

- ◆ At bedtime
- ◆ At naptime(s)
- ◆ In the morning (perhaps)

If you want to wean your baby, at least partially, and she doesn't start to give up meal-time breast or bottle feedings on her own, you may have to give her a little nudge.

- ◆ Do it gradually, one meal at a time.
- ◆ First, eliminate the premeal nursing.
- ◆ Offer up a solid meal and be sure to offer her a cup (not a bottle, unless you intend to wean her from the breast to the bottle) of juice or water with the meal. Offer your breast (or a bottle) only after the meal.
- ◆ Within a week or two, she will probably eat more solids and no longer need any breast milk or formula after the meal.

After you've replaced all daytime breast or bottle feedings with meals in this gradual, systematic way, your baby will probably nurse or take a bottle only in the morning (when she's so hungry that a solid meal might not fill her up) and before bed (when she probably wants the security more than the nutrition). Many babies give up their single nighttime feeding somewhat willingly at around a year. But you don't need to rush it if you want to continue with this nursing.

When you do want to wean your baby completely, you can try either of two methods. You may find it easiest to use the switch method, replacing the final nursing of the evening with a final bottle feeding. (Of course, this method means you'll later need to wean her from the bottle, using the cold turkey method.) To wean from the breast to a bottle, simply substitute the bottle for the breast.

If you still breast-feed your baby more than once a day, then eliminate just one nursing session at a time. Offer the bottle instead of the breast at your baby's hungriest feeding. He's most likely to accept the substitute then, and eliminating this feeding will prompt the greatest reduction in your breast milk production.

Q-Tip _____

Because your baby no doubt associates you with breast-feeding, especially at certain times of the day, it will help to have your partner or another person give your baby the bottle for the first week or two, until she is weaned. If no one can help you, try facing your baby away from you while giving the bottle. That way, she won't have to stare at the now-taboo breast while getting used to the bottle.

If you don't want to wean your baby from the breast to the bottle, or if you've decided to wean her from the bottle, try the cold turkey method. Give your baby a big meal an hour or so before bedtime and then, if she's still hungry, a snack right before bed. Have a sipper cup of water ready next to your baby's crib. Then, if you haven't yet done so, establish a regular bedtime routine that will serve as an affectionate, comforting replacement for the routine of the breast or bottle. (See Chapter 17.)

Q-Tip

You will have an easier time weaning your baby from the bottle if, from the very beginning, you treat the bottle as if it were a breast. Make the bottle a "part of you" so that your baby associates it solely with being fed formula while in your arms. Do not let your baby carry the bottle around with her. As your baby becomes more active toward the end of the first year, she will probably want to crawl or walk more than she wants to eat—and this desire can motivate her to wean herself.

Try to show your baby a little extra love, affection, and understanding during this period. She needs to know that you still care.

The Least You Need to Know

◆ Let your baby practice feeding himself as early as 6 months or even younger. Giving him his own spoon, his own cup, and plenty of finger foods will help him enjoy mealtimes and grow more independent.

◆ An eating baby is a messy baby, especially if he helps to feed himself. Pay no attention to his barbaric table manners for now.

◆ As meals of solid foods begin replacing breast or bottle feedings, aim to provide a balanced diet.

◆ Gradually wean your baby whenever you are ready. The timetable depends more on your needs than on any other factor.

Chapter

17

To Sleep, Perchance to Dream

In This Chapter

- ◆ Creating bedtime rituals and a cozy sleep space
- ◆ Getting your baby to go to sleep (by himself, if possible)
- ◆ The pros and cons of the family bed
- ◆ Dealing with naps and midnight awakenings

As a newborn and early infant, your child established a sleep pattern determined partly by her sleep needs and partly by hunger. Your baby may have been as regular as clockwork or as unpredictable as the weather. But after 6 months without a single good night's sleep, you're probably more than ready for your baby to begin sleeping more consistently and predictably.

If Your Baby Sleeps so Much, How Come You're So Tired?

How much sleep does your baby need? The amount of sleep a baby gets varies greatly with the individual (see the following table). Age plays a factor; your baby will probably need 2 to 3 hours less sleep at the end of her first year than she did at the beginning. But your child's individual nature plays much more of a role in determining how much she will sleep.

In looking at the following table, keep in mind that the average accounts for individuals at both extremes. The range is so wide that your baby may sleep much more or much less than the average.

How Much Does Your Baby Sleep?

Age	Average	Range
0–1 months	16 ½ hours	10–22 hours
1–4 months	15 ½ hours	10–20 hours
5–8 months	14 ½ hours	9–20 hours
9–12 months	13 ½ hours	9–18 hours

Some blissful babies start out sleeping more than 20 hours a day and continue sleeping nearly that much throughout the first year. On the other hand, very active babies may, after their first few days, sleep less than 12 hours a day. Unfortunately for their exhausted parents, the sleep needs of these infants are not likely to increase as they grow older. Your baby will let you know through her sleeping patterns just how much sleep she needs. As long as she can function throughout much of the day without fatigue, general misery, and crankiness, she's getting enough sleep—no matter how little that is.

Because your baby probably sleeps somewhere around half the day, you may wonder why you feel so tired all the time. The reason is that babies don't get their sleep all at once, as most adults do. If your baby slept 13 hours in a row, you'd be the most rested new parent in the world. Unfortunately, they don't.

Even at 6 months, most infants sleep only 6 to 8 hours at a stretch. But after half-waking at 4:00 or 5:00 A.M., your child can drift back to sleep fairly easily after some comforting or feeding.

Just because she can sleep that long, however, doesn't mean that she will. Your baby's schedule may seem entirely random to you, with no set patterns to sleeping, waking, or eating. If so, don't despair. You can take steps to make her schedule more predictable.

Good Night, Moon: Bedtime Rituals and Routines

Most babies like routines. It provides them with a sense of security. By establishing dependable bedtime routines for your baby, you can therefore make the evening proceed much more smoothly. By around the sixth or seventh month, every baby should have a sleep routine in place. You can start establishing a bedtime routine much earlier, but if you haven't done so yet, start one now.

A helpful bedtime routine begins with a set, although not necessarily rigid, bedtime. Certainly, your baby is somewhat flexible. You've no doubt seen him fall asleep almost anywhere when he gets tired. But the more you disrupt your baby's bedtime, the more you will disrupt his entire sleep schedule.

If you keep your baby up to go to a party, for instance, he may fall asleep on the way home (or at the party itself). But if he later wakes up when you try to transfer him to the crib, don't be surprised if he acts as though he had just taken a nap instead of beginning the night's sleep. It may be hours before he is ready to go to sleep again. This situation doesn't necessarily create a problem, as long as you remain as flexible as your baby and you enjoy having him stay up late with you. But if you want and need to establish a regular sleep schedule, you'll need to stick pretty close to a set timetable.

Calming Influences

The other elements of your bedtime routine should all aim toward establishing a calm, quiet, and happy atmosphere. Your bedtime routine can include any of the following:

- Taking a long walk with your baby after dinner (yours or hers). The rhythmic motion of riding in a stroller can soothe your baby and approaching darkness can draw a curtain on the day.

- Taking a warm bath an hour or so before bedtime. A bath will not only get your baby clean, but will probably relax her as well.

- Changing into nightclothes. Having certain clothes that your baby wears only at bedtime can help her get in the right mood.

- Reading books or nursery rhymes. Reading simple storybooks or reciting nursery rhymes allows you to soothe your baby with the calm of your own voice.

- Rocking in a rocking chair; walking with a slow, swaying motion; or holding your baby and doing gentle, rhythmic knee bends. The rhythmic swaying of these actions can have an almost hypnotic effect on your baby. (That's why so many babies fall asleep in a car seat or an automatic baby swing.)

- Snacking before bed. If your baby eats solid food, a snack—especially one that includes formula, milk, or other protein—will help fill your baby's stomach.

◆ Nursing or bottle-feeding before bed. A full stomach can often bring on a case of drowsiness. (Just think how you feel after Thanksgiving dinner.)

◆ Making music. Your own singing or a tape or CD of lullabies (or folk rock or country songs) can carry your baby off to dreamland. Don't be shy about singing to your baby. Even if you're tone-deaf, she'll love to hear you singing to her.

◆ Using comfort items or transitional objects. A soft blanket, a favorite stuffed animal, or anything that your baby finds calming should stay in the crib with her.

◆ Giving a massage. A brief and gentle in-bed massage or some loving caresses can relax your baby's body and mind.

◆ Sucking. Giving your baby a pacifier or directing her to her thumb will allow her to soothe herself through sucking.

◆ Saying good night. Gentle parting words offered with hugs and kisses can end your quiet time together on a calming note. You might want to encourage your baby to "say good night" (with a hug, a wave, and/or a kiss) to you, too. She can also say good night to a few stuffed animals, dolls, and other objects (à la *Good Night, Moon*).

Q-Tip

During most of the first year, you may find a pacifier more trouble than it's worth. If it falls out of her mouth while she's going to sleep or later, in the middle of the night, she probably won't be able to find it herself. Who do you think she'll call for help?

It may help to scatter half a dozen pacifiers all over her crib. If she rolls over on top of one, it's not likely to disturb her sleep. But if she loses the one in her mouth, she may be able to find another without your help.

Pick a few of these suggestions (or add a few of your own) and build a bedtime routine around them. Keep it simple and soothing. Remember, you'll be doing this every night for months—or even years—to come.

Wait! I'm Not Finished Yet!

If your child still falls asleep during nursing or bottle-feeding, the period from 6 to 9 months, when your baby will feed less and less from the breast or bottle, may provide a good opportunity to break the habit of nursing your baby to sleep.

Even if your baby still falls asleep while feeding, though, that does not mean that she doesn't need a bedtime ritual. Work out a routine you both enjoy and then go through all the elements before you begin feeding your baby. In a few months, when your baby's ever-increasing alertness prevents her from falling asleep in your arms, the elements of her bedtime routine will already be in place.

Try to keep the bedtime ritual relatively simple. Remember that you're creating a routine: something you'll do pretty much the same way every night for months or even years to come. Choose activities (with the exception of nursing) that either you or your partner can do with your child. If you keep it simple enough, you might even be able to get a friend, relative, or sitter to substitute for you every once in a while. (Don't expect your baby to welcome this change as eagerly as you do.)

> **Q-Tip**
>
> Turn down the bedding in the crib before beginning your bedtime ritual. Whether your baby falls asleep while feeding or during some earlier stage of the routine, you'll find it much easier to slip her into the crib if you don't need to hold her with one hand and fumble for the sheets with the other.

Most of the bedtime routine—certainly the last half-hour or so—should take place in your baby's bedroom (or, if you share space, in your bedroom). That way, you can establish an atmosphere of calm in the place where your baby sleeps and also make it easier to move her into her crib without creating much of a disturbance. The bedtime routine should end with you laying your baby gently in her crib, ideally while she's still awake. If you can manage to put your baby down while she's drowsy but not quite asleep yet, she will gain valuable practice in falling asleep on her own.

The Right Atmosphere

All your efforts to soothe your baby through a calming bedtime ritual will be sabotaged if your baby's corner or bedroom and crib are not conducive to sleep. From about 3 months on, your baby will probably sleep better in a room of his own. What will disturb his sleep is not the sounds that you make that accidentally wake him up, but rather the sounds that he makes that wake you up. Every time your baby shifts his body in the crib, you may jump. With every cough, whimper, or sigh, you may want to run over to the crib to make sure he's all right. This quick response is what will no doubt wake him.

If you plan on eventually moving your baby into his own room, do it earlier rather than later. Your baby will more easily adapt to the change now, when his memory is short, than he will later, when he will regard the move as abandonment.

Q-Tip

If your baby's bedroom is far from your own (or from other rooms where you spend time after he falls asleep), you'll find it worthwhile to invest in a baby monitor. If he does start to cry, and especially if he cries hard, you'll want to know it.

If space considerations make a room of your baby's own impossible, then at least consider dividing the room in some way. Sturdy full-size bookcases, a screen, or a drape can give you a sense of privacy while you share the same room. Or you might use a similar divider to partition off space in another room. For example, if you enjoy spending most of your time with your partner in your bedroom at night, whether you're reading, watching TV, or making love, you might want to put the crib in the living room rather than in the bedroom.

Make sure the room isn't too hot or too cold. A surrounding temperature in the low to mid-70s is comfy for your baby. But you don't need to heat the entire room (or house) to that temperature. Each blanket and quilt on your baby raises the surrounding temperature by about 2° or 3°.

Silent Night?

For most babies, the right atmosphere for sleep requires relative (but not necessarily complete) darkness. Window blinds or shades will help keep out moonlight, streetlights, and the morning sun. If your child dislikes complete darkness, a night light will help. (It can also help you avoid bumping into the furniture and waking your baby when you check on him in the night.)

Babyproofing

Don't forget that as soon as your baby can sit up, you'll need to adjust the level of his crib mattress, lowering it to a level where the guard rail is as high as his shoulders when he is standing. When your baby first uses his crib posts to pull himself up to standing, you'll want to know that the railing is high enough to prevent him from spilling out of the crib.

Your baby does not need total silence in order to sleep. Indeed, you're doing him a disservice if you attempt to muffle all noises. Such extreme measures condition your baby to wake at the least disturbance. Certainly, if your baby wakes at most sounds, then it makes sense to try to quiet things down a bit. But don't assume your baby needs complete quiet to sleep before seeing any evidence of it.

In fact, a steady, predictable hum of background noise, such as a dishwasher, a distant TV, a fan, an air conditioner, a white-noise machine, or a CD of music and/or intrauterine sounds, may help your child sleep more restfully than complete silence will. (Perhaps such sounds remind your baby of the sounds he heard from inside your belly before he was born.)

The Family Bed: Is It for You?

The family bed, where everyone sleeps not only in the same room but in the same bed, has worked for generations of babies in other cultures. Although this practice is less common here, some parents find it very practical. If your baby still wakes several times a night for food or comfort, for example, you may find it easier to keep her in the same bed with you. For this reason, a family bed makes the most sense when your baby is very young and still feeding around the clock.

Of course, your baby may still wake you up if she's in bed with you, but you won't need to wake up as fully as you would if you had to go to her room and get her. And she may just wake, snuggle up closer to you, and fall asleep again on her own. A family bed can in this way offer your baby a special degree of warmth and security.

Yet family beds have drawbacks, too. The lack of privacy means that you and your partner will have to find a separate place to do your own cuddling. The lack of privacy may also make you feel hemmed in: even when you're both sleeping, you won't have any refuge from your baby.

A family bed probably has a psychological impact on your baby, too. Unfortunately, there's no consensus about what that impact is. Some say the family bed causes more sleep problems; others say it reduces them. Some say that because, even when asleep, the baby is never alone, a family bed may increase separation anxiety. Others insist that the special sense of warmth and security created by the family bed decreases separation anxiety.

Some parents worry about the potential hazards of the family bed. What if you roll over on top of your baby? Well, unless you're drunk or an extremely heavy sleeper, you probably won't. A lingering consciousness will prevent you from crushing or smothering your child. But for argument's sake, suppose you do roll over on top of your baby. One of you will surely notice. If it's you, you'll wake up and move over; if it's your baby, she'll start screaming, and then you'll wake up and move over.

Babyproofing

Avoid very soft mattresses and waterbeds, which can result in accidental smothering. In addition, the waves created by your movement in a waterbed may throw your baby off the bed.

Although the risk of accidentally smothering your baby is slight, it can—and very rarely does—happen. (Many more babies die of SIDS in their own cribs than die of suffocation in their parents' bed.) Nonetheless you should take this possibility, however slight, into account when deciding whether to invite your baby into your bed.

The final drawback of the family bed is the ever-looming question: how long will this go on? Once you've established a family bed, it will be very hard to get your baby to agree to sleep anywhere else. The older she gets, the more entrenched this habit will become. Why would she agree to sleep in her own cold, lonely crib or bed when she can enjoy the cozy closeness of sleeping next to you?

Despite the drawbacks, some parents feel perfectly comfortable with the advantages of a family bed. But before you try it yourself, think about it carefully and discuss it fully with your partner. Keep in mind that it's a virtually irreversible decision. So don't simply give in to your desperation for uninterrupted sleep by taking your baby into bed with you on a regular basis.

To Bed, To Bed, You Sleepyhead

Sharing in a bedtime ritual is the fun part of getting your baby to sleep. Putting him down and getting him to go to sleep is the hard part. After rocking, cuddling, nursing, feeding, reading, singing, telling stories, sitting together, leaving, punishing, and every other trick in the book, you may understandably throw up your arms in surrender. For many parents, the only solution seems to involve the torture, as bad or worse for parents than for the babies, of letting the baby cry himself to sleep.

Letting your baby cry himself to sleep makes no sense in the early months of his life. When a young baby cries, he needs something (see Chapter 6). By 6 months, however, your baby cries not only when he needs you, but when he wants you as well. Although it's nice to fulfill your baby's desires whenever you can, you need not gratify his wants as much as you need to satisfy his needs.

Baby Talk

"There never was a child so lovely but his mother was glad to get him asleep."

—Ralph Waldo Emerson

Your baby wants you to stay with him until he's asleep. He wants you to rock him, to sing to him, to suckle and soothe him. But no matter how entrenched these habits have become, he does not need them in order to get to sleep. Your baby does need to learn how to go to sleep by himself, however. The sooner he learns, the easier it will be for him. The longer you allow him to fall asleep in your arms, the harder it will be to break this habit.

You may think it selfish to put your needs for sleep and serenity above your child's. But it's also selfish to prolong your baby's exclusive dependence on you and to spare yourself from enduring your baby's cries as he learns how to go to sleep without you.

Ultimately, getting your baby to sleep on his own serves not only your own selfish interests, but your baby's well-being as well.

If you haven't yet done so, start putting your baby in his crib before he falls asleep. To get started, you need to time it just right. If your baby's wide awake, he will pop right up and start screaming his head off. On the other hand, if you wait too long, your baby will fall asleep before you get him in the crib, and you will have missed your opportunity. So try to put your baby down when he's drowsy but still awake. Oh, your baby won't like it at first. He'll probably react with mournful and sometimes desperate crying. How you respond to those cries will make all the difference.

Abandon Ship

One response, the Spock method, involves sweating out the crying. Steel yourself, go through your bedtime routine, and then after saying good night, don't go back in, no matter how much your baby cries. Your baby's cries may become more and more desperate as time drags on, but if you can bear it, she will eventually wear herself out or give up and fall asleep.

A warning is in order, however: on the first night, the crying is likely to last at least 20 to 30 minutes and perhaps more than an hour. (You may find it necessary to take refuge from your baby's cries by using a white-noise machine of your own: ear plugs, stereo headphones, or a TV or radio program.)

This method may seem unbearably cruel to you. When parents remain resolute, however, this strategy usually works. The amount of crying gradually subsides over the course of several nights until it's down to 5 minutes or less. Believe it or not, in less than a week, your baby will learn how to go to sleep on her own.

Baby Doctor

If your baby won't calm down no matter what, or if the cries continue for hours and don't seem any shorter the next night, you might want to check with your baby's doctor. If your baby has an ear infection or other illness, now might not be the best time to teach her to sleep on her own.

Checking In

An increasingly popular alternative involves periodically checking in to let your child know you're still there and to make sure he's okay. After saying good night and leaving the room, stay away for a set amount of time—say, 5 minutes to start. After the agreed-upon time has passed, you or your partner should go in, check on your baby, and try to soothe him without picking him up. Instead, offer kind, soft words and perhaps a pat on the back.

Don't stay for more than a minute or two. Then whisper good night and head out of the room again. Continue to check on him every 5 minutes, but never for more than a minute or so, until he stops crying and falls asleep. On the second night, hold out a little longer, maybe 10 minutes this time. Over the next week or two, gradually increase the amount of time spent away from your baby's cribside before you return.

With enough parental resolve, this method also seems to work most of the time. The only problem is that it may be worse torture for your child to see you every 5 minutes, only to have you refuse to pick him up, than to not see you at all. Your baby may cry louder and harder each time you leave. Eventually, however, the crying will stop.

Q-Tip _____

If your baby has almost always been nursed to sleep, then Daddy should put him to bed when you decide to try to get him to sleep on his own. Your baby will want to suckle if he even catches a glimpse of Mommy. To avoid upsetting the baby further, Daddy needs to go through the bedtime routine and do all the checking in, at least for the first week or so.

Fade to Black

If you want to ease your baby into sleeping on her own, turn the lights out after her bedtime ritual, put her in her crib, and then sit with her for 5 or 10 minutes. You may want to rock in a chair where your baby can see you, or you may choose to sit right next to her crib and stroke her back for a few minutes. When she seems groggy but not quite unconscious, get up matter-of-factly, whisper good night, and leave. If your baby immediately pops up and starts crying, however, you'll still need to resort to one of the methods described previously: total withdrawal or periodic check-ins.

Still too cruel for you? Well, don't do it unless you're convinced it's the best thing for your baby (and you). If you are unable to maintain your resolve, you will send mixed signals to your baby. If you break down and pick her up, she may end up "learning" that if she cries long enough or hard enough, she will ultimately get what she wants.

A Refresher Course: Nap Time

Your baby doesn't get all the sleep he needs at night. To get the other 2 to 6 hours of necessary rest, most 6-month-olds still take two to three naps a day. The lengths vary from 1 to 3 or even 4 hours. Toward the end of the first year, though, your baby is likely to cut down to just one or two naps a day.

If your child resists taking a nap no matter how tired he seems, then follow a routine similar to your bedtime ritual. First, set the mood by drawing the blinds and/or shutting the curtains to darken the room. Make sure that your baby has a full stomach and a clean diaper. Then play, sing, or read quietly to relax your baby. When you're done with the ritual, leave the room. If you have decided to let your baby cry himself to sleep, use the same method you've chosen for nighttime slumber, but don't let it go on as long. You've got all day, so you can always try again later when he seems more tired.

Q-Tip

Feel free to let your baby nap regularly in a stroller or a car seat, as long as it's not the only place he can fall asleep. You may find it easiest, especially if your baby tends to resist naptime, to sandwich a nap into long drives or extended walks with a stroller.

Keep in mind that your baby needs the sleep he gets during his naps. Too much napping can sometimes interfere with nighttime sleep, but don't deny your child a nap when he's tired during the day. If your strategy is intended to make bedtime easier and help your baby sleep soundly through the night, it may backfire. An overtired baby tends to sleep much more restlessly than a well-rested one. In addition, overtiredness tends to cause crankiness and may lead to more accidents. If you deny your baby the daytime sleep he needs, he may conk out at bedtime, but he's almost sure to rise sooner and more often during the middle of the night. Instead, try limiting the time he naps to 3 or 4 hours (unless, of course, he's sick). It may seem like a sin to wake a sleeping baby, but you're going to need your sleep, too.

It's Crying Time Again: Midnight Wake-Up Calls

Every baby (and every adult) wakes up during the night. REM (rapid eye movement) sleep, which involves lots of dreams and movement, often ends with a brief awakening. Waking, however, isn't the problem. It's the inability to fall back asleep that causes all the trouble. Your baby needs to learn, as all adults have, to fall back asleep on her own when she wakes briefly in the night.

Baby Doctor

Indulge premature or very small babies with nighttime feedings a little longer. They may need nighttime feedings for several months more than full-term or larger babies.

To learn how to do it, your baby needs you to give her a chance. Try to stop yourself from jumping up at the slightest whimper or sound. Instead, go to your baby only when she cries loudly and steadily. When you make a midnight visit, don't try to entertain your baby. Just be there and try to calm her down. If she's hungry, by all means, feed her. But try to maintain conditions conducive to sleeping: relative quiet (whispers and soft lullabies), darkness (don't turn on the lights), and calm (the middle of the night is for sleeping, not playing).

No More Midnight Snacks

By 6 months, your baby should no longer need the breast or bottle in the middle of the night—at least, not because he's hungry. If your baby still wakes to eat, it's more a matter of habit than of hunger. He's used to having midnight snacks, so he wakes up for them, regardless of whether he's hungry.

If you want to put an end to your baby's waking you up to order a midnight snack, try one or more of the following strategies:

◆ **Fill that tummy.** Nurse your baby longer (or give him more formula) right before bed, or offer him a before-bed snack of cereal or toast. If your baby falls asleep before "finishing" the bottle or before nursing for very long, gently wake him and encourage him to eat more.

◆ **Eat hearty.** Encourage your baby to eat more during daytime meals: more solid foods, more breast milk, and/or more formula. Your baby may be making up for too little food during the day by feeding at night. Don't add more feedings because that may make your baby more likely to want frequent feedings at night, too. Instead, try to feed him more at each established meal.

◆ **The kitchen is closing.** Wake your baby for a feeding at your convenience: right before you go to bed. Although this strategy doesn't exactly take care of the problem, it makes nighttime feeding less likely to disturb your sleep.

◆ **Going, going, gone.** Gradually cut back on the amount you feed your baby when he wakes you in the middle of the night. Cut back on the amount of time you spend nursing or the amount of formula you prepare. Then stop midnight feedings altogether and use other methods to soothe your baby.

◆ **Don't be so sensitive.** Wait until whimpers become cries before going to your baby in the middle of the night. When you do go to him, try something else before resorting to feeding (or even picking him up). For example, try lullabies or gentle caresses on his back or hair. If that doesn't work, pick him up, but still try to avoid feeding him. Feed your baby only as a last resort. Even if you do end up feeding him, your other attempts at intervention will have stalled enough to stretch the time between feedings. This stretch may give you an extra half-hour or so before his call the next night.

Q-Tip

If you still breast-feed your baby, designate your partner as the first-response team for middle-of-the-night calls. When your baby catches sight of you in the middle of the night, he sees a neon sign emblazoned across your chest: "All You Can Eat!" You'll need to replace this with a new sign: "Under New Management!"

If you can eliminate (or come close to eliminating) midnight feedings, you can then tackle the problem of midnight awakenings. Feeding, rocking, rubbing, patting, singing, and/or shoving and reshoving a pacifier in your baby's mouth all prolong his dependence on you to get him back to sleep. Gradually stop helping him get back to sleep, just as you stopped helping him get to sleep in the first place.

Anticipated Awakenings

When trying to eliminate midnight awakenings, you do have an alternative to letting your baby cry it out. Anticipate her awakenings and strike first. Your baby probably wakes at approximately the same time(s) every night. If you know when, then set your alarm and wake her up a half-hour before she would normally wake you up. When you wake her, do whatever you normally do to get her to go back to sleep: nurse, rock, sing, whatever.

Your baby may soon begin to rely on you to anticipate her nighttime needs. So after preempting her awakenings for a few nights, start to push back the time you wake your baby by another half-hour or so every couple days. This method does take a while (2 or 3 weeks) to implement. In the meantime, you'll need to wake at some odd hours (as if you haven't been doing that since your baby was born). Yet this program may help you to condition your baby out of midnight wakings in less than a month. After so many months of conditioning, however, you may continue to wake in the middle of the night for some time longer.

The Least You Need to Know

◆ Your baby may sleep more or less than the average baby. What matters is not how much sleep she's getting, but how well she seems to function on that amount of sleep.

◆ A bedtime ritual that establishes a calm, quiet, happy atmosphere will help prepare your baby for sleep.

◆ The family bed—a staple in many cultures—may work for you, too. But it can be a hard habit for a young child to break.

◆ The sooner you get your baby to go to sleep on her own, the easier it will be. Nonetheless, this process inevitably involves some tears.

◆ Your baby still needs from one to three naps a day to get enough sleep.

Chapter **18**

Recording Your Baby's Life

In This Chapter

- ◆ Taking photos of your baby
- ◆ Sharing your baby pictures with others
- ◆ Photo albums, scrapbooks, and baby books
- ◆ Videotaping or digitally recording your baby

Your baby, of course, is the cleverest, the funniest, the most beautiful and most precious baby who ever lived. So naturally, you want to capture—and share—the moments when your baby is at her cleverest, funniest, most beautiful, or most precious.

With your baby amazing you at every turn, however, coming up with something new, delightful, poignant, or astonishing almost every moment she's awake—and sometimes even when she's asleep—you may find it hard to decide when *not* to record her life. Every moment is a photo op; every minute worthy of video recording; every "milestone"—and anything your baby does is a milestone—worth jotting down in a baby book. How could you possibly leave anything out?

Baby Pictures

Whether you're still working with a film camera or have joined the hundreds of millions of people worldwide who have switched to digital photography, you will want to have your camera handy throughout the first year of your baby's life. Photographs will allow you to capture and preserve family memories—not only for you and your partner—but for your baby and your grandchildren and generations to come.

When your baby first arrived on the scene, everything seemed so vivid and new and striking that you no doubt felt you would remember each moment forever, whether or not you had a photographic record. Memory, however, is an uncertain faculty. Your memories, like those of many parents, may begin to blend together and go blurry around the edges—especially if you have a second or third or tenth child.

Baby Talk

"Long ago it must be,
I have a photograph,
Preserve your memories,
They're all that's left you."

—Paul Simon

When memory fades, even just a little, photographs can help spark those memories and make them as vivid as ever. So even if every moment of your baby's life seems unforgettable to you now, you may want to make sure they remain unforgettable in the future by preserving some of them on film or digitally.

Film Forum

Although the number of American households with film cameras is dwindling, many of you no doubt still have—and use—your old-fashioned camera. If so, you are helping to maintain a tradition that has preserved family memories for generations.

Many photographers actually prefer film over digital as a medium. Film may have few advantages over digital cameras, but to its adherents, these advantages are significant:

◆ Film allows more artful contrasts of light and darkness.

◆ Film photography, especially in black-and-white, is an established art form.

◆ Film cameras are significantly less expensive than digital cameras.

◆ Development of film always yields a tangible object (a photograph or a slide).

◆ Tangible photographs are easier for many to organize and arrange in a photo album or scrapbook.

Despite these advantages, most new parents today are turning their backs on film to embrace the new digital technology available to them.

Q-Tip _____

One area in which almost all parents still prefer film to digital photography is the formal studio portrait. No matter how many beautiful candid snapshots you take of your baby, you may decide that you want a studio portrait of your baby dressed to the nines and looking his "very best." If so, you can find family portrait studios in your telephone book's Yellow Pages or in most mall department stores.

The Digital Age

As the price of digital cameras has fallen in recent years, more and more parents (and other amateur photographers) have replaced their old film cameras with digital ones. After all, digital photography has its advantages, too:

◆ Digital photography offers instant gratification, displaying onscreen an instantaneous image of what you have shot.

◆ Digital photography allows you to "edit out" the bad photos as you go rather than paying for them all to be developed and then having to weed out the bad ones.

◆ Digital photography allows easier interface with other media (such as PCs) that permit cropping, editing, retouching, and more.

◆ The ease of media interface facilitates sharing photos with distant family members.

◆ Uploading them to your computer allows you to make professional prints or holiday cards (if you have a photo-quality printer) without having to go outside the house.

If you haven't switched to a digital camera yet, you may want to look into digital the next time your camera breaks down. In fact, soon you may not have a choice. Japanese camera makers Canon and Nikon announced in 2006 that they would no longer develop new models of film cameras—a sign that the shift to digital is becoming permanent.

Since both film and digital cameras have their advantages, however, you may want to own both—a film camera for the artier, more permanent shots and a digital camera for instantly capturing the moment and sharing it with those you love.

Baby Proofing _____

No matter how cute your baby looks in the bath, do not leave her there to run and get the camera. (The same advice applies to the changing table or any potentially dangerous place for your baby.)

Photo Ops

Whether you stick with film photography or make the switch to digital, your baby will present you with plenty of photo opportunities. During the first year alone, you will want to capture these moments:

- The first time she suckles
- Her first nap
- Her first bottle
- Her first diaper change
- Her first smile
- Her first cry
- Her first bath
- Her first laugh
- The first time she wears a new outfit
- The first time she rolls over
- Her first book (reading or eating)
- Her first solid meal
- Her first trip (anywhere)
- Her first tooth
- The first time she sits up
- The first time she crawls
- The first time she stands
- The first time she creeps along the furniture
- Her first steps
- Her first birthday party

That's just the firsts. Your baby will, of course, also provide photo ops with her second smile, her third bath, her fourth meal, and almost every other thing she does. Every moment of your baby's first year could be looked at as a photo opportunity.

Q-Tip _____

We cannot offer you expert advice on how to take professional photographs of your baby, since we are by no means professional photographers. However, we can point you to two very good books that will help you make the most of your baby's photo ops:

The Complete Idiot's Guide to Photography Like a Pro, by Mike Stensvold

The Complete Idiot's Guide to Digital Photography Like a Pro, by Steven Greenberg

Sharing the Moment

Of course, the fact that every moment could be viewed as a photo op—and that you can share them with almost everyone you know in a matter of minutes—is part of the problem that many new parents face. Just a generation ago, sharing baby pictures was a much more private affair. New parents would perhaps make duplicate prints and regularly send a few select photographs to the baby's grandparents, as well as an occasional shot to other family members or friends. The only mass mailing would come near the end of the year, when the parents would carefully choose the cutest picture of their baby for a holiday card.

With digital cameras, however, all that has changed. Digital cameras make it relatively easy to upload every picture taken onto the family computer. Once you've got your baby pictures stored on your computer, it's simple to send them over the Internet to everyone in your e-mail address book.

With more and more families and friends separated by hundreds or even thousands of miles, you—and your extended family—may appreciate this newfound ability. Not only can you share pictures of your baby with those who love him, but you can share these photos just a few minutes after you take them.

It's natural to want to share your baby's most precious moments with each other, with your baby (when he gets older), with your parents, with your siblings, and with one or two hundred of your closest friends. At the same time, you know—deep in your heart, if you'll only admit it—that no one loves your baby quite so much as you do. Could it be possible that for other people, sharing your baby pictures could become too much of a good thing?

That, of course, depends on who the other people are. It's a safe bet that your parents (and your partner's parents) want to see as many pictures as possible of your baby. And your baby's aunts and uncles will probably welcome occasionally updated photos, too. With all but your closest friends, however, you may find it wiser to show a little more restraint.

> **Q-Tip**
> Instead of overwhelming your friends and family members with a monthly barrage of five or six dozen digital photos, you may want to take advantage of photo-sharing sites like Flickr.com or Kodakgallery.com. These websites allow you to share your baby pictures with anyone in the world. When you have a new set of photos, you can post them on the website, e-mail everyone you know with an invitation to look at them if they'd like, and put a hyperlink in the e-mail that will take them directly to the site. This gives your loved ones the opportunity to browse through your photos without obligating them to do so.

Preserve Your Memories

Another problem with the wealth of photo opportunities your baby offers you—and the ease with which digital technology allows you to capture each and every one of them—is how to organize them all. In the old (predigital) days, parents selected the best photos to put in a photo album and socked away the rest in shoeboxes. As digital capacity multiplies the number of photographs taken, however, organization often falls by the wayside.

Digital photos provide a much more ephemeral means of recording your family memories than film photos. Sure, you can save every photo you take of your baby by uploading them onto your computer, but in all likelihood, there they'll sit, stored in a file that—after you send it to family members and friends—may rarely, if ever, get opened again.

Unfortunately, creating a computer file does not even guarantee the permanence of your photos. Each time you upgrade your computer or software and each time a new digital technology is introduced, you may lose—or lose track of—a significant portion of your digital photos. And if your hard drive breaks down, you'll find it next to impossible to retrieve your photos, so back them up regularly.

You can't depend on your friends and family members to be curators of your baby photos either. For the most part, those who receive your digital photos attached to an e-mail will browse through them quickly and then delete them. Digital photos don't have the tangible substance of film photos, so people don't take as much care to preserve them.

You will definitely want a more permanent record of your child's baby photos than digital storage can provide, however. Your family photos matter to you, maybe more than you think. We've all heard news stories of people who gather up their family photos or photo albums during an earthquake, in the face of an approaching hurricane, or even while their house is on fire. Their explanation for risking their safety for the family photos? Everything else can be replaced, but family photos are irreplaceable.

Baby Talk

"A photograph is a secret about a secret. The more it tells you the less you know."

—Diane Arbus

Let's Get Organized!

Just because you've gone digital doesn't mean you can't create a more permanent record of your baby's early life. Simply treat your digital photos as if they were film ones.

If you had a film camera—or if you actually do still use a film camera—you would simply select the best of your photos to put in a photo album, reproduce as wallet photos, or enlarge and frame. Then you'd put the rest away in a safe place. So do the same if you've gone digital.

First, organize your digital photos on the computer. Whenever you upload your pictures, take a few minutes to pick out your favorites. Store these in a special "Favorite Photos" file that you can augment with each upload. In addition to sharing these favorite photos through e-mail, you can print your special favorites for a more permanent record. You can print them yourselves if you have a photo-quality printer and good photo-stock paper. Or you can take them to an outside service, available through local photo shops, pharmacies, or grocery stores, that will print them for you.

If you're feeling creative, you can even use photo-editing software to crop, resize, retouch (to eliminate red-eye, for example), lighten, or darken your photos to make them as perfect as your baby. You can also create photo montages that, when printed, will make ideal pages for a photo album or scrapbook.

Prints of your favorite digital photos will provide a permanent record that you will cherish for decades to come. As for finding a safe place for the rest of your photos, remember to create back-up files of all your uploads. Although disk failure is not uncommon, the chances that your hard drive will crash and your discs fail at the same time are slim.

Put It in the Books!

Once you've made at least a selection of your photos permanent, you can begin to think about presentation. A traditional photo album offers the simplest, most basic format. Most parents organize their family photo albums chronologically, moving week by week or month by month from the baby's birth to her first birthday. This scheme works well for a baby's photo album because it suggests a narrative. In looking through the album later, the pictures will serve as prompts, encouraging you or your partner to tell the story of your baby's first year as you leaf through the pages with a friend, a relative, or your baby herself.

Of course, you don't have to follow a chronological format if you have other ideas on how to arrange your photo album. You could organize it anyway you want: by milestone "firsts," by themes, by those in the picture with your baby, or by some principle of your own. You could also use a commercially produced "Baby Book" to help organize your photos for you. These books usually have pages with inscriptions like "Baby Comes Home" or "Baby's First Meal"—with space left for the insertion of baby pictures.

Alternatively, you can use some of the ideas from books like these to create your own scrapbook dedicated to your baby. Sandwiched around such items as your baby's birth notice; a copy of her birth certificate; thoughts penned by you, your partner, friends, or family members about your baby; and lists of her accomplishments (dates of various milestones, her vocabulary at various ages), you can arrange photographs either chronologically or thematically. A thematic approach to your baby's scrapbook might contain pages on …

- Baby at peace (nursing, serene).
- Baby's floor show (lying on her back or stomach, lifting her head up, crawling).
- Reading time (your baby's first books).
- Baby in the bath (shampoo in her hair, splashing).
- Baby at rest (napping, sleeping).
- Baby at play (handling various toys).
- Life of the party (playing with or being held by friends and family members).
- Baby's holidays.
- Baby in the park (on the swings or slide).
- Baby goes exploring (looking around, wide-eyed).
- High-chair high jinks (eating, making a mess).
- Baby fashion show (wearing brand new clothes, before they get coated with spit up or baby cereal).
- Baby's milestones (sitting, standing, first steps).
- Baby's first birthday.

You, of course, will have many ideas of your own on how to organize your baby book or scrapbook. If you need ideas on additional themes, design elements, or composition, *The Complete Idiot's Guide to Scrapbooking*, by Wendy Smedley, will take you through every step of the process.

> **Q-Tip**
>
> Even if you're not the type of parents who like to create scrapbooks or put together photo albums, you might want to try your hand at journaling: writing down your own thoughts, feelings, observations, and memories to provide a permanent record of your baby's first year. A journal about your baby will be not only something you enjoy when you're feeling nostalgic, but an invaluable resource for your baby when she grows a little older and wants to know what she was like as a baby.

Making Home Videos

Home videos offer many of the same opportunities, challenges, and temptations as baby pictures. Video cameras have become increasingly less expensive and more portable over the last decade. This has increased the opportunities and made it much more convenient for parents to record and share the significant—and often not-so-significant—moments of their baby's life.

Not only can you easily make videos of your baby's day-to-day life, you can make really good videos. Camcorders are now able to record directly onto DVDs, and both hardware and software for digital recording have become more powerful and much easier to use. So even if you're not Steven Spielberg or Quentin Tarentino, you can still make professional-looking movies of your baby's happiest moments, milestones, and disappointments.

Unfortunately, we do not have the expertise to instruct you on the lighting, shooting, and editing techniques that will turn you into the Martin Scorsese of baby videos. A terrific tutorial in these techniques, however, can be found in *The Complete Idiot's Guide to Making Home Videos*, by Steven Beal.

> **Q-Tip**
>
> A nice alternative to videotapes are audiotapes of your baby. Your own parents may enjoy getting a tape, CD, or audio file with several minutes of his babbling, cooing, and yammering. As the years go by, you—and your baby—will also enjoy reliving these preverbal babbles. And once he starts saying real words, keep that tape rolling—for records of his talking, chattering, and singing.

Once you've made the perfect video of your baby, broadband and digital technology have made it easier for you to share your baby's milestones with family members and friends. In years past, videotape made it possible for you to gather everyone around the TV to share your baby videos. If you have a digital camcorder, however, you don't all need to be in the same place to watch your videos; it's easy to send video and audio files to anyone in the world who has their own broadband access.

The ease with which you can create digital videos—like the ease of taking digital photos—makes it more likely that you will accumulate so many images of your baby that you will have more than enough. You may want to take the time every couple of months to organize your videos and even edit together a highlight reel of his best, funniest, or most amazing moments.

Q-Tip _____

Broadband technology makes it possible for you not only to share memories of significant events in your baby's life, but also to broadcast them live, allowing grandparents and other distant relatives or friends to see his first steps, for example, as they happen. All you need is a broadband computer and a webcam pointed in the right direction.

As with photos, discretion is advised in determining how much of your video record you will share with family members and friends. When considering whether to send a digital video over the Internet, for example, if you think you *might* be overdoing it, then you probably are. Try to stick to the old rule of vaudeville performers: *Always leave them wanting more!*

The Least You Need to Know

◆ Make the most of your baby's photo opportunities. Have a camera ready to go at all times.

◆ Be sensible. Don't leave your baby in a dangerous situation for even a second to run and get the camera.

◆ No matter how much other family members or friends love your baby, they probably don't want to see as many pictures and videos of her as you do.

◆ Figure out the way to preserve and organize your baby's photos and videos that best suits you and do it.

Drawing a Line in the Sandbox

In This Chapter

◆ Does your baby know right from wrong?

◆ Setting consistent, fair, and reasonable limits on your baby's behavior

◆ Enforcing rules and limits

◆ Is it ever appropriate to punish a baby?

◆ Alternatives to "No!"

If your baby has already started to crawl, congratulations! If she's shown signs that she's just about to crawl, watch out! Crawling and other forms of mobility usher in a new talent for your baby as well: making "mischief" and getting into trouble.

Oh, sure, your little darling may have knocked over her juice before—or even thrown it. She may have pinched or bitten or pulled hair as part of her early explorations. But now that she's mobile, your baby's ability to get into places she shouldn't be and to do things she shouldn't do has multiplied. The days when you could blithely put your baby down and know that she and your possessions were safe are now over.

You may find your baby systematically emptying the bookcase and ripping the pages out of your favorite novels. You may catch her chasing after the dog and repeatedly pulling its tail. Perhaps you'll discover her halfway up the stairs, turning and responding to your alarmed gaze with a "who, me?" grin. Maybe there's a mysterious grape juice stain on the living room couch. Or you may find out that she has spooned oatmeal into the VCR. It makes a parent proud, doesn't it?

No matter how much initiative and ingenuity your crawler shows in the mischief she creates, you are much more likely to be upset, exasperated, and just plain angry at your baby than to feel proud or amused by her when she "behaves badly." Clearly, the time has come to begin setting limits on your baby's behavior. Certainly, you don't want to curb your child's adventurous spirit, her thirst for discovery, or her eagerness to explore her surroundings. (Okay, maybe sometimes you do.) But at the same time, you can't let your infant do anything and everything she wants to do.

Beyond Good and Evil

When your baby has broken a treasured lamp or spilled blueberries on your favorite shirt or ripped through the photos in the family album, you may forget that he doesn't yet know the difference between right and wrong.

Your baby is just beginning to grasp the concept of cause and effect. For the rest of this year (and most of the next), he will do experiments that will help further his understanding of this concept. Your baby cannot possibly anticipate what will happen when he behaves in a certain way until he gains knowledge of cause and effect through his experience and his experiments:

- He drops a ball; it bounces.

- He drops a spoonful of mashed potatoes; it splats.

- He drops a sipper cup; it pops open and juice sprays everywhere.

How could he discover all these different effects without performing these experiments?

To move beyond these simple results and realize that dropping each of these things produces different effects not only on the objects themselves, but on you, too, is beyond his capacity to reason. You laugh and clap when he drops a ball. You scowl when he drops the mashed potatoes. Can it possibly be that his actions are prompting these different responses on your part?

Because your child lacks a fundamental understanding of both cause and effect and the difference between good behavior and bad behavior, it is impossible for him to "misbehave." Your baby is entirely amoral. He doesn't behave well or misbehave; he simply behaves the way he behaves, with no thought about whether his behavior might be right or wrong.

Because your baby lacks any understanding of right and wrong, he cannot be held responsible for his actions. Experience (a lot more than he has had up to now) and your teaching will help your baby develop an understanding of the effects and consequences of his actions and learn how to behave accordingly. Although your teaching should begin now, that understanding won't come for some time yet.

Baby Talk

"Father asked us what was God's noblest work. Anna said men, but I said babies. Men are often bad; babies never are."

—Louisa May Alcott

Remember, no matter how bad or unruly your baby's behavior becomes, your baby is not bad. Indeed, most infant behavior that gets labeled "bad" is simply a matter of the child exploring the world and perhaps testing certain limits. Avoid labeling your baby a "bad girl" or a "bad boy." Your child, especially as he grows older, is likely to accept this damaging characterization without question. Heard often enough, it can become a self-fulfilling prophecy, establishing a pattern that may last throughout childhood and beyond.

Q-Tip

You may want to avoid labeling both your baby and his behavior as "bad." Remember, strictly speaking, his behavior is not bad, although it may be dangerous, harmful, destructive, or unfair. Opt instead for expressions that provide a brief explanation of why your baby shouldn't behave that way, such as these:

- "Ow! That hurts!"
- "No! That's dangerous!"
- "No grabbing! That's not fair!"
- "You hurt her!"
- "Don't bang that, it will break!"

Now Junior, Behave Yourself

If your baby isn't responsible for her actions, where does that leave you? How can you discipline an amoral child? Because your baby lacks responsibility, you need to take responsibility for her actions. You need to make sure that she will not harm herself or others and will not destroy anything of value to you or to others.

Even babies need limits. Precisely because she doesn't know what's safe and unsafe, right and wrong, fair and unfair, your baby needs you to steer her in the right direction. Through both your words and your own actions, you need to teach your baby safety, respect, fairness, and eventually morality. (Be patient. Even when she does begin to develop these concepts, which won't be for several years, your child will not always be able to control her impulses and behavior to conform with this new knowledge.)

Where do you draw the line between acceptable and unacceptable behavior? That, of course, depends on your priorities. But whatever limits you set, try to make sure they meet the following criteria.

Consistency. Your baby will not learn your rules from a single lesson. How can she when she has a very short and very selective memory? She cannot carry the lessons of one experience into a similar situation later or even the same situation. So you will need to repeat the same moral lessons over and over and over again.

For this reason, your rules must be consistent. Whatever rule you establish needs to apply at all times and in all situations. If you scolded her for hitting yesterday but ignored it today because "nobody got hurt," you will confuse your baby. Consistency—similar actions always leading to similar results—will allow her (eventually) to draw conclusions about her behavior from similar experiences: "Oh, Mommy and Daddy don't like it when I hit someone."

Fairness. Your baby cannot yet consider the wants or needs of other people before she acts, so she cannot possibly weigh everyone's needs and desires and come up with a fair, balanced solution when they conflict. You need to serve as the arbiter of fairness. You have to encourage her to take turns and stop her from grabbing toys or food from others. Fairness also means being fair to your child, though. Keep in mind that she's just an infant. If your rules don't allow her to be an infant, if they presume that she's a little adult, they aren't fair to your baby.

Reasonableness. Although your baby's capacity for reasoning is still limited at best, the rules and limits you set should still be reasonable. Your long-term goal in setting limits is to teach your child moral responsibility, but you cannot achieve this goal if you impose arbitrary rules—the kind that you will later explain with "Because I said so!"

Even though your child cannot yet understand it, every rule and limit you set must have an underlying rationale. With an infant, each rule should aim to accomplish one of the following ends:

- Keeping your baby safe. Examples: You cannot ride in the car unless you're strapped in the car seat. No playing with knives or other sharp objects.

- Keeping others safe from your child. Examples: No hitting. No biting. No kicking. No hair pulling.

- Keeping your property intact. Examples: No drawing on the walls. No food in the living room. No handling of fragile objects.

- Nurturing respect for other people and for their rights and feelings. Examples: No grabbing. Wait your turn.

If you can justify all of your rules with one or more of these four rationales, then they all set reasonable and necessary limits on your child's behavior.

Q-Tip _____

Don't set too many rules, especially for an infant. For a baby, a lot of rules breeds confusion. In addition, the more rules you have, the more likely they are to conflict on occasion. This kind of conflict puts your baby in an awful bind: she has no basis for deciding which rule is more important.

Baby Police: Enforcing the Law

How should you enforce the limits you set? Most parents start by saying, "No!" More often than not, this warning in itself is effective in stopping your baby from doing something dangerous, harmful, or destructive. The tone you use (even more than the word itself) probably stops your infant in his tracks. With this single word, he instantly gets the message: what he was doing, or was about to do, was unacceptable and you don't like it when he does that.

Depending on his personality, your baby may collapse into tears when you say "No!" If so, then go to him and offer him comfort and the reassurance that you love him even when you don't like what he's doing. Remain firm about your limits: don't let him resume the behavior when he's calmed down, but demonstrate your love at the same time.

When you say, "No!" try to sound stern without yelling or getting angry. Keep in mind that your baby is only a baby. Don't let him get away with murder, but don't get really angry at him for behaving like a baby either. The sharpness and sternness of your voice will startle your baby; yelling or anger will frighten him. And once you scare your baby—no matter how appropriate it may seem after he's bit someone or been caught halfway up the stairs—you lose him. Any chance of teaching a lesson about safety or fairness is gone.

Baby Doctor

If you often lose your temper at your baby, try to figure out why. Could you be angry about anything else? Or angry at someone else? Are you angry at yourself? Do you feel abandoned and/or overwhelmed? Have you set standards for your baby's behavior that are unreasonable? You may need the help of a professional to sort it all out.

Don't Get Mad, Get Even (Tempered)

You may be surprised how angry you can get at an innocent little baby. Even though she can't be held responsible or be blamed for her behavior, you have every right to get angry at your child. At times, especially when she does something unsafe or something that hurts others, you may even lose your temper and yell at your infant.

No doubt you feel terrible; you should. Your anger almost certainly frightens your baby. But occasional angry outbursts will do her no lasting harm. In fact, letting your anger out may do less long-term harm than holding it in. Bottled-up anger and resentment can eat away at the good relationship you're trying to maintain with your baby. By contrast, an isolated outburst of anger (if handled properly) can quickly be put behind you, allowing you and your baby to relish each other's company again. So don't worry too much about your tirades unless they become habitual.

Q-Tip

If you do blow up at your baby, give yourself a few minutes to calm down and regain control of your emotions. Then immediately go to your baby (and your partner) and apologize. Your baby needs reassurance that you love her no matter how angry you feel.

If your anger does seem out of control, calm yourself down rather than try to discipline your child at that moment. When coupled with rage, "discipline" can quickly escalate into abuse. By waiting, you may miss the chance to connect your scolding with the "misbehavior" that occasioned it because your child will no longer remember what she did that was so bad. But better to deal with correcting her behavior next time than to do damage to your child now.

By regaining control of your anger, you will (eventually) serve as a role model for your baby. She will learn from you more constructive ways of expressing anger than through yelling or hitting. Isn't this part of the discipline you want to teach her, too?

Don't Just Say "No!"

When you first start setting limits, simply saying "No!" may do the trick. Because your baby probably hasn't heard this word much before, especially delivered in such a stern tone, it may stop him from doing whatever he's doing. But as he grows older, he may begin testing this limit. He may turn, smile sweetly at you, and then continue on his merry way.

No matter how cute your baby is when he does this, don't let him get away with it. If saying "No!" doesn't stop your baby from doing something that's dangerous, harmful, or destructive, you must follow through immediately with actions that back up your words. What actions are appropriate before your baby's first birthday? It depends on the situation:

- ◆ If he has somehow gotten his hands on something that's dangerous, remove it. Take it from your baby's hands (or mouth) and put it way up high where he can't reach it.

- ◆ If he's exploring something dangerous that you cannot take from him, for instance, if he's chewing on an electric cord, then remove him from the area.

- ◆ If he's hitting, biting, or otherwise hurting another child, then quickly separate the children. Keep them apart for 5 minutes or so until calm has been restored and they can play nicely together again.

- ◆ If he's bent on destroying something of value, take it away or take him away from it.

Whatever you choose to do to back up your words, explain your rationale to your baby as you're taking action:

- ◆ "No peanuts! You might choke."

- ◆ "No biting on the cord! It could shock you."

◆ "No biting! That hurts."

◆ "No paint on the couch! That ruins it."

Will your baby understand all of this? Probably not. Even if he does understand your words at that moment, chances are that he won't remember them for very long. The next time your baby sees a peanut or the electric cord, for instance, she may again be tempted to chew on it.

It doesn't matter whether your baby understands everything you say. But these brief explanations lay the groundwork for the ultimate objective of all discipline: teaching your child the differences between safe and unsafe behavior and right and wrong.

Does Punishment Fit the Crime?

Because your baby does not yet know the difference between "good" and "bad," it's neither fair nor reasonable to discipline her as if she did. (You'll have plenty of time for that later.) Neither punishment nor the threat of punishment helps to discipline an infant. When your baby doesn't do as she's told, she isn't necessarily trying to defy you or your rules. She simply doesn't understand or remember them.

Baby Talk

"Lacking all sense of right and wrong, a child can do nothing which is morally evil, or which merits either punishment or reproof."

—Jean-Jacques Rousseau

Your baby doesn't know any better. Ignorance of the law may not be a defense that works in court, but it should count for a lot in the home. Because your baby is incapable of making connections between her own (unacceptable) actions and your (punitive) reactions, any kind of punishment is inappropriate before her first birthday. At this age, "No!" will teach her much more about behaviors to avoid than any kind of punishment will.

Infants learn little or nothing from any kind of punishment, whether time-outs, the withholding of treats, or spankings. Your baby just doesn't get it. To her, these punishments are unpleasant, unfair, and cruel things *you* do to *her*, not consequences of anything that she's done herself. Because punishment makes absolutely no sense to your baby, it shouldn't make any sense to you either. Punishment has no positive impact whatsoever on an infant.

Spanking a baby is particularly odious. Although a slap on the wrist may occasionally be necessary to prevent your baby from sticking a fork into an electric outlet (or another child), spanking (a punishment for willful misbehavior) does not make sense with infants. Your baby is not yet capable of willful misbehavior.

In addition to being unfair and unreasonable to your baby, spanking …

◆ Teaches your baby nothing about right and wrong.

◆ Sends the message that might makes right, that problems are best dealt with through force rather than persuasion.

◆ Is dangerous when done in anger.

◆ Is cold and cruel when done calmly.

Ain't Misbehavin'

Another reason to avoid explicitly punishing your baby is that his misbehavior, strictly speaking, is seldom really misbehavior. Although throwing food, for example, might warrant punishment in an older child, an infant cannot help doing it. A preschooler knows what will happen when he drops or throws mashed potatoes on the floor; an infant has to do it to find out.

Similarly, most actions that your infant takes that might deserve punishment later are things that he cannot help doing now. Your baby is becoming increasingly curious. He wants to explore his world and experiment with the objects in it. That's how he learns about the world.

If your baby bites you or pulls your hair, he doesn't intend to hurt you. He does it because he wants to discover more about you, just as he explores the other objects in his world. How does he find out about a new toy? He grabs it, pulls it, pokes it, scratches it, bangs it, kicks it, and bites it. When he does this to another person, don't assume the worst. He wasn't being mean-spirited. He was just being a baby. And punishing a baby just because he behaves like a baby isn't fair.

"No!": Don't Overuse It

Once your baby has begun to crawl, she needs the opportunity to explore her environment. Exploring and acquiring knowledge adds to her growing independence and confidence. But to make the most of these adventures, she needs the freedom to roam (within limits, of course) wherever her interests take her. She needs to be able to make discoveries and experiment with the objects in her world on her own.

Without intending to do so, you can easily douse the flame of your baby's passion for exploration and discovery. All you need to do is say "No!" 20 or 30 times a day. Saying "No!" discourages your child from exploring her environment, or at least parts of it.

The more often you use the word "No!" the less effective it becomes. Your baby will quickly tire of hearing that word all the time, and it will lose its shock value. Your child may end up ignoring your repeated prohibitions.

Beware of turning "No!" into a game, which it can easily become if you overuse the word. If your baby starts to challenge your authority, you may admire her spunk, but try not to let her see your admiration. Your baby needs to know that this is serious business, that you say "No!" only when you mean it. For all of these reasons, try to use "No!" only for the most serious offenses—those that represent an immediate danger to your baby or to others (and perhaps to your property as well).

Constantly saying "No!" not only discourages your infant from exploring her world and gradually strips the word of its effectiveness, but it may also damage your baby's sense of security, acceptance, and self-confidence. To your baby, displeasing you feels dangerous. Your baby naturally equates any expression of disapproval on your part with rejection. This sense of rejection, in turn, heightens any abandonment fears she already has.

Baby Talk

"Children need love, especially when they do not deserve it."

—Harold S. Hulbert

So do whatever you can to cut down on the number of times you say "No!" to your baby. Whenever you do say it, make sure to follow up your expression of disapproval with expressions of warmth and affection. Comfort your child, who may be devastated at the thought of having done something wrong (although she may not quite understand what she did). Above all, emphasize that even when you get angry at her, even when you don't like what she's doing, you still love her.

Infants, thoroughly anchored in the present moment, often have a hard time realizing that someone can shout at them and still love them. Your baby does not yet know this fact through either instinct or experience. Because she cannot separate a person from his or her behavior, you have to show her how to do it.

Just Say "Yes!"

An infant, as noted earlier, is not capable of behaving a certain way just because it's "good" (or avoiding certain behaviors because they're "bad"). Infants behave according to the urges and interests of the immediate present. They cannot do otherwise.

Your baby will behave himself (in your eyes) only if he wants to behave the way you want him to behave. Of course, this doesn't mean that you should let your baby do anything he pleases. You still need to provide the guidelines of acceptable behavior—again and again, if necessary.

You cannot possibly get your infant to renounce bad behavior at this age, but you can get him to embrace good behavior. How? By tricking or enticing him into wanting to do what you want him to do. With a little creative redirection, you can put a positive spin on negative prohibitions, turning a sharp "No!" into a resounding "Yes!"

Your baby has a very short attention span. If something's out of sight, it's out of his mind as well. So if you can distract him, you can probably steer your baby relatively easily away from unsafe or unacceptable behavior. Try to get your child interested in something else, something that's safe and nondestructive. He'll probably forget all about that unsafe thing he wanted to do within seconds.

Similarly, you can redirect your baby's energies from mischief or unsafe behavior toward a safer behavior that involves the same action. For instance, if your baby starts hitting you, offer him an alternative: something safe to hit. You might say, "Oh, you want to hit something now? Okay, these are for hitting." Then steer him toward drums or a tower of soft blocks to knock down. If he's biting, offer him a teether or a biscuit that he can bite on. If he wants to throw something valuable (and breakable), trade it for a ball or a beanbag. That way, your child can hit or bite or throw as much as he wants, but in such a way that no one gets hurt.

Q-Tip _____

When all else fails, try banishment. Despite hearing you say "No!" your baby may continue to live dangerously. Ignoring your attempts at distraction, he may remain obsessed with a particular forbidden behavior. If this is the case, put him in exile. Pick him up and physically remove him from the "scene of the crime."

If he persists in his efforts to go back and repeat the objectionable behavior, create a physical obstacle (perhaps a safety gate) that blocks him from returning. You may find him much more willing to accept the alternatives you offer once he's in a different room.

Another positive way to steer your child toward good behavior is through babyproofing (see Chapter 10). By limiting your toddler's choices only to safe ones, babyproofing can steer him away from dangerous actions and toward safe behavior without his even knowing it. Thorough babyproofing takes care of two of the four aims of setting rules: keeping your baby safe and your property intact. If babyproofing takes care of these, you can focus your rules and your "No's" on keeping others safe from your baby and on nurturing respect for the rights and feelings of others.

The Power of Positive Thinking

Finally, keep in mind that the ultimate goal of disciplining your child is to nurture and promote moral behavior, to teach the difference between right and wrong or good and bad. Setting and enforcing limits and saying "No!" (or "Don't" or "Never …") deal with only half of this equation. They point out what's wrong or bad, but they teach nothing about what's right or good.

Try to be positive about your child's behavior as well. Pay attention to your baby's behavior not just when she's being a devil, but also when she's being an angel. After all, good behavior warrants praise just as much as bad behavior calls for criticism. When your child does something right or good, don't forget to praise her and reward her.

As your crawler moves toward toddlerhood, her social behavior will be motivated not only by an urge to avoid displeasing you (and select others), but by a sincere wish to please you as well. So show your baby when her behavior pleases you. Don't let her good behavior go unnoticed while you focus all of your attention on correcting her bad behavior. If you take the time to praise and reward her good behavior often enough, your baby will eventually make an effort to repeat the behavior.

The Least You Need to Know

- A baby does not have the ability to understand the difference between right and wrong, good and bad. Babies have no morality.

- Because your baby is amoral, punishment makes no sense. You can't reasonably punish your baby for acting like a baby.

- Any limits you set should be consistent, fair, and reasonable.

- In enforcing limits, try to teach your baby, even before she can fully understand you, the differences between right and wrong and between safe and unsafe behavior.

- You can use your wiles to steer your child away from dangerous or hurtful behavior.

Part 4

The Pre-Toddler: 9–12 Months

You made it through the first month or two of crawling with your home and your baby both intact? Congratulations! But don't expect things to get easier in the coming months. Your baby will soon be on her feet. Even if she doesn't take her first steps until after her first birthday (most babies don't), she'll probably be standing before then. This position gives her greater opportunities to explore and to get into trouble.

As your baby approaches her first birthday, she becomes more and more independent and perhaps more and more insecure. Offer reassuring words as your baby strikes out on her own. If you're lucky, she may even offer a few priceless words in return: Mama and Dada. These words, and the loving way your baby says them, will provide a sumptuous reward for all of your efforts and worries over the past year.

Chapter 20

Walking and Talking (Almost): 10 to 12 Months

In This Chapter

- ◆ Moving toward mobility: balanced sitting, pulling up to standing, and standing without support
- ◆ On the move: cruising and tentative walking
- ◆ Making falls safe
- ◆ Translating first "words"

If you thought crawling was like a roller-coaster ride, thrilling but scary, you ain't seen nothin' yet. In the next 3 months, your baby will probably pull herself up to a standing position for the first time, if she hasn't already. Then she'll start to *cruise* (use chairs, tables, couches, bookcases, and other furniture to support her standing as she inches along the edge).

Once in a while—when absorbed in some toy, perhaps—your baby may let go of the furniture and stand unsupported for several seconds before plopping down or reaching out for support again. By her first birthday, she may even embark on that nonstop thrill ride: her first tentative steps.

Of course, you'll be proud and excited as she gradually progresses toward toddlerhood. But with each of these steps also comes new dangers. Standing, cruising, and walking all lead inevitably to another new skill your baby will need to master: falling. So pack away those coffee tables and other low furniture with sharp edges. Buy some rugs or wall-to-wall carpeting. Steel yourself for the awful sight and sound of your baby's head crashing down against the floor. And get ready to applaud; your baby's nearly on her way.

Steps Toward First Steps

Your baby will probably figure out how to work himself all the way around from lying on his stomach to sitting up during the ninth, tenth, or eleventh month. Even if he can't get there himself, if you sit him up, he should probably be able to sustain a sitting position for some time by the tenth month.

The key has always been maintaining balance. Throughout this year, your baby has learned to coordinate his muscles from the top down. First came control over his neck and head, then his shoulders and upper torso. After that, he began to use his arms and his hands with ever-increasing dexterity. Then came the hips, thighs, and knees, and suddenly your baby was crawling. By now, your baby has control over nearly every muscle in his body. All he needs to do is practice keeping everything in sync so that he can maintain balance.

Q-Tip

Your child still needs plenty of time to practice his moves. Let him crawl around to his heart's content in safe rooms; don't constantly transfer him from high chair to walker to stroller to crib. Put him on the floor for most of the day. Encourage him to wander and explore and then to stop and examine whatever he finds (though make sure beforehand that anything he's likely to find will be safe). Try not to discourage him; give him room to roam and babyproof thoroughly enough so that you won't constantly be saying, "No!"

Not only can your 9- or 10-month-old baby now sit for quite some time without toppling over, but he can use only one hand to support himself, so he can use the other to pick up toys (or other objects) and play with them.

Of course, your baby is not content to just sit around anymore. During the next 3 to 6 months, your baby will make developmental leaps and bounds. (Actual leaps and bounds come later in the second year.) Your child will probably achieve the following milestones very soon:

Baby Doctor

If you're worried that your child may be developmentally delayed, consult your pediatrician. The doctor will probably reassure you that your child is perfectly normal, but it doesn't hurt to ask. After all, this reassurance may be just what you need to hear.

- Pulling himself up to a standing position (9 to 12 months)

- Cruising along the edges of furniture (9 to 13 months)

- Standing on his own with no support (9 to 14 months)

- Walking (10 to 15 months)

Again, please keep in mind that all the ages included here represent average ranges. Your baby will progress at his own individual pace. His development may fall at the beginning or end of the range, or even outside the range, without cause for concern on your part. Just because he pulls up at 7 months and walks at 9 months doesn't mean he's from the planet Krypton, and just because he still hasn't done any of these by his first birthday doesn't mean anything is wrong.

Standing Up ...

By around 10 months, your baby will probably be able to use her legs to support her own weight. She'll still need you or something else to help her maintain her balance, however. She will plant her feet and straighten her legs, for example, if you hold her hands or help her wrap them about a table leg. But if you let go, or if she lets go, she'll plop down onto the floor.

Around 10 or 11 months, your baby will be delighted to discover that she can pull herself up to a standing position whether you help her or not. (Remember, some babies do this months earlier and some months later.) By holding on to the vertical bars of her crib, the leg of a chair or table, or your pants or legs, she can gradually pull herself up by putting one hand above the other and then successively moving the lower hand to a higher position. In less than half a minute, she'll be on her feet. As

Baby Doctor

Don't worry if your child appears to be bowlegged when she first stands. Nearly all babies are. Even when she stands with her feet together, her knees probably won't touch. Rest assured that this is perfectly normal. Your child will probably remain bowlegged for at least another year.

long as she holds that support tightly, she will be able to stand and maintain her balance for quite a while.

When your baby pulls herself up on her feet for the first time, she will no doubt be excited and very pleased with herself. She'll proudly look around as if she were Sir Edmund Hillary at the top of Mount Everest. A whole new world of expansive vistas has opened up before her.

Unfortunately, after surveying the territory for a minute or so, your baby will suddenly realize that she's stuck! She doesn't yet know how to walk. She hasn't figured out how to move her hands and feet to inch along the edge of a piece of furniture. She can't even remain standing unless she continues to hold on to something, and she may need both hands to do it, so she can't play with anything either.

To make things worse, your baby doesn't even know how to sit down yet. Your baby can't and won't move anywhere until her legs give way, she falls, or she gets you to help her. Obviously, of these three alternatives, your baby would prefer the last. So once she figures out that she's stuck, she'll probably start to cry.

Q-Tip

Give your baby an incentive to stand if you think she's almost ready. Place a favorite toy on the seat of a tall chair, the third shelf of a secure bookcase, or some other perch high enough out of reach that in order to get it, she'll have to stand up. (Make sure you haven't put it so high that she won't be able to reach it even if she does stand.) Then encourage her to get the toy. If she does stand, shower her with applause and affection. Don't let this game go on too long, however. If she starts to get frustrated because she can't yet stand and doesn't know how to begin, quickly and cheerfully intervene and get the toy for her.

... and Falling Down

When your baby stands there crying, you will, of course, go over, rescue your darling by gently sitting him down, and praise him for his courage and skill. Yet almost immediately, he'll pop up onto his feet again, repeating his new trick. This time, it won't take nearly as long for him to figure out that he's stuck again. He'll cry out again, and you'll help him sit down again. But as soon as his bottom hits the floor, he may do it all over again. Now it's become a game for him—and hopefully for you, too.

Q-Tip _____

When you "rescue" your child from a standing position, don't just scoop him up. Show him a better way: sitting down. Gently bend your baby's knees and lower his bottom as far as it can go without having him let go yet. Then gently pry his clinging fingers from his support, take his hands in yours, and lower him until his bottom hits the floor.

After building his confidence with this approach, try letting him drop down on his bottom. Take his hands in yours, but if his bottom stays close to the ground, let him go. Just make sure your baby lands safely. Be ready to catch him if he starts to topple over to one side or the other with the impact.

Whether or not you help your baby discover how to sit, he will quickly learn how to do it on his own. Probably within a week or two of first standing, your baby will lower himself as far as he can go and then bravely drop the last few inches. It won't take more than one drop for your baby to figure out that he won't get hurt (as long as he lands on his well-padded bottom). He may even start to have as much fun dropping down with a thump on the floor as he did pulling himself up in the first place.

Until your baby learns how to fall safely, you may tire of the pulling up, getting stuck, and calling for help game long before your child does. After helping him sit back down half a dozen times, you may be ready for something new. If your baby seems obsessed with this game, try to distract him. Move him away from whatever he's using as a support and sit him down with one of his favorite toys—or try giving him a new toy that he's never played with before.

If your baby immediately leaves the toy and crawls back to his standing spot to pull himself back up, you'll have to indulge him or resort to more drastic measures. Try taking him completely out of the house, maybe for a walk in his stroller or a ride in the car. By the time you get back, your baby may have forgotten his new trick—but not for long.

Baby Proofing _____

As soon as your baby starts to practice pulling himself to a standing position, secure all the furniture he might use as support. Because lightweight furniture will probably not bear your child's weight as he tries to pull himself up, he may end up on his back on the floor with the piece of furniture on top of him. Though your baby probably won't get seriously hurt this way, he could become scared or discouraged.

When your baby first learns to stand (or cruise or walk), it will be nerve-racking for you. You'll see dangers long before your child does. (When you do, remove them or steer your baby away from them.) You'll see he's about to fall, but know you can't get across the room in time to catch him. (Don't worry—as long as you've removed sharp-cornered furniture. Your baby doesn't have very far to fall.)

Although your baby's first weeks of standing, cruising, and walking will be hard on your nerves, don't react by banishing him to a playpen. With practice, he'll get better at maintaining balance and avoiding dangerous falls. But he won't get any practice at all while cooped up in the prison of a playpen. (A playpen with mesh sides may not even allow him to pull himself up.)

Cruise Control

About a month after your baby first pulls herself up to a standing position, she will start *cruising*. (No, that doesn't mean she will start frequenting bars and looking for dates.) Your baby will start by pulling herself up to standing using a couch, chair, or low table for support. Then, using sideways shuffling steps, she'll slowly, carefully move along the edge of that piece of furniture. Without letting go, your baby will slide both hands in the direction she wants to go. Then she'll move her lead leg over without lifting it off the ground. Finally, she'll catch up with the trail leg, sliding it over next to the lead leg.

If your little cruiser finds a piece of furniture that she can move without pulling it down on top of herself—a kitchen or dining room chair, for example—she may even fashion her own makeshift walker. By pushing the chair in front of her as she totters along, she can now walk all the way across a room.

Within a few weeks of first cruising, your baby will lift her trail leg instead of sliding it. Though this may seem like a small thing, it represents an enormous developmental leap. At least for a moment, your baby has supported herself on just one foot—a feat she must master before she can walk.

After a month or so of cruising, your baby will probably need only one hand for support. This new skill will free her to move from one piece of furniture to the next—if it's close enough for her to reach. Tentatively, your baby will let go of her support with one hand and reach out for another piece of furniture to support her.

Q-Tip

You can encourage your baby to cruise from one support to another by moving furniture closer together in rooms where your baby plays. If you put enough low, solid pieces of furniture next to one another, your cruiser can move all the way around the room while remaining on her feet!

Releasing one hand from her support will not only give your baby greater freedom of movement, but it will also give her the freedom to play while cruising. She can reach out, pick up a toy, bring it to her mouth, or even throw it from her new lofty height. When she becomes especially absorbed in play, your baby may even let go of her support with both hands. Without even realizing it, your baby may be standing and maintaining her balance on her own!

Sshhhh! Don't scream or shout. You'll surely startle your baby into falling. Just watch and admire with pride. After a few seconds, she'll drop down and (hopefully) land on her bottom. Sadly, your baby won't be able to repeat this trick on demand. But now that she's done it, you'll know that your baby is almost ready to start taking her first wobbly steps.

Step by Step

Once you've seen your baby stand on his own, even by accident, it's tempting to try to push him to walk, too. You may sit in the middle of the room calling to your baby to come to you. Meanwhile, your baby stands holding on to the sofa, wondering what the heck you're talking about (or perhaps dropping down and then crawling toward you).

Although it isn't easy, try to be patient. Encourage your baby, but don't push. Let your baby develop at his own pace. If your baby fails to do something that you're trying to get him to do before he's ready, he will see your disappointment and that will be a blow to his self-esteem. But if he does something (like walking) successfully according to his own timetable, his confidence in himself will skyrocket.

If he's like most babies, your child won't take his first steps until the months after his first birthday. But even if your baby isn't walking until about 17 months, there's probably no cause for concern. Though you should consult your pediatrician if your baby isn't walking by 18 months, your baby is probably just fine. He's just not in any hurry to walk.

Q-Tip

Whether your baby is a cruiser or an early walker, he doesn't yet have any use for shoes when he's inside. In fact, shoes can be detrimental to your child's development. Your baby needs to be able to feel the shift of weight on his feet in order to maintain his balance, and shoes make this more difficult. In addition, walking in bare feet will help strengthen your baby's ankles and build his arches. If it's too cold for bare feet in your home, try slipper socks with skid-proof soles instead of shoes or regular socks (which can be too slippery). For safety, your baby will need shoes outside. But even then, choose shoes that are flexible rather than stiff. Again, skid-proof soles will help.

Help! I've Fallen and I Can't Get Up!

Inevitably, standing, cruising, and, of course, walking all mean one thing: falling. Your baby will almost definitely suffer more bumps, bruises, and even cuts over the next 3 months than she has during the previous 9. As your baby's mobility increases, babyproofing again becomes very important (see Chapter 10). Do everything you can to ensure that when she falls, she falls safely.

Supervision at all times becomes even more important once your baby is on her feet. Gently steer her away from dangers. But at the same time, don't constantly hover over your child trying to prevent all accidents. (Thorough babyproofing will make hovering unnecessary.) Try to avoid sending the overprotective message that the world, and even your home, is unsafe or threatening.

Try not to overreact when your baby falls. If you cry out and rush over to her, you'll spook your child, who will probably cry as much or more in response to your alarmed reaction as from the fall itself. Unless you know your child is really hurt, try to shrug it off with a "Whoops! You're okay, try again." If you can train yourself to take it in stride, your child is much less likely to become shy of falling.

Speaking (More or Less)

By the time your baby has his first birthday party, he won't be a baby anymore. Not only will he be (almost) walking, but he'll be (almost) talking, too. For many infants, first words often come around the tenth or eleventh month. But don't worry if your baby hasn't spoken a recognizable word by his birthday. Some babies don't speak at all until they're 15 months or older.

What's in a Name?

Your baby's first word will undoubtedly refer to some special object. Like Adam in the garden of Eden, your baby will assign names to the things in his world. Of course, you may not understand these names at first. His favorite teddy bear may be a *gimmy*; his spoon may be his *boo*.

If he showed any consistency at all, you'd quickly catch on. You'd know that no place setting is complete without a boo and that your baby won't go to sleep without his gimmy. But that would make it too easy. Your baby will, apparently on a whim, change the names of certain things. Overnight his gimmy will be transformed into a *mata*. (What's a mata? Nothing, what's a mata with you?)

Why the inconsistency? You may think your baby is trying new names in an attempt to find the right one. Yet your baby doesn't seem particularly frustrated when he picks a "wrong" name, so that's probably not it. He may be using different names as a way of trying out new sounds. Or perhaps he merely enjoys the power of naming the world around him. Whatever the cause, the era of shifting names will pass within a few weeks. Though your baby still might not have hit upon the "real" name yet, at least he'll be more consistent: from now on, a bobo will always be a bobo.

A Rose by Any Other Name

Does it matter that your baby doesn't use the same word that you would use? It can. If you have no idea what your baby is talking about, then her choice of vocabulary has made communication impossible—and that can be frustrating for both of you. But if you are attentive and manage to decipher your baby's code, then it shouldn't matter at all. If she says something and you figure out what she means, that's communication! She has accomplished just what she had intended: using "language" to convey an idea to you.

Until your baby starts using the same words you do—and even after, when in the presence of others not as familiar with your child's particular way of enunciating—you will need to serve as her translator. Listen carefully to what your baby is saying and how she says it. Babble, which will continue for many months to come, sounds different from "speech" (no matter how unintelligible). Babble often comes in a long, sing-song stream. But when your baby is trying to communicate, when she desperately wants you to understand, her voice will sound more insistent. She will say the "word" and stop, waiting for your response. Then she'll repeat it, perhaps more urgently.

Of course, no matter how insistent your baby becomes, you won't necessarily understand exactly what she's trying to say. Give her some help. When your baby says "findin," try to figure out what she means. If she's intensely looking or pointing somewhere, go to that general area and begin holding out possibilities. Pick up or put your hand on anything that might be a findin. As you touch each object, ask her if that's what she means: "Findin? Findin? Findin?"

If you don't get it relatively soon, both you and your baby will start to get frustrated. If the frustration level begins to rise too high, give up for now and try to distract your baby with something else of interest. But if you do get it, you'll know it right away. Your baby will beam and offer up a much more satisfied "findin." If what she wanted is safe, by all means give her the findin. Reward her with affection and praise, too. After all, she just found a creative way to communicate her ideas or desires to you.

Q-Tip

You can help your baby learn the "right" names for things. When you talk to your baby, continue to emphasize nouns. Don't just repeat a word over and over again, however. Your child may echo your word without having the slightest idea what you mean. Instead, teach her the names of things through everyday conversation, through a narration of events as they unfold, and through reading books together.

While emphasizing nouns, don't neglect adjectives. Start to point out the colors of things as well as simple descriptive words like *big* and *little, hot* and *cold, wet* and *dry.* You might also want to start pointing out cause-and-effect relationships to help expand her understanding.

The "Right" Word?

Especially during these first few months of speech, avoid explicitly correcting the words your baby uses. Your baby is trying hard to communicate with you. Trust that he's doing the best he can. Your baby has plenty of time to learn the "right" words for things. For now, celebrate his delight in having communicated his needs, desires, or observations to you. The more encouragement you give him, the more eagerly he will try to communicate in the days to come.

A baby who is constantly corrected by his parents, or even worse, a baby whose parents deny him things unless he says it "correctly," may become reluctant to talk at all. He'll become particularly averse to trying new words. At least for now, accept the way your baby talks and the words he chooses to use.

This acceptance does not mean that you need to adopt your baby's words as your own or to mimic his way of speaking. Baby talk is fine—for your baby! It won't do any harm for you to adopt a few particularly entertaining words that your baby invents. But he will learn much more from you if you talk like an adult. So without explicitly correcting your baby's vocabulary, use the correct word when you talk about it.

For instance, unless you choose "findins" as one of your baby's special pet names for real words, when you find them, don't say, "Here are your findins." On the other hand, don't make a blatant point of correcting him either, by saying something like, "Not findins. Raisins." Instead say, "Oh, findins! Of course you can have some raisins." If you continue to use the word *raisins* in everyday speech, then your baby will soon adopt that word as his own.

Q-Tip _____
Don't be surprised if you (and your partner) are the only ones who understand what your baby is saying. Not only have you cracked your baby's code; you also have the experience to understand your child's inflections and speech patterns. Others who have much less experience deciphering your baby's words will naturally find it more difficult to understand him, even after he has started to use the same words adults do.

Trust that your child will discover the "right" word in his own time. Until he's ready to do so, attempts to force proper language and usage on him will only inhibit his efforts to speak. If you understand his words, respond in kind. If you don't, make an effort to try to find out what your baby means. If you succeed, you will have helped to create not only a mutual understanding—but also mutual delight.

The Least You Need to Know

◆ Allow your child to develop at her own pace. Encourage and applaud her new mobility, but don't apply pressure.

◆ Standing, cruising, and walking all lead to falling. Renew your babyproofing efforts to ensure that your baby falls safely.

◆ Try to take your baby's falls in stride. If you overreact, you'll condition her to overreact, too.

◆ Do your best to figure out what your baby is trying to say when she invents a new word. Your understanding will be your baby's reward.

◆ Try to avoid correcting your baby's words (or grammar). Repeated correction may inhibit her fledgling attempts at speech.

Chapter 21

Fun for the Whole Family

In This Chapter

- Terrific toys for pre-toddlers
- Rhymes, songs, and other word play
- Nurturing a love of reading in your baby
- TV and pre-toddlers
- Are playdates possible?

During the second half of your baby's first year, you will start to have lots of fun together with toys and games. You can build things together (actually, you can build things and your baby can knock them down). You also can play "catch" with her (actually, you can roll the ball between her legs and it will stop—but that's close).

Even though she won't quite master building, throwing, or catching yet, your baby will develop a new appreciation for toys in the second half of the year. In any case, she will play with them differently. Your baby will no longer be content simply to handle her toys, put them in her mouth, perhaps shake or bang them, and otherwise explore them. Now she will begin to use toys as vehicles for learning new skills.

Toy Story

In the last half of his first year, your baby will still enjoy many of the toys he enjoyed during the earlier half of the year. The best toys for this age are those that illustrate the principle of cause and effect in fun ways. These toys respond with sound or movement when your baby does something to them. Popular cause-and-effect toys include these:

◆ Rattles

◆ Squeak toys

◆ Balls with bells inside

◆ Pop-up toys where hidden figures (cartoon characters and so on) pop up when your baby spins a tiny drum, turns a telephone dial, pushes a button, or pulls on a lever

◆ Pull toys

◆ Pull-string musical toys

◆ Toys that allow pouring of water or sand

◆ Cribside activity centers (by about 10 months, your baby should be able to master most, if not all, of the activities, such as spinning telephone dials, ringing bells, and pushing buttons)

Baby Talk

"Never help a child with a task at which he feels he can succeed."

—Maria Montessori

Even a light switch can entertain your infant for much longer than you'll want to hold him up to the switch.

Cause-and-effect toys help your child develop a sense of his own power. His initial discovery of this power will no doubt surprise him. The first time he turns a rotary telephone dial and makes Mickey Mouse pop out of a busy box, or squeezes a rubber puppy and hears it "yelp," for example, it will probably be unintentional.

But after two or three such accidents, your baby realizes that what he does prompts Mickey to pop up or the dog to squeak. From then on, your baby will spin the dial and squeeze the puppy on purpose because he wants to see or hear the same effect again. For the first time, your child will appreciate that he has some control over the world around him.

Fill It Up

Household containers (plastic tubs, various boxes, baskets, coffee cans, and so on) or other toys that allow filling and emptying are lots of fun for children during the second half of the year.

> **Q-Tip** _____
>
> Although shape boxes may be too advanced for the first year, you can cut a slot in the plastic top of a coffee can to make a "slot box" instead. Encourage your baby to push lids of baby food jars, blocks, safe (big) beads, and other toys in through the slot or the holes you've cut. Where'd they go? Into the can or box, of course. Your infant will find this game entertaining every time you bring out the container.

Nesting cups are also great fun at this age for filling and dumping, for stacking, or for nesting within one another. You can buy a colored set (usually eight cups) or just use paper or plastic cups of the same size. Store-bought stacking cups also allow you to build a tower for your baby to knock down. In time, she will use them to build towers of her own.

Blocks, Beads, and Balls

Blocks are great for building things, too. Your baby will also have fun just holding, "eating," throwing, and dropping blocks. You can buy or make a wide variety of blocks: cushy foam-rubber blocks, hard wooden blocks, lightweight cardboard blocks, or single-serving cereal box blocks.

Large-scale beads that snap together are also great fun for putting inside containers, for pulling apart, for filling with water and dumping out, and later, for building necklaces and chains.

Balls of various sizes will also entertain your baby at this age. During the final month or two before her first birthday, your baby may be able to roll a big ball (a beach ball or kickball) to you and then stop it if you roll it back. In this way, the two of you can play catch. Smaller balls (anything larger than your baby's fist should be safe) are fun to roll through open-ended cardboard mailing tubes. Your baby will love watching the balls disappear and then reappear at the other end of the tube.

You and your baby can begin playing a primitive form of catch anytime after she can sit up. First, hand her a ball or favorite toy. Then smile, put your hand out, and say,

"Could I please have the ball?" (Don't forget to thank her if she hands it to you.) Repeat this back-and-forth transfer as often as it retains interest.

Exercise Equipment

Your baby will love to climb stairs shortly after he begins to crawl, so provide him with safe stairs to climb. You might find a set of wooden nursery steps, which doubles as a wonderful boat or seesaw when flipped over, at a garage sale or consignment shop. Another good practice device for climbing is a toddler-size plastic slide with no more than four or five steps.

A riding toy, which allows your baby to propel himself by using his own feet, may delight your child near the end of the first year. In addition to giving your baby an opportunity to coordinate use of his feet and legs, a riding toy will also help him practice balancing.

Around your child's first birthday, you may want to try your hand at setting up a miniature "obstacle course." Try using toddler slides that your baby can climb up and slide down, play tunnels or tables or chairs draped with sheets that he can crawl through, and cardboard boxes and pillows to climb over.

Q-Tip

An exercise game that consistently entertains crawlers and toddlers is the "chase game," which can be played on all fours or, once he's got some stability as a toddler, on two feet. Start by having your baby chase after you. Crawl away just out of reach and encourage him with words like, "Try to catch me!"

When your baby gets the hang of the game, you try to do the catching. Try to avoid making it too threatening. Use a playful tone of voice and say, "I'm gonna catch you!" Whether catching or being caught, winning the game will give your baby a boost in confidence, so be sure to let him catch you and to let him lead you on a merry chase before you catch him.

Word Play

Does language play—finger and toe rhymes, nursery rhymes, sing-along songs, and circle-time activity songs—improve the developing language skills of an infant? Probably. After all, hearing words in many different contexts expands your baby's understanding of language in general and of particular clusters of sounds (in other words, words and phrases).

But regardless of whether it advances your baby's language development, the playful use of words entertains your infant. Finger and toe games, for instance, use rhymes that, through repetition, allow your baby to anticipate what will happen next. The repetition of nursery rhymes, songs, and books also combine entertainment, anticipation, and stimulation.

Music to Your Baby's Ears

Your baby loves to listen to your voice. Whether you're talking, reading, or singing, your baby finds your voice entrancing. So sing to your baby—not just to soothe her with bedtime lullabies, but also to stimulate her with fun songs. Try not to feel self-conscious about singing silly and fun songs to your baby. Remember, your baby is no music critic. She just loves that you're taking the time to sing to her.

By about 8 to 10 months, when she becomes obsessed with making her own sounds and mimicking sounds she hears, your baby may start to enjoy "singing along" with you. Try singing a few notes over and over again to your child. See if she tries to echo them back to you. If your baby does start "singing," it will give her practice using her voice in a new way. And this may soon lead to language because babies often sing many of their first words.

> **Q-Tip** _____
> You can expand your baby's interest in music by playing CDs or tapes and by giving her musical instruments of her own during the last 3 months of her first year. Most infants particularly enjoy rhythm instruments like tambourines, drums, maracas, and the ever-popular pot and wooden spoon combo. Your child may also plink out a few notes on a xylophone or toy piano before her first birthday.

Singing not only shows off language in a new setting, but introduces concepts of loud and soft, as well as high and low notes. Like nursery rhymes, most good children's songs wrap language up in a rhythmic package, which makes them not only more enjoyable for your baby but more memorable, too.

Rhymes with Reasons

Rhyming games, which combine actions with either poems or songs, are more than just play. Like most games, they encourage your infant to be more social. In addition, circle-time songs like "Wheels on the Bus," "Itsy Bitsy Spider," and "Open/Shut Them" can help him begin to coordinate words and actions. Counting rhymes like "This Old Man," "One, Two, Buckle My Shoe," "Five Little Speckled Frogs," and "Four Little Ducks" may pave the way for learning numbers. Other rhymes and songs may help your baby learn the names of body parts or the alphabet. Best of all, all of them will be fun for you, and eventually your baby, to sing.

Here are some favorite rhymes and songs:

- With "Pat-a-Cake" and other clapping songs, you can help your baby learn to clap his hands by lightly holding his wrists and clapping his hands together.

- "This Little Piggy" is just plain fun, especially if you finish with a total-body tickle.

- "Itsy Bitsy Spider" can help teach your baby fine motor skills as he uses his fingers to show the spider walking or the rain falling. Until your baby can do these movements himself, don't hesitate to help him out a little.

- When you sing "I'm a Little Teapot," help your child form a handle with one arm and a spout with the other. When it comes time to pour, tilt his body to the spout side.

- When you sing "Where Is Thumbkin?" help your baby raise the appropriate finger with each hand and then have the two fingers introduce themselves to each other with a little "bow."

- Help your baby accompany "One, Two, Buckle My Shoe" by pantomiming the actions described.

- When you sing "If You're Happy and You Know It," your baby will love clapping, stomping his feet, and jumping up high to show how he feels.

- Once your baby can stand, you can begin playing "Ring Around the Rosy."

By the Book

If you want to cultivate a love of reading in your child, start as soon as possible. Books, like rhymes and songs, allow you to share language with your baby in a new, enjoyable, and stimulating way. Reading allows her to make more connections between words and the objects she sees on the page. It will also open up entire worlds to your baby, providing an opportunity to teach about colors, shapes and textures, body parts, people, animals, and every other thing under the sun.

A Picture Book Is Worth a Thousand Words

In choosing books for infants, pick ones that have bold, colorful illustrations or photographs that capture his interest and hold his attention. At this age, good pictures are worth much more than a thousand words. Many board books and bath books for infants don't even bother telling stories. They just show one object per page and name it—and that's probably just what your baby will enjoy.

Books that feature lots of babies or faces will appeal to your child, as will books that highlight animals; cars, trucks, and trains; toys; and things he sees every day in the home, the neighborhood, or the park. Although books that have long stories (more than 10 or 12 words per page) and few pictures will not hold your baby's interest, simple stories may work toward the end of the first year. If you try to read stories at this age, however, watch your baby for signs of intolerance: boredom, shifting, wandering off. After all, most babies at this age have an attention span of less than 5 minutes.

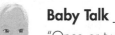

Baby Talk

"Once or twice she had peeped into the book her sister was reading, but it had no pictures or conversations in it, 'and what is the use of a book,' thought Alice, 'without pictures or conversations?'"

—Lewis Carroll

The Durability Factor

If you want to make reading inviting to your baby, you'll need to make books accessible, so make sure to get at least some books sturdy enough for her to handle by herself. Try plastic books and bath books at first. Then introduce sturdy board books that allow your baby to explore them without destroying them (at least, not right away). Fabric books can be fun, too. You might even want to make your own by sewing different fabrics together into a "book."

> **Q-Tip**
>
> You can make your own sturdy, durable, child-safe books. Cut out some bright, colorful magazine pictures that your baby likes. You might also choose copies of some favorite family photos or baby pictures. Trim these pictures so that they'll fit inside a sealable plastic sandwich bag. Then put two back to back in each bag, facing out. (A piece of cardboard between the pictures will make the book sturdier.) Sew the "pages" together—or punch holes in the bags and tie them together with colored yarn. What could be better than a book you made—especially if it's about your baby or your family?

Reading Aloud

When reading simple books to your baby, don't simply read them. Unless he can see the pictures, reading aloud is just words in a vacuum to him. Sit your baby on your lap, point to the various objects shown, and name them two or three times. Take full advantage of the "cuddle factor": the opportunity to curl up with each other and share in the experience. Make reading a special quiet time for both of you.

> **Baby Talk**
>
> "You may have tangible wealth untold;
> Caskets of jewels and coffers of gold.
> Richer than I you can never be—
> I had a mother who read to me."
>
> —Strickland Gillilan

Don't be enslaved by the text—the least important part of the book for infants and young toddlers. Your child may become bored if you just try to read the words as written: "In. Out. Up. Down. Wet. Dry." Instead, encourage your baby to take part in the reading. In enthusiastic tones, talk about the pictures you both see: "The puppy's *in* the basket now. See? Oh, look. Now the puppy got *out* of the basket."

You might also ask for your baby's help in finding certain objects in the illustrations: "Do you see a mouse? I can't find the mouse." Even though your baby can't name it, he may very well understand you and be able to point to it. If he doesn't, take the time to point it out yourself so that he learns the meaning: "Oh, there's the mouse!"

Don't become a fanatic about reading pages in order. Since books for infants seldom tell linear stories, who cares if you skip a few pages—or even skip all the way from the first page to the last (or vice versa)? With books that have more text, don't worry about reading every single word. When your baby gets bored with one page, turn to the next. By 6 or 8 months, he might start reaching out and trying to turn the pages, or at least grab the book, himself. And if your baby wants you to read the book again after you've read the last page, by all means go ahead and do it.

The Electronic Sitter

The amount of television your baby watches, and the content of the programs, shouldn't be an issue until the end of the first year or even later. Until about 9 or 10 months, your baby sees TV as nothing more than a blur of flashing lights and colors. With most shows, even children's shows, the images change too often to permit your baby to focus. (Some infants find this blur somewhat hypnotic, but most find it boring.) Even after your baby starts to "watch" TV, it probably won't sustain her interest for very long. After all, your child still has an extremely short attention span.

Not all television programs are bad. Children's shows on public television and Nickelodeon can teach even very young children shapes, songs, and social mores. Undeniably, sitting your baby down in front of the TV can be useful at times. When you need to make dinner, for instance, and your crawler or toddler would otherwise be wrapped around your ankles as you try to carry a pot of boiling pasta to the sink, TV may seem like an appealing option.

It's not that watching TV is such a bad thing to do. But your baby could be doing so many other things. So when TV does become a viable option, try to limit viewing time. Just as important (if not more important), limit your baby's viewing choices. In general, stick with public television, shows on channels like Nickelodeon, and well-chosen video. Almost all of these choices permit commercial-free viewing of nonviolent, somewhat educational programming.

> **Baby Proofing**
>
> Don't count on TV's hypnotic powers to keep your crawler or toddler safe. Your child still needs supervision. Even if she seems entranced by a particular show, she may lose interest and wander off. Make sure the TV's in a child-safe room, that all stairs are blocked off, and that you can see your baby from where you will be.

Playdates and Play Groups

How much of a social life does your infant need? Put it this way: even if you give your child the opportunity to meet hundreds of other babies, he'll make little use of these opportunities during the first year or two. At this age, even if he's not naturally shy, your baby is not likely to engage another infant in anything approaching cooperative play. Nonetheless, your baby may communicate with another child through looks, smiles, babbles, and touches that may be surprisingly gentle—or surprisingly rough, so take care.

Your child is not yet capable of playing, much less sharing, with others, so don't try to force him to play with others. About the best you can hope for, at least until age 2 or 3, is parallel play: playing next to another child, but having little or no interaction with the other child. (Even this kind of play requires supervision—for example, to mediate struggles over toys.)

Baby Talk

"Fresh air and liberty are all that is necessary to the happiness of children."

—Thomas Love Peacock

This doesn't mean you should immediately cancel all the playdates you've scheduled over the next year or two. Playdates still serve important functions. For one, they can help you establish a network of potential playmates for later years, when he will be ready and eager to play with others. For another, they can help you maintain friendships with parents of children the same age as your baby.

What about joining an organized play group? Certainly, a "Mommy and Me" or "Daddy and Me" class may be fun for your baby. Depending on his emerging personality, your baby may enjoy seeing other children, or he might be somewhat overwhelmed. Either way, he probably won't have any more fun than he would have doing similar activities (climbing, singing, finger and toe play, "circle time" activities) at home alone with you.

Although your baby will reap few significant benefits from organized play groups, they can nonetheless be a valuable resource for you. Enrolling in a class gives you and your baby a regularly scheduled reason to get out of the house. In addition, you might learn some new songs or games you can play at home with your baby. Most important, an organized play group may give you a rare opportunity to talk to other parents of children your baby's age. (Most organized groups extend an equal welcome to either fathers or mothers.)

You can also reap some of these benefits through less organized activities. If you take your child out almost every day to a local park or playground, chances are, you'll meet at least a few other parents of infants, and either the adults or the children will hit it off. You can always start your own play group, too. Try to avoid getting too big, though. (Three or four kids is probably plenty.) You can then rotate playdates from house to house to give your baby (and the other children) new and safe places to explore and new toys to discover. You may even be able to work out some sort of baby-sitting trade-off with some of the other parents.

The Least You Need to Know

◆ Simple toys that illustrate cause and effect—they do something when your child does something to them—will be your baby's favorites.

◆ The rhymes and rhythms of children's verse and songs can make them more memorable and therefore easier for your child to learn than dry prose or even conversations with you.

◆ Set aside time to read with your child every day—and have fun with it.

◆ Your baby may play next to another infant, but don't expect her to play with anyone else for years to come.

Chapter 22

Look Out, World! Getting Ready for Your Toddler

In This Chapter

- ◆ Celebrating your child's first birthday
- ◆ Anticipating the year to come
- ◆ Childproofing for the toddler and the climber
- ◆ Keeping your 1-year-old safe

Congratulations! In less than a year, you and your baby have gotten to know and love each other. As he approaches his first birthday, you must feel proud of all your baby has accomplished. A year ago, your baby was bawling and helpless—dependent on you for everything from such basics as eating, cleaning, and dressing to more complex needs such as comfort, conversation, and other stimulation. Today, although he still needs you for most of these, he can probably eat with some degree of independence and move around with a great deal more.

A year ago, your baby could communicate only through cries. Now he has a wide array of smiles and other facial expressions, gestures, and even some fledgling "words" to convey his feelings or desires. From a creature of pure instinct, your baby has become a child of reason—at least some of the time. He wants to explore and experiment, to find out what's out there and discover how the world works.

Baby Talk

"If a child is to keep alive his inborn sense of wonder, he needs the companionship of at least one adult who can share it, rediscovering with him the joy, excitement, and mystery of the world we live in."

—Rachel Carson

While acknowledging the incredible development your baby has undergone, take some pride in all you have accomplished, too. You have learned what particular cries mean and have built a basis for verbal communication. You have discovered, at least in part, what sort of person he is—for indeed he *is* a person now. You have stimulated his development of physical and mental skills, encouraging him to expand his abilities. Most important, you have kept him happy, healthy, and safe. So have a happy birthday—and many, many more!

Your Child's First Birthday Party

Planning a birthday party for your almost-1-year-old? If so, do your baby a favor: keep it simple. At this vulnerable time in her life, when she's getting ready to take her first steps (or has already taken her first steps), your baby's anxiety around other people may be stronger than it has ever been before. In such a state, your child will not appreciate a room full of people, whether friends or strangers. Make the party a family affair, with at most two or three playmates (if she has any yet). Think of it more like a special playdate than a party. All you need to do is have safe toys on hand for your baby and her young guests.

Baby Talk

"A truly appreciative child will break, lose, spoil, or fondle to death any really successful gift within a matter of minutes."

—Russell Lynes

As with any occasion at this age, timing is everything. Don't schedule the party at naptime or mealtime. She will more likely be social if she's well fed and well rested. Even then, an hour or 90 minutes will probably be your baby's limit.

Your baby doesn't need elaborate decorations or paid entertainment at her party. Indeed, a guy dressed up like Spongebob Squarepants is more likely to traumatize your child than to enchant her. You don't even need to buy a whole lot of gifts for her first birthday. After all, your baby is just as likely to enjoy a cardboard box filled with packing peanuts as the expensive gift that came in it.

Your baby's first birthday may seem the ideal time to introduce her to cake. Again, keep it simple. Save the three-tiered cake with the figures on top for her wedding. A cupcake will do for this occasion.

In short, try not to work yourself up too much about your child's first birthday party. Relax. It means much more to you than it does to your baby at this age.

A Sneak Preview

What will the next year bring? For one thing, your child will probably double (or even triple) the number of teeth in his mouth. The new teeth include the painful advent of two new sets of molars, one around the beginning of the year and one near the end. As the year goes on, your toddler will sleep less at night and cut down on daytime napping. In fact, by his second birthday, he may be down to just one nap a day.

Your child will also master many new skills in his second year. Physically, he will become increasingly graceful and confident. From tottering first steps, he will walk with increasing self-assurance. Within a few months, he'll not only be walking, but running and climbing everything in sight. He may even try his hand at walking backward!

His expanding mobility and improving dexterity mean your 1-year-old will need more stimulation in your home. You'll need a few new toys, especially containers (including shape boxes), puzzles, dress-up clothes and props for make-believe play, and crayons, paints, and other art supplies.

Baby Doctor

Don't worry if your 1-year-old goes through periods when he seems to forget how to do things that he once did with ease. Although true regression is possible, your child has more likely moved on to some new ability than lost an old one.

Your baby will need more outside stimulation, too. You should continue taking him to parks, playgrounds, and stores, and perhaps add special trips to children's museums, art museums, malls, and other places where there's a lot going on.

The growth in your baby's language skills will be very exciting. Words will come slowly at first, but your baby will pick up the pace during the last few months of the year. From 20 to 40 words at 18 months, your child may speak 150 to 200 by his second birthday. He will probably even begin to put two words together to form simple sentences.

Baby Talk

"The worst stage a kid ever goes through is the one he is going through right now."

—Sam Levenson

Unfortunately, his favorite word may soon be "No!" Expect to hear it a lot and try to accept it with good grace. Your 1-year-old will be trying to establish his independence in one of the few ways open to him: refusing to do what you want him to do.

Throughout the year, he will probably test your limits and challenge your authority. Get used to these challenges. Your child will issue them for many years to come.

Prepare Yourself (and Your Home)

Although it may seem inconceivable when you consider how many scrapes, cuts, bumps, and falls you have already prevented since your baby began to crawl, your 1-year-old will require even more vigilance. You'll need to "spot" her on the slide or anything she starts to climb—and she's likely to climb almost anything. If you're unable to spot her, you'll need to do what you can to make anything she can climb inaccessible to her.

Anything that represents a danger to your toddler, such as poisons, choking hazards, and sharp objects, now needs to be kept inside locked cabinets. As your toddler begins to climb like a monkey, even things stowed away in high cabinets will no longer be totally inaccessible.

You'll need to be especially vigilant near roads and driveways and in parking lots. Don't depend upon drivers to see someone as small as your toddler as she darts out into the street. Never let her walk into the street without holding your hand, and don't let her play anywhere near the street.

Childproofing

As mentioned in Chapter 10, babyproofing is not a one-shot deal, but rather an ongoing process. Throughout the infant and toddler years (and the preschool years as well), you'll need to reevaluate and update your safety measures repeatedly to reflect your child's growing abilities. Now is one of those times. As your child changes from a crawler into a toddler, he will develop the ability to get his hands on anything that isn't nailed down. Although all of your babyproofing measures also apply to young toddlers, you'll need to move beyond them to childproofing.

Running into Danger

Your toddler's walking and running will make it necessary to introduce a number of new safeguards. To help prevent falls, for instance, you may want to take the trouble to secure any rugs.

If your home has sliding glass doors or plate-glass windows, put decals or window stickers on them to make them more visible. A running toddler who can't see the glass may crash right into or through it. Because this amount of glass would be so danger-ous, you might even find it well worth the expense to replace them, at least temporar-ily, with Plexiglas or safety glass.

Now that your baby can stand, he can probably reach most of the doorknobs in your home. You'll have to take steps to prevent your toddler from locking himself in or, even worse, letting himself out. A strip of electrical tape or duct tape can prevent most lock-ins. Tape the door latch flush against the side of the door to make it impossible to pull the door shut in a way that locks it.

You'll also need some way of knowing if outside doors have been opened. You won't want your toddler to wander outside without adult supervision. Hanging a bell that jingles when the door opens or closes should provide adequate warning that your child has gone outside or is at least seriously thinking about it.

Climbing Hazards

Another new talent that will get your adventurous toddler into trouble will be her improved climbing skills. Freestanding shelves represent a significant hazard to small climbers. To your 1-year-old, shelves will look like a ladder or staircase, and the top shelves will invariably have the most interesting objects. To prevent your child from tipping shelves over on top of herself, take the time to secure any freestanding shelves to a wall.

Your child's climbing and her ability as an escape artist may also put her in increased danger when she's in a stroller, car seat, or high chair. Even when she's strapped in, you'll need to keep a close eye on your climber. Once she can toddle about, walk, run, and climb, your baby may have little patience for such confinement. She may wriggle out from under the safety straps and begin to climb out of the high chair or the moving stroller.

Q-Tip

If you want to discourage your young climber from scaling the pantry shelves and kitchen counters, store foods that are safe for her on lower shelves and in lower cabinets.

Once your toddler becomes a climber, even cribs and playpens will no longer be as safe as they once were. Your child may find ingenious ways to climb out, and she'll get better and better at it the more she practices. If your toddler becomes a particularly adept climber, you may need to consider moving her out of her crib and into a bed. After all, it's a long way down from the top of the crib railing to the floor.

Q-Tip

If your child becomes a talented escape artist, you may decide it's time to begin exploring alternatives to high chairs and strollers. (There is no alternative to a car seat, but luckily, car seats are also much more difficult to escape.)

Instead of strapping your baby into a stroller, try doing a lot more walking hand in hand. It will be slower, but you won't have to worry about her falling out of the stroller. As for the high chair, it may be time to put it away when your child can consistently get out from under the safety strap. Your child will probably enjoy a miniature table and chairs that allow her to come and go as she pleases and eliminate the risk of serious falls.

Safety Rules

Although your baby may speak only a handful of words (if any) when he turns 1, he understands much more than he can say. So don't hesitate to begin teaching him safety rules. Whenever you encounter any danger, tell your toddler the safety rule. For instance, make it a strict rule that he must hold a trusted grown-up's hand before stepping into the road.

Babyproofing

When your toddler moves out of her crib, you can minimize the chance that she'll fall out of bed by using temporary side rails or by using a single side rail and placing the other side of her bed against the wall. Or you may want to eliminate the possibility of falls altogether by placing your child's mattress directly on the floor.

When possible, use a dramatic flourish, sharp tones, and pantomime to amplify your words. When cooking, for example, you might pretend to touch the pot or stove, pull your hand back quickly and say, "Ow! Hot! Don't touch!" If you're slicing vegetables, you might show your 1-year-old the blade, touch it, and say, "Ow! Sharp! Don't touch!"

Don't rely on a single safety lesson to teach your child what to do and what to avoid. Repeat the lesson whenever you encounter an everyday danger. If you send a consistent message, even a 1-year-old can learn to avoid many dangers. Unfortunately, even after your child seems to have learned the lesson, even after he can repeat your words or fill in the blanks when you pause in midsentence, he may forget your warnings in his fascination with some forbidden object.

Nothing will take the place of careful supervision, and your 1-year-old will need a lot of it. But as long as you can keep him safe, you have a fun and exciting year ahead of you—and many more to come.

The Least You Need to Know

◆ Your baby will never remember her first birthday party, so don't bother making it a huge deal—or a huge ordeal.

◆ Your baby will become increasingly mobile, and more likely to get into dangerous situations, during her second year.

◆ Your baby will also become increasingly verbal. Unfortunately, her favorite word is likely to be "No!" Keep a sense of humor and recognize this as an essential step in establishing her independence.

◆ Childproofing is an ongoing process that must continually take into account your child's growing abilities.

◆ Despite all your safety measures, you will need to maintain constant vigilance.

Part 5

Partners in Parenting: Issues for First-Year Parents

No matter how old your baby is, certain decisions and problems seem inescapable. When should you or your partner return to work, or should you return at all? What's the best way for a dad to stay involved in the joys and responsibilities of parenthood? How can you and your partner share in parenting without stepping on each other's toes or using your baby to play tug o' war? Do you even remember how your child was conceived (it was sex, wasn't it)? And is it too much to ask to get 15 minutes to yourself once in a blue moon?

Parenting works best as a partnership. Sure, it's possible to do it alone, as many good parents have proved. But both you and your baby will find your life together more fulfilling if you have a willing and able partner to lighten the burdens and to delight in the treats of parenting. Don't be shy. Offer help if you feel underutilized; ask for help if you feel overwhelmed. But whatever you do, try to do it together.

Chapter 23

The Great Juggling Act

In This Chapter

- ◆ Whether and when to go back to work
- ◆ Alternatives to full-time work or full-time parenting
- ◆ Day-care options
- ◆ Finding a good sitter, nanny, or day-care provider
- ◆ Handling separation and separation anxiety

Deciding whether and when to go back to work can be an agonizing decision for most parents. First, you face the choice of whether to go back to work at all. Balancing your baby's needs, your own needs, your partner's needs, and your financial needs is not easy. You're a good parent. You want to do what's best for your child. But what is best?

Unfortunately, this question has no easy or universal answer. What's best for your sister or your best friend or me may not be what's best for you. You will need to struggle to reach a personal decision based on careful consideration of the factors discussed in this chapter—and other considerations unique to you and your circumstances. No matter what decision you make, it will involve some degree of compromise because that's what balance is all about.

Everything's Up in the Air

Fortunately, if you want and/or need to work outside the home, you can combine work and family in many different ways. Each alternative has its own particular benefits and drawbacks. Here are some of the options:

◆ You could stay at home with your baby full-time.

◆ Your partner could stay at home with your baby full-time.

◆ You or your partner could work at home, trying to squeeze work time into the hours when your baby is sleeping (which will decrease as the year goes on) or in the other's care.

◆ You and your partner could iron out work schedules that allow you to share baby and home care while both working at least part-time (or one of you full-time and the other part-time).

◆ One of you could work part-time and the other full-time, and find a good caregiver for the hours when both you and your partner are not home.

◆ Both of you could work full-time and leave your child in the care of a warm, sensitive caregiver.

If you've decided to work, even part-time, or if you have no choice but to work, you still face a long line of logistical hurdles:

◆ When should you go back to work?

◆ Who will take care of the baby when you and your partner are both working? How do you know a good day-care provider from a bad one?

◆ What kind of day-care situation is best for your baby?

◆ Who will take the baby to his day-care provider? And who will pick him up?

◆ Who stays home if the baby is sick? Or if the day-care provider gets sick? Who will take care of the baby if and when the day-care provider goes on vacation?

To keep all these balls in the air—family time and baby care, work, your relationship with your partner, and a smidgen of time for yourself—you'll have to become quite a juggler. It won't be easy, especially at first, but you'll get better with practice. So don't punish yourself if you drop one or more of the balls once in a while; just pick it up and keep trying.

Working It Out

Should you return to work after your baby is born? If you can even ask this question, consider yourself lucky. Many parents have no choice about whether to go back to work. Among parents of children under the age of 1, nearly 60 percent of mothers and about 90 percent of fathers work (not counting the unpaid labor of housework and child care). Not all of these do so by choice. Whether single parents or dual-earning couples, many parents find that they have to go back to work just to make ends meet.

Of course, just because you're lucky to have a choice doesn't make that choice any easier. Whether you decide to make a full-time commitment to one or the other or split your time between child care and paid work, you'll be forced to sacrifice something important. Any choice you make may involve a sense of loss.

In making your decision, you and your partner will need to try to find a balance between your baby's needs and your own (whether financial or personal). This choice is very personal, but here are some issues you may want to consider:

◆ **Money.** For many parents, the issue of money proves decisive. Can you afford to take extended time off? If you would prefer to stay home, can you economize to compensate for lost earnings? If you go back to work, how much extra money will you really be bringing into the household budget? How much will the added costs of child care, house cleaning, and business-related expenses (commuting, clothing, lunches, and so on) eat away at your earnings?

◆ **Priorities.** What are the most important things in your life? So many possibilities suggest themselves: family, independence, living comfortably, your baby's well-being and healthy development, your relationship with your spouse, career progress, self-confidence, adequate and (somewhat) affordable health-care coverage, personal growth, and many others. Rank your priorities and consider which decision best serves those at the top of the list.

Baby Talk _____

"At work, you think of the children you've left at home. At home, you think of the work you've left unfinished. Such a struggle is unleashed within yourself: your heart is rent."

—Golda Meir

◆ **Emotional issues.** Don't dismiss these issues as unimportant. You, your partner, and your baby will all suffer if you make a decision that leaves you feeling miserable. In which role, parent or wage-earner, do you feel most confident? In which does your partner? Which is most stressful?

Will you feel guilty for "neglecting" your baby if you go back to work? Will you feel dissatisfied if you don't work at least some of the time outside of the home? Will you feel pressed to provide "quality time" in the hours you spend with your child if you're away working 20 or more hours a week? How will you feel if you miss special firsts: first laughs, first steps, first words? Will you feel jealous of your day-care provider (even if it's your partner)?

◆ **Trust.** Do you have someone you trust to care for your baby? If not, are you confident you'll find someone trustworthy? Will anyone ever earn your trust as your baby's caregiver?

◆ **Shared care.** Will your partner share in child care and household chores? Can you depend on your partner to ease some of the burden? Or will you not only be working outside the home, but doing all the work inside as well?

◆ **Career goals.** Will extended time off significantly retard your job advancement? Can your employer offer you assurance that you'll have a job if you take more than its standard parental leave?

◆ **Employer flexibility.** How understanding is your employer? Will your employer (or your partner's) allow you time off when your baby or baby-sitter is sick? Can you leave early or come in late? How much time will your job really require? Can you work at home?

In making your decision, keep in mind that unless you're financially strapped, any choice you make is reversible. If things don't work out the way you had hoped, you can always change your mind. If you work full- or part-time and find it unbearable to be away from your baby, take an extended leave or quit your job, if you can afford it. If you decide to stay at home and find that you miss the money, the camaraderie, the status, or the sense of accomplishment that you once got at work, try to find some work outside the home.

Baby Doctor _____

If you breast-feed your baby and want to continue until she has begun eating solid foods, you'll probably want to wait until your baby is at least 6 months old before returning to a full-time job. Although you can, in theory, express milk during breaks and your lunch hour, it may be difficult to find an environment where you can relax enough to let milk flow easily.

It's All in the Timing

When's the best time to return to work? Again, if you can even ask this question, consider yourself lucky. Many parents have little choice about when to return to work.

The 1993 Family and Medical Leave Act mandates up to 12 weeks of unpaid leave for family emergencies or the birth of a baby. If you work for a company with fewer than 50 employees, however, the law doesn't apply to your company. Smaller companies don't have to offer parental leave. Even if your company grants 12 weeks of leave, financial considerations may necessitate a quicker return. So if you have the option to take a longer leave, you're one of the lucky ones.

If you can set your own timetable, the best time to return to work depends on your individual situation and your baby's. Ideally, you should allow enough time to bond with your baby. By forming a solid bond during your baby's infancy, you establish a basis for a close relationship throughout her childhood. If you fail to bond with your baby now, you may never gain confidence in your own parenting skills. This lack of confidence may haunt your relationship with your child for years to come.

Your baby also needs time to bond. She needs your day-to-day care in order to develop basic trust in you. Your ability to satisfy her wants and needs provides the foundation for basic trust. Your baby's ability to trust others in future relationships may depend on the amount of trust she builds in her relationship with you and your partner now.

But how long does it take to form this bond? You may have formed a solid bond by 2 months, or it may take 6. It depends on your personality and that of your baby. In addition, you may be able to return to work part-time relatively soon after your baby's birth and still have plenty of time to work on bonding. No one answer applies to all parents and infants. The best possible answer is to return to work when you and your baby both seem ready.

> **Q-Tip**
>
> Although there may not be a single "best time" to return to work, there are times to avoid. If possible, don't return to work when your baby is experiencing some other major change. If you've just moved into a new home, if your baby has just started to crawl or walk, or if you're just now trying to get her to sleep through the night, your baby needs you to provide a strong sense of stability and security. You will notice how clingy your baby becomes during these times. For this reason, these are all lousy times to add the stress of separating from you and getting used to another caregiver.

Isn't There Another Way?

In considering whether and when to return to work, you don't need to make a definitive choice between job and family. If you're struggling to make the "right" decision at all, then you must have the option of not returning to work full-time. So consider part-time employment instead.

When affordable, part-time work probably represents the best of all possible worlds for mothers and fathers of young children and the children themselves. It allows you to maintain a primary role in your child's care, it brings in additional household income, and it affords the opportunity for some sense of accomplishment both inside and outside the home.

Combining full-time baby care with part-time employment does have drawbacks. For one, part-time work may not produce enough household income. Also, with the exception of child care during the hours you work, your job-related expenses (commuting, clothing, and the like) will probably be almost as high for part-time work as they are for full-time work. Finally, getting benefits as a part-time worker is difficult, though not always impossible, depending upon the demand for your skills.

Q-Tip

If you decide to work part-time, you might prefer working 4 to 6 half-days rather than 2 or 3 full days. Although you will spend more time and money commuting, you will never be away from your baby for very long.

If you think part-time work might be the best decision for you and your family, ask your employer (or potential employer). Your employer may surprise you by being more sensitive to your concerns and more flexible in his or her demands than you might anticipate, especially if you have very marketable skills. In any case, you'll never know if you don't ask.

Other alternatives you might want to consider include …

◆ **Flex-time scheduling.** Many employers, especially large ones, allow flex-time scheduling, but few U.S. employees take advantage of this opportunity. If you work an 11-to-7 day and your partner works from 7 to 3, you'll cut your child-care costs in half. Such an arrangement also gives both of you more time to spend with your baby. The downside: you'll have less time for each other.

◆ **Telecommuting.** Ask your employer if you can do any or all of your job at home. With nearly half of U.S. companies now offering at least some telecommuting options, this setup has become an increasingly viable alternative to spending all day in an out-of-home office. The downside: you'll need to discipline yourself to get down to work as soon as your baby goes down for a nap or your partner gets home—in short, whenever you have a free hour or two.

◆ **Starting your own business.** You may decide to start your own part-time or freelance business with your base of operations at home. The downside: it won't work unless your skills are in demand. Also, it will require even more discipline than if you were working at home for an outside employer.

Who's Minding the Baby?

No matter how much you decide to work, you'll almost definitely be in the market for child care. Once upon a time, grandparents, aunts, or cousins handled child care for working parents. But fewer and fewer new parents today live close enough to their parents or siblings to make this a viable option, so you'll probably have to find someone to care for your baby when you can't be home with him. Whether you and your partner are working full- or part-time, you will basically have three child-care options available to you: a nanny or baby-sitter, a home day-care provider, and a day-care center.

Despite all the horror stories you may have heard, child care doesn't have to be a nightmare. For every notorious day-care institution, there are hundreds of adequate ones and dozens of good ones. For every baby-sitter caught beating a child on camera for the evening news, there are dozens of sensitive, caring sitters who would never dream of harming a baby.

If you do your homework—by conducting interviews, visiting day-care sites, checking references, and so on—you will almost certainly find one of the good ones.

The Gold Standard: Nannies and Sitters

Having a nanny or sitter come into your home to care for your baby has certain advantages:

◆ Your baby remains in the environment most familiar to her and doesn't have to get comfortable in new surroundings.

◆ Your child needs to get used to only one new person (rather than an entire staff).

◆ Your baby will probably get sick less often because she won't have daily exposure to other babies (germ-carriers all—except yours, of course).

◆ You don't need to lug supplies and clothing back and forth from your home to the day-care site.

◆ You don't need to make special arrangements or stay home yourself if your baby gets sick.

◆ A nanny or sitter offers more flexibility in terms of hours because you get to set them yourself.

◆ During your baby's naps, your sitter may do some light housework, an invaluable blessing.

In-home care has some disadvantages, too. It makes you entirely dependent on one caregiver. If your sitter gets sick, gets caught in traffic, or—aaargh!—quits with little or no notice, you're stuck. A single caregiver has a greater potential to spark feelings of jealousy or rivalry on your part, too. Also, sitters are neither licensed nor subject to supervision, and you'll need to work hard at building a relationship with your baby's sitter just to find out what they've been doing all day.

A major drawback of in-home care is the cost. Hiring a full-time nanny or a part-time sitter is the most expensive child-care option. In addition to a decent salary, a full-time caregiver may expect (and deserve) medical benefits, vacation time, and periodic raises in pay. Also, by law you are required to withhold federal, state, and local taxes, as well as half of the Social Security and Medicare "contributions" of any household employee. You have to ante up the other half of your nanny's Social Security and Medicare payments yourself—and if you or your partner ever hope to hold an elected or appointed government office, you'd better do so.

Q-Tip

Any paid child care is tax-deductible to the degree that it allows both parents (or a single parent) to work or look for work. Ask your local IRS office for Form 2441: Child and Dependent Care Expenses. Because the form requires you to provide the Social Security numbers of any child-care workers you hire, it may give you the incentive to put your nanny or sitter on the books.

If you've decided to hire someone to care for your baby in your home, start looking early. Finding a good one is not always easy. Holding on to a good one, is even harder. Adult caregivers often find that they need more money than child-care workers are usually paid. Teenage sitters often have busy social lives of their own. So if you find a good caregiver, treat her or him like gold.

Prospecting for Gold: The Search

You'll need to do some work just to find viable prospects for an in-home child-care position. Here are some of the things you can do:

◆ **Word of mouth.** Ask neighbors, your pediatrician, coworkers, and clergy members. You can try asking other parents, too, but don't expect too much of a response: it's like asking a miner where to find gold around these parts.

◆ **Classified info.** Check the want ads in your local paper(s) or try placing one yourself.

◆ **Post-it notes.** Check community bulletin boards at the town hall, the grocery store, the drug store, and so on, and post your own ad there, too.

◆ **On campus.** If you need only part-time help, register with the employment, career counseling, or housing office of the nearest college or university. If you have an extra room, you might be able to find a college student who wants to trade 10 to 15 hours of child care a week for a free room and perhaps some meals.

◆ **Student employment.** For part-time help in the evenings and on weekends, or for an occasional sitter, call the guidance counselor at your local high school or junior high school and ask if your school district offers baby-sitting training programs. If it does, the guidance office will gladly offer you a list of prospects.

◆ **Grandparents for hire.** Check with your local senior citizen centers. Many older people are capable of caring for a baby (although a toddler may be harder to keep up with).

Q-Tip

If you have a spare room and need full-time child care, consider hiring live-in help. You can usually offer a lower salary if you add room and board. Au pair agencies (see Appendix F) can find you young adults (usually 19 to 24 years old) from other nations who will provide child care in return for room, board, and a token salary (plus a hefty agency fee).

Panning for Gold: The Interview

Even if you feel desperate, don't hire the first prospect you get. Instead, collect a handful of prospects and then invite each of them to your home for an interview.

What should you look for? It depends on your own needs and preferences. If promptness is important to you, for instance, you won't want to hire someone who shows up late for the interview. But no matter what your personal preferences, you want someone who seems warm and comfortable with young children. At least some training or knowledge of infant development, including knowledge of infant CPR, can be a plus, but keep in mind how much knowledge and training you had when your baby was born. You may also want to consider how well your sitter's and your baby's personalities mesh. A shy infant and a pushy or overbearing sitter won't match up well, for example. But neither will a very social infant and a withdrawn, passive sitter.

The most important quality that a nanny or sitter should have is the ability to communicate well. You want someone who will not only be sensitive to your baby's preverbal communication, but also be at ease when talking to you about your baby. A good prospect will not only listen attentively to you, but will ask questions about your baby, your child-rearing philosophy, and his or her job responsibilities during the interview and/or tour of your home.

During the interview, ask about the person's beliefs regarding setting limits, feeding habits, and so on. Make sure they're at least close to your own. You might also find it useful to offer up a few hypothetical situations to see how the interviewee would handle them. Find out how the person would handle not just an emergency (although you certainly want to know that), but also such everyday crises as crying jags, crankiness, and the refusal to eat or nap.

Q-Tip

During the interview, excuse yourself from the room for a minute, leaving the prospective sitter and your baby alone together. When you return, come back in quietly. Observe how the prospect is interacting with your baby. If the sitter isn't interacting with your baby at all, forget it. If the sitter is trying, however, give the two of them a couple of minutes to get to know each other. You can use this time to form some initial impressions about the sitter's rapport with infants. (Your baby may "sabotage" this tryout if he sees you. No matter how great the sitter, he prefers you.)

If the sitter seems warm without being pushy, offers a narrative of what your baby is doing, and/or tries to engage your child but lets him proceed at his own pace, you may have a good prospect.

Trust your instincts in hiring a nanny or sitter. If something doesn't feel right, even though you can't quite put your finger on it, don't hire that person. (However, if this feeling arises with every interview, reevaluate whether you really want to hire a sitter at all. *You* may not be ready to leave your baby in someone else's care.)

Even after a successful interview, consider hiring the sitter for a trial period of 1 or 2 weeks before you really need child care. This trial period will give you a chance to observe your baby and the sitter together. It will also give you a chance to ease your baby into child care by leaving for short times at first and building up from there.

Q-Tip

Check any potential sitter's references! Follow up by contacting the references by phone; don't be satisfied with just a written letter. Call the letter writer to find out what the interviewee did for the family and for how long. Find out why the person left and whether that family would consider hiring her or him again.

Child Care Outside the Home

A full-time nanny or part-time sitter may not suit your particular needs or situation. You may not be able to afford in-home care. Or you may be unable to find anyone who meets your standards for in-home care. If, for any reason, in-home care won't work for you and your baby, you'll need to explore the world of child care outside the home.

You will find two basic alternatives: family day care and day-care centers.

A Home away from Home: Family Day Care

A family day-care provider takes care of just a few children in her or his own home. (The number of children, including those who live there, should not exceed five.) The small size of this kind of day care can make it feel like a family. Smallness also allows more excursions—to a local park or playground or even a grocery store. Because the caregiver is usually a parent, the home will almost always be well baby-proofed. Last but not least, family day care is usually the least expensive child care option available—no small consideration to many working parents.

Family day care, however, like in-home care, forces you to depend on just one person for care. If she or he can't do it for any reason, you'll need to cancel your own plans or commitments or find an alternative quickly. You cannot send your child when she gets sick either, and she will get sick: exposure to other children almost always means more colds, flus, and illness in general. Finally, most family day-care providers are not licensed—and therefore are not subject to any type of supervision or periodic review.

Q-Tip

You may want to join a babysitting co-op or try your hand at forming your own. Co-ops are essentially family day care with rotating caregivers, including you whenever your turn comes up. You can ensure that every parent participates equally by employing a rigid rotation schedule. Or you could establish a system of credits that members earn by taking their turns at caregiving and "spend" by taking advantage of another member's services. (You'll probably need to set a limit on how deeply any individual member can go into "debt" before having to pay it off in services rendered.) Although it can be exhausting to take your turn, it's a small price to pay for having child care available when you need it.

Day-Care Centers

Center-based day care has the advantage of being almost always available. Because day-care centers do not depend on just one person to provide care, they don't shut down if one staff member gets sick. In addition, staff members are almost always trained and experienced. Because all day-care centers must be licensed, you'll know that yours meets the safety requirements mandated by your state. Spaces in child-care centers are often designed for a specific age group of children. Finally, if your employer offers an on-site day-care center, you can probably visit your baby (and perhaps even nurse her) during lunch hours or coffee breaks.

Baby Talk

"A baby who spent certain hours of every day among other babies, being cared for because he was a baby and not because he was 'my baby,' would grow to have a very different opinion of himself from that which is forced upon each new soul that comes among us by the ceaseless adoration of his own immediate family."
—Charlotte Perkins Gilman

Unfortunately, finding a day-care program that accepts kids under age 1 is difficult. (In fact, many day-care centers won't accept children who are still in diapers.) Although center-based care doesn't cost as much as in-home care, it does cost more than family day care. The biggest drawback of most large day-care centers, however, is their rigidity. Programs are often very structured, an approach that isn't suitable for most infants. Many large centers are also inflexible in terms of scheduling drop-off and pick-up times.

Navigating the World of Day Care

Although it can be somewhat easier to find a good family day care or day-care center than to find someone who will care for your baby at home, this search also takes time. Start looking as soon as you've made the decision to go back to work. You'll be glad you took the time to do it right.

You can find a good day-care provider using many of the same resources used to find a nanny or sitter. For instance, the classified section in your local newspaper probably has dozens of ads for child-care centers and family day-care providers. Check under *Day Care* in the Yellow Pages of your phone book. You should find both centers and family providers there, too.

Word-of-mouth is the best way to find family day-care providers, so ask clergy members, your pediatrician, and your neighbors. Consult other parents, too; they are often much more willing to share information when talking about out-of-home care than when asked about nannies or sitters.

If you're looking for a day-care center, don't forget to ask your employer. Employers, such as hospitals, corporations, and sometimes unions, often provide the best center-based care. Large employers recognize that providing quality day care can help attract valuable new employees and retain the employees they already have.

Exploring the Brave New World

Whether looking for family day care or a day-care center, always take the time to visit the site with your baby before registering. See what the caregivers are doing with other children your baby's age. Do they seem attentive to the infants in their care? Do they talk to the babies? Form an overall impression and ask yourself: will you feel comfortable leaving your baby there?

As you tour the site and talk to the caregivers, pay particular attention to the following considerations:

◆ **Space.** Does it seem adequately babyproofed? Do you see equipment to climb and plenty of stimulating, age-appropriate toys? If the day care has a playground, is it safe for babies? Is the space divided into separate areas or separate rooms for sleeping, eating, changing diapers, and playing?

Is the changing area well away from the eating and playing areas? Does the staff clean and disinfect the changing table after each use? Do they wash their hands before and after each changed diaper?

◆ **Size.** Count the number of infants (including your own) and the number of caregivers. With infants, who need a lot of individualized attention and do not participate in group activities, the ratio should not exceed three children for each caregiver.

◆ **Staff.** Ask about the staff's training and experience. Find out how many work full-time and how many part-time. (Hiring part-time workers who get no benefits is a cost-saving measure that may indicate less training, dedication, and overall quality from the center.) You might also want to know how management conducts background checks on its staff members and the turnover rate among the staff.

◆ **Licensing.** All day-care centers should have state licenses. (Few family day-care providers do.) Have state reviews ever turned up any violations? If so, what were they and what changes were implemented to address the problems?

◆ **Program and philosophy.** Does the caregiver offer the flexible, individualized program that infants need? What's the balance between group activities and individual play time? Do the caregivers do anything special to help a new child adjust? Do they encourage the use of security blankets or other comfort objects?

◆ **Logistics.** You'll also want answers to practical matters. What happens if you're late to pick up your baby? Who supplies food for snacks and meals? Can they accommodate sick children? If so, what do they do to curb the spread of illness? Are toys regularly scrubbed and disinfected to keep them relatively germ-free?

◆ **Cost.** What can you expect to pay for day care? Does the provider charge an hourly rate? Are half-day rates available? Or is a single price set regardless of how many hours you use the service?

Q-Tip _____

Check references as thoroughly with day-care providers as you would with someone you're bringing into your own home. After all, if your darling will be spending a significant amount of time there, you'll want to know what other parents think of it.

Parting Is Such Sweet Sorrow

No matter how fantastic your sitter or day-care provider seems, both you and your baby may suffer from separation anxiety when it comes time to part.

Especially toward the end of your baby's first year, as her memory begins to develop, separation anxiety may become almost unbearable for both of you. Your 10-month-old will know that as soon as the baby-sitter steps in the door or as soon as you walk into the day-care room, you'll soon be going. Your baby may cry almost hysterically when it's time for you to leave. And she may repeat this scenario day after day.

Q-Tip

It may ease separation anxiety later if you at least occasionally employ a sitter during the first 6 months of your baby's life. She may feel more comfortable with separation if it has already been a familiar aspect of her life.

If your child suffers from separation anxiety, try to ignore the hysterics and make parting as short and sweet as possible. Say good-bye with a smile and a hug and step outside the door. Then come back 5 minutes later. Don't go back into the room (or house); just stand outside the door or perhaps look in through a window. Chances are that your baby will already have quieted down and adjusted to her day-care situation. If, over the course of a week or two, she doesn't calm down within 10 minutes or so of your departure, you can always reconsider your decision—either about putting her in day care at all or about using this particular day-care provider.

The worst part for your baby (and therefore for you) is the act of separation. Your baby may remember similar situations from the past and anticipate the separation. But in her focus on the immediate moment's anxiety, she may not remember the happy reunion that always followed in the past. She may think you won't ever come back.

After you're gone, however, your baby may forget that you've gone at all. (Focusing on the immediate moment does have its advantages.) Or maybe she calms down enough to remember now that you always do return. Fortunately, your baby should cry less and less each day (though hysterics may escalate again if she's sick, tired, in the middle of a developmentally challenging period, or otherwise susceptible to teariness).

As great as your baby's anxiety may seem, your own anxiety may be even worse. You may plague yourself with questions like these:

◆ Will she survive without you?

◆ Will she miss you?

◆ Are you being selfish?

◆ Will the separation harm your baby?

Try to be grateful that your baby has someone else who also wants to care for her. After all, if you have formed a loving relationship with your child and continue to bond well with her during your time together, what harm will it do to have other warm, sensitive, loving caregivers bond with her, too? Your baby is perfectly capable of bonding with more than one or two people. (If you nonetheless feel jealous of your baby's caregiver, you may want to reevaluate your priorities and take more "time off" before returning to work.)

> **Baby Proofing**
>
> Should you ever have second thoughts about the quality of care your child receives, whether from a nanny, family day care or day-care center? Yes—if you see any of these signs:
>
> - Bruises, cuts, or signs of abuse
> - Profound hunger, dirty diapers, or signs of neglect
> - Crying, signs of withdrawal, or listlessness toward the day-care provider(s)
> - The absence of any smiles or affection for the day-care provider, even after several weeks together
>
> If you *consistently* or *repeatedly* observe any of these signs, you should start looking for another day-care provider immediately.

Take heart. Separating usually gets easier after the first few times. You'll learn that your child did survive and will survive. You'll recognize that she appears relatively unscathed. And you'll be relieved to see that she seems just as happy to see you as ever.

What's Your Hurry?

With any new sitter or day-care situation, give your baby time to get used to the idea before running off and "abandoning" him. Ideally, you will leave him with someone he knows. Arrange to have the sitter arrive at least 15 minutes early (paid, of course) or, even better, have the sitter come for one or two visits while you're both there before you leave him or her alone with your baby.

In a day-care situation, plan to stay for at least half an hour on the first few days and perhaps even the entire first day. Again, before you enroll, try to arrange extended visits to the site before he has to go it alone. Then, on his first days, give your baby the opportunity and the encouragement to get involved in some activity before you go.

For both your baby's sake and your own, start small. Ease your baby into longer separations by first going on short outings: perhaps a half-hour or hour apart (or even as little as 15 minutes). This process allows both you and your baby to build trust in his caregiver in small stages. Then gradually extend your time apart until you reach the amount of time you'll regularly need.

Q-Tip

If your baby has a security blanket, a special stuffed animal, or another object that makes him feel safe, by all means let him bring it to day care or have it available when the sitter arrives (and when you leave). Don't ever discourage his use of it or, as he gets older, tease him about it. Just because your baby needs something else to feel safe, especially when you're not around, doesn't mean that you haven't done your part to nurture his sense of security. On the contrary, your baby wouldn't be able to take advantage of such a substitute if you hadn't given him a sense of security.

When it comes time to go, don't try to sneak out of the house (or the day-care center). If you do, your baby will never know when you're leaving, and he may become more clingy than ever—even in situations when you're not going anywhere.

Make good-byes short, sweet, and predictable. Strive to create a parting ritual similar to your bedtime ritual. Don't insist that he stop crying before you leave. (Think what power that gives him.) Smile, offer reassuring words, give him a hug and a kiss, let him know you'll miss him, and then go already. Your baby relies on you to determine whether everything is safe, so he needs to see that you have confidence that everything will be all right. That's why warmth and smiles at parting are so important.

The Least You Need to Know

♦ If you have a choice about whether or when to return to work after your baby is born, recognize how lucky you are.

♦ There's no "best" time to return to work, but there are "worst" times. If your baby has just gone through a major change in circumstance (new house, one parent away on business for a while) or a major development toward independence (crawling, walking), she probably needs you more than ever for security.

♦ Although good caregivers are out there, it can take some time to find one. Start looking at least a month before you need one.

♦ Check references for both in-home sitters and out-of-home day-care centers by phone. Don't rely on testimonial letters.

♦ Ease your child into day care by having your sitter come over while you're still at home or through extended visits to the day-care site before you leave her alone there. Then start with small periods of time and work up to the amount of time you'll need.

Chapter **24**

Making Time for Yourself

In This Chapter

◆ Attending to your basic needs

◆ How and when to find 15 minutes for yourself

◆ Guidelines for maintaining sanity during your first year as a parent

Making the adjustment from being part of a couple (or an individual) to being a parent is not always easy. Parenthood brings with it an awesome burden of responsibilities, both long-term and immediate. Hold that little darling of yours while feeding him just before bed, and you realize how much he depends on you for everything: for food, for shelter, for sleep, for day-to-day care, for companionship, for stimulation, for protection, for comfort, and above all, for love. At times, you no doubt feel overwhelmed by the juggling of responsibilities and the neediness of your baby. The constant toll of sleep deprivation certainly doesn't help the situation.

No matter how fulfilling you find parenthood, you may feel neglected and lost in the shuffle. What you want for yourself doesn't seem important anymore: not to you, not to your partner, and certainly not to your baby (who doesn't yet realize that you are not merely an extension of him). At such times, you may want to scream out, "What about me? Don't I matter? When will I ever get a moment to myself?"

... If You Try Sometimes You'll Find You Get What You Need

Your wants and needs do matter, but in the first blush of parenthood, you probably shifted your priorities to give precedence to your baby's wants and needs. This shift is perfectly natural, generally expected, and, to some extent, beneficial for both you and your baby. After all, if you didn't intend to make your baby a priority, why did you have one in the first place?

But as much as you can, you need to make your own wants—and certainly your own needs—a priority, too. A good caretaker has to take care of herself or himself as well as the baby. If you don't eat right, if you don't exercise, if you don't get the bare minimum of rest you need, you won't have the fitness, energy, and stamina you need to attend to your baby's needs and make the most of your time together. If you don't have at least a little time to yourself, you may begin to resent the time you devote to caring for your baby. Taking the time you need to eat properly, exercise, and relax will make you a better parent, not a worse one.

Eating Right

Eating well is essential for any parent, whether you are a nursing mother, a non-nursing mother, or a father. Diet certainly affects the quality of the breast milk a nursing mother produces. (See Chapter 4 for dietary guidelines for nursing mothers.) But even if you're not nursing, you need the energy and the health benefits that come from a good diet just to keep up with your baby.

What does eating well mean? First, a good diet begins with eating as regularly and consistently as you possibly can. If all your meals involve snacking on the run, you probably aren't getting the nutrition you need. Regular meals make it easier to ensure that you eat quality foods and help maintain your energy at a consistent level.

Try to eat well-balanced meals. To gain the fuel you need to juggle all your parenting responsibilities (not to mention your other responsibilities), aim for a diet...

- High in complex carbohydrates (whole-grain breads, cereals, and pastas; and brown rice, peas, beans, lentils, and other legumes).

- High in protein (low-fat milk, yogurt, or cottage cheese; eggs; meat; poultry; fish; tofu; and peanut butter).

- Rich in vitamins, especially vitamin C (citrus fruits and juices, melons or berries, tomatoes, fresh peppers, and broccoli).

◆ Rich in minerals, especially calcium (dairy products, some fish, and green, leafy vegetables) and iron (spinach, beef, sardines, soy products, chick peas or garbanzo beans, and other legumes).

◆ Low in fats (especially saturated fats), sugars (including corn syrup, sucrose, dextrose, and fructose) sugar substitutes (aspartame and saccharin), and sodium (salt).

Drink plenty of fluids, too. If you're nursing your baby, you need to drink about a half-gallon per day. But even if you're not nursing (or you're the father), you should drink almost that much.

Remember, if you're nursing, you need extra calories, just as you did during your pregnancy. But at the same time, you should avoid consuming so many extra calories that it prevents you from losing most of the excess pounds you put on during your pregnancy. If you're not losing your pregnancy pounds, then cut down to your prepregnancy caloric intake.

Finally, new parents need plenty of calcium and iron (nursing mothers need zinc, too). Though you can get these minerals through your diet, you may want to consider taking vitamin and/or mineral supplements. Talk to your doctor about what you're eating and see whether he or she recommends any supplements.

Baby Doctor

If you're nursing, try not to drink *too* much fluid. Drinking much more than half a gallon a day may actually inhibit rather than augment the production of breast milk.

Q-Tip

If you're a breast-feeding mother, reduce the number of calories you consume during the second half of the year, when your baby depends less and less on breast milk to meet her nutritional needs. You are no longer eating (as much) for two.

Just Say No to Drugs

If you breast-feed your baby, consult your pediatrician and your own doctor before taking any drugs. Any drug that a nursing mother takes invariably enters the milk supply. Even if you are not a nursing mother, drug use may affect your ability to function and provide for your child's needs. And drug abuse (whether of legal or illegal drugs) can inflict serious and long-term physical and emotional damage on both you and your child.

Drink only moderate amounts of alcohol (no more than two drinks) and caffeine. Too much alcohol or caffeine saps you of the energy you need to care for yourself and your child properly. In addition, alcohol dehydrates you instead of hydrating you. Worst of all, both alcohol and caffeine can be passed to your baby through breast milk.

Baby Doctor

If you didn't stop smoking during the pregnancy (and you should have), quit it now! Tobacco adversely affects your health, and if you nurse, the tobacco poisons your baby's health, too. If you smoke indoors (especially in a car), the second-hand smoke will damage the health of both your partner and your baby. Do yourself and your family a favor: stop smoking.

Fit to Be a Parent

Exercise offers important benefits to everyone: mothers, fathers, and even babies. Exercise can help new mothers lose pregnancy weight faster. It can also help flatten your abdomen, returning your figure to its prepregnancy form (or a reasonably close approximation). In addition, moderate and regular exercise in the immediate wake of labor and delivery accelerates healing.

Baby Doctor

Always consult your doctor before beginning any exercise program, especially one begun in the weeks after giving birth. Avoid sit-ups, leg lifts, and strenuous exercise for the first 6 weeks after childbirth. These exercises may put too much strain on your healing body.

For both mothers and fathers, aerobic exercise (walking at a brisk pace, jogging, swimming, or bicycling), if done regularly (20 minutes or more, three to four times a week), will improve your circulatory and respiratory systems. Exercise also promotes relaxation, making you better able to handle the stresses of new parenthood and possibly warding off or alleviating postpartum depression.

If you can't manage a full-fledged workout, at least do regular stretching. Stretching (though not to your full extent in the first 6 weeks postpartum) reduces the incidence of muscle strains, pains, and spasms. The straining of muscles, especially back muscles, is common among new parents who find themselves lifting and putting down their baby 40 or 50 times a day.

Being physically fit makes you better able to handle the demands of parenthood, so make it a priority to get the exercise you need. Arrange with your partner (or, if necessary and affordable, a baby-sitter) to give you the time for three or four 1-hour exercise sessions a week. Setting aside an hour gives you time to warm up with gentle stretches, exercise for 20 to 30 minutes, cool down with walking or light stretches, and perhaps even take a shower.

Q-Tip

If you are nursing your baby, offer her the chance to drink from your breast before you begin exercising. Vigorous exercise may increase the levels of lactic acid in your breast milk, making it taste sour for 90 minutes or more after your workout.

Rest Up

Forget about sleep. Virtually all new parents are deprived of sleep. Even in the early months of your baby's life, when he sleeps 10 to 14 hours a day, you certainly don't. For one thing, he probably never sleeps for more than 4 or 5 hours in a row—and not necessarily at night when you sleep. For another, too many other chores get in the way of a regular nap or rest when your baby sleeps during the day.

If you're constantly feeling exhausted and somewhat overwhelmed, take better advantage of your baby's nap schedule. Especially during the immediate period of recovery from labor and delivery, nap—or at least try to relax—whenever your baby naps.

Give Yourself a Break

Unfortunately, you may be the type of person who, despite your exhaustion, feels you have to get something done while you have two free hands (and eyes and ears). If so, that's fine. Do what you feel you have to do.

But before you take care of anything else, take care of yourself. Get into the habit of taking at least 15 or 30 minutes for yourself every time your baby takes a nap. Use this time to do whatever relaxes you or makes you feel good:

- Take a nap.
- Lie down, or if that makes you antsy, at least sit down.
- Listen to your own breathing.
- Meditate.
- Stretch out any muscles that ache from extended baby care.
- Take a warm bath.

- ◆ Make love.

- ◆ Read something just for pleasure.

- ◆ Watch some TV.

- ◆ Listen to music.

In short, give yourself permission to do something that relaxes you and clears your mind. You will be more able to accomplish your other objectives if you first get some rest and give yourself some time to think (or, just as important, not to think). Take this time as soon as you have put your baby down and are relatively certain that she's drifting off to sleep. Don't miss out on the opportunity to relax by telling yourself you'll put your feet up just as soon as you've finished doing a few chores. Two factors will conspire against this strategy.

First, household chores have a way of multiplying. You may plan just to put the breakfast dishes away and make the beds. But in doing the dishes, you'll notice that the counters need cleaning and maybe the floor needs mopping. And in making the beds, you may see that the furniture needs dusting or notice that the laundry has begun to pile up.

Second, your child—through no malice of her own—will no doubt wake up just as you finish up your chores and settle down to relax for a few minutes. Many babies seem to have a kind of radar that rouses them into action as soon as their parents allow themselves to take a few personal moments. But this radar usually shuts down during the first 30 to 60 minutes after your baby goes to sleep—so that's the best time to get some rest yourself.

Maintaining Your Sanity

Many new parents try to do too much. You may want not only to be a super parent, but also to take care of all household chores and make some money, too. If so, try to relax. Let some things slide for a while. With the exception of getting dinner on the table, most household chores can almost always be put off until later. You don't have to pick up all the toys and prepare a gourmet meal for visitors. Almost everyone will understand that you have a baby to take care of and that he must take precedence over daily chores.

Q-Tip _____

If, as a new parent, you have a tendency to try to do too much, take the following three rules to heart:

Rule #1: You don't have to manage everything all at once.

Rule #2: You don't have to do everything right.

Rule #3: You don't have to do everything yourself.

If you can convince yourself to live by these rules, you will maintain a much more relaxed and fulfilling attitude toward your new role as parent.

Living with a baby can be insane. Because you will be juggling so many responsibilities, a set of guidelines may help make them seem more manageable—and help to preserve at least a little of your sanity. As you struggle to adjust to the demands of new parenthood, the following strategies may ease the transition:

- **Prioritize.** Focus your attention on enjoying your baby and allowing your baby to enjoy you. He will never be this age again, so don't miss out on your chance to get the most out of this year. Make yourself and your partner a priority, too. Don't neglect your basic needs or your relationship with each other. Next to loving your baby, the greatest gift you can give him is to love each other. Everything else—no matter how important it seems at the moment—is secondary.

- **Organize.** Even if you're not a list keeper, you might find it helpful to list things you need to do. A little organization will help you prioritize and focus your efforts. (By the time your baby finally gets to sleep, you may need a list simply to remember anything else you had to do.)

- **Simplify.** Make your life easier. Treat yourself to an occasional take-out meal. Consider using paper plates instead of dishes. Feed your baby solid foods before your own dinner or during the meal, whichever seems easiest to you. Cut down on your schedule as well. Your baby probably won't let you go everywhere you want to go anyway, so you might as well drop some events from your calendar.

- **Forgive and learn.** Your baby will forgive any and all mistakes, as long as you continue to show him that you love him. Let his example inspire you. Don't be so hard on yourself (or your partner). Parenting is an endless course of on-the-job training. Don't expect to do everything perfectly—at least, not the first time. Instead, expect to make mistakes and try to learn from them. If you make good use of them, your mistakes can make you a better parent.

◆ **Laugh at yourself.** Maintain a sense of humor. Laughing at pitfalls and obstacles that come your way, especially the ones you create for yourself, will help you maintain your sanity. Besides, your baby will love to hear you laugh, even if he doesn't understand why.

◆ **Take it slow.** You won't have any choice but to take it slower this year. Your baby will invariably slow you down and make you late. Fortunately, most people who understand the demands that babies put on parents will expect you to be late. So don't be in such a rush and allow extra time for everything.

◆ **Get out and about.** Do something outside the house with your child. Plan special outings (or regular walks to the park) every day when weather permits. Do anything you can to escape the cozy confines of your home. (See Chapter 13 for tips on making outings with your baby work.) If you go out, the household chores that you haven't gotten to yet won't get done, but they won't be staring you in the face all day either.

Baby Talk

"Of course, I don't always enjoy being a mother. At those times, my husband and I hole up somewhere in the wine country, eat, drink, make mad love, and pretend we were born sterile and raise poodles."

—Dorothy DeBolt

◆ **Ask for help.** You don't necessarily need to hire a nanny or a house cleaner to ease your burden. Ask for what you need, and you'll be pleasantly surprised at how many people are willing to chip in. Friends, relatives, and your partner may all want to help you out, as long as you let them know that you need help.

If you use these strategies to maintain your balance and your perspective, you will begin to appreciate that you don't have to be Wonder Woman or Superman to manage a household with an infant. And you don't have to go nuts either. All you need to do is the best you can—and ask for help when you need it.

The Baby Blues: Postpartum Depression

If you're one of those parents who welcomes the new joys that your baby has brought and feels great about them, that's terrific. After all, you've brought a new life into the world, and caring for him can be both challenging and exhilarating. But if you feel terrible as a new parent, you're not alone. As many as one out of four new mothers suffers from postpartum depression that persists for several months after the birth of their baby. In addition, at least half go through a brief period (about a week) of depression immediately after delivery.

Because depression may be linked to the postpartum drop in estrogen and progester-one, your doctor may attempt to treat your depression medically by controlling your hormone levels. This process involves getting shots to replace these hormones and then *titrating* (gradually decreasing) the dosage over several weeks.

Despite common belief, however, postpartum depression is not all due to hormones. New parents often have plenty of good reasons to be depressed. Becoming a new parent creates a tremendous physical and emotional strain. If you're feeling depressed, try dealing with some of these factors:

◆ **Fatigue.** Studies have shown that sleep deprivation and exhaustion can lead to depression. The link between exhaustion and depression underlines the importance of getting whatever rest you can. Nap or just rest when your baby takes a nap. Also, allow yourself to let nonbaby chores slide a bit.

◆ **Letdown.** After 9 months of pregnancy, labor and delivery have brought the big build-up of energy, excitement, and anxiety to an end. In addition to missing the feeling of having your baby growing inside you, you may feel a letdown now that the exhilarating anticipation is over. Or you may be disappointed that you don't feel as much as you wish you did. It might help to recognize that every end also represents a beginning. Yes, the pregnancy is over, but you still have years of challenges, defeats, triumphs, and joys ahead of you. (Of course, this prospect also might be precisely what depresses you.)

◆ **Isolation.** During the final weeks of pregnancy, friends and relatives may have flocked to your side. Even strangers may have offered to hold the door for you or give up their seat on a bus or park bench. After your baby's birth, you may face all the chores you used to do, plus all the new responsibilities of parenthood, and have no help to deal with it all. You may end up feeling overwhelmed, inadequate, abandoned, unappreciated, and/or resentful—and, to make matters worse, guilty about these feelings. You have every right to feel this way. The responsibilities of new parenthood are never-ending and largely thankless.

Again, it's important to ask for the help you need. Ask your partner, other relatives, and friends to do what they can. If you can afford it, hire someone for a few hours a week to help with nonbaby chores like housecleaning.

> **Baby Doctor**
>
> If depression persists and has a negative impact on your appetite and your ability to sleep, or if it leads to feelings of apathy, hopelessness, suicidal urges, or urges to harm your baby, get professional help immediately! Such profound and lasting depression not only represents a threat to you, but will also adversely affect your relationship with your baby and may interfere with his development.

You may even want to hire someone to take the baby for an hour or two so that you can take care of yourself.

◆ **Invisibility.** Most people, perhaps even your partner, will now focus most (if not all) of their interest and attention on the baby: "How's he doing?" "Oh, he's so cute." "Wow, what an appetite he's got." "Who does he look like?" In the eyes of many, new mothers fade into the background. If you feel ignored and neglected, let your partner and others close to you know how you feel. Remind them that you need a little attention, too.

Also, treat yourself to some special time just for you—every day, if you can do it. Get some exercise. Go out to dinner with your partner once in a while. Or have your partner take the baby while you take a long, hot bath (hopefully, in a relatively soundproof bathroom).

Q-Tip _____

Don't hang around the house all day. Despite your baby's company, keeping yourself housebound only increases your sense of isolation. Especially during the first year, your baby is portable. Go on a long walk, visit a museum, visit with friends, or go shopping. In short, do anything you can to get out and about.

Guard against letting the baby blues drag you too far down. Seek help, if you need it—from your partner, your family, your friends, or professionals. Do it for your baby as well as for yourself. After all, he needs you to take care of yourself—so that you can take care of him.

The Least You Need to Know

◆ Your wants and needs matter; set aside at least a few minutes a day to devote to them.

◆ Make sure you eat right, exercise, and get enough sleep to maintain your energy levels.

◆ The first 15 minutes of your baby's nap should be your special time. Do whatever relaxes you or makes you feel good.

◆ You don't need to do everything yourself, to do everything right, or to do everything right now.

◆ Postpartum depression is understandable, but try not to let it go on too long. Do what you can to lift it and don't hesitate to ask for the help you need.

Parents as Partners

In This Chapter

- Sharing the joys and burdens of parenting
- Accepting and appreciating your partner's child-care efforts
- Finding time for each other
- Reviving romance in your lives
- Remembering how you conceived a child in the first place (oh, yeah … sex)

No doubt about it. Having a baby changes the dynamics of your home. It means less time for yourselves and less time for each other. It means taking on the new responsibilities of caring for the new baby and planning for her future. As early as the first year of your baby's life, you'll begin asking yourself whether you should consider moving to an area with better schools. You'll start thinking about—and, if possible, doing something about—putting money away for her college education.

For most couples, having a baby also transforms them into a more traditional couple or solidifies traditional roles already adopted. The new mother spends more time and energy taking care of the baby and home; the new father assumes even greater responsibility as a breadwinner (especially if, prior to the birth, his partner had contributed her earnings to the family budget).

But no matter how you and your partner choose to divide up the responsibilities of work and home, you'll need to keep one thing constantly in mind: you're in a partnership. Both of you will need to work together in order to achieve your common goals. If you haven't taken the time to define those goals with your partner, you may want to do so in the early months of your baby's life. No doubt some of these goals are unique to you, your partnership, and your family. But like virtually all parents, you probably share these goals:

◆ Doing what's "best" for your child(ren)

◆ Protecting the health and well-being of your family

◆ Continuing to grow as individuals, as a couple, and as parents

◆ Building on the love that's already in your home and family

◆ Thriving (or at least surviving) financially

◆ Nurturing your child(ren)'s physical development, intelligence, emotional well-being, and dedication to certain values

At times, these goals will conflict. Child-care responsibilities, for instance, may interfere with your relationship with your partner. Your dedication to financial goals may necessitate sacrificing some personal goals. Your devotion to spending time with your child may require making financial sacrifices.

Baby Talk

"Having a child is surely the most beautifully irrational act that two people in love can commit."

—Bill Cosby

When goals conflict, that's when you really need to work together as a partnership. If you or your partner sets priorities unilaterally, if either of you makes important family decisions without consulting the other, not only will you erode the foundation of your partnership by creating anger and resentment, but you also will deprive yourself of the opportunity to benefit from the other's wisdom.

So rededicate yourself to this partnership. Work together, value each other as individuals, maintain a loving atmosphere, and share responsibilities as much as you can. You may not achieve all of your family goals, but you will surely have a better chance if you strive for them together.

Share Care

As much as you can, try to share child-rearing (and housekeeping) duties in whatever way suits you both best. Your baby will benefit greatly from having both parents involved in his care. You can share responsibilities in many different ways. If you both want to do everything (or if both of you find one particular chore especially odious), you might want to try alternating nights. Mommy gave the baby a bath and got him ready for bed last night, so Daddy will get him changed, rock him, and sing him some lullabies tonight.

Alternatively, you might want to divide the chores and joys when both of you are home according to your separate interests and abilities. Your partnership may work best if each of you contributes according to your individual talents, knowledge, and abilities. Perhaps one of you loves to splash in the bath with your baby, while the other loves to sing lullabies. Maybe one of you learned to cook at the Sorbonne, while the other mastered making beds at West Point. If you do divide the household labor according to talents and interests, though, try to make sure that one of you doesn't get stuck with all the chores that neither of you wants to do, such as housecleaning or laundry. Ideally, both of you should have a similar mix of fun time and chore time.

No matter how you and your partner decide to share child care, don't be shy about asking each other for help when you need it. So what if it's your partner's turn to change a diaper? If your baby's diaper has leaked all over the bed, your partner could use some help. One of you can change and clean up the baby while the other strips the sheets and remakes the bed.

Take turns as much as you can during the wee hours, too. Each of you can change a diaper in the middle of the night, of course. If your baby drinks from a bottle, even if most of his nutrients come from breast milk, then Mommy doesn't always have to be the one to give 4 A.M. feedings. (Okay, maybe one of you has to get up to go to work in the morning, but just because one of you may be staying home doesn't mean you'll get the chance to sleep in.) Even if your baby drinks nothing but breast milk, Daddy can share some of the nighttime duties. Daddy can always give the baby a bottle of expressed milk or get up to bring the baby to Mommy and later take him back to his crib.

Temper your enthusiasm for fairness and equal sharing with logic, however. Although some mothers don't need to wake up all the way in order to nurse their babies, others become fully alert as soon as their babies attach to their breasts. If Mommy is going to be fully awake anyway, it may make more sense for you as a couple to let Daddy get some shut-eye now and perhaps get up early with the baby in the morning. Talk it over with your partner and come up with a plan to share caregiving in the way that works best for both of you.

Q-Tip _____

In your devotion to sharing care and taking turns, don't forget to spend time together as a family, too. Three is not always a crowd when you're talking about Mommy, Daddy, and baby (although sometimes it is). So don't just hand off your baby like a hot potato. Make time for the three of you to play together, sing together, read together, and just cuddle up together.

No Silent Partners!

Sharing care is not always as easy as it sounds. The division of power in American parenting is shifting a little more toward mutuality every year, yet mothers still assume the bulk of responsibility for child rearing and child care. Of course, many new fathers today welcome the responsibilities of parenthood, but some fathers seem reluctant to participate in baby care.

If you and your partner share time with your baby more evenly than most parents, or if yours is the rare household where the father does most of the child care, that's great. If Daddy consistently volunteers to take the baby, terrific! Mommy should probably take him up on his offer right away. But what should you do if your partner never volunteers? What if your partner seems content to stay on the sidelines rather than getting into the game?

(**Authors' note:** Although it may involve a sexist assumption, the following paragraphs on "silent partners" are addressed to mothers whose partners shy away from sharing in their babies' care.)

Every new mother could use some help caring for her baby, and the first person you turn to should, of course, be your partner. So if your partner doesn't make the first move, don't keep waiting for him to volunteer. Enlist him to share both baby and household responsibilities with you.

Q-Tip _____

Of course, your partner works hard all day. Naturally, he's tired when he finally gets home. Certainly, he could use some peace and quiet. (Certainly, you could, too.) But try not to think of it as overburdening your partner to ask for his help with the baby when he's home. On the contrary, think of it this way: why should you have all the fun with your baby? Playing with your baby and taking care of her may relax your partner and help him get his mind off work.

Your partner may be more than willing to share in baby care even if he has never volunteered for duty. Fathers who shy away from baby care do so not necessarily due to laziness, but for a wide variety of reasons:

◆ Your partner may regard baby care as your turf and is therefore reluctant to step on your toes.

◆ Your partner may not have offered because you seem to be handling everything so well that he didn't know you needed help.

◆ Your partner may lack a certain degree of confidence in his ability to handle the responsibilities of child care.

Like any other problem in your relationship, you won't get anywhere if you don't talk about it. Conversation is the grease that makes partnerships run smoothly. Avoid accusations that put your partner on the defensive; instead, talk to him about what you want and need from him. Then listen carefully to his response and try to hammer out a solution that both of you can live with. If the problem is lack of awareness, make your partner aware of the help you need. If the problem is fear of invading your domain, invite him in. If the problem is self-doubt regarding his parenting abilities, help him realize that he's not going to become more confident unless he participates more.

 Q-Tip _____

If your partner feels he doesn't know which way is up with your baby, ease him into child care by working (and playing) together with your baby before asking him to go it alone. Teach him what you know. Let him watch the way you feed your baby a bottle, or change her diaper, or rock her to sleep. Then encourage him to take a turn. Be sure to ask your partner whether he'd prefer you to stay or whether it would make him even more nervous to have you looking over his shoulder. When he feels more comfortable with her, arrange for more time that your partner and your baby can spend alone together.

Vive la Difference

If you want your partner to have confidence in his or her parenting skills and if you truly want to share in the care of your baby, then try to appreciate everything your partner does with the baby. Try to be grateful that both of you have partners who are willing to share in the joys (and hardships) of baby care.

As a general policy, this appreciation means taking a hands-off approach to your partner's child-rearing methods. Don't expect your partner to change diapers, comfort your baby, play with him, put him to bed, or do anything else in exactly the same way you do. Mothers and fathers are different people, and they do things in different ways. When your partner has the baby, remind yourself (through clenched teeth, if necessary) that your way of doing things is not the only right way.

Certainly, you can point out the different ways that each of you does things, especially if your partner asks for advice. But when you do, try to raise the subject as a point of interest, a recognition of difference, or, at most, a suggestion rather than as a criticism. (Belittling your partner's parenting abilities is certainly out of bounds.) If you can avoid triggering each other's defenses, you have the chance to learn something from each other. You don't need to approve of everything your partner does, of course. But carefully weigh any objections you may have before you raise them with your partner. In general, you'd probably be wise to avoid direct criticism of your partner's child-rearing style unless he or she is doing something that truly poses a danger to your baby.

> **Baby Talk**
>
> "Children are supposed to help hold a marriage together. They do this in a number of ways. For instance, they demand so much attention that a husband and wife, concentrating on their children, fail to notice each other's faults."
>
> —Richard Armour

Parenting is often a thankless job. At salaried work, you may get some form of recognition: a raise, a promotion, a party or other celebration of a job well done, even just a "Good job!" or "Well done!" But at home, you not only don't get a salary, but you don't get any commendations or sense of recognition either. (Your baby's smiles and giggles no doubt provide a priceless reward, but some other recognition would be nice, too.) So make a point of praising your partner when you see him or her do something particularly wonderful or creative or loving for your baby (or for you). Commend your partner for a job well done. After all, if you don't do it, no one else will.

Alone Together

If approached with mutual openness and honesty, the upheaval that a baby creates in your lives and your relationship can bring you two closer together (although, at times, this possibility will seem hard to accept). If, however, you both try to shoulder your new burdens with solitary stoicism, your silence can drive a wedge into your relationship.

After having a baby, you and your partner may spend more time together than ever before. Yet at the same time, you'll probably spend less time than ever alone together. Your baby leaves you and your partner very little time to have fun as a couple. You may no longer have any chance to relax—unless you count flopping down on the couch together after finally getting the baby off to bed.

Baby Talk

"The most important thing a father can do for his children is to love their mother."
—Theodore M. Hesburgh

Yet you need at least some time to yourselves. With all the other priorities in your life, it's easy to let your relationship with your partner slide. You may take each other for granted and no longer put in the energy needed to sustain and continue to build your relationship. But one of the greatest gifts you can give your child is two parents who love each other deeply, so make each other a high priority, too.

Don't depend on those chance moments that you may have to spend some time devoted to each other. With a demanding baby in the house, you and your partner have virtually no chance for spontaneity. Everything from going to the park as a family to getting dinner on the table requires planning now. So plan to spend some time with each other. What these dates lack in spontaneity, they may make up in preciousness.

Somehow you'll need to find some time for each other:

◆ Try putting your baby to bed at a reasonable hour (easier said than done) so that you can spend at least a couple of hours alone together before one of you falls asleep—or the baby wakes up again.

◆ If that doesn't work, give up trying to get together at night, when you're probably both exhausted. Instead, try setting an early alarm to wake you half an hour or an hour before you expect your baby to wake for the day. Have a peaceful, loving breakfast together—maybe even breakfast in bed (and who knows where that might lead …).

◆ Try to romance each other at least once a month. Get a sitter (or a relative) and arrange for a date with each other—if it makes you feel better, after the baby has gone to sleep. Go out to dinner together, take in a movie, go to a party, go out dancing. (Don't feel that you've failed yourself or your partner if the evening doesn't end with a marathon lovemaking session. Making conversation and nurturing your relationship is just as important as making love.)

When you're alone together, don't spend all of your time talking about the baby. Talk to each other about each other, about your needs, your feelings, and what you're doing when you're not together. Try to be patient, understanding, and complimentary toward your partner. The overall purpose of these times together is to let your partner know that he or she still matters to you.

A Fine Romance

Don't be surprised if you don't feel as romantic as ever following the birth of your baby. An array of physical, emotional, and logistical factors may have dulled your sexual appetites somewhat. These are just some of the obstacles you're up against:

◆ **Exhaustion.** It's hard to feel romantic when you can't even see straight, and both of you are no doubt exhausted most of the time. Especially in the early months, your baby has you on call every minute of the day and night, so you seldom (if ever) get more than 3 hours of uninterrupted time for each other—or for yourself.

◆ **Lack of privacy.** You may literally no longer have a room of your own. Even if you do, your baby is probably in your bed almost as much as you are, and three is definitely a crowd in the marital bed.

◆ **Hormones.** The postpartum drop in your (or your partner's) hormone levels (estrogen and progesterone) during the first weeks of your baby's life may result in decreased sexual desire. In addition, postpartum hormonal changes can inhibit vaginal secretions, leaving the vagina dry and more sensitive to abrasion and other sources of pain.

◆ **Nursing.** Breast-feeding can also dry up both desire and lubrication. In addition, breast-feeding may inhibit, or even satisfy, some of your sexual needs. (For the record, however, nursing mothers tend to enjoy postpartum sex sooner on average than bottle-feeding mamas.)

◆ **Body image.** You may not feel very sexy until you lose most of the weight you put on during pregnancy. (This comment is not addressed solely to women because many men gain weight during pregnancy, too.)

◆ **Depression.** Either or both of you may be experiencing a case of postpartum depression. Even a mild case of depression will inhibit your sexual desire and certainly your feeling of sexual desirability.

◆ **Jealousy.** Your partner's (or your) intense relationship with your baby may satisfy needs for intimacy in a much less complicated way than the intimacy between two adults. In turn, this intense relationship can make your partner (or you) jealous of the time and devotion you (or your partner) lavish on your baby.

◆ **Fear.** During the initial postpartum months, you (or your partner) may fear that intercourse will cause tearing, pain, or (yikes!) another pregnancy. Unfortunately, none of these fears is entirely groundless.

◆ **Pain.** In the first few months after giving birth, intercourse may indeed cause some pain until (or even after) the *perineum* heals. (The perineum—the soft external tissue between the vagina and the anus—gets stretched, bruised, and sometimes torn during childbirth.) Decreased lubrication may also cause some discomfort.

◆ **Divided attention.** You may not be able to relax or stop thinking about your baby long enough to entertain sexual desire, especially if your baby sleeps in the same room with you. With so much of your energy and emotions focused on your baby, you may feel drained of loving impulses toward anyone else, even your partner.

◆ **Different priorities.** Making love may not be at the top of your list of priorities. If you have any time at all to spare, you may prefer to do something else (sleep, take a relaxing bath, exercise, whatever).

◆ **Attitude.** Your partner's (or your) feelings about the breasts and vagina may have changed in the wake of childbirth and breast-feeding. After seeing your baby drawing nourishment from them, for example, you or your partner may view breasts in a different light. The apparent shift in function (although actually it's a split in function) from sexual stimulation to nurturing might inhibit your sexual foreplay. Likewise, the feeling or sight of your baby emerging from the birth canal may have altered the way you or your partner feel about the vagina. Either of you may feel certain inhibitions about intercourse as a result.

If you have any of these problems or concerns, don't leave them unspoken. Talk to your partner openly about the obstacles that stand in the way of resuming sexual intercourse. Don't let your partner think it's him (or her). If your partner doesn't know the reasons for your reticence, he or she may end up feeling unattractive, abandoned, and resentful.

Baby Doctor

If you notice any vaginal spotting, regardless of whether you've resumed making love, report it to your doctor.

So talk about sex even if you're not doing anything about it. You may find out that your partner shares your concerns or has worries of his or her own. Bringing them out into the open may not solve all of these problems, but it will allow you to decide together when you want to try to pick up where you left off.

Nuts-and-Bolts Problem Solving

Some of the factors inhibiting your sexual relationship—stabilizing hormone levels, the effect of nursing, your body image, and postpartum depression and healing—

should improve on their own with the passage of time. When you are both ready, you also can take steps to overcome most of the other obstacles to renewed lovemaking (although exhaustion may be something you'll have to learn to live with). You can get past a lack of natural lubrication, for instance, by using an artificial lubricant until vaginal secretions resume.

Baby Doctor

If necessary, you can always seek counseling. Professional sex therapists and/or marriage counselors can often get to the root of communication problems or sexual relationship difficulties in just a few intense sessions.

If pain is the problem, then try different sexual positions until you find one (or more) that are more comfortable for you. For example, women have more control over the depth of penetration and so feel less pressure on the perineum if they are on top or side to side rather than on the bottom. If you can't find any position that's comfortable, talk to your doctor. A topical estrogen cream (available by prescription only) may alleviate some of your soreness and pain.

If you are finding it difficult to relax enough to make love, try your favorite relaxation techniques before you get into bed:

◆ Take a warm bath.

◆ Meditate.

◆ Try some of the relaxation exercises practiced during pregnancy.

◆ Share a glass of wine with your partner (although you should avoid overindulging in alcohol).

Try to expand your sexual horizons, too. Just because one or both of you doesn't feel like intercourse, you can still find many other ways to express your love for each other: talking, wining (not too much) and dining, holding hands, lying in bed together, cuddling, and engaging in a wide variety of sexual foreplay.

In the Mood

Take your time. Don't force yourself to fake sexual feelings or have sexual intercourse before both of you are ready for it. After all, the normal balance of maternal hormones may not return for months after delivery. What's more, you may do more long-term damage to your sexual relationship by rushing into postpartum sex and having bad sexual experiences than you would by waiting until you both feel good about it. So try not to obsess about sex; give yourself and your partner time.

Whenever you resume your lovemaking, you may need to lower your expectations somewhat. It may be weeks or even months, for example, before you (or your partner) have an orgasm again. In the meantime, both of you need to remain as patient, loving, and understanding as you can. You need time to recapture both the mutual ardor and the gratification that marked your sexual relations before your baby arrived.

Sexual spontaneity does become more difficult once you have a baby, but it's not impossible. If you and your partner find yourselves alone at last, entertain the possibility of mutual seduction. If you're both feeling in the mood, for example, schedule a "date" for baby's next naptime. Or if your baby has a fairly regular nighttime sleep schedule, pencil your partner in for the slot right after bedtime. Whether you drop everything at the spur of the moment or schedule time for each other, try to make the most of your opportunities. They may be short-lived.

Almost every new parent has a story about the baby's bad sense of timing. Your baby may wake up just before you achieve sexual climax. She may pull herself up to standing for the first time and peer over the crib railing at you while you and your partner are having intercourse. Or she may find some other creative way to interrupt or inhibit the sexual act. Try to hold on to your sense of humor if and when it happens to you.

Baby Doctor

Don't resume having sexual intercourse until your doctor gives you the okay. If you and your partner are feeling romantic before your doctor has said it's okay, find some other way to satisfy each other. Because only intercourse is inadvisable during the first postpartum weeks, the range of possibilities extends all the way from hand-holding to oral sex.

How important is sex to you? Only you and your partner can answer that. Establish your priorities with your partner and arrange your schedule accordingly. If something else is lower on your list of priorities than making love, then let it go and devote that time to each other. But if something else is higher, by all means do the other thing first.

Most important, talk—and listen—to your partner. Talk about your emotions, the new sources of stress in your life, and anything else that might be affecting your sexuality. Work at seeing things from your partner's point of view, too. Do whatever you can to keep your sexual relationship going despite the lack of sexual relations. Until you're both ready to resume sexual intercourse, work on maintaining trust, patience, understanding, open lines of communication, and loving feelings.

Even after you have resumed sexual relations, continue talking honestly to your partner about sex. If you don't feel like making love because you're exhausted (or for any other reason), let your partner know. If sexual intercourse feels uncomfortable or painful, don't just grit your teeth. Let your partner know so that you can both try something different. If something new (or old) feels particularly good, share this information, too. If you let your partner know what feels best to you, then you won't have to wait for another happy accident to feel that good again.

The Least You Need to Know

◆ Just because your partner hasn't volunteered to share baby care doesn't mean he's unwilling or unable. Your partner may just need a little encouragement, a little advice, a little understanding, and a little patience.

◆ Your way of feeding, changing, rocking, or any other aspect of baby care is not necessarily the only way, or even the "right" way. So appreciate and applaud your partner's efforts with your baby.

◆ You can learn new ways of handling your baby by observing your partner with an open mind and vice versa. But neither one of you will learn anything if you watch each other with a critical eye.

◆ Your relationship with your partner matters to you, to your partner, and not least of all to your baby. Make each other a high priority in your lives.

◆ Take your time resuming sexual relations. Remain as open, patient, loving, and understanding with each other as you can.

Chapter 26

Tips for Today's Dads

In This Chapter

◆ Forming a paternal bond with your baby

◆ The value of paternity leave

◆ Care and feeding of your new baby

◆ Paternal post-partum depression

Once upon a time, a father had strictly defined responsibilities. He was expected to work hard (up to 50 or 60 hours a week) to make enough money to put food on the table and a roof over his children's heads. He was the family protector, watching out for his family's safety and well-being. He was the head of the household, the man who imposed discipline and meted out punishment on his children. ("Wait 'til your father gets home!" was often a mother's ultimate threat.) Except for breadwinning, protection, and discipline, however, a father's job in the household was pretty much over once the baby was conceived. He wasn't expected to change diapers, feed the baby, do laundry, or clean up the toys.

With little child care expected of him, a father had free rein to do what he pleased when he got home. Many took advantage of the opportunity to play whenever they had time to spend with their children. Evenings were devoted to games of peekaboo; "catch me, catch me"; catch the ball; and whoops-a-baby. But when bedtime rolled around, mom stepped in again to bathe the baby, get her in her pajamas, and put her to bed.

> **Baby Talk**
>
> "To become a father is not hard. To be a father is, however."
>
> —Wilhelm Busch

Though this arrangement did allow for warm moments between fathers and children, most fathers today are no longer satisfied with this limited notion of paternal duties. Many men now want (or their partners want them to take) more than just a supporting role in family life; they want to be costars. They want to be more actively involved in their babies' lives; they want a better chance to demonstrate their warmth, tenderness, strength, caring, and competence.

In addition, with more and more mothers of infants returning to the workforce, more and more fathers are being pressed into taking on more child-care duties whether they initially like it or not. (In time, nearly all fathers are grateful for the opportunity—not at every moment, certainly, but in the overall scheme of things.)

Whether you embrace the expansion of paternal duties or accept it only reluctantly, your active involvement in child rearing from the earliest days will prove a blessing for every member of your family:

◆ Your baby will benefit from having the opportunity to relate to two parents, each of whom has his or her own style, strengths, and weaknesses.

◆ Your partner will be relieved of the full burden of child care, which can be overwhelming even if she doesn't also work outside the home. By reducing your partner's fatigue, you may also help ease any postpartum depression she may experience.

◆ Your active paternal involvement will work to your benefit, too. Forming a strong bond with your baby through day-to-day care can be a source of great pleasure and emotional gratification. As you grow into the role of fatherhood, you will feel more comfortable, confident, and capable not just as a parent, but in other aspects of your life as well.

Jack of All Trades

Anything your partner can do for your baby (except for breast-feeding), you can do, too. Among many other things, you can …

- Feed him from a bottle.

- Change his diapers.

- Give him a sponge bath (or later, a tub bath).

- Get him dressed.

- Rock him to sleep (or just to calm him).

- Take him on walks.

- Take him to the doctor.

- Sing lullabies and songs to him.

- Read to him.

- Play with him.

Of course, just because you're now expected to share in baby care doesn't mean you'll be a natural at it (though you may very well be). You may have to work on building the patience, tuning in the radar, expressing the gentleness, and unleashing the playfulness that caring for an infant often demands. But it may surprise you to find that many mothers, including your partner, probably need to develop these skills, too.

On-the-Job Training

Feeling like a big know-nothing boob (or a complete idiot) when it comes to your baby and child care? Well, we'll let you in on a little secret: your partner probably doesn't know what she's doing either. Oh, she may have read a bit more about babies than you have. She may have done some baby-sitting earlier in her life. But unless she has children already from a previous relationship, she probably has little more experience in taking care of a baby than you do.

So why do you assume she has a leg up on you? Or maybe that's the wrong part of the anatomy. Yes, your partner has breasts that can nourish your baby and you don't, but that's the only thing that she can do for your baby that you can't do. You may argue that child care is an inbred, gender-specific skill. Baloney! Nurturing and parenting do involve skills, but they're acquired ones that have nothing to do with gender.

Baby Talk

"If the new American father feels bewildered and even defeated, let him take comfort from the fact that whatever he does in any fathering situation has a 50 percent chance of being right."
—Bill Cosby

Like any other skill, parenting will get better with practice—but you won't get the practice you need if you sit and twiddle your thumbs instead of getting up and getting to know your baby. Parenting is a crash course of on-the-job training for both fathers and mothers. Like any hands-on learning, the more you do, the more you learn and the more confidence you acquire.

If you want or need a tutorial, then read all of this book. The more you know, the more confidence you'll have. Book knowledge has its limits, though. No matter how much you read about baby care, what really counts is your hands-on experience. For this reason, you'll learn more from your baby about baby care than from any other source.

Your baby will not look at you and your parenting skills through critical eyes. (Your partner, however, might. If she does, encourage her in a nice way to lighten up a little.) In fact, your baby will forgive almost any mistake you make. After all, she doesn't have any other father to compare you with; you are the best father your baby will ever have.

So do things your own way and trust that, at least most of the time, your instincts, love, and compassion will steer you in the right direction. You don't need to be perfect, and you don't need to do everything just the way your partner does (or the way your father did). Just do your best to be loving, giving, and caring. Who knows? In time, you may become more adept at certain aspects of parenting than your partner.

Q-Tip

If you still think you need some sort of private instruction in parenting skills, talk to your partner (unless she's going through the same self-doubts) or to other parents you know. Encourage them to share "trade secrets" that you might find useful as a father. Be open to their suggestions and use the ones that make the most sense to you.

Bonding Does Not Mean Watching *Goldfinger*

When your baby is first born, you may be concerned that you don't feel any bond or even any love for your child. If you feel it right away, that's great. Work on strengthening that bond through daily care. But if you don't feel a paternal bond right away, give it time.

Every relationship takes time to build. You're building a brand-new one with your baby, and neither of you knows the other yet. Fortunately, parental love and caring is a circular process that builds on itself. You feed, change, hold, rock, and comfort your baby because you love him; and you love him because you feed, change, hold, rock, and comfort him. The more you care for your baby, the sooner he will get to know and love you—and the sooner you will get to know and love him.

Baby Doctor

If, despite taking care of your baby, you still feel no bond, and if any anger, resentment, and hostility you feel grow to a point where violence seems a possibility, seek help immediately from a family therapist, psychologist, psychiatrist, or medical doctor.

The "We" Hours

In addition to love and caring, all you need to become a good father is time. You've got to put in your hours, whether it means changing diapers, bathing your baby, feeding her, putting her to bed, hugging and kissing her, or playing, singing, and reading with her.

If you already feel pressed for time as the family breadwinner, this can seem like a big demand. Even if you work 60 hours a week, however, you can still probably manage to set aside at least 3 or 4 hours a day to spend with your baby. (Time when one or both of you are sleeping doesn't count.) But you have to make your baby and family a real priority in order to accomplish this scheduling feat. You may need to cut back on leisure activities, for example. Set aside blocks of time—daily, if possible—when you will have absolutely nothing to do but devote yourself to your baby. Your baby will come to cherish these special times with her daddy—and you probably will, too.

Given enough time, your baby is just as likely to attach to you as to your partner. Indeed, when hurt or scared, your child may even begin to turn to you for comfort as often as or even more often than she turns to her mother. But again, you need to put in your hours. That's the only way to win your baby's confidence, build her trust in you, and help her to feel secure in your presence.

Paternity Leave

If you possibly can, take a good chunk of paternity leave shortly after your baby is born. Both you and your partner could use the extra rest you'll get by sharing baby care in the first weeks. In addition, you'll have the opportunity, perhaps never to be repeated, to get to know and enjoy your new baby in a relaxed, leisurely way. Paternity leave affords you the chance to get comfortable with your child. If leave is not available or not affordable, then take some vacation time or personal days.

Q-Tip

The 1993 Family and Medical Leave Act applies to you as well as your partner, provided that you work for a company with 50 or more employees. By law, you can take up to 12 weeks of unpaid leave per year for family reasons, yet few new fathers take advantage of this law.

If spending time with your baby is a priority for you, consider some of the alternative employment options discussed in Chapter 23. You, too, can perhaps customize your work schedule to spend more time with your family. You may be able to take advantage of telecommuting, flex time, or part-time work (at least for a month or two). If you have a marketable skill, you might consider starting a freelance business from your home. Or you and your partner might work out an arrangement in which you both work part-time or stagger your work hours to share baby care.

Even if you cannot or will not alter your work schedule after your baby is born, try to make yourself available for emergencies. After all, you are just as capable of taking time off from work to take your baby to the doctor or to stay home with him when he's sick (or the baby sitter is unavailable).

Breast-Feeding! How Can You Compete with That?

Some new fathers wonder whether their inability to nurse will prevent them from bonding as completely with their babies as their partners do. It's true that if your partner breast-feeds, you can't bond with your baby in quite the same way she does, but you can demonstrate your love in so many other ways besides nursing that this one area should not interfere with your ability to get to know and love your baby.

Your baby will bond with both you and your partner not just through feeding, but through smiling, clinging, seeing, hearing, and crying. If you respond to your baby in

Q-Tip

Your willingness to feed your baby from a bottle will become especially helpful at weaning time. You can give your baby a bottle while your partner stays out of sight—and hopefully out of mind.

a loving way, she will love you regardless of whether you have the ability to lactate. Besides, you can still feed your baby by giving all, or at least most, of the bottle-feedings used to supplement breast-feeding or to give your partner a break from baby care.

When you do feed your baby, take full advantage of the opportunity to bond with her in a special way. Don't nonchalantly prop a bottle in your baby's mouth while you watch TV or read the newspaper or talk with friends. The food you give your baby—whether formula or expressed breast milk—is important. But even more important is the warm physical contact that comes with holding her close. Loving, gentle touch gives your baby an all-encompassing sense of support, calm, security, and love. So cradle your darling in your arms, hold her against your chest, and stare into her beautiful eyes.

> **Q-Tip** _____
> Whether feeding your baby, playing with her, or doing any other activity with her, try to maintain as much eye contact as possible. Eye contact is as important as physical contact in creating and sustaining an intimate relationship with your child. Singing or cooing softly to her while feeding her or cuddling her can not only keep her gazing up at you, but can also deepen your relationship. A warm smile will also keep your baby's eyes glued to your face.

If your baby gets fed breast milk exclusively, you can still participate in the feeding process. You can help, for instance, by getting your baby out of her crib when she cries in the night. You can also help out with any other middle-of-the-night activities: changing soggy diapers, for instance, or getting your baby to go back to sleep.

> **Q-Tip** _____
> You may be able to put your baby back to sleep in the middle of the night more easily than your partner can. Precisely because you don't have breasts, your hugging, rocking, and singing lullabies may have a more soothing effect on her than your partner's attempts to do the same. Your partner's breasts can become a distraction or obsession no matter how tired your baby seems.

If you can feed your baby an occasional bottle, great! If not, then make the most of all your other opportunities to care for your child. When your partner is nursing your baby, admire the miracle of breast-feeding (as long as it doesn't make your partner feel too self-conscious). But try not to feel jealous or left out. You are not in a competition for your baby's affections or attention.

A Baby! How Can You Compete with That?

You're not in a competition for your partner's love and attention either, though you may at times feel as if you were. If you're feeling jealous of your baby, here's some advice you won't find in any other parenting guide: grow up! Right now, you can't afford the self-absorbed luxury of wallowing in your jealousy. Your baby needs not only your partner, but you, too. Your partner needs you as well, maybe more than ever before.

Certainly, you should let your partner know your feelings. Let her know that you miss the time you once shared alone together. Perhaps the two of you can come up with some ways for you to feel more included. But don't expect your partner to fix everything; she can't. She already has one baby to take care of.

You need to come to terms with the fact that you're no longer just a couple. Don't expect many moments together, just the two of you. When these rare treasures do pop up (or when you can schedule them), make the most of them. Talk to each other, share with each other, give each other massages, and if you're in the mood, try a little romancing.

Baby Doctor

If your depression persists for more than a couple of months, you may find it worthwhile to seek professional help.

Keep in mind, however, that you're a family now, so try to enjoy life as a family. Spend time together as a threesome. Try to be patient as both you and your partner adjust to your new circumstances. The sense of distance that sometimes crops up between new parents is almost always temporary.

Postpartum Depression: Not for Women Only

Feeling depressed? Wishing that you could share in the joy of having a new baby, but for some reason you're left cold? You're not alone. More than half of new fathers experience their own version of postpartum depression. Fortunately, the depression of new fathers, like that of new mothers, usually passes quickly.

Although you have ample reason to feel happy and exhilarated, you probably have plenty of good reasons to feel depressed, too. The following sections address some of the most common causes of depression for new fathers.

Changing Roles

Having a baby changes relationships within the whole family. You may find it difficult to adjust to these changes. For one thing, you probably won't make love to your partner as often as you did before having the baby. Even worse, you will both have less energy to invest in each other physically, emotionally, spiritually, and intellectually.

With all the dramatic changes that your tiny new tenant has wrought in your household, you may wonder, "Where do I fit in?" With no clear sense of purpose in your home, you may suddenly feel like an observer of events that seem outside your control. If so, then stop sitting on the sidelines. You may be able to shake a good deal of your depression by taking action. Define your role more clearly by participating as an equal partner.

If you're out of the house working most of the day, try to assume more than your share of caregiving when you get home. Especially if your partner works outside the home, too, you should increase your share of child care and other parenting responsibilities. Help out with household chores, too. Recognize that your partner has a full-time job even if she's "only" with the baby all day. Do some cleaning and cooking and diapering, and work your way out of depression.

Baby Talk _____

"If men do not keep on speaking terms with children, they cease to be men and become merely machines for eating and earning money."

—John Updike

Makin' Bacon

Any financial worries you may have had before the conception of your child have only gotten worse since. Hospital bills, setting up a nursery, buying clothes—none of these comes cheap. (And then there's the cost of a college education down the road.) You undoubtedly have a greater financial burden, especially if you've lost a portion of your household income because your partner is staying home to care for the baby.

Breadwinning is an enormous responsibility for new fathers. Even if your partner plans to return to work in just a few months, you probably feel as though the entire burden of bringing money into the home falls on your shoulders.

Do whatever you can to alleviate some of the financial burden you feel. Cut down on whatever expenses you can, at least until you feel afloat once again. (You certainly won't be going out as much as you once did, and that should help a little.)

Utter Exhaustion

Too many late-night calls and all-nighters (even if you're not physically getting up) may leave you feeling extremely fatigued, and exhaustion contributes greatly to depression. Try to take good overall care of yourself so that you can better take care of both your baby and your partner. Get as much rest as you can, eat right, and try to get at least 2 to 3 hours of exercise a week.

Isolation

You may have almost no social life anymore. If you work outside the home, you may have no social contacts whatsoever that aren't related to your job, especially if, as a conscientious parent, you rush straight home after work to be with your family. If, on the other hand, you work part-time, work at home, or have taken time off (temporarily or permanently) from outside work to devote more time to baby care, you may feel a different kind of isolation: gender isolation. You may be the only dad at your local "Mommy and Me" group or the only man you see at the playground in the middle of the morning.

Baby Doctor

If you and your partner still feel isolated from each other during the second half of your baby's first year, you may need some help repairing the breach. Consider short-term marriage, couples, or family counseling.

If you feel cut off from others, seek out support groups for new fathers. You might also want to check with your local adult education program, a community college, or the YMCA to see if they offer courses aimed exclusively toward fathers. Don't give up on your relationships with other men. Arrange with your partner to trade off nights every 2 or 3 weeks so that you can have a "boys' night out" with some of your friends and she can have a "girls' night out" (though this trade-off may be difficult to manage until your child is weaned).

Whatever the cause of your depression (if any), you owe it to yourself, your partner, and your baby to deal with it. Seek out financial counseling, emotional support, and the good advice of your partner. Take good care of yourself, emotionally as well as physically. Make your emotional, physical, and spiritual health a priority. After all, you want to stick around for as much of your baby's life as possible, don't you?

Q-Tip

Many people still don't know how to regard a man who participates fully in baby care. Many mothers are very accepting of fathers that they get to know through playgroups with their babies. Yet in the playground, many mothers are very wary of "strange men," even those accompanied by a baby.

Complete strangers may approach you in the grocery store and ask if you're baby-sitting today. (Would they even think of asking a mother the same question?) You can't control other people's responses and reactions to your involvement in your baby's care, but you don't have to feel awkward just because other people don't know what to make of you.

The Least You Need to Know

◆ Your active involvement in home and family life will benefit your baby, your partner, and you.

◆ With the single exception of breast-feeding, you can do everything for your baby that your partner can.

◆ The best way to get to know and love your baby—and to let her get to know and love you—is to devote time to caring for her.

◆ If available and affordable, paternity leave can be a blessing in the first weeks (or even months) of your baby's life.

◆ You may be able to get past the baby blues by taking better care of yourself, talking to others about your feelings and concerns, and plunging as wholeheartedly as you can into baby care.

Chapter 27

Opinions: Everybody's Got One

In This Chapter

- Handling unsolicited advice
- Asking for advice
- Accepting—or rejecting—advice you've solicited
- Trusting your judgment

You can't burp him like that—you'll make him sick! Don't change her on the floor—it's so dirty! That's no way to bathe a baby! By the time my Brittany was 3 months old, we had her sleeping through the night. Don't run in there every time he cries! You're just teaching him to cry whenever he wants something. You can't let your baby crawl around naked. We never put Matthew down without a diaper. She obviously needs some fresh air. Why don't you take her out for a walk?

If you haven't yet heard critical comments like these, don't worry   you will. For some reason, parenting is one of those vocations—like driving or card-playing or fashion—that almost everyone feels free to kibitz about. Now, you might be able to shrug off someone telling you to discard a six instead of a jack, to put your turn signal on sooner, or even that your eyeglasses make you look like a fuddy-duddy (okay, that one might set you off a little). But you might find it much harder to take with good grace the not-so-subtly-veiled suggestion that you are doing something wrong as a parent.

Baby Talk

"The most consistent gift and burden of mother-hood is advice."

—Susan Chira

A critical comment about your parenting style or tech-niques may come from almost anyone—your partner, your parents, your siblings, friends with children, friends without children, and even strangers. In most cases, it will be offered as a "friendly word of advice" or a "word to the wise." But you may not see these comments as friendly—and as a result, may completely reject any wis-dom that they do have to offer.

Did I Ask for Your Opinion?

A lot of people won't wait for you to ask before offering their opinions on your par-enting skills—and, of course, your parenting faults. What makes people feel they have the right to offer unsolicited advice and criticism about something as personal as par-enting depends on the individual:

◆ The majority of the time, parents, siblings, and friends may be sincerely trying to help.

◆ Your own parents—and your partner's—may feel entitled to voice their opinions on your parenting because they "taught you everything you know about parent-ing."

◆ People who feel insecure or inadequate about their own parenting skills may offer "advice" as a way of undermining your confidence and sense of security regarding your parenting.

◆ Some people think they know everything about everything and cannot stop themselves from trying to "improve" everyone else they see.

◆ People who don't have children of their own tend to think parenting is easy and therefore feel free to share their uninformed wisdom with you.

◆ In any relationship that centers on a power struggle (which may or may not characterize your relationship with your partner, your parents, your siblings, or some of your friends), criticism in the form of unsolicited advice can serve as a weapon used to gain the upper hand.

◆ Other parents may have genuine wisdom gained through their own experience and may offer it solely in the hope that you will benefit from what they've already been through (perhaps by not repeating their mistakes).

When strangers or mere acquaintances offer you parenting advice, you have no clue about their motivation. So you might as well give them the benefit of the doubt, considering their "words of wisdom"—no matter how unwelcome—as well intentioned.

With friends and family, you may have a much better idea of what prompts their unsolicited advice. You have a history with these people and no doubt understand their motivations better than we do. Nonetheless, unless you want to escalate their critical remarks into a full-fledged war of words, you may do well to give them the benefit of the doubt, too. Think of them as simply trying to help by sharing their wisdom.

Handling "Friendly" Advice

Even if you believe that the people offering you parenting tips are well intentioned, that doesn't mean you need to take their advice. If you believe in the virtue of civility, you have the obligation to listen respectfully to what other people have to say. (Who knows? You may actually learn something.) But you have no obligation to embrace their opinions or act accordingly.

Curiously, it's often easier to handle advice from a stranger than to deal with suggestions offered by friends or family. If a stranger comes up and tells you you haven't dressed your baby warmly enough, for example, you might answer politely, "Thank you. You may be right." If you disagree with the stranger's advice, you'll probably ignore it and move on with your life.

If this same comment were made by someone in your family, however, you might react very differently. The stereotypical example is the meddling mother-in-law in whose eyes her daughter-in-law cannot do anything right as a wife or mother. Maybe you get along very well with your mother-in-law—but your relationship with your own mother or sister has been fraught with competition or tension.

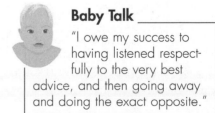

Baby Talk

"I owe my success to having listened respectfully to the very best advice, and then going away and doing the exact opposite."
—G. K. Chesterton

If you have a history of antagonism or even ambivalence with your "critic," you will probably react very defensively to any comment on your parenting. Even if the advice offered has some value, you probably won't hear it because you'll see it as an attack—and you may be right.

Even when you suspect your critic of ulterior motives, however, try not to react defensively. You don't need to respond in kind to a perceived attack. Treat family and friends who offer unsolicited advice with just as much respect and decorum as you would a stranger. Listen politely, respond thoughtfully, and then accept or reject the advice without working yourself up about it.

Granted, this is easier to put into practice when you have limited contact with your critic. If you don't have to subject your parenting skills to critical eyes for more than a day or two every few months, you will probably find it relatively painless to shrug off their comments.

If your critics drop in on you several times a week—or worse, every day—with unwanted advice, then this laissez-faire attitude will not work. Sooner or later, you will need to confront your critic. If you don't, your hidden anger will slowly destroy any relationship you have. (This applies to your partner as well as other family and friends. See Chapter 25.)

One of the most effective ways to bring up the subject is to begin by granting the other person the benefit of the doubt: "Mom (or Dad or Marge or Homer or who-ever), I know you're trying to help and that you want me to be the best parent I can possibly be …." By opening the discussion in this way, you're defusing any defensiveness with a compliment.

Baby Doctor

If you remain unsatisfied after confronting a critical family member, you might find issue-oriented family therapy helpful. A few sessions that bring you and your partner together with your critic and perhaps his or her partner may help bring out the tension in a safe atmosphere and help you all arrive at an agreeable solution.

Then get into the heart of the subject. Talk about how these "friendly suggestions" make you feel. Assert that you want to make your own mistakes and have your own triumphs as a parent. Finally, admit that at times you may have questions and want advice, and he or she may be the first person you ask when you do.

If your critic is at all reasonable, this approach will have an impact. Your critic will understand your point of view and (at least try to) respect your wish for more freedom to succeed or fail on your own.

Asking for Advice

Of course, there actually will be times when you want advice. Whether you're tearing your hair out because your baby is colicky, walking into walls because she won't go to sleep, worrying about a diaper rash that won't go away, or just wondering whether you can try introducing raspberries into her diet, you will realize that no matter how much and how fast you're learning, you don't always have all the answers.

Asking for advice when you've run out of things to try can give you new ideas that you may (or may not) want to try with your baby, or reassure you that what you wanted to try all along is okay. But just as important, it can relieve some of the isolation and loneliness that parents of infants often feel.

So where can you turn for advice? Well, if you had critics who honored your request to back off a little, it would be nice if you felt comfortable turning to them to give you pointers. After all, you already know they want to help and aren't shy about sharing their opinions. But if you let their "helpful suggestions" go on too long, you may still harbor some ill feelings that will prevent you from turning to them.

Fortunately, there are endless sources of parenting advice:

- ◆ Your partner
- ◆ Your parents (or your partner's)
- ◆ Your grandparents (or your partner's)
- ◆ Siblings who have children
- ◆ Friends who have children
- ◆ Favorite aunts or uncles
- ◆ Neighbors
- ◆ Other parents at baby classes
- ◆ Websites on the Internet
- ◆ Books like this one

Baby Talk

"I started relying on the expert advice of other mothers—especially those with sons a few years older than mine. This great body of knowledge is essentially an oral history, because anyone engaged in motherhood on a daily basis has no time to write an advice book about it."

—Mary Kay Blakely

All of these sources can offer you valuable new perspectives on parenting issues. How you choose to put this wealth of advice to use is, of course, up to you.

Well, You Asked for It

Do you have to accept advice just because you asked for it? Of course not. You owe it to the people you asked for advice to consider seriously any suggestion they make. If you think it sounds like something that's at least worth a try, that's terrific. You've gotten just what you were looking for.

If you disagree with someone else's suggestion, you are under no obligation to try it just because you asked that person's opinion. You might (consciously or unconsciously) have sought out advice merely to confirm your own convictions. In this case, the "wrong" answer will serve you just as well as the "right" answer. The fervent rejection of a suggestion probably means that you already had an idea in mind about what you wanted to do; you just needed to hear someone else's opinion in order to help you make up your own mind.

Although you do not have to take people up on their suggestions after asking for their advice, you might find it helpful to use them as a sounding board. For example, you might let them know that you're thinking of doing something else and finding out why they suggested what they did. They may have sound reasons for their advice. Even if you don't find these reasons persuasive, they may open you up to new ways of thinking about parenting.

If you still don't want to do what has been suggested after hearing your advisor's reasoning, that's fine. Understand, however, that in rejecting his or her ideas, you have the potential to create some hurt feelings. To help minimize this risk, be sure to thank the person for their suggestion and explain why you plan to do something else instead.

You Could Look It Up

Do you have to take the advice of experts found on the Internet or in books like this one? Of course you do! Not!

In some respects, trying to get advice from books or sources on the Internet is much easier than asking relatives or friends. After all, you don't need to worry about hurting anyone's feelings if you choose not to accept this advice.

Baby Talk

"Parents ought to get some idea of how the so-called 'experts' have changed their advice over the decades, so that they won't take them deadly seriously, and so that if the parent has the strong feeling, 'I don't like this advice,' the parent won't feel compelled to follow it."

—Dr. Benjamin Spock

You can't have a conversation with a book in order to find out the reasoning behind an author's advice, as you could with a friend or family member. But the best books on parenting provide a fairly complete grounding in the author's thinking anyway. If, after reading a parenting book or parenting website, you don't know why the authors make the suggestions they do, then you probably should find another source of expertise.

Use knowledge gained through books or websites just like a friend's or family member's advice—solely as a resource to help you decide what's best for *you* to do. If you like a suggestion you've read, go ahead and do it; if you don't, feel free to ignore it. You just don't need to be as polite about it.

Trusting Yourself

Whether you seek out advice or someone offers it to you out of the goodness of their heart, you (and your partner) need to make the final decision about what's best for your baby. After all, no matter what the situation, there is no "one best thing" to do. Parenting is all about choices—the ones you make and the ones you don't make.

When you need help, you should certainly seek advice. Ask your parents or siblings or friends and listen to what they have to say. Look at this book (okay, and *maybe* one or two other sources) and see what we have to say. But when it comes down to it, you're the ones who will have to decide what to do.

Gather all the information and advice you can get—but then make a decision and trust in your judgment. After all, who knows your baby better than you and your partner do? No one does. In fact, when it comes to your own baby, you *are* the expert.

The Least You Need to Know

- ◆ You can shrug off most people who offer unwanted suggestions about your parenting. If you must deal with them on a regular basis, however, a firm but polite confrontation may be needed.

- ◆ When you need parenting advice, don't feel reluctant to ask someone for their opinion or consult a book or website.

- ◆ Just because it's written down in a book or on a website doesn't make something the gospel truth. Feel just as free to reject "expert" advice as you would a friend's or family member's.

- ◆ No matter what anyone else advises, do what you think is right as a parent. When it comes to your own baby, you *are* the expert.

Glossary

apnea   A temporary cessation of breathing. An episode of apnea that lasts more than 20 seconds is associated with an increased risk of Sudden Infant Death Syndrome (SIDS).

au pair   A young adult from a foreign country who provides live-in child care in return for room, board, and a small salary.

Babinski reflex   A newborn reflex that causes a baby to bend her foot upward, spread her toes, and raise up the big toe in response to strokes on the sole of her foot.

Babkin reflex   A newborn feeding reflex that causes a baby to open his mouth in response to pressure on his palm.

breast abscess   Infection and painful inflammation of breast tissue, often the result of an infection that entered the breast through an untreated crack in the nipple.

colic   A pattern of intense and inconsolable crying that recurs around the same time every day (often the late afternoon or early evening). Colic begins in the early weeks of a baby's life and may continue for as long as 3 months. The cause of colic is unknown.

colostrum   Immature or early breast milk, which is higher in protein and lower in fat than later breast milk. Also called first milk, colostrum matures into breast milk over the first couple of weeks of breast-feeding.

cradle cap   Flaky skin found most often on the top of a newborn's head.

cruising   A stage in the development of walking skills. A pre-toddler cruises by using furniture for support while creeping along the edges.

diphtheria   A bacterial infection, commonly immunized against during the first year, that attacks the throat and airway.

engorgement   Too much milk in the breasts, which can cause swelling, hardening, heat, or pain in the breasts. Engorgement is a common complaint in the early months of breast-feeding.

expressing milk   Drawing milk out of the breast manually or with a breast pump for later use in bottle feedings.

fine motor skills   The ability to perform small, delicate movements such as grasping.

fontanels   Two soft spots in a baby's skull at birth. The fontanels close as the bones of the skull mature and join. The fontanel located at the back of the head closes at 4 months; the one on top of the head closes within 2 years.

grasping reflex   A newborn reflex that causes a baby to close her palm around any object placed on it.

gross motor skills   The ability to perform big movements such as rolling and crawling.

hemophilus influenzae type B (HIB)   A bacterial infection that can cause meningitis (inflammation of the membranes that envelop the brain and spinal cord).

hepatitis   A disease characterized by inflammation of the liver.

meconium   A black sticky substance that fills a baby's intestines while in the womb. A newborn's first bowel movements often consist primarily of meconium.

melanin   A natural pigment that darkens the skin.

milia   A temporary rash of white dots resembling pimples, commonly found on the nose or face of a newborn.

mongolian spots   Bluish-gray birthmarks commonly found on the backs or bottoms of dark-skinned infants. They generally disappear within 4 years.

Moro reflex   Also called the startle reaction, this newborn reflex causes a baby to stiffen his body, thrust out his arms and legs, and then immediately pull them back in whenever any loud noise, sudden movement, or loss of support startles him.

object constancy   The recognition that an object can disappear from sight without ceasing to exist.

perineum   Soft external tissue located between the rear of the vagina and the anus. The perineum often suffers from bruising, stretching, or even tearing during child-birth.

pertussis   An infection, also called whooping cough, that can cause inflammation of airways and serious difficulty breathing, especially among infants.

polio   A viral infection that attacks the central nervous system, causing nerve damage and possible paralysis.

rooting   A newborn feeding reflex that causes a baby to turn her head toward a finger or nipple that strokes her on the cheek or the side of the lips.

rubella   German measles.

shutdown response   A defense against overstimulation, this reflex causes a baby to fall asleep instantly when confronted with too much noise or too many visual stimuli.

SIDS   Sudden Infant Death Syndrome, the unexplained death of an infant during sleep. SIDS claims the lives of 1 in 600 healthy infants in the United States every year.

stork bites   Tiny pink birthmarks, often found on or around the head, that usually fade and disappear within the first 6 months.

strawberry marks   Small red bumps found on the head or face of newborns. Although they sometimes grow larger during the first year, they usually disappear in the second year.

Sudden Infant Death Syndrome   See *SIDS*.

tetanus   A bacterial infection, also called lockjaw, commonly immunized against during the first year.

tonic neck reflex   A newborn reflex that causes a baby to assume a "fencing posture" (with his arm extended in line with his eyes) if he is laid on his back and his head is turned to one side.

umbilicus   The remainder of the umbilical cord after it is clamped, cut, and tied. The umbilicus falls off (leaving the belly button) within 3 weeks of birth.

varicella   Chicken pox.

vernix   A white, waxy, or greasy substance that protects a baby's skin while still inside the womb. This coating may still be present at birth, especially in skin folds and under fingernails.

Height and Weight Charts: The First Year

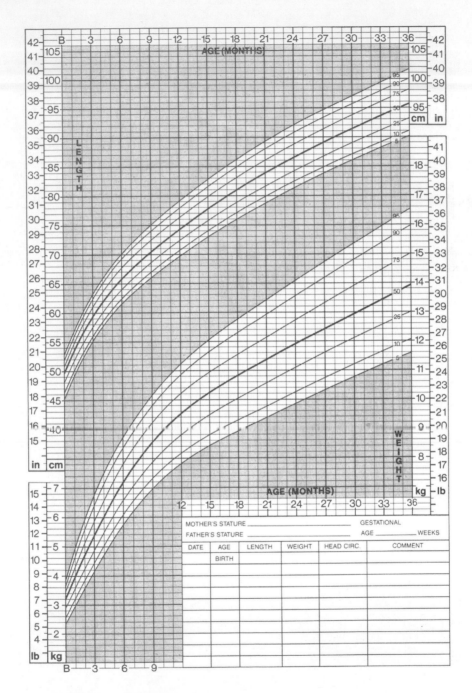

Height and Weight Ranges, 0–36 Months, Girls
Adapted from: Hamill, P. V. V., T. A. Drizd, C. L. Johnson, R. B. Reed, A. F. Roche, W. M. Moore: Physical
Growth: National Center for Health Statistics Percentiles. AM J CLIN NUTR 32:607-629, 1979. Data
from the Fels Longitudinal Study, Wright State University School of Medicine, Yellow Springs, Ohio.

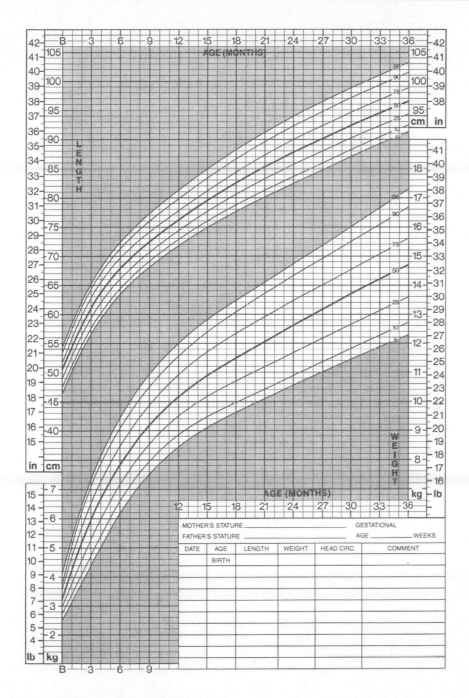

Height and Weight Ranges, 0–36 Months, Boys
Adapted from: Hamill, P.V.V., T. A. Drizd, C. L. Johnson, R. B. Reed, A. F. Roche, W. V. Moore: Physical
Growth: National Center for Health Statistics Percentiles. AM J CLIN NUTR 32:607-629, 1979. Data
from the Fels Longitudinal Study, Wright State University School of Medicine, Yellow Springs, Ohio.

Vaccination Schedule: The First Year

Your pediatrician will probably recommend that your child adhere to the immunization schedule outlined in the following table.

Vaccine	Birth	*1* month	*2* months	*4* months	*6* months	*12* months
Hepatitis B	Hep B	Hep B		Hep B	Hep B	
Diptheria, Tetanus, Pertussis			DTaP	DTaP	DTaP	
Haemophilus influenzae type B			Hib	Hib	Hib	Hib
Inactivated Poliovirus			IPV	IPV	IPV	
Measles, Mumps, Rubella						MMR
Varicella						Var
Pneumococcal			PCV	PCV	PCV	PCV
Influenza					Influenza	
Hepatitis A						Hep A

Recommended childhood immunization schedule, United States, January–December 2006

Vaccines are listed under the routinely recommended ages. **Bold type** indicates a range of acceptable ages for vaccination. (When **bold type** appears in the final column [12 months], the recommended age range for this immunization continues into the first year.) The influenza vaccine is *not* recommended for all children. Approved by the Advisory Committee on Immunization Practices (ACIP), the American Academy of Pediatrics (AAP), and the American Academy of Family Physicians (AAFP).

First Aid and Treatment of Common Childhood Illness

As the parent of an infant, you can't possibly be prepared for everything that will happen. Yet you *can* take precautions that will help prepare you for the most common accidents and illnesses that babies experience during their first year of life.

In this appendix, you will find pointers on how to provide first aid and what to do in case of common childhood accidents and emergencies. In addition, you will find a description of symptoms that may indicate the need for a visit to your pediatrician, and advice on how you might treat such symptoms and illnesses—under your pediatrician's supervision, of course.

A general word of advice regarding both accidents and illnesses: if you have any hesitation about calling your pediatrician or 911 for treatment of an illness or accident, make the call. Do not hesitate where your baby's health or safety is concerned. After all, it's better to call for help when you may not need it than to fail to call when you do need help.

First Aid for Accidents and Emergencies

No matter how careful you are as the parent of a newborn or infant, accidents happen. And when an accident happens, you may need to act quickly. You may need to perform emergency first aid, call 911 to contact emergency personnel, or consult your pediatrician at once. This section will tell you what to do in case of accident or emergency—and when you need to contact your doctor or emergency personnel.

Ideally, you won't ever have any reason to use the information contained in the following pages. With any luck, the worst accident you'll run into during your baby's first year will involve a minor insect bite or sting.

If your baby does have an accident or emergency, however, you will want to know what to do—starting with how to administer first aid. So here's what to do in case of common accidents or emergencies.

Accidents: Bites and Stings

Babies in their first year rarely get bitten by wild animals; more commonly, babies are bitten by a family pet or another small child. Because any bite that breaks the skin can lead to infection, you should seek a doctor's care immediately after *any bite*—whether the biter was a **human, a domestic animal, or a wild animal.** (Wild animals do increase the risk of infection and disease transmission, but about half of all cat bites lead to infection, too.)

First, attend to the wound itself. If your baby is bleeding, clean the wound and stop the bleeding as you would any cut or other wound that breaks the skin (see page 362). If the bleeding is massive or uncontrollable, maintain pressure on the wound with a clean towel, sheet, or other large cloth and immediately call 911 or get someone to drive you to the nearest emergency room. (You will need to maintain pressure on the wound until medical personnel take over.)

If an animal that bit your baby is unfamiliar to you, try to restrain it for testing—but don't allow yourself to get bitten, too.

After treating your baby's wound, your pediatrician will probably prescribe antibiotics, especially if the biter was a cat or wild animal. Although dog bites less commonly cause infections, your doctor should decide whether antibiotic treatment is appropriate and necessary.

Unlike animal bites, **insect bites or stings** seldom require a doctor's attention, unless they become infected or your baby shows a high sensitivity to insect venom. To relieve itchiness caused by bites from mosquitoes, flies, fleas, or bedbugs, apply calamine lotion—but *do not* apply calamine lotion around your baby's eyes or genitals. To relieve pain and swelling after a wasp or bee sting, apply a cold compress (a clean washcloth soaked in cold water or an ice pack). Remove a bee's stinger by scraping it horizontally with a credit card. Avoid squeezing the stinger, which could cause the injection of more venom into the wound.

Call your pediatrician immediately if an insect bite or sting is followed by severe pain, extreme swelling of the face and lips, difficulty breathing, an outbreak of hives, weakness, dizziness, or unconsciousness. Your baby may be experiencing an anaphylactic reaction to the insect venom and need immediate medical attention.

Following any insect bite or sting, watch for signs of infection (red streaks, pus, dramatic swelling) and consult your pediatrician if they appear.

Accidents: Burns and Scalds

During the first year of her life, if your baby is burned, whether by heat, fire, chemicals, or electrical shock, **call your pediatrician or 911 immediately.**

While waiting for medical attention, soak the burn in cool water and keep the cool water running over the burn until your baby no longer seems in pain (as long as half an hour). *Do not* use ice, butter, grease, ointments, or powder on a burn; all of these can worsen an injury caused by a burn. Cover the burned area with a sterile gauze pad, a clean towel or sheet, or other nonadhesive material.

With any severe burn, remove all clothing from the burned area unless it sticks firmly to the skin. *Do not attempt to pull away clothing that sticks to the skin.* Instead, cut away the clothing around the burned area and seek immediate medical attention.

If the burn was caused by an electrical shock and your baby has stopped breathing, **begin infant CPR** (see page 353) at once.

In case of a **mild sunburn** (red, warm, sensitive skin), you can treat your baby on your own. Cool compresses (a cool, damp washcloth) or a cool bath can help ease your baby's discomfort. If she still seems in pain, you can give your baby the proper dosage of acetaminophen (check the package—or better still, check with your doctor—to determine the correct dosage for your baby's *weight* rather than age). If your baby develops secondary symptoms (blistering, fever, or vomiting), call your pediatrician at once.

If your baby has **severe sunburn,** it should be treated like any other serious burn. Consult your doctor immediately for proper treatment.

Accidents: Choking

If your baby has something caught in his throat and is coughing, let him cough, since coughing may dislodge the object from his throat. However, if your baby is unable to cough, cry, or talk, if he is making high-pitched wheezing or crowing sounds, if he cannot breathe, or if his complexion turns from red to blue, **begin infant CPR immediately** (see page 353) and yell for help (someone to call 911 or other number for emergency medical care). If no one is available to help, administer infant CPR for 1 minute, then bring your baby to the phone (where you can continue CPR) or take out your mobile phone and call for help between CPR repetitions.

If you can see an object blocking your baby's throat or if you know he has something caught in his throat, you will first need to try to **clear his airway**.

1. Hold your baby face down on your forearm, with his head firmly supported in the V formed by your thumb and forefinger and angled lower than his trunk. (With a larger baby, you can hold him face down across your lap, but again, with his head supported and lower than his trunk.) If you are standing, you can support your forearm on your thigh for extra support.

2. Use the heel of your free hand to deliver five firm and rapid blows between your baby's shoulder blades.

3. If no foreign object pops out and your baby is still not coughing or breathing, turn him over on his back, rest him firmly in your forearm or lap and, with his head and neck supported, apply five rapid chest compressions. *Using just two fingers*, placed one finger's width below the nipple line (an imaginary line drawn between the nipples), push the sternum (the breastbone midway between the nipples) down about $1/2$ an inch, and repeat rapidly five times.

4. If you have not seen the object dislodged and your baby is still not breathing or coughing, open his mouth by placing your forefinger under his lower jaw and your thumb inside his mouth to hold down his tongue. If you can see the foreign object obstructing your baby's throat, try to remove it by sweeping it out with your finger. *Do not* attempt to pinch the object, which might end up pushing it farther into his airway.

5. If your baby is conscious but still not breathing normally, repeat the entire sequence of five back blows, five chest compressions, and an examination of the airway. Keep repeating this sequence until the object is dislodged from your baby's airway or your baby loses consciousness. If the object is dislodged, monitor your baby's breathing and let her rest quietly until help arrives.

6. If your baby loses consciousness, **begin CPR immediately** (see following box).

CPR (Cardiopulmonary Resuscitation) for Infants

If you have a baby (and you do), you—and your partner—have a responsibility to learn baby and infant CPR. Although a description is provided, a description is *not* a course and it offers you no practical experience.

For the sake of your baby, you need to be absolutely certain that you can do CPR *before* you need it. So if you haven't yet done so—and you should have taken the course during pregnancy—take a course in baby and infant CPR (available through the Red Cross, your local Y, or other community organizations)—*now!*

As of July 1, 2006, the American Heart Association adopted new guidelines for CPR. The new guidelines call for the following steps, which apply to all children before their first birthday:

Check your child's airway, breathing, and circulation (ABC).

A) **Airway:** Look to see if your baby's chest rises and fall. Listen for any breath sounds. Feel air being exhaled by your baby as you put your cheek next to her open mouth while watching her chest.

B) **Breathing:** If your baby is breathing, call 911 and wait with your baby until help arrives. If you cannot detect any signs of breathing, attempt two rescue breaths: cover your baby's nose and mouth with your mouth, puff up your cheeks, and give two gentle breaths lasting 1 second each.

If rescue breaths do not cause your baby's chest to rise, reposition her head by gently tilting her forehead back and lifting her chin. Try two more rescue breaths.

C) **Circulation:** If the chest rises, check her pulse by placing two fingers on the inside of your baby's upper arm between the elbow and the shoulder and pressing gently for no more than 10 seconds. If you cannot feel a pulse, begin chest compressions. Locate your baby's sternum by imagining a line between her nipples and placing your ring finger at the midpoint. The sternum is located one finger's width below this point, so use your middle and index fingers to compress the chest. Compress the chest by pushing down with two fingers one third to one half the depth of your baby's chest. Compress very rapidly at a rate of approximately 100 pushes per minute. After every 30 compressions, give two more rescue breaths, and return immediately to compressions.

After five complete cycles of compressions followed by rescue breaths, check your baby's pulse again for at least 5 seconds, but no more than 10 seconds. If you detect a pulse, continue rescue breathing (one breath every 5 seconds) until emergency personnel arrive, your baby resumes breathing on her own, or you become too exhausted to continue. If you do not detect a pulse, repeat five more cycles of compressions followed by rescue breaths. Check the pulse again after five cycles and repeat as needed or until emergency personnel arrive.

Accidents: Heatstroke

If your baby is suffering from heatstroke, his body temperature has risen to dangerous levels, usually due to very hot conditions: for example, a humid midsummer beach day; too many clothes on a hot, humid day; or too much time spent in a closed, overheated car. (*You should never leave your child unattended in a car, whether hot or cold.*)

Heatstroke can often be confused with a high fever, which is actually only one symptom of heatstroke. Other symptoms may include convulsions, lethargy, and/or loss of consciousness. If your baby is suffering from heatstroke, he needs immediate cooling and emergency medical assistance. Cool your baby immediately by removing extra layers of clothing; sponge-bathing him in cool water; wrapping him in a cool, soaked towel; and/or fanning him. While applying these cooling methods, call 911 or wrap him in a cool, soaked towel and take him to the nearest emergency room at once.

Accidents: Poisoning

Medicines, household cleaners, and certain household plants can be toxic. If your baby has ingested poison, she may demonstrate any or all of the following symptoms:

- ◆ Sudden behavior changes, including lethargy, agitation, or irritability
- ◆ A racing pulse
- ◆ Rapid or difficult breathing
- ◆ Vomiting or diarrhea
- ◆ An abnormal amount of drooling, often accompanied by a bad odor
- ◆ An abnormal amount of sweating or eye watering
- ◆ Dilated or constricted pupils
- ◆ Convulsions or loss of consciousness

If even a possibility exists that your baby has ingested a toxic substance, **seek emergency care immediately**. Call your local poison control center (this number should be posted next to all of your phones), the national **Poison Control Center (1-800-222-1222), or 911** at once. As you are calling, look for clues that might tell you what she ingested: an open or empty container of any toxic substance (medicines or household cleaners, for example) or household plants within your baby's reach. Even if your child has not shown any symptoms yet, call the poison control center at once if you see these kinds of empty or open bottles anywhere that your baby might have reached.

When you call, the poison control center or emergency personnel will need to know your baby's name, age, weight, any medical conditions, and the name of the suspected toxin, including when and how much you think she swallowed.

Check your baby's mouth for any traces of what she ingested and remove those that remain with your fingers. Keep this to give to your doctor or emergency personnel. Also, give the bottle of any toxin (with its label intact) you suspect your baby may have ingested to the doctor or emergency personnel.

If you suspect poisoning, *do not give your baby syrup of ipecac or any other emetic.* Forcing the toxin to come back up by inducing vomiting can cause more damage to your baby's throat.

Accidents: Poison Ivy, Poison Oak, Poison Sumac

Poison ivy, poison oak, and poison sumac can cause an especially itchy, red, blistering rash. As soon as you know or suspect your baby has come in contact with any of these, wash the exposed skin with soap and water for at least 10 minutes. In addition, wash with soap and water anything else that may have come in contact with the poison ivy, poison oak, or poison sumac. This includes especially clothing and shoes. (While washing these items, protect yourself, if possible, by handling them with gloves or a clean cloth diaper.)

If a reaction (called contact dermatitis) develops, treat the rash—red and itchy, perhaps with blistering, oozing, or swelling—with calamine lotion. Apply this lotion three or four times a day. Avoid lotions that contain antihistamines or anesthetics, which may cause allergic eruptions. (Your pediatrician may prescribe oral antihistamines to control the itching, but these are very rarely prescribed for babies in their first year of life.) Cool compresses and acetaminophen may help relieve your baby's itching, too.

If your baby's rash is severe, persistent, or located near the eyes, face, or genitalia, consult your pediatrician about appropriate treatment.

Accidents: Shock

In case of injury, trauma, or severe illness, your baby may go into shock. Shock is characterized by one or more of the following:

◆ A rapid, weak pulse

◆ Clammy, cold, and pale skin

◆ Chills

◆ Nausea or vomiting

◆ Extreme thirst

◆ Difficulty breathing

◆ Convulsions

Do not attempt to treat shock yourself. Call 911 and try to make your baby comfortable until help arrives. Lay him down on his back, elevate his legs to help blood flow to his brain, and cover his body lightly with a baby blanket. *Do not attempt to give him any food or drink.*

Accidents: Swallowed Foreign Objects

Many swallowed objects—marbles, coins, game pieces—will not do your baby any harm unless they obstruct her airway. Just examine your baby's dirty diapers until the object has passed through the digestive tract.

However, if your baby has swallowed something she shouldn't have, you will need to **call your pediatrician and take your baby to the emergency room** under any of the following circumstances:

◆ The object swallowed was sharp (such as a pin or a small toy with sharp edges).

◆ Your baby has difficulty swallowing (which may indicate obstruction).

◆ Your baby gags, vomits, drools, or wheezes after swallowing the object (which may indicate obstruction).

◆ Your baby has difficulty breathing or is choking. In this case, call 911 and begin trying to clear the airway using the method described earlier under "Choking" (see page 352).

First Aid for Injuries and Emergencies

Injuries: Bone Fractures

Broken bones—fractures—are a common occurrence among young children. Fortunately, most do not require surgery; if immobilized, they will repair themselves.

If your baby breaks a bone, he will probably cry hysterically from the pain. You may notice swelling around the fracture and your baby will probably not want you to move the affected limb. If you suspect your baby may have broken a bone, contact your pediatrician at once. Immobilize the injured limb by improvising a splint: roll a magazine or newspaper around the suspected break and secure it with bandages or ties (but don't secure it so tightly that you cut off circulation to that limb).

With a particularly bad fracture, the bone may protrude through your baby's skin. If so, *do not touch the bone* or attempt to put it back under the skin. Instead, cover the wound with sterile gauze; apply pressure, if necessary to control bleeding; call 911; and wait for emergency personnel to arrive.

If you suspect a broken leg, neck, or back, do not try to move your baby at all. Try to comfort or soothe your baby while keeping him still. Call 911 and wait for emergency personnel to move your baby safely. Do not give your baby food or drink while waiting for medical care.

Injuries: Bruises

Bruises are almost never serious, although your baby may find a bruise painful enough to warrant a flood of tears. If your baby has a bruise, apply a cold compress, a cold pack, or an ice pack wrapped in a towel for 30-minute intervals. This should numb the area enough to relieve the pain while simultaneously reducing the swelling.

Injuries: Cuts and Gashes (Wounds That Break the Skin)

Wounds that break the skin can be major (with massive, uncontrolled bleeding), large (with a significant flow of blood), small (with some blood), or minor (with very little bleeding).

If your baby has suffered a severe injury and blood is gushing out or coming out in such volume that you cannot stop it, apply pressure on the wound with a clean towel or sheet to slow the flow. **Call 911 or get someone to drive you immediately to**

the nearest emergency room (you cannot drive yourself because someone needs to care for your baby during transportation). Maintain constant pressure until medical personnel take over.

With large wounds, with a steady flow of blood, first stop the bleeding by covering the cut with a sterile gauze pad, a clean cloth diaper, or a washcloth and applying firm pressure. Elevating the wound may also help stop the bleeding. If you cannot stop the bleeding within 15 minutes, apply additional covering to the wound, continue to apply pressure, and contact your pediatrician immediately. Your doctor will probably direct you to seek treatment in his or her office or the nearest hospital emergency room.

If your baby has suffered a small cut, with some blood but not a steady flow, place sterile gauze over the wound and apply firm pressure until the bleeding stops. Then wash the wound gently with soap and water, apply antibacterial ointment or spray, and put a bandage over the wound. If you are at all concerned about the wound, call your pediatrician, explain the injury, and see if an office visit is necessary.

If your baby has suffered a minor cut, wash it with soap and water and flush the wound with running water to clean it of any debris. Apply a dab of antibacterial ointment or antiseptic spray and cover the wound with a bandage or sterile gauze.

After any open wound, pay attention to how it heals. If you notice redness around the wound, swelling or tenderness, drainage, or pus, the wound may have become infected. Consult your pediatrician at once.

Injuries: Ear

If a bug or other object becomes lodged in your baby's ear, *do not* attempt to pry it out with your finger, a cotton swab, tweezers, or any other tool. This could push it deeper into your baby's ear. Even worse, overly vigorous attempts to clear the ear can damage your baby's eardrum and ultimately her hearing. Instead, contact your pediatrician or take your baby to your local emergency room, where your baby's ear can be cleared safely.

If your baby's ear shows signs of injury (bleeding from inside the ear, difficulty hearing, and so on), call your pediatrician.

Injuries: Eye

If a small object (dust, a gnat or other small bug, sand, or an eyelash, for example) becomes lodged in your baby's eye, tearing will probably wash it out. If necessary, you can try flushing out the object with warm (not cold or hot) water. With your baby lying on her side, place your fingers about $1/2$ inch above and below her eyelids to keep them open while flushing them out. Rinse from the inside of the eye to the outside, keeping the affected eye lower than the unaffected eye.

If this attempt is unsuccessful—you can still see the object or your baby keeps trying to rub it out of his eyes—call your pediatrician and go to the doctor's office or the nearest emergency room. *Do not* try to remove the object yourself because you might accidentally scratch his cornea. Before leaving for the doctor's office or hospital, cover your baby's eye with a sterile gauze pad to relieve some of his discomfort and keep him from rubbing it.

If your baby's eye has been exposed to toxins (household chemicals, for example), immediately flush the eye with warm water for 15 to 20 minutes, holding it open as described above. Then take your baby to the nearest emergency room or your pediatrician's office, or call your doctor or the local or national **Poison Control Center (1-800-222-1222).**

If your baby gets a black eye, apply a cold compress or cold pack to the eye for 20 minutes. Then call your pediatrician to arrange for an examination to check for internal damage or broken bones around the eye.

Injuries: Finger(s) or Toe(s)

Injuries to toes—and especially fingers—are not common among babies under a year old. It does sometimes happen, though, that a baby's fingers will get crushed by a closing drawer, door, or car door. If your baby's fingers have been crushed, immediate swelling and bruising are likely. The injured fingers will turn blue, and there may be some bleeding. If the bleeding is under your baby's nail(s), a blood clot will form, the area under the nail will turn black or blue, and pressure under the nail will likely become very painful. You may need to take your baby to the nearest emergency room, where the blood clot can be drained to relieve the buildup of pressure.

If a crushed finger is bleeding, wash the wound with soap and water and cover it with a small sterile gauze pad. Applying an ice pack or soaking the finger in cold water may help reduce the swelling and relieve some pain. *Do not* leave fingers or toes in cold water for more than 15 minutes without a 5-minute break to allow the fingers or toes to get warm again.

If the pain subsides and your baby calms down, you may not need to consult your pediatrician. Over the next few days, however, you should be alert for signs of infection—increased swelling, resurgent pain or discomfort, redness, drainage around the wound, or post-traumatic fever. Any of these symptoms should prompt a call to your baby's doctor.

If you think it's possible that your baby has a broken finger or toe, *do not* attempt to straighten it out yourself. Instead, consult your doctor or take your baby to the nearest emergency room immediately.

You should also contact your pediatrician at once if the injury causes excessive swelling or bleeding under the nail.

Another common injury involving fingers or toes is a torn or detached nail. If your baby has torn or ripped a fingernail or toenail, keep the finger or toe clean and covered as much as possible until it heals. A bandage can help keep the torn nail in place until it can be trimmed away at the tear. If your baby has a detached nail, you need not tear it off, since it will eventually fall off by itself.

Until the nail has grown back completely, keep the unprotected fingertip or toe clean but *do not* soak the digit (which can promote fungal infections). Keep the cleaned fingertip or toe protected with a bandage and regularly change the bandage to keep it clean until the nail grows back (which could take up to 4 months). Until the nail has grown back, watch for signs of infection (swelling, redness, or heat) around the wound.

Injuries: Head

A standing, toddling, or climbing baby is often a falling baby, and banged and bruised heads are not uncommon among babies under 1 year of age. After any head injury—a fall on the head or a blow to the head—pick up your baby and comfort her with kisses and care. Your child will probably stop crying and resume normal activity within 5 or 10 minutes.

If your child has sustained a bruise on her head, treat the bruise with a cold compress or cold pack to relieve any swelling or pain.

If your child has a cut on her head, stop the bleeding as you would any other wound: by pressing a sterile gauze pad against the wound. After the bleeding has stopped, gently wash the cut with soap and water. If you can't stop the bleeding, keep the wound covered with fresh gauze and maintain pressure while getting your partner or someone else to drive you and your baby to the doctor or emergency room, where she will probably get stitches.

Because the effects of head trauma sometimes take time to appear, you should observe your baby carefully for a day or two following any head injury. **Call your doctor or head straight to the nearest emergency room** if any of these symptoms arise within two days of a head injury:

◆ Loss of consciousness. If consciousness does not return within a few minutes, move your child as little as possible (except to remove him from a dangerous situation), especially if you suspect a possible neck injury in addition to head trauma. If your baby has stopped breathing, begin CPR at once (see page 353) and have someone call 911. Continue CPR until emergency personnel arrive.

◆ Inability to be roused from sleep. "Test" your baby by waking her once or twice on the first night after the head injury, as well as once in the middle of any day-time naps.

◆ Lethargy or extreme sleepiness.

◆ Extreme irritability, which may indicate a persistent headache.

◆ Persistent vomiting. Vomiting once or twice after a head injury is common, but this should pass within a few hours.

◆ Convulsions (seizures).

◆ Swelling of your baby's skull or a depression in her skull.

◆ A significant change in your baby's coordination, strength, or mental abilities— for example, a loss of balance, weakness in her arms or legs, crossed eyes, or the inability of her eyes to constrict or dilate.

◆ Blood or other fluid leakage from the nose or ears.

◆ Apparent loss of mobility of an arm or leg.

Any of these symptoms could indicate a serious head trauma and the possibility of internal bleeding. You should **take your baby to an emergency room at once.**

Injuries: Limb or Digit Severed

If your baby has had a limb or digit completely severed, bleeding will be massive and uncontrolled. Cover the wound with sterile gauze, a clean cloth diaper, or a clean washcloth and apply heavy pressure in an attempt to control your baby's bleeding. While maintaining pressure, have someone perform CPR (see page 353) if your baby has gone into shock and stopped breathing. Call 911 or get someone to take you and your baby to the nearest emergency room at once.

If possible, preserve the severed digit or limb by wrapping it in a wet clean cloth, putting it in a bag, and packing it in ice. *Do not* put any ice in direct contact with the severed body part.

Injuries: Puncture Wounds

With any puncture wound (a sharp object that penetrates your baby's skin), soak the wound in warm, soapy water for 15 minutes. If large, *do not* remove the cause of the puncture wound, since removal could lead to uncontrolled bleeding. Instead, place padding around the object to keep it from moving. Then call your pediatrician or 911, or get someone to drive you and your baby to the nearest emergency room.

As with any open wound, be alert for signs of infection (redness, swelling, or drainage around the wound) in the days following the injury. If any of these symptoms appear, call your pediatrician for a follow-up examination.

Injuries: Scrapes and Abrasions

In their first months on their feet, babies do not always fall in a safe, well-padded space. If your baby falls and scrapes a knee, elbow, or other body part, take a few minutes first to pick him up and hold him until he calms down. Because the top layer(s) of skin have been scraped off, the scraped area will be tender or sore. A scrape may also involve slight bleeding.

If your baby has a scrape, clean it gently with soap and water, keeping in mind the tenderness of the scraped area. If your baby finds washing too painful, he may find it more comfortable to soak in a tub. After cleaning the scrape, cover it with a sterile bandage or (with bigger scrapes) a large sterile gauze pad taped in place.

Injuries: Splinters

If your baby gets one or more splinters, wash the area gently with soap and water, which will not only clean the area but may soften the skin around the splinter. If the splinter seems painful, numb the area with an ice pack before trying to remove it.

To remove a splinter, sterilize tweezers by holding them over a flame for several seconds or cleaning them with a cotton ball soaked in rubbing alcohol. If the end of the splinter protrudes, try to remove it with the tweezers. If the end is inaccessible, sterilize a sewing needle (again with a flame or alcohol) and try to pick the splinter loose (you will probably need your partner or someone else to keep your baby still while you're trying to get at the splinter). After removing the splinter, wash the area again with soap and water.

If you cannot remove a splinter, soak the area three to four times a day in warm, soapy water. If the splinter still doesn't come out or if the area around the splinter becomes red, swollen, or hot (which could indicate infection), call your doctor for further instructions.

Injuries: Teeth

Despite the fact that your baby won't have many teeth in her first year, those she does have will be right up front and vulnerable. If a tooth gets chipped or broken due to a fall or a blow to the mouth (for example, getting hit by a ball), use sterile gauze or a clean washcloth and warm water to clean your baby's mouth around the broken tooth. Check to make sure all tooth fragments have been removed from her mouth, since they could be a choking hazard for your baby. A very cold damp washcloth can help minimize swelling and relieve any pain around the area of the broken tooth. Call the dentist, if your baby already has one, or your pediatrician, who will probably refer you to a dentist.

If one of your baby's teeth has been knocked out entirely, contact your dentist or pediatrician. If you have recovered the tooth, take it with you to the dentist, pediatrician, or emergency room. If the tooth is not whole, your dentist will want to make sure any fragments have been cleared from your baby's mouth to guard against choking. However, since the dislodged tooth was not permanent anyway, the dentist will probably not attempt to replace it. This means your baby will probably need to do without that tooth until a permanent one grows in (probably around her sixth birthday).

Treating Common Symptoms of Illness During the First Year

Unless you have a medical degree, you cannot diagnose illnesses. But as a parent, you can certainly recognize symptoms of illness. This section will give you some pointers on how to treat or ease common symptoms of illness during your baby's first year or at least keep him as comfortable as possible despite his symptoms.

Constipation

Constipation is rare during the first several months, especially if your baby is exclusively breast-fed. After starting solid foods, however, your baby may suffer from occasional constipation.

In trying to determine whether your child is constipated, keep in mind her usual defecation patterns. Some babies may go more than a day without a bowel movement, yet still not be constipated, while others may have difficulty passing stools despite having frequent bowel movements.

Instead of looking at frequency, look at your baby's stools for signs of constipation. In the first months, firm stools with bowel movements less than once a day may indicate constipation. Later in your baby's first year, symptoms of constipation might include …

◆ Hard, dense, often pellet-size stools with several days between bowel movements.

◆ Apparent abdominal pain during bowel movements.

◆ Soiled diapers between bowel movements (which could be leakage around a bowel obstruction).

◆ Blood in or around the stools.

If you do notice blood in your baby's stools, or if she suffers from frequent constipation, consult your pediatrician.

You can relieve occasional constipation with a simple change of your baby's diet. Add more water, prunes, raisins, plums, apricots, peas, beans, and whole-grain breads and cereals. You could also try introducing apple juice or prune juice into her diet in small amounts (an ounce or two). Feed your baby less rice, cereal, and bananas, and if you've started to introduce cow's milk before her first birthday (which is not recommended), switch back to formula, breast milk, or water.

Because exercise can also relieve constipation, you might also try to give your baby more running around time or free play time.

Unless your pediatrician tells you to do so, however, *do not* give your baby a laxative or stool softener.

Convulsions (Seizures)

Although scary for a parent to witness, convulsions are not dangerous in themselves and almost never do damage to the brain or nervous system.

Some convulsions can be brought on by fever. Febrile convulsions can cause the eyes to roll upward, cause the limbs or entire body to stiffen, or cause twitching, jerky movements that involve the whole body. Febrile convulsions usually last only a minute or two.

In addition to seizures associated with fever, there are two common types of convulsions. Grand mal seizures consist of rapid, violent movements that often begin in just one part of the body and then spread to the entire body, occasionally involving a loss of consciousness. Petit mal seizures, which consist of a vacant stare and attention lapse that rarely lasts more than several seconds, are much more subtle and may even go unnoticed for several years.

Most convulsions will stop on their own. However, if your baby is having a convulsion, you will want to keep him safe until it passes. Place him on the floor or on a bed and clear the area of any hard or sharp objects (though these really shouldn't be on the floor or baby's bed anyway). Lay him on his side with his hips higher than his head. This will prevent him from choking if he vomits during the seizure.

Do not restrain your baby unless he is in danger of injuring himself. *Do not* try to give him food or drink. *Do not* leave your baby until a seizure stops.

After convulsions have ended, call to inform your pediatrician that a seizure has occurred. The doctor may or may not want you to bring your baby into the office for an examination.

Although you should stay with your baby during a seizure, ask your partner or someone else to call 911 or your pediatrician right away if …

♦ The seizure causes difficulty breathing.

♦ The seizure causes choking.

♦ The seizure causes blueness.

♦ One seizure follows another.

♦ A seizure last more than 5 minutes.

If your baby stops breathing, begin CPR (see page 353) at once.

If your baby's convulsions are associated with a fever, after the seizure has ended, your baby should return to normal behavior, although he may seem sleepy or actually fall asleep. After the convulsions have stopped, you may treat the fever with acetaminophen or ibuprofen as directed by your pediatrician. You can cool your baby with a cool sponge bath, but *do not* put your baby in a bathtub, since a second seizure, if it happens, could cause him to inhale water.

Diarrhea

In trying to identify diarrhea, keep in mind that breast-fed and formula-fed babies, on an exclusively liquid diet, do not have firm stools. After introducing solid foods, however, stools tend to become firmer. If bowel movements at this point become loose, watery, and more frequent, this is diarrhea.

There's not much you can do to make your baby's diarrhea go away. Because diarrhea can irritate the skin quicker than normal stools, however, you should keep your baby's bottom clean by frequently changing her diaper and applying a diaper cream with every change.

Diarrhea, especially when coupled with vomiting, depletes the body of water and salt, so you will probably need to increase your baby's fluid intake. However, *do not* give your baby undiluted juice (especially apple and pear juice, which can exacerbate diarrhea). Your pediatrician may recommend an over-the-counter electrolyte solution (Pedialyte, for example) to help replenish low levels of water and salt. Depending on the severity of the diarrhea, your doctor may recommend giving your baby *only* electrolyte solution for 12 to 24 hours. Breast-fed babies can continue breast-feeding, while bottle-fed babies might need to drink formula diluted with water to half-strength for 24 hours.

If your baby already eats solid foods, she can start eating bananas, rice cereal, toast, potatoes, and/or pasta after 12 to 24 hours. *Avoid fruits* other than bananas until diarrhea has passed.

Unless told to do so by your pediatrician, *do not* give your baby any antidiarrheal medication.

If your baby has diarrhea, watch for signs of dehydration:

◆ Less frequent urination (although this can be hard to determine when your baby has diarrhea because you'll be changing watery diapers often)

◆ Dry mouth

◆ Fewer tears when crying

◆ A decrease in play

◆ A sunken fontanel

If you notice any of these signs, **notify your pediatrician at once.**

Chronic diarrhea—diarrhea that continues for 2 weeks or longer—also requires a pediatrician's examination. So if your baby's diarrhea persists for this long, contact your pediatrician.

Call your pediatrician immediately if your baby's diarrhea is accompanied by …

◆ A persistent fever (lasting more than 24 hours).

◆ Repeated vomiting (lasting more than 12 hours).

- ◆ Bloody stools.

- ◆ Jaundice (yellowing) or rash.

- ◆ A refusal to eat or drink.

- ◆ A swollen abdomen or apparent abdominal pain.

Any of these symptoms coupled with diarrhea could indicate a serious medical problem.

Fainting/Loss of Consciousness

If your baby loses consciousness, check his airway to make sure it's clear. Then check his breathing by placing your ear next to your baby's mouth and watching to see if his chest rises and falls. If he has stopped breathing, give two rescue breaths to begin CPR (see page 353) at once and yell for someone to call 911. (If no one is available to call, bring your baby to the phone or use a cordless or mobile phone to make the call yourself between CPR repetitions.) Continue CPR until your baby resumes breathing or help arrives.

If your baby is still breathing, lay him flat, turn his head to the side, and check for any objects or food in his mouth. Gently use a finger sweep to clear anything out of his mouth. *Do not* give your baby food or drink in an attempt to revive him. **Call 911 or your pediatrician immediately** and, if you suspect poisoning (for example, you find open medicines or household cleaners), call the **Poison Control Center (1-800-222-1222).**

Fever

Although a high fever always calls for treatment, fever is actually a good thing. A fever indicates that your baby's immune system is fighting an infection or illness. Fever is a sign that your baby's internal defenses are hard at work, trying to protect her body and fight infection by destroying germs and other disease-causing agents. (A high temperature makes the body less hospitable for viruses and bacteria.)

Mild fever in itself therefore demands no treatment. Unfortunately, fever can also cause discomfort, increase the need for fluids, and accelerate your baby's breathing and heart rate. In infants, it can also trigger convulsions (see page 364).

Knowing whether a fever is mild or severe requires an accurate temperature reading. *Do not* rely on feeling your baby's forehead to determine fever. Instead, take her rectal temperature using a digital thermometer coated in a nonpetroleum lubricant or her tympanic temperature using a tympanic (ear) thermometer. (Because the accuracy of a tympanic thermometer depends on your ability to place it correctly [but always gently] in the ear canal, most pediatricians prefer rectal temperatures taken with a digital thermometer.) *Always sterilize the thermometer before and after use* with rubbing alcohol or soapy water followed by a cool water rinse.

The American Academy of Pediatrics recommends that you call your doctor if your baby's (rectal) temperature reaches higher than:

◆ 100.4°F if your baby is under 2 months old

◆ 101°F if your baby is 3 to 6 months old

◆ 103°F if your baby is 7 months old or older

If your baby's fever gets this high, your pediatrician will need to examine her to confirm or rule out serious infections. Most calls to your pediatrician, however, will not be prompted by fever itself, but by other symptoms: an earache, a cough, recurrent vomiting or diarrhea, a rash, irritability, or excessive sleeping or fatigue.

You should also contact your pediatrician at once if your baby's fever follows exposure to an exceedingly hot place (the beach or a standing car in summer, for example), which may indicate heat stroke (see page 354), or if the fever is associated with a convulsion (see page 364).

Again, because a fever indicates that your baby's body is fighting an infection, unless your baby has a history of febrile convulsions, *you do not necessarily need to treat a fever.* Watch your baby's behavior. If she is behaving normally, you don't need to treat the fever at all. However, if your baby appears uncomfortable or irritable, can't sleep, or shows other signs of pain, or if her (rectal) temperature rises above the limits outlined above, call your pediatrician. Your doctor will probably recommend treatment with acetaminophen or (usually not until your baby is over 6 months old) ibuprofen.

Never give your baby ibuprofen if she is repeatedly vomiting or otherwise dehydrated.

Never give your baby aspirin or any product with aspirin as an ingredient.

Too much acetaminophen can cause a toxic reaction, which may include nausea, vomiting, and abdominal pain. So as with any medication, check the dosage chart on the bottle *very carefully* and determine the dosage based on your baby's weight rather than her age. (Better still, tell your pediatrician how much your baby weighs when you call and ask the appropriate dosage. Until she is 2 years old, make it a point always to check the dosage with your doctor before giving your baby acetaminophen, ibuprofen, or any other medication. Also, if your doctor prescribes antibiotics to treat an illness that has caused the fever, ask whether you can still give your baby acetaminophen or ibuprofen, since some antibiotics contraindicate fever-reducing medications.

If you're waiting for your pediatrician to call back and give you the okay on acetaminophen or ibuprofen, if your baby still seems uncomfortable after medication, or if she is vomiting and thus not retaining the medication, try cooling her off with a sponge bath using slightly warm water. (A cold-water sponge bath may increase your child's fever by causing her to shiver, which will raise the body temperature.) Support your baby as you sit her in the baby bath or tub. Using a washcloth, cover your baby's body from the neck down with a thin layer of warm water and allow it to evaporate before repeating. Continue this sponging until her temperature has dropped to an acceptable level (this may take as much as 30 to 45 minutes). However, if your baby seems upset, remove her from the tub. Remember, *fever itself is not harmful* unless it reaches extremes (higher than 104°F).

If your baby has a fever, you will need to make sure she drinks plenty of fluids (that is, more fluids than usual). You should also try to increase her calorie intake since a feverish body breaks down stored fat to produce heat.

Finally, do your best to help your baby feel comfortable despite her fever. *If your baby is not shivering* (which would indicate that she is chilled and may want another layer of clothing or a blanket to be comfortable), keep her comfortable by dressing her in light clothing while indoors. Also, try to keep the indoor temperature comfortably cool by using a fan or air-conditioning.

Sore Throat

If your baby's throat tissue becomes inflamed, often due to a viral infection, he will have a sore throat. Your baby cannot tell you that he has a sore throat, of course. However, you can look for signs: irritability, often accompanied by a loss of appetite, difficulty swallowing, excessive drooling, and a mild fever and/or cold. If you notice these signals, check your baby's throat for unusual redness or swollen tonsils.

If your baby has the signs of a sore throat, call your pediatrician, who may want to take a throat culture to rule out strep throat (see page 380).

To treat a sore throat, your pediatrician may recommend acetaminophen to relieve pain. Your baby should also drink plenty of fluids while he has a sore throat. If he already eats solids, soft, cold foods can be easier for your child to eat until his sore throat goes away.

Vomiting

In a baby, it's important to distinguish vomiting from spitting up. After breast-feeding or bottle-feeding, many babies spit up, often because they've ingested more than their stomach can hold. Spitting up should not cause any concern on your part. Vomiting, by contrast, involves a much greater volume of regurgitation. If your baby is vomiting, she will *empty* her stomach contents.

Vomiting often results from a viral infection, although it may also follow an extended bout of coughing or head injury (see page 360). Vomiting will usually stop without any targeted treatment after it runs its course. Unless told by your doctor to do so, *do not* use over-the-counter medications to stop vomiting.

Focus on keeping your baby safe. Keep your baby lying on her stomach or side when vomiting, to minimize the risk of aspiration (inhaling vomit into her lungs).

Because vomiting can dehydrate your baby, make sure she drinks extra fluids (but not if drinking prompts more vomiting). Test your baby's tolerance with sips of fluids about 2 hours after her last vomiting episode. If she tolerates sips, give your baby 1 or 2 ounces of fluids every half-hour or so, beginning 2 to 3 hours after the last vomiting episode. For the first 2 hours, give her water only. If this doesn't prompt further vomiting, you can progress to an electrolyte solution (such as Pedialyte) or clear liquids for another hour. Then you can try breast milk or half-strength formula.

If your baby has begun eating solids, you can try popsicles 4 to 6 hours after she last vomited, too. From 12 to 24 hours after your baby's last vomiting episode, you can gradually return to her normal diet, supplemented with plenty of clear fluids. As with diarrhea, start with starchy foods: rice cereal, toast, pasta, bananas, and so on.

Care During Common Childhood Illness

Although the following section describes symptoms of and treatment for common childhood illness, if you suspect your child has any of these illnesses, call your child's doctor at once. These descriptions may help you correctly diagnose your child based on his symptoms. However, illness does not always follow the exact same course for every child.

A complete and accurate examination and diagnosis should be made by your doctor in order to prescribe the best and most effective treatment. Your pediatrician has the medical training and expertise to give you the best possible advice on how to handle any childhood illness. So even if you think you've figured out what your child has, consult your doctor to find out what to do about it.

Bronchiolitis

Bronchiolitis, an inflammation of the lung's breathing tubes (the bronchioles), often starts with the same symptoms as a cold or upper-respiratory infection: a runny nose, a cough, and sometimes a fever. As the illness advances, however, the cough will progress and your baby may have difficulty breathing.

Symptoms that demand a pediatrician's attention include …

- Wheezing (high-pitched whistling exhales).
- Difficulty breast-feeding, sucking, swallowing, or drinking fluids due to difficulty breathing.
- A blue tint developing on the lips or fingertips, which indicates a failure of the lungs to deliver enough oxygen to the blood.

In addition to following your pediatrician's prescribed care, you can help your baby feel more comfortable by giving her plenty of fluids, especially clear ones. The use of a cool-mist humidifier, nasal aspirator, and/or mild saline nose drops (if your pediatrician recommends them) may help relieve some of your baby's nasal congestion.

Chicken Pox (Varicella)

Chicken pox usually starts with a mild fever accompanied by a very itchy rash of red spots that turn into pimples that blister before crusting over and turning into scabs. The rash can soon cover your baby's entire body, spreading from his torso and scalp to his face, arms, and legs.

If your pediatrician confirms the diagnosis of chicken pox, do your best to keep your baby comfortable and prevent him from scratching. Acetaminophen may reduce your baby's fever and lessen the itch (and the urge to scratch). *Do not* give your baby an oral antihistamine unless your doctor prescribes it.

Oatmeal baths and lukewarm baths can also help relieve some of his itchiness. Bathe your baby regularly with soap and water, and trim his nails to keep him clean and help prevent scratching and secondary infection. When you put your baby down for a nap or for the night, cover his hands with mittens or socks to prevent him from scratching in his sleep.

If you or your partner is pregnant, contact your own physician at once, since chicken pox can pose a risk to a developing fetus.

Common Cold/Upper-Respiratory Infection

Everybody knows what a cold looks like: a runny nose (with discharge often starting clear, then becoming thicker and taking on a greenish or yellowish tinge), sneezing, coughing, a sore or scratchy throat, a mild fever (less than 102°F), irritability, loss of appetite, and fatigue. Colds are common and uncomfortable, but almost always relatively harmless. They usually go away by themselves within a week to 10 days and rarely lead to complications.

Until your baby is 3 months old, however, call your pediatrician whenever she has cold symptoms. In very young babies, colds can develop into croup, bronchiolitis, or pneumonia.

After your child is 3 months old, call your pediatrician if …

- Your baby seems to have pain in her ear (you may notice her tugging, rubbing, or flailing at her ear).

- Her temperature rises above 102°F.

- She has difficulty breathing.

- Her lips or fingertips turn blue (which indicates difficulty breathing).

- Her cough persists for more than a week.

- Nasal congestion lasts more than 10 days.

Your pediatrician may or may not want you to bring your baby into the office after you describe her symptoms.

Whether or not you see the pediatrician, try to keep your baby as comfortable as possible during her illness. Give your baby extra fluids and do what you can to see she gets extra rest. With your doctor's okay, you can give your baby acetaminophen or, if appropriate, ibuprofen for treatment of fever (see page 367) or discomfort.

Do not give your baby an over-the-counter cold or cough medicine unless your pediatrician tells you to do so.

To clear nasal passages, especially before nursing, bottle-feeding, or bedtime, use a suction bulb. Squeeze the bulb first, then stick the tip inside your baby's nostril and release the bulb slowly to withdraw the mucus. If your baby's mucus has become hard, mild saline nose drops can help loosen it.

A cool-mist humidifier—cleaned every day and set close to your baby's crib—will help keep her nasal discharge flowing. Running a hot shower in a small bathroom can fill the room with warm steam, which can also help relieve congestion. Simply stay with your baby in the bathroom until she breathes more easily.

Finally, your baby may sleep more easily if you raise her head by putting one or two pillows *under* the crib mattress (but not on top of the mattress, since babies should *never* have pillows in their crib).

Conjunctivitis (Pink Eye)

Conjunctivitis—more commonly called pink eye—is an inflammation of the lining of the eye. Conjunctivitis usually appears first in just one eye but may be easily transmitted from one eye to the other. Symptoms include bloodshot eyes, tearing, discharge, and itching in the eyes, and often sensitivity to light.

If you suspect that your baby has pink eye, contact your pediatrician for a full examination and diagnosis. The doctor may prescribe eye drops or ointment to relieve discomfort and prevent secondary infections.

If your baby has pink eye, you can relieve some of his discomfort by applying a clean, warm wet washcloth to his eye for several minutes. Because conjunctivitis is highly contagious, *do not* use the same washcloth more than once until it has been thoroughly laundered, and wash your own hands thoroughly with soap and water after treating your baby's eyes. Also, use a separate towel just for your baby (and regularly change it for a new one), to keep the infection from spreading.

Croup

Croup—an inflammation of the larynx (voice box) and trachea (windpipe)—often begins as a simple stuffy nose, perhaps with a mild fever, but soon turns into a sharp, barking cough that worsens at night, usually accompanied by a high-pitched noise when inhaling. Croup is often accompanied by hoarseness or laryngitis. If you suspect your baby has croup, call your pediatrician at once. Because continued inflammation could narrow her windpipe, making it extremely difficult for her to breathe, eat, or drink, your baby needs immediate medical attention.

Running a hot shower in a small bathroom can help ease your baby's breathing. Hold her in this makeshift "steam room" and keep the shower running for 15 to 20 minutes or until her breathing becomes easier. Taking your baby for a walk outside at night may also help ease her breathing. A cool-mist humidifier, which you should clean daily, placed next to your baby's crib may help her sleep more easily. When your baby goes to sleep, use a baby monitor or sleep in the same room until she gets better so that a coughing attack will wake you and allow you to treat her quickly.

If your baby has croup, she needs emergency medical care if ...

♦ She seems to struggle for every breath.

♦ She makes a high-pitched whistling sound that gets louder with every breath (which indicates extreme constriction of the trachea).

♦ She turns blue when coughing.

If your baby has any of these symptoms, call 911, drive her to the nearest emergency room, and/or contact your pediatrician at once. *Do not* attempt to open your baby's airway with your finger, since the swelling is beyond the reach of a finger.

Encephalitis

Encephalitis, a swelling of the brain that can lead to permanent neurological damage or even death, demands immediate medical attention. Symptoms include a high fever, often accompanied by vomiting and extreme drowsiness. If you suspect encephalitis, call your pediatrician or go to the nearest emergency room at once.

Influenza (Flu)

The symptoms of influenza are well known:

♦ The sudden onset of fever (usually over 101°F)

♦ Chills and shivering

♦ A dry, hacking, unproductive cough

♦ Extreme fatigue

♦ Occasionally, vomiting or diarrhea

♦ Often aches, pains, and stiffness (which will make your baby more fussy and irritable)

These initial symptoms may be followed by a stuffy nose, persistent (and often more productive) coughing, and a sore throat. Influenza may sometimes be distinguished from a common cold by more coughing and nasal stuffiness rather than a runny nose.

Call your pediatrician if your baby has flu symptoms and is under 6 months old, if symptoms persist for more than 2 days, or if his fever exceeds 102°F. Because influenza is a viral infection, it cannot be treated with antibiotics, but your doctor will want to rule out a bacterial infection (which can be treated with antibiotics).

If your baby has the flu, be sure to give him extra fluids, light meals, and lots of rest. A cold-steam vaporizer placed next to his crib may help your baby breathe easier. If your pediatrician recommends it, you can give your baby acetaminophen or, if over 6 months of age, ibuprofen (always in the proper dosage) to ease his fever or discomfort. *Never give your baby aspirin or any product containing aspirin. Do not give your baby ibuprofen if he is repeatedly vomiting or dehydrated.*

Lyme Disease

Lyme disease, caused by the bite of a deer tick, can lead to arthritis if left unchecked. Initial symptoms of Lyme disease remain localized around the site of the tick bite: a red rash surrounded by a light ring, making it look like a bull's eye. The rash may then spread or appear elsewhere on your baby's body. The rash may be followed by flulike symptoms: fever, chills, fatigue, swollen glands, and aches and pains.

If you suspect your baby may have Lyme disease, call your pediatrician to make an appointment. If administered within a month of the tick bite, antibiotics are very effective in preventing complications. Even if diagnosed later than 1 month after the bite, antibiotics can help—so if you suspect this might be the case, take your baby to your pediatrician to get an accurate diagnosis.

Measles (Rubella)

Since the introduction of the measles vaccine, measles—characterized by a high fever and a rash of red bumps—has become exceedingly rare, yet it still does occasionally appear.

The symptoms of measles resemble those of a common cold at first. The initial signs of illness may include a dry, hacking cough; a runny nose; and/or conjunctivitis (pink eye) or red, watery eyes. Within a few days after the appearance of these symptoms, your baby may develop a high fever (103°F or higher), which may persist for several days. A fever (see page 367) this high, of course, calls for a visit to the pediatrician. Other prerash symptoms may include swollen glands or diarrhea.

After 2 to 4 days of these symptoms, a rash of tiny white spots that resemble grains of sand may appear inside your baby's mouth. A rash of very small red bumps will then appear, usually beginning on her face (often on the forehead) and then spreading to her neck, trunk, arms, and legs.

If you suspect measles, call your pediatrician and arrange for an office visit so that (s)he can confirm the diagnosis and be watchful for pneumonia or other complications. When you call for an appointment, let the office know that you suspect measles so that they can keep your baby quarantined from other children during the visit. If your baby does have measles, keep her away from anyone who has not developed immunity (either through vaccination or by having the disease) until both her fever and her rash have disappeared.

Try to keep your baby comfortable until the illness passes. Give her extra fluids. A warm bath or sponge bath may help ease her discomfort, or, with your pediatrician's okay, you can treat the discomfort or fever with acetaminophen (in the correct dosage, of course). If your baby has conjunctivitis, which can make her extremely sensitive to light, dimming the lights in her room can help.

Return to your pediatrician for a second visit if you suspect that your baby's measles have led to any complications: an ear infection (see page 378); Pneumonia (see page 379); or Encephalitis (see page 374).

Meningitis

Meningitis is an inflammation of the tissues that cover the brain and spinal cord. There are two distinct types: viral meningitis is rarely serious, except in babies under 3 months of age. Bacterial meningitis, however, is very serious, with possible complications including deafness, and, less commonly today, neurological or brain damage or death. Because prompt diagnosis and treatment can minimize the risk of complications, if you even suspect your child may have meningitis, **call your pediatrician at once.**

If your baby is under 2 months old, contact your pediatrician or go to the nearest emergency room immediately if you notice the following symptoms:

- High fever
- Listlessness (extreme inactivity)
- Excessive crying or irritability
- Loss of appetite
- Swelling or bulging at the site of either fontanel (the two soft spots on your baby's skull)

Although your baby most likely does *not* have bacterial meningitis, your pediatrician needs to see your child at once to rule it out. In the case of meningitis, it's better to be safe than sorry.

If your baby is over 2 months old, you should contact your pediatrician or head to the nearest emergency room immediately if you observe these symptoms:

◆ High fever

◆ Excessive drowsiness

◆ Vomiting

◆ Loss of appetite

◆ Unusual irritability or crankiness

◆ A stiff neck

◆ The swelling or bulging of either fontanel

If your pediatrician confirms a diagnosis of bacterial meningitis (through a blood test and a spinal tap—a procedure in which a sample of spinal fluid will be removed from below your baby's spinal cord), your baby will need to be hospitalized for the administration of intravenous antibiotics and fluids. Your baby's hospitalization may last from several days up to 3 weeks, depending on his age and the strain of bacteria identified through the spinal tap.

Mumps

A swelling of salivary glands below and in front of ears and above the jaw, mumps has become much less common since the introduction of the MMR (measles-mumps-rubella) vaccine. Because the vaccine is not given until your baby's 1-year check-up, however, she may be susceptible.

If your baby has mumps, the swelling may affect either or both of the salivary glands. The area around the swelling will be tender (your child will probably cry if you touch her) and may also cause pain when she opens her mouth or eats. Your baby may also have secondary symptoms, including fever, weakness, ear pain, loss of appetite, nausea, and, occasionally, vomiting. Swelling and tenderness may also affect your baby's joints and, if he is a boy, his testes. If your baby appears to have these symptoms, contact your pediatrician to confirm the diagnosis.

If your baby does have mumps, try to make her as comfortable as possible. If your doctor gives you the go-ahead, treat your baby's fever with a proper dose of acetaminophen. Your baby will need lots of fluids, but she probably won't want to drink because swallowing may be painful. If your baby seems reluctant to drink, encourage her to take frequent sips of liquid. If your baby has begun eating solids, switch to soft foods (such as soupy cereals) that require minimal salivation in order to digest.

To relieve some of her gland tenderness, you might try applying a cool or warm, slightly damp washcloth. Finally, your baby will need lots of rest.

If you notice any complications—including extreme fatigue, severe abdominal pain, or painful testes—you should take your baby for a second visit to the pediatrician.

Otitis Media (Middle Ear Infection)

Otitis media, more commonly known as an ear infection, is very common among infants and toddlers. It often follows as a complication of a cold or flu.

Some ear infections don't produce any symptoms. Because your baby can't tell you that his ear hurts, you will need to watch for signals he may give you:

- Tugging or rubbing at his ear
- Increased crying, especially during breast- or bottle-feeding (because sucking alters pressure in the middle ear and may cause pain)
- Difficulty sleeping
- Possibly a fever
- Apparent hearing loss or diminishment
- Yellow fluid draining from his ear, which indicates a slight perforation of the eardrum (which will heal with treatment)

If your baby has an ear infection, your pediatrician may prescribe antibiotic treatment or may take a wait-and-see approach. If the doctor prescribes antibiotics, they should take effect within 2 to 3 days, although—as with any antibiotic—your baby should continue taking the full course of antibiotics (usually 10 days).

Whether or not your pediatrician prescribes antibiotics, you can help relieve some of your baby's symptoms. With your doctor's okay, acetaminophen can help reduce fever and ease any ear pain. Sponge baths may also help relieve fever, while a warm compress applied to his ear (unless it upsets your baby) can help relieve the pain.

When your baby is sleeping, it might help to elevate his head by placing a pillow *under* the crib mattress (but not in the crib).

Do not use eardrops of any kind unless authorized to do so by your pediatrician.

Your pediatrician will probably want to see your baby to recheck his ears when he has completed a course of antibiotic treatment. You can take your baby back earlier, however, if ear pain still seems to bother him 3 days after beginning antibiotic treatment. (Your doctor may need to prescribe a different antibiotic.) You will also need to consult your pediatrician if your baby's hearing loss seems to persist after treatment has been completed.

Pertussis (Whooping Cough)

Although uncommon since the introduction of the pertussis vaccine, whooping cough has not been completely eradicated—and is very dangerous for babies in their first year because it could lead to severe respiratory problems.

Pertussis causes a severe inflammation of the lining of the air passages, resulting in a narrowing of the airway. If your baby has whooping cough, her shortness of breath will cause her to inhale deeply and rapidly between coughs. The "whooping" sounds these breaths often make give whooping cough its name.

Whooping cough may start with cold symptoms, but your baby's cough will then worsen and the whoops may start soon afterward. A lack of oxygen may cause your baby's lips and extremities (her fingertips and toes) to turn bluish. Other symptoms may include drooling, tearing, sometimes vomiting, poor appetite, and extreme exhaustion due to her constant shortness of breath.

Treatment of whooping cough often requires hospitalization to guard against such complications as pneumonia or other secondary infections. Your baby may also require oxygen and suction of her respiratory secretions.

Your baby will need lots of rest. A cool-steam vaporizer may help loosen her respiratory secretions and ease her breathing to some degree. *Do not* give cough medicine to your baby.

Pneumonia

Pneumonia, a lung infection, may follow a cold, flu, or other viral infection or may be caused by a bacterial infection. Symptoms of pneumonia may include any of the following:

- Fever, chills, or sweats

- Flushed or pale skin

- Wheezing or other difficulty breathing (rapid or raspy breaths)

- Phlegmy cough

- Lethargy

- Loss of appetite

- Discomfort and crying

- Bluish lips or fingertips

If you think your baby might have pneumonia, call your doctor at once—especially if your baby is turning blue or having difficulty breathing.

Because it may be difficult to determine whether a viral or bacterial infection has caused the pneumonia, your pediatrician may prescribe an antibiotic. If the infection is bacterial, antibiotics may eliminate the pneumonia within several days (though your baby should complete the full course of antibiotic treatment). His cough, however, may linger for several weeks.

At home, help your baby get lots of rest and drink plenty of fluids. As with any fever, you can treat it with acetaminophen or ibuprofen, subject to your pediatrician's approval, or—if your baby does not object—cool sponge baths. Because your baby needs a productive cough to clear secretions from his lungs, however, *you should not give him cough suppressant.*

If your baby's fever lasts more than 2 to 3 days after beginning antibiotics, if your baby has difficulty breathing, or if his joints become red or swollen, which may indicate a spreading of the infection, contact your pediatrician to arrange for a follow-up examination.

Strep Throat

Strep throat, an inflammation of the throat and tonsils, is caused by a bacterial infection—and therefore responds well to antibiotic treatment.

If your baby has strep throat, she will usually have a low-grade fever or fluctuating temperature as well as a runny nose. She may also appear pale, seem irritable, or suffer from a loss of appetite.

If a throat culture confirms that your baby has strep throat, your pediatrician will prescribe antibiotics. As with any antibiotic, it is important to complete the full treatment even after the symptoms have gone away. Your baby's doctor will probably want to schedule a follow-up visit to recheck her throat about 10 days after your initial visit. However, if your baby's fever or other symptoms fail to clear up within 3 days of beginning antibiotics, you should probably arrange for an earlier follow-up.

At home, you can treat your baby's symptoms. Give her lots of fluids and feed her soft, cold foods (soupy cereal, cold liquids, popsicles, and so on). Fever and pain can be treated with acetaminophen or ibuprofen (as directed by your pediatrician).

Viral Infections

The symptoms of viral infections not already described depend on the part of body infected. If the respiratory tract becomes infected, for example, symptoms could include cold symptoms, coughing, or a sore throat. If the intestinal tract becomes infected, symptoms might include vomiting or diarrhea. In addition, a viral infection of any area of your baby's body can cause fever, general achiness, and loss of appetite (often due to a sore throat or breathing difficulties).

No treatment exists for viral infections; instead, you (and your baby) must allow the illness to run its course. All you can do in the meantime is try to make your baby more comfortable by treating his symptoms—for example, fever (see page 367), sore throat (see page 369), vomiting (see page 370), or diarrhea (see page 365). While waiting for the viral infection to subside, however, be alert for the appearance of new symptoms, which could indicate a secondary infection or the spread of the viral infection.

The Complete Diaper Bag

Use this checklist to make sure you have everything before you go out with your baby.

All Year

- ❑ Cloth or disposable diapers (lots of them)
- ❑ Diaper wipes (for bottom and hand cleaning)
- ❑ Diaper cream
- ❑ Several cloth diapers (for spit-up and other spills)
- ❑ A waterproof changing pad
- ❑ Large plastic bags (for dirty things)
- ❑ Extra baby clothes
- ❑ Socks or booties
- ❑ A light jacket or sweater
- ❑ A sun hat (in summer) or warm hat (in winter)
- ❑ Pacifiers (optional)
- ❑ A baby blanket, stuffed animal, or other comfort object
- ❑ A few small, simple toys
- ❑ Bottle(s) of formula *or* bottle(s) of water and a small container of powdered formula (for bottle feeders)

After 6 Months Old

❑ A bottle of sunblock

❑ Two or three teethers

❑ Snacks and/or baby food

❑ A baby spoon

❑ A bib

❑ A spare set of electrical outlet covers

❑ Water or juice in small plastic bottles

For Longer Trips or Vacation Travel

❑ A new toy

❑ Board books or visually stimulating toys

❑ Extra snacks

❑ First-aid travel kit (thermometer, bandages, gauze, tweezers, antibacterial cream, liquid acetaminophen)

❑ Any medications (and prescriptions)

❑ Medical insurance cards and medical records

❑ Baby monitor (optional)

❑ Night light (optional)

Resources for New Parents

If, as a new parent, you sometimes don't know where to turn, you can get almost any question answered either online or by making a phone call. The following list features organizations that will answer your questions about medical and safety issues or connect you with parental support groups. In addition, you will find a select list of companies that offer a variety of safe products.

Medical Information

The most pressing questions facing many new parents revolve around issues of health and medical care. Whether you have general medical questions or questions regarding specific medical conditions or illnesses, one of the organizations listed here will probably be able to answer them.

General Medical Care

American Academy of Pediatrics
141 Northwest Point Blvd.
Elk Grove Village, IL 60007-1098
847-434-4000
Fax 847-434-8000
www.aap.org

Provides information and publishes brochures on children's health issues.

American Red Cross
2025 E St., NW
Washington, DC 20006
202-303-4498
www.redcross.org

The American Red Cross offers courses in CPR (cardiopulmonary resuscitation) for infants and children, as well as other parenting classes. Contact your local Red Cross chapter for more information.

La Leche League International
1400 N. Meacham Rd.
P.O. Box 4079
Schaumburg, IL 60168-4079
1-800-LALECHE (1-800-525-3243)
Fax 847-519-0035
www.lalecheleague.org

Provides information and support to nursing mothers.

The National Association of Children's Hospitals and Related Institutions
401 Wythe St.
Alexandria, VA 22314
703-684-1355
Fax 703-684-1589
www.childrenshospitals.net

Provides information on local children's hospitals.

National Health Information Center
P.O. Box 1133
Washington, DC 20013-1133
1-800-336-4797
Fax 301-984-4256
www.health.gov/nhic

Provides publications and referrals on health and medical questions.

Nursing Mothers Counsel, Inc.
P.O. Box 50063
Palo Alto, CA 94303
408-291-8008
www.nursingmothers.org

Provides information and assistance to nursing mothers.

Medical Conditions and Illnesses

American Diabetes Association
1701 N. Beauregard St.
Alexandria, VA 22311
1-800-DIABETES (1-800-342-2383)
www.diabetes.org

Answers questions and provides publications on juvenile diabetes.

Asthma and Allergy Foundation of America
Consumer Information Line
1233 20th St., NW
Suite 402
Washington, DC 20036
1-800-7-ASTHMA (1-800-727-8462)
www.aafa.org

Provides information to parents of children with asthma, reactive airway disease, or allergies.

Cystic Fibrosis Foundation
6931 Arlington Rd.
Bethesda, MD 20814
1-800-FIGHT-CF (1-800-344-4823)
Fax 301-951-6378
www.cff.org

Offers information on cystic fibrosis.

Juvenile Diabetes Research Foundation
120 Wall St.
New York, NY 10005-4001
1-800-533-CURE (1-800-533-2873)
Fax 212-785-9595
www.jdrf.org

Answers questions on juvenile diabetes.

Sickle Cell Disease Association of America
231 E. Baltimore St.
Suite 800
Baltimore, MD 21202
1-800-421-8453
www.sicklecelldisease.org

Provides information on sickle cell disease.

Terminal Illnesses

American SIDS Institute
509 Augusta Dr.
Marietta, GA 30067
1-800-232-SIDS (1-800-232-7437)
Fax 770-426-1369
www.sids.org

Provides information and referrals regarding Sudden Infant Death Syndrome.

Children's Hospice International
1101 King St.
Suite 360
Alexandria, VA 22314
1-800-24-CHILD (1-800-242-4453)
www.chionline.org

Provides information on hospice care and resources for terminally ill children.

The Compassionate Friends
P.O. Box 3696
Oak Brook, IL 60522-3696
1-877-969-0010
Fax 630-990-0246
www.compassionatefriends.org

This organization offers support to families who have experienced the death of a child.

Child Safety

Keeping your baby safe is, of course, one of your primary concerns as a new parent. The following organizations offer information, advice, and help that will allow you to keep your baby safe. Many offer hotlines that can provide you with immediate assistance in case of emergency.

Child Help USA (National Child Abuse Hotline)
15757 N. 78th St.
Scottsdale, AZ 85260
Hotline 1-800-4-A-CHILD (1-800-422-4453)
Fax 480-922-7061
www.childhelpusa.org

This hotline provides advice and help to end child abuse.

The Children's Defense Fund
25 E St., NW
Washington, DC 20001
1-800-CDF-1200 (1-800-233-1200)
www.childrensdefense.org

This organization offers many publications on parenting, child abuse, child care, and other subjects of interest to new parents.

The National Highway Traffic Safety Administration
400 Seventh St., SW
Washington, DC 20590
Vehicle Safety Hotline 1-888-327-4236
www.nhtsa.dot.gov

This organization offers information on seat belts, child safety restraints, and other auto-safety issues.

National Safety Council
1121 Spring Lake Dr.
Suite 100
Itasca, IL 60143-3201
1-800-621-2855
Fax 630-775-2213
www.nsc.org

This organization provides information and publications on a wide variety of child safety issues.

Safe Kids Worldwide
1301 Pennsylvania Ave., NW
Suite 1000
Washington, DC 20004-1707
202-662-0600
Fax 202-393-2072
www.safekids.org

This organization provides publications on child safety and childproofing.

U.S. Consumer Product Safety Commission
4330 E. West Highway
Bethesda, MD 20814
1-800-638-CPSC (1-800-638-2772)
Fax 301-504-0124
www.cpsc.gov

This organization establishes and monitors safety standards for children's products; it provides safety information and lists of recalled products.

U.S. Environmental Protection Agency
National Lead Information Center
422 S. Clinton Avenue
Rochester, NY 14620
Fax 585-232-3111
Hotline: 1-800-424-LEAD (1-800-424-5323)
www.epa.gov/lead/pubs/nlic.htm
www.nsc.org/ehc/lead.htm

This organization offers pamphlets on lead and lead poisoning, and operates a hotline to provide immediate answers to questions about lead and lead poisoning.

General Parental Support Groups

New parents sometimes just need a good listener or a helping hand. The following groups can put you in touch with support groups for mothers, fathers, and parents (regardless of gender), offer information on postpartum depression and other issues facing new parents, or help you find child-care providers in your area.

The Fatherhood Project
Families and Work Institute
267 Fifth Ave.
Floor 2
New York, NY 10016
212-465-2044
Fax 212-465-8637
www.familiesandwork.org/fatherhood/index.html

This organization promotes increased involvement of men in child-rearing and offers books, seminars, and training.

MELD (Minnesota Early Learning Design)
219 N. Second St.
Suite 200
Minneapolis, MN 55401
612-332-7563
Fax 612-344-1959
www.meld.org

MELD is a nationwide organization of local parent support groups.

National Association of Mothers' Centers
64 Division Ave.
Levittown, NY 11756
1-800-645-3828
Fax 516-520-1639
www.motherscenter.org

This organization can direct you to a local support center for new parents—or help you start your own.

Parents as Teachers National Center, Inc.
2228 Ball Dr.
St. Louis, MO 63146
1-866-PAT-4YOU (1-866-728-4968)
Fax 314-432-8963
www.parentsasteachers.org

This organization oversees a network of support and education groups for new parents and offers select safety and health products, as well as books, audiotapes, and videotapes that promote child development, nutrition, and safety.

Postpartum Support International
927 N. Kellogg Ave.
Santa Barbara, CA 93111
Hotline 1-800-944-4PPD (1-800-944-4773)

This organization may be able to refer you to a postpartum depression support group in your area.

Child Care

Child Care Aware
3101 Wilson Blvd.
Suite 350
Arlington, VA 22201
1-800-424-2246
Fax 703-341-4101
www.childcareaware.org

This organization will refer callers to local agencies who can provide lists of family day-care providers and child-care centers. It also offers brochures on child care.

AuPair Care
600 California St.
Floor 10
San Francisco, CA 94108
1-800-4AU-PAIR (1-800-428-7247)
Fax 415-434-5415
www.aupaircare.com

This agency will help you find an au pair.

AuPair in America
River Plaza
9 W. Broad St.
Stamford, CT 06902
1-800-928-7247
www.aupairinamerica.com

This agency will help you find an au pair.

Au Pair Programme USA
6965 Union Park Center
Suite 100
Midvale, UT 84047
1-800-255-7722
1-800-574-8889
www.aupairprogrammeusa.com

This agency will help you find an au pair.

EF AuPair
EF Center Boston
Cambridge, MA 02141
1-800-333-6056

This agency will help you find an au pair.

EurAuPair
Eastern office: 1-800-901-2002
Southern office: 1-800-618-2002
Midwestern office:1-800-960-9100
Western office: 1-800-713-2002
www.euraupair.com

This agency will help you find an au pair.

InterExchange AuPair USA
161 Sixth Ave.
New York, NY 10013
1-800-AUP-AIRS (1-800-287-2477)
www.aupairusa.org

This agency will help you find an au pair.

Intellectual Stimulation

It's never too early to get your child in the habit of reading. The following organization offers strategies that will help you nurture your baby's love of reading.

The American Reading Council
20 W. 40th St.
New York, NY 10018
212-730-0786

Selected Child Mail-Order Companies

If you're looking for safety products, you can find a mail-order company that will suit your needs. The list below, although far from comprehensive, includes a number of companies that can get you started in your search for the perfect products for your baby.

Toys

Back to Basics Toys
2707 Pittman Dr.
Silver Spring, MD 20910-1807
1-800-356-5360
www.backtobasicstoys.com

Childcraft Education Corp
P.O. Box 3239
Lancaster, PA 17604
1-800-631-5652
www.childcrafteducation.com

Constructive Playthings
13201 Arrington Rd.
Grandview, MO 64030
1-800-448-7830
www.constplay.com

F.A.O. Schwarz
200 Toy Lane
Blairs, VA 24527
1-800-876-7867
www.fao.com

Sensational Beginnings
987 Stewart Rd.
Monroe, MI 48162
1-800-444-2147
www.sensationalbeginnings.com

Toys to Grow On
2695 E. Dominguez St.
Carson, CA 90895
1-800-874-4242
www.toystogrowon.com

Books, Music, and Videos

Chinaberry
2780 Via Orange Way
Suite B
Spring Valley, CA 91978
1-800-776-2242
www.chinaberry.com

Gryphon House
P.O. Box 207
Beltsville, MD 20704
1-800-638-0928
www.gryphonhouse.com

HearthSong
P.O. Box 1050
Madison, VA 22727
1-800-533-4397
www.hearthsong.com

Just for Kids Books
664 Milwaukee Ave.
Suite 209
Prospect Heights, IL 60070
847-229-8783
www.justforkidsbooks.com

Music for Little People
P.O. Box 1720
Lawndale, CA 90260-6620
1-800-727-2233
www.musicforlittlepeople.com

Clothes

Hanna Andersson
1010 N.W. Flanders
Portland, OR 97209
1-800-222-0544
www.hannaandersson.com

Mia Bambini Inc.
360 Merrimack St.
Riverwalk Building
Lawrence, MA 01843
1-800-766-1254
www.miabambini.com

Olsen's Mill Direct
1641 S. Main St.
Oshkosh, WI 54902
1-800-537-4979
www.olsensmilldirect.com

Babyproofing and Safety Equipment

One Step Ahead
Box 517
Lake Bluff, IL 60044-0517
1-800-274-8440
www.onestepahead.com

Perfectly Safe
7090 Whipple Ave.
North Canton, OH 44720
1-800-898-3696
www.perfectlysafe.stores.yahoo.net

Practical Parenting
15245 Minnetonka Blvd.
Minnetonka, MN 55345
952-912-0036
www.practicalparenting.com

Right Start
Right Start Plaza
5334 Sterling Center Dr.
Westlake Village, CA 91361
1-888-548-8531
www.rightstart.com

The Safety Zone
Hanover, PA 17333
1-800-999-3030
www.safetyzone.com

Index

C

F

Q-R

S

Expert tips and

THE COMPLETE **IDIOT'S** GUIDE TO

Proven methods to give your child the good night you're dreaming of

Sleep Training for Your Child

Melissa M. Burnham, Ph.D. and Jennifer Lawler, Ph.D.

THE COMPLETE **IDIOT'S** GUIDE TO

Feeding Your Baby & Toddler

More than 200 recipes for baby- and toddler-friendly dishes

Elizabeth M. Ward, M.S., R.D.

ISBN: 978-1-59257-540-4

ISBN: 978-1-59257-411-7

All from the complete reference series

THE COMPLETE **IDIOT'S** GUIDE

ALPHA

insighttful advice

 ISBN: 978-1-59257-517-6

 ISBN: 978-1-59257-469-8

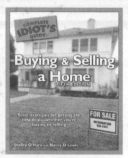

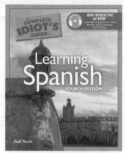

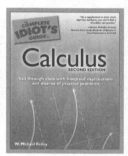